The American Critical Archives is a series of reference books that provide representative selections of contemporary reviews of the main works of major American authors. Specifically, each volume contains both full reviews and excerpts from reviews that appeared in newspapers and weekly and monthly periodicals, generally within a few months of the publication of the work concerned. There is an introductory historical overview by the volume editor, as well as checklists of additional reviews located but not quoted. This volume, a significant contribution to the reception history of *Leaves of Grass, Specimen Days*, and other works, reproduces the full range of the contemporary reviews of Whitman's books. Brash and iconoclastic, revered and reviled at various times, Whitman—because of his bold literary experiments and frank treatment of sexuality—was accorded an astonishing array of commentary, ranging from sympathy with his "hearty wholesomeness" to hostility toward poems that were a "mass of stupid filth." Reviews by Rufus Griswold, Fanny Fern, John Burroughs, William Dean Howells, Henry James, Hamlin Garland, Oscar Wilde, and (writing anonymously) Whitman himself, as well as a host of lesser-known writers, clarify much about both the poet and nineteenth-century American culture and its tastes and preoccupations, its myopia and acuity. These reviewers, the first to frame the issues for critical debate about Whitman, shaped his long-term reputation.

AMERICAN CRITICAL ARCHIVES 9
Walt Whitman: The Contemporary Reviews

The American Critical Archives

GENERAL EDITOR: M. Thomas Inge, Randolph-Macon College

1. *Emerson and Thoreau: The Contemporary Reviews*, edited by Joel Myerson
2. *Edith Wharton: The Contemporary Reviews*, edited by James W. Tuttleton, Kristin O. Lauer, and Margaret P. Murray
3. *Ellen Glasgow: The Contemporary Reviews*, edited by Dorothy M. Scura
4. *Nathaniel Hawthorne: The Contemporary Reviews*, edited by John L. Idol, Jr., and Buford Jones
5. *William Faulkner: The Contemporary Reviews*, edited by M. Thomas Inge
6. *Herman Melville: The Contemporary Reviews*, edited by Brian Higgins and Hershel Parker
7. *Henry James: The Contemporary Reviews*, edited by Kevin J. Hayes
8. *John Steinbeck: The Contemporary Reviews*, edited by Joseph R. McElrath, Jr., Jesse S. Crisler, and Susan Shillinglaw
9. *Walt Whitman: The Contemporary Reviews*, edited by Kenneth M. Price

Walt Whitman

The Contemporary Reviews

Edited by
Kenneth M. Price
College of William & Mary

CAMBRIDGE
UNIVERSITY PRESS

Published by the Press Syndicate of the University of Cambridge
The Pitt Building, Trumpington Street, Cambridge CB2 1RP
40 West 20th Street, New York, NY 10011–4211, USA
10 Stamford Road, Oakleigh, Melbourne 3166, Australia

First published 1996

Printed in the United States of America

Library of Congress Cataloging-in-Publication Data
Walt Whitman: the contemporary reviews / edited by Kenneth M. Price.
p.   cm.— (American critical archives)
Includes index.
ISBN 0–521–45387–9 (hardcover)
1. Whitman, Walt, 1819–1892—Criticism and interpretation.
I. Price, Kenneth M.   II. Series.
PS3238.W3693   1996
811'.3—dc20   95–597
CIP

A catalog record for this book is available from the British Library.

ISBN 0–521–45387–9 hardback

For Gillian

Contents

Series Editor's Preface   ix
Introduction   xi
Editorial Note and Acknowledgments   xxiv

Leaves of Grass (1855)   1
Leaves of Grass (1856)   57
"A Child's Reminiscence" (1859)   69
Leaves of Grass (1860–1)   77
Drum-Taps (1865)   109
Leaves of Grass (1867)   133
Poems by Walt Whitman (1868)   145
Leaves of Grass (1871), *Passage to India* (1871),
    Democratic Vistas (1871)   179
Two Rivulets (1876)   209
Leaves of Grass (1881–2)   221
Specimen Days & Collect (1882–3)   271
November Boughs (1888)   305
Complete Poems & Prose of Walt Whitman (1888)   331
Democratic Vistas, and Other Papers (1888)   339
Good-Bye My Fancy (1891)   345

Index   355

Series Editor's Preface

The American Critical Archives series documents a part of a writer's career that is usually difficult to examine, that is, the immediate response to each work as it was made public on the part of reviewers in contemporary newspapers and journals. Although it would not be feasible to reprint every review, each volume in the series reprints a selection of reviews designed to provide the reader with a proportionate sense of the critical response, whether it was positive, negative, or mixed. Checklists of other known reviews are also included to complete the documentary record and allow access for those who wish to do further reading and research.

The editor of each volume has provided an introduction that surveys the career of the author in the context of the contemporary critical response. Ideally, the introduction will inform the reader in brief of what is to be learned by a reading of the full volume. The reader then can go as deeply as necessary in terms of the kind of information desired—be it about a single work, a period in the author's life, or the author's entire career. The intent is to provide quick and easy access to the material for students, scholars, librarians, and general readers.

When completed, the American Critical Archives should constitute a comprehensive history of critical practice in America, and in some cases Great Britain, as the writers' careers were in progress. The volumes open a window on the patterns and forces that have shaped the history of American writing and the reputations of the writers. These are primary documents in the literary and cultural life of the nation.

M. THOMAS INGE

Introduction

The contemporary reviews of Walt Whitman indicate that he was always in a swirl of controversy. He made for good press by violating poetic norms, treating taboo subjects, and acting in various audacious ways, including (early in his career) meshing together the roles of "rough" and artist. The contemporary fascination with Whitman only increased when publishers pirated *Leaves of Grass*, British and American newspapers exchanged barbs over his reception, the secretary of the interior fired him from his government clerkship, and the district attorney of Boston suppressed *Leaves* as "obscene" literature. Journalistic pieces about Whitman—both human-interest stories and, even more, literary reviews—were important because Whitman's long-term critical reputation began to take shape in this context of controversy.

To many commentators, the 1855 edition of *Leaves of Grass* was downright quirky. Issued without an author's name on the title page and without titles for individual poems, everything about the book—from its unorthodox punctuation to its startling assertions—challenged readers. Some of the initial reviews were harsh, but, for an experimental book, *Leaves* garnered a surprising amount of measured criticism and some outright praise. On 23 July 1855, in the New York *Daily Tribune*, for example, the first reviewer, Charles A. Dana, commented insightfully on the "anonymous bard": He noted the "pensive insolence" of the frontispiece, quoted extensively from the preface, and (though concerned about "reckless and indecent" language) credited the poems with being "certainly original in their external form." A few days later, an anonymous reviewer for *Life Illustrated* followed Dana's example by describing the frontispiece and stressing the importance of Whitman's preface.[1]

In August 1855 no reviews of *Leaves* appeared, a silence that Whitman responded to by writing three of his own unsigned reviews, two appearing in September and another in October (discussed later). These acts of self-promotion contributed to—and to some extent helped provoke—the sudden outpouring of praise and condemnation showered on Whitman. Both Charles Eliot Norton and Edward Everett Hale wrote discerning analyses. Norton thought *Leaves* conveyed a mixture of Yankee transcendentalism and New York rowdyism, and Hale, writing in the *North American Review*, admired the poetry's "freshness, simplicity, and reality."[2] The Washington *Daily National Intelligencer*, in contrast, put a negative construction on Whitman's link to transcendentalism, asserting that if Emerson admired the work "its hieroglyphs would be as unintelligible to our ken as was the inscription around the sacred ibex to the erudite Mr. [George Robins] Gliddon." Rufus Griswold, both supercilious and sanctimonious, thought Whitman produced a "mass of stupid filth" and wondered if the poet were not "possessed of the soul of a sentimental donkey that had died of disappointed love." Griswold's attempts at humor quickly gave way to moral condemnations when he had recourse to Latin in order to chastise Whitman as a same-sex lover: "*Peccatum illud horribile, inter Christianos non nominandum*" (that horrible sin not to be named among Christians). Fanny Fern retorted, in the earliest review signed by a woman, that *Leaves of Grass* was "unspeakably delicious" and an "unmingled delight." She scorned those false purists who charged that the book was coarse and sensual: "Let him who can do so, shroud the eyes of the nursing babe lest it should see its mother's breast."[3]

The first British reviewer, in the London *Weekly Dispatch*, took a view similar to Fanny Fern's and applauded the "hearty wholesomeness" of the 1855 *Leaves of Grass*. Disoriented by the lack of "every condition under which poetry is generally understood to exist," the *Dispatch* nonetheless found in Whitman's lines a melody "peculiar and appropriate to themselves alone." Less than a week later, however, the *Saturday Review* condemned Whitman as obscene and concluded that his book ought to be thrown "instantly into the fire." Other harsh British reviews were quick to appear. On 22 March 1856 the *Examiner* described Whitman as a poet "perpetually haunted by the delusion that he has a catalogue to make." Dubbing the poet a "wild Tupper of the West," its reviewer was the first of a series of commentators (British more often than not) who linked *Leaves of Grass* with *Proverbial Philosophy* by Martin Farquhar Tupper.[4] The *Leader*, for example, thought neither poet effective, because their "external form . . . is startling, and by no means seductive, to English ears, accustomed to the sumptuous music of ordinary metres." Worse yet, the "central principle" of *Leaves of Grass* is "staggering," for it "seems to resolve itself into an all-attracting egotism—an eternal presence of the individual soul of Walt Whitman in all things, yet in such wise that this one soul shall be presented as a type of all human souls whatsoever."[5] The London *Critic* judged Whitman to be as "unacquainted with art, as a hog is with mathematics." Ridicule gave way to panic when its reviewer wished to have bodily harm inflicted on Whitman: "The man who wrote page 79 of the *Leaves of Grass* deserves nothing so richly as the public executioner's whip" (an indignant reaction to Whitman's account of "loveflesh swelling and deliciously aching, / Limitless limpid jets of love hot and enormous").[6]

Whitman strove both to protect himself from zealous reviewers and to advertise his book when he interjected his own anonymous reviews into the ongoing discussion of *Leaves of Grass*.[7] He battled to get his book a hearing and to frame key interpretive questions. His anonymous self-reviewing is as fascinating for the energy and inventiveness it displays as for what it reveals about his ability to conceive of himself as other,[8] to regard his poetic self as apart from himself. This habit of mind had many effects, including, for example, the renaming of himself as "Walt" as opposed to Walter and his development of a shifting, multifaceted persona.

In addition, Whitman's self-reviews show his desire to manage public perception of his relation to "literature" itself. "An English and an American Poet" contrasted *Leaves of Grass* with the work of Tennyson, who Whitman believed displayed symptoms of overrefinement and "ennui" characteristic of English culture as a whole. In "Walt Whitman and His Poems," the poet describes himself as "talking like a man unaware that there was ever hitherto such a production as a book or such a being as a writer." He also published "Walt Whitman: A Brooklyn Boy" in the Brooklyn *Daily Times*. This review opens with the claim that "to give judgment on real poems, one needs an account of the poet himself." He then describes himself so as to stress his bond with working-class Americans.[9]

Unlike the original *Leaves of Grass*, which was widely noticed, the second edition, of 1856, received only three reviews, two mixed and one sharply negative.[10] Audaciously, in the second edition, Whitman had printed without permission Emerson's famous letter of greeting and extracted one sentence ("I greet you at the beginning of a great career") to serve as a gold-lettered puff on the spine of the book. The *Christian Examiner* judged these actions to be the "grossest violation of literary comity and courtesy that ever passed under our notice." More generally, its reviewer found Whitman's "self-applause" to be nearly as repugnant as his "pantheism and libidinousness." The Brooklyn *Daily Times* focused on the "new, enlarged and stereotyped edition," which puts forth Whitman's "two-fold assertion of individuality . . . of himself personally, and of himself nationally." The work is "altogether *sui generis*, unless we may call it Emersonian."[11]

Whitman's literary manners, specifically his self-reviewing, also came in for sharp attack. On 17 December 1856, the New York *Daily Times* (in assessing simultaneously the first two editions) commented on turning to the "forepart" of one volume to find "proof slips of certain review articles written about the *Leaves of Grass*."[12] Two of these reviews, when compared with the 1855 preface, provided "unmistakable internal evidence that Mr. Walt Whitman . . . was not content with writing a book, but was also determined to review it."[13] His poetry scorns hypocrisy, yet Whitman himself "perpetrates a lie and a sham at the very outset of his career."[14] The *Times* also rankled at Whitman's use of Emerson's letter, terming it nothing better than "literary fraud." Despite its occasional harshness, this review deserves close attention, for the critic struggles, fascinatingly, to reconcile his own divided responses to

Whitman. On the one hand, he asserts that Whitman puts forth the "emblems of Phallic worship" and produces a "muck of abomination"; on the other, he notes that Whitman "has expressed certain things better than any other man who has gone before him." For all his misgivings, the reviewer appreciates the "singular electric attraction" and the "wondrous, unaccountable fascination" of *Leaves of Grass*.[15]

The debate over the quality of the third edition, of 1860, began, in effect, with a preliminary scuffle in the preceding year, when the Cincinnati *Daily Commercial* reviewed the magazine publication of "A Child's Reminiscence" (later entitled "Out of the Cradle Endlessly Rocking"). The *Commercial* describes the poem as "a shade less heavy and vulgar than the 'Leaves of Grass,' whose unmitigated badness seemed to cap the climax of poetic nuisances. But the present performance has all the emptiness, without half the grossness, of the author's former efforts." Moreover, Whitman is excoriated as an "unclean cub" whose lines are "stupid and meaningless twaddle." In direct response, the poet wrote "All About a Mockingbird," his own anonymous evaluation of "Cradle" (published in the friendly pages of the New York *Saturday Press*). He described the treatment he received in the *Commercial* as "tip-top cutting-and-slashing criticism, which we have conned with unfeigned pleasure." He then takes the occasion to announce "the true 'Leaves of Grass' [the third edition], the fuller grown work of which the former two issues were the inchoates."[16]

In general, the third edition was sharply criticized by English reviewers;[17] nonetheless, they found the book fascinating as a tangible object. The *Saturday Review*, for example, commented that "the type is magnificent, the paper is as thick as cardboard, and the covers, ornamented with an intaglio of the earth moving through space and displaying only the American hemisphere.... It is a book evidently intended to lie on the tables of the wealthy." The "splendid" features of the book seemed, however, curious adornments for "one of the most indecent writers who ever raked ... filth into sentences." The *Westminster Review* also noted the expense the American publisher went to in its "outward setting-forth." The *Spectator*, in turn, commented on this "Protean, ubiquitous, and multitudinous person" and wondered:

> Where are the phallic emblems, and the figures of Priapus and the Satyrs that should have adorned the covers and the pages of this new gospel of lewdness and obscenity? Its frontispiece should have been, not the head and shoulders of the author, but a full-length portrait drawn as he loves to depict himself in his 'poems'—naked as an Anabaptist of Munster, or making love like Diogenes *coram populo* [in front of the people].[18]

American reviewers tended to be far more positive in their responses. Although the New York *Times* objected to Whitman's "indecencies" and "self-conceit," the Boston *Banner of Light* countered that Whitman, better than any other writer, has "seized hold of the *spirit* of things."[19] Moncure Conway concluded of the 1860 edition that "Whitman has set the pulses of America to music." His "profanity is reverently meant, and he speaks what is unspeakable with the simple unreserve of a child." An equally effusive long review appeared in the *Saturday Press*, which judged Whitman to be a "great Philosopher." Whitman's "expression seems always the suitable and natural result of the thought. It is indeed tame and prosy in the conveyance of any commonplace idea or feeling, but it rises and melts into sweet and thrilling music whenever impelled by the beautiful impulse of a grand thought or emotion."[20]

In 1865, several reviewers preferred Whitman's new volume, *Drum-Taps*, over *Leaves of Grass* because of the "propriety"[21] of his subject matter and the appearance of "greater . . . beauty of form."[22] *Watson's Weekly Art Journal* enthused that "for the first time, the full strength of our American life receives expression—receives assertion." The *Radical* also admired the work, explaining that the "true poet discovers new and unsuspected laws of art, and makes his own rules," and Whitman is "unquestionably a true poet." The most insightful review, by John Burroughs, offers a lengthy account of Whitman's life, the publication and reception history of *Leaves of Grass*, and an analysis of *Drum-Taps* itself. A discriminating admirer of Whitman's work, Burroughs responds especially powerfully to "When Lilacs Last in the Dooryard Bloom'd":

> By that curious indirect method which is always the method of nature, the poet makes no reference to the mere facts of Lincoln's death—neither describes it, or laments it, or dwells upon its unprovoked atrocity, or its political aspects, but quite beyond the possibilities of the art of the ordinary versifier, he seizes upon three beautiful facts of nature which he weaves into a wreath for the dead President's tomb.[23]

Other reviewers remained convinced, however, that Whitman's work was inartistic. The New York *Times* sputtered disapproval of Whitman's "poverty of thought, paraded forth with a hubbub of stray words." The two most famous reviews of *Drum-Taps*—by William Dean Howells and Henry James—were also negative. Howells judged the artistic method of *Leaves* to be "mistaken." Considering his popular success, Whitman's theory must be wrong: He has enjoyed the "fructifying extremes of blame and praise," yet he remains little known to the popular mind. James regarded *Drum-Taps* as the effort of an "essentially prosaic mind to lift itself, by a prolonged muscular strain, into poetry."[24]

Robert Buchanan reviewed *Drum-Taps* and *Leaves of Grass* (1867) after Whitman was fired from his job in the Interior Department. Buchanan's review, little more than a puff of Whitman's image, is important because it is one of only two known reviews of the 1867 *Leaves of Grass*. (The other review, probably by John Burroughs, appeared in the Boston *Commonwealth*.)[25] Even more surprising, the 1876 *Leaves of Grass* apparently was not reviewed at all and *Democratic Vistas* (1871) only in England.[26] At first glance, the lack of reviews seems curious because many general treatments of Whitman were appearing in these years: In 1876 alone, for example, four books and at least seventy-one periodical items discussed the poet. Two main factors contributed to the dearth of reviews: First, reviewers tended to ignore volumes entitled *Leaves of Grass* because they seemed to repeat previous work. (Thus, when the 1876 *Leaves of Grass* was published with its companion volume, *Two Rivulets*, it was *Two Rivulets* that received critical notice.) Whitman's unusual publication history also hurt his chances of gaining publicity through conventional reviewing channels. Along with *Leaves of Grass*, Whitman published eleven separately titled volumes, and in six cases he served as his own publisher.[27] For much of his career, Whitman lacked the aid powerful publishers routinely offered in helping arrange for reviews of books.

Whitman had compensations, however. His unorthodox entrance into the English literary world—through William Michael Rossetti's publication of selections from *Leaves of Grass*—led to increased attention from abroad. The London *Sunday Times* of 29 March 1868 reviewed Rossetti's selections. Noting that "unreflective readers will see nothing but a harsh and over-daring Tupper," the reviewer argued that a genuine affinity existed between Whitman and Rabelais and Montaigne: "The greatest works of all times, from the earliest literature of Greek and Hebrew, to the latest of France and England, are offensive to English prudery." Rossetti, responding to prevailing mores, printed some poems in their entirety and others not at all. Hence he is "no Bowdler"; his efforts go "to herald the entire work rather than to render it unnecessary." *Lloyd's Weekly London Newspaper*, on the other hand, called Rossetti a disciple and wondered whether his selections were always judicious. Its reviewer admired what had been made available from *Leaves of Grass*. He found it paradoxical, however, that Whitman's other writing could be "so disfigured by violation of morality and decency, as to be rather too much for the English reader; and, stranger still, to hear Mr. Rossetti praying for a complete edition." The most favorable review, "Walt Whitman's Poems," appeared in the London *Sun*. For its reviewer, reading the Rossetti selections "yielded. . . . exquisite pleasure." The reviewer was particularly impressed by Whitman's "thoughts, emotions, aspirations, expressed as in a new language, and, once so expressed, never afterwards to be altogether forgotten."[28]

Much discussion centered on whether Whitman deserved the name "poet." The *Saturday Review*, critiquing the Rossetti volume, remarked, "To call a man a poet merely because he holds forth in rhapsodical style about one man being as good as another, everything being all right, every one having a right 'to do as he dam pleases' . . . and other dogmas of the same sort, is to confuse the functions of the poet and the stump orator."[29] *Chambers's Journal of*

Popular Literature, Science, and Art acknowledged being predisposed against Whitman because of the "extravagant praise" he had been given but conceded that he was "really noteworthy," the "first characteristic poetical writer the United States have produced." He "does not write verse at all" but has "invented a certain rolling changeful metre of his own."[30]

The English gave three reviews to *Two Rivulets*, while the American press failed to notice the book. The earliest commentator, Edmund Gosse, tried to achieve a moderate position, viewing Whitman as a "pure man of excellent intentions, to whom certain primitive truths with regard to human life have presented themselves with great vividness, and who has chosen to present them to us in semi-rhythmic, rhetorical language, which rises occasionally, in fervent moments to a kind of inarticulate poetry, and falls at others into something very inchoate and formless." J. H. McCarthy, in the *Examiner*, noted that in this volume Whitman had turned away from love and passion: the "present volume is distinctly a political, a historical, or, perhaps more correctly still, a prophetic book, and it deals with and treats of the mighty future of America." The reviewer found in Whitman "virtues and strength sufficient for claiming laureateship of the great American nation." Paradoxically, Whitman was better known and appreciated in the "land of the stranger than at home." W. Hale White, writing belatedly in the *Secular Review* in 1880, observed that *Two Rivulets* received little recognition in England. He regretted that lack of attention because "this book contains, perhaps, the best defense of Democracy which has been offered of late years . . . and some of the truest poetry."[31]

The agreement Whitman reached to have the 1881–2 *Leaves of Grass* published by James R. Osgood marked a breakthrough for the poet, promising a new level of acceptability and literary prestige. The importance of an established publisher is suggested by the many reviews the 1881–2 *Leaves of Grass* received even before the suppression controversy. The New York *Sun*, in "Walt Whitman and the Poetry of the Future," finds in *Leaves* an "egotism that reaches the verge of sublimity," and proceeds to compare, side by side, passages from Whitman and the Bible. (Unusually for the time, this review held that the "three or four poems which have rhyme are of the crudest and the stanzas are fetters.") The *Liberty* of Boston respectfully reviewed the volume, saying that Whitman's work was now tastefully "got up" without losing its "original native simplicity, freshness, and vigor." The *Critic*, in addition to applauding Whitman's promotion of "universal love," noted the anomaly that Whitman had been the champion of democracy and the working man, despite being "caviare to the multitude." That is, "his admirers have been almost exclusively of a class the farthest possibly removed from that which labors for daily bread by manual work."[32]

The *Dial* of Chicago was representative of those that found little merit in Whitman: His "lack of a sense of poetic fitness, his failure to understand the business of a poet, is certainly astounding. . . . In view of his savage contempt for anything musical in poetry, it will be a fine stroke of the irony of fate if he shall be destined to be remembered only by the few pieces which are marked by the 'piano tune' quality that he derides—the true and tender lyric of 'My Captain' and the fine poem on 'Ethiopia Saluting the Colors.'" Somewhat surprisingly, this reviewer also considered "Lilacs" a magnificent threnody. The *Literary World* objected to "passages which sound like a lecture on the obstetrics of lust . . . and the apotheosis of the phallus."[33] The Detroit *Free Press* granted that Whitman was "genuine and thoroughly believes in himself," yet its reviewer felt that "Children of Adam" was an "outrage upon the decencies of literature," and concluded that "when such a work . . . has free circulation and transmission through the mails, an argument . . . is furnished for the professional perverters of youth whose vile trash is really less indecorous in form." Similarly, the New York *Examiner* commented that "we are not sure that the book is not amenable to the laws against sending obscene literature through the mails." And T. W. Higginson joined the chorus of people predicting legal trouble for *Leaves of Grass*. The *Free Press*, *Catholic World*, and the Chicago *Tribune* were united in chastising Whitman for "beastliness."[34]

In March 1882 *Leaves of Grass* was officially designated as obscene literature by the district attorney of Boston, and the city's postmaster (temporarily) banned the book from the mails. Rees Welsh & Co. of Philadelphia (largely through the efforts of David McKay) stepped in quickly to publish *Leaves of Grass*, and the book sold well. On 12 August 1882, T. Francis Gordon offered in the *American* "views concerning the propriety of issuing the volume in its present shape." Gordon asserted that "good art" is the "noble expression of noble ideas" and that poetry such as "Children of Adam" displays a "realism [that] has no place in art." Lafcadio Hearn, in the New Orleans *Times-Democrat*, went farther and asserted that "'Children of Adam' . . . condemn[s] him beyond redemption." The Boston *Commonwealth*, however, argued that Whitman's claim to the rank of poet may be questionable, but "it is absurd . . . to rank the work as an obscene or reprehensible one in the broad and literal sense."[35]

The earliest review of *Specimen Days and Collect* appeared in the New York *Tribune*. Acknowledging Whitman's freshness and individuality, the *Tribune* nonetheless found that "no perfectly sane person" could conclude that "Whitman has any new message to deliver to the world." More appreciative reviews quickly followed, however. The Boston *Sunday Herald* reviewer felt that *Specimen Days* alone "would be enough to establish the author's fame as a great poet." The New York *Times* agreed that *Specimen Days* made an "important contribution to our literature." The reviewer joined others in noting that Whitman's prose is not sharply to be distinguished from his verse: More rhapsodist than poet, Whitman is most poetic when "inspired by night." The *Literary World*, in a contradictory manner, argued both that Whitman's prose is "interchangeable" with his poetry and that his "prose is better than his poetry. It is clear. It is sane. It is intelligible. It is often readable." The *Critic*, in "Walt Whitman's New Book," focused on Whitman's word "ensemble" as a key to his project. Here Whitman was seen as a great failure despite the admiration expressed for his development of an "elastic system of poetry-prose."[36]

Many of the most important reviews of *Specimen Days* came from England. The *Westminster Review* observed that Whitman saw everything in two categories—democratic or feudal—and democracy seemed to exist nowhere but in the United States. The review, near its close, stated: "Our sense of the importance of the work has led us to extend to an undue length." Edward Dowden commented on *Specimen Days and Collect* for *Academy* in 1882. This account describes (more than it evaluates) the volume. The tone, however, is favorable, and the piece closes with hope that Whitman will visit England, where he would receive "friendly greetings" from many of that nation's literary figures. The *Spectator*, on the other hand, was sharply critical of Whitman's "ignorance": his "scrawled title-page, furnishes abundant evidence that its author knows next to nothing of the many things which he unhesitatingly exalts or denounces and that he has no adequate conception of the many problems he so confidently solves."[37]

In the final years of his life, Whitman attained a degree of majesty and renown. This stature did not save him from criticism, but even his harshest critics in the 1880s and 1890s rarely matched the boiling fury of some of his early reviewers. Commentary on his final works was generally respectful, at times even adulatory. For example, Sylvester Baxter regarded Whitman's *Complete Poems & Prose* (1888) as "a book to be prized by the bibliophile as well as treasured by Whitman's friends."[38]

The friends of *Leaves of Grass* came to include an increasing number of prominent writers. Oscar Wilde wrote a long and appreciative review of *November Boughs* for the *Pall Mall Gazette* in which he argued that "Whitman is at his best when he is analyzing his own work, and making schemes for the poetry of the future." Another noteworthy author, Hamlin Garland, commented on *November Boughs* for the Boston *Evening Transcript*. He found it an "admirable book" and judged that the "number of people who begin to understand and admire this great personality is increasing." Garland remarked that the "controversy about poetry is mostly a contention about a word." What Garland called poetry someone else might call passionate descriptive speech, but the terminology "does not matter." Howells, too, commented on *November Boughs*, registering a more positive opinion than he did of *Drum-Taps*: Whitman's "literary intention was as generous as his spirit was bold, and . . . if he has not accomplished all he intended, he has been a force that is by no means spent."[39]

Most other commentators on *November Boughs* either were negative or were relatively restrained in their praise. Many reviewers, whatever they thought of Whitman's work as a whole, recognized "A Backward Glance O'er Travell'd Roads" as a significant accomplishment. The *Saturday Review*, the *Critic*, and the *Scottish Review* were struck by the "singular modesty" and eloquence of "A Backward Glance." Yet some remained ready to dismiss Whitman: the *Literary World* declared that Whitman "has failed and failed lamentably in his attempt to construct a new technique in verse," and the San Francisco *Chronicle* predicted that *November Boughs* "will prove tedious to all except his admirers."[40]

The New York *Tribune* reviewed *Good-Bye My Fancy* on 16 August 1891. Though free of hostility, the review is nonetheless negative. For example, it asserts that "when Walt Whitman tries to be profound he commonly becomes unintelligible." The *Independent* was far harsher: "There is nothing of any value whatever in this book. . . . That the great magazines were right and Walt Whitmon [*sic*] wrong the contents of this thin, crazy-quilt volume amply prove." Favorable reviews, however, outnumbered negative ones. Sidney Morse in the *Conservator* found that, despite Whitman's "strange form," his poems yielded "full satisfaction." The *Critic* added that in this volume "Whitman's beliefs come out singularly strong and triumphant." The *Literary News* also praised the work of the "grand old fellow." And the *Literary World* found *Good-Bye* to be both "very pathetic and courageous," closing his career "firmly and fitly."[41]

In one of his early anonymous reviews, Whitman claimed that he accepted with "easy nonchalance" the chances of his work's "present reception, and, through all misunderstandings and distrusts, the chances of its future reception." Actually, of course, he never relaxed about the fate of *Leaves of Grass*. As we have seen, he included press notices of his book in some of the later printings of the 1855 edition.[42] Whitman's own reviews should be seen both as a vital part of his overall project and as a characteristic effort to blur the boundaries of his text. Moreover, he reprinted the comments of several early reviewers in a section called "Opinions," appended to the second edition of *Leaves of Grass* (1856) and again in a pamphlet of press notices entitled "*Leaves of Grass* Imprints" (1860), a brash effort to promote the third edition of his book. His fascination with reviews is apparent when we consider that he reviewed his book, reprinted his reviews (along with others), and then reviewed those reviews.[43]

The contemporary reviews were important to Whitman, but what do they say to us now? The reviews open up any number of intriguing questions, two of which bear mentioning here. First, the widespread conviction in the nineteenth century that there was a fundamental link between Tupper and Whitman deserves renewed consideration. At this particular moment in criticism, when popular and sentimental works are open for reevaluation, we can profit from a close look at the ground that both links and divides these two writers. A second feature of the reviews, running consistently from the opening review to the end of Whitman's career, is a tendency to highlight as having special poetic value Whitman's apostrophe to the "tender and growing night" in "Song of Myself" (section 21). Intriguingly, reviewers return again and again to the passage. Edward P. Mitchell observed that Whitman "exults in showing side by side the sublime or the beautiful that has always been acknowledged as such, and the sublime or the beautiful unacknowledged and unrecognized by everybody but himself."[44] Mitchell then contrasts section 21 of "Song of Myself" with the passage on the "calm and commanding" black drayman. Mitchell is right, of course, to suggest that the "tender and growing night" invokes standard visions of beauty, including moonlight and mottled water. These standard appeals no doubt go far toward accounting for the resonance the passage had for so many nineteenth-century readers. Nonetheless, there is an only partially submerged eroticism about the passage, too, an eroticism many of these reviewers objected to elsewhere, but which, in the right kind of context, they responded to despite themselves.

Notes

1 [Charles A. Dana], "New Publications: *Leaves of Grass*," New York *Daily Tribune*, 23 July 1855, p. 3, and *Life Illustrated,* 28 July 1855. The latter item is reprinted in James K. Wallace, "Whitman and *Life Illustrated*: A Forgotten Review of *Leaves*," *Walt Whitman Review*, 17 (December 1971), 135–8.

2 [Charles Eliot Norton], *Putnam's Monthly*, 6 (September 1855), 321–3, and Edward Everett Hale, *North American Review*, 83 (January 1856), 275–7.

3 "Notes on New Books," Washington *Daily National Intelligencer*, 18 February 1856, p. 2; Rufus Griswold, *Criterion*, 1 (10 November 1855), 24; Fanny Fern [Sara Payson Willis Parton], "Fresh Fern Leaves: *Leaves of Grass*," New York *Ledger*, 10 May 1856, p. 4.

4 London *Weekly Dispatch*, 9 March 1856, p. 6; *Saturday Review*, 1 (15 March 1856), 393–4; *Examiner*, 2512 (22 March 1856), 181. Comparisons of Whitman and Tupper appeared also in "Walt Whitman and His Critics," *Leader and Saturday Analyst*, 30 June 1860, pp. 614–15; "*Leaves of Grass*," *Literary Gazette*, n.s. 4 (7 July 1860), 798–9; *Saturday Review* (7 July 1860), 20; *Critic*, 21 (14 July 1860), 43–4; *Westminster Review*, 74, n.s. 18 (1 October 1860), 590; [Henry James], "Mr. Walt Whitman," *Nation*, 1 (16 November 1865), 625–6; "Walt Whitman's Poems," *Literary World*, 12 (19 November 1881), 411–12.

5 "Transatlantic Latter-Day Poetry," *Leader*, 7 (7 June 1856), 547.

6 *Critic* [London], 15 (1 April 1856), 171. The reference to page 79 of the 1855 edition is to the untitled poem ultimately known as "I Sing the Body Electric."

7 The poet did not invent the practice of self-reviewing, of course. Before writing *Leaves*, he clipped and carefully preserved an article about Leigh Hunt's analysis of his own poetry and the "same sort of self-criticism by other poets" (William R. Perkins Library, Duke University).

8 For a discussion of this matter, see Onno Oerlemans, "Whitman and the Erotics of Lyric," *American Literature*, 65 (December 1993), 708.

9 "An English and an American Poet," *American Phrenological Journal*, 22, no. 4 (October 1855), 90; "Walt Whitman and his Poems," *United States Review*, 5 (September 1855), 206; "Walt Whitman: A Brooklyn Boy," Brooklyn *Daily Times*, 29 September 1855, p. 2.

10 The second edition contained much that was new, increasing the number of poems from twelve to thirty-two. Yet Whitman's decision to market twenty new works under an old title—to conceive of these works as an expansion or organic growth out of the first edition—apparently led people to view this as a repeat performance.

11 *Christian Examiner*, 60 (November 1856), 473, and "New Publications," Brooklyn *Daily Times*, 17 December 1856.

12 This unorthodox promotional tactic was mentioned in other reviews also.

13 In conducting his detective work, the reviewer referred to the *American Phrenological Journal* and the *United States Review*.

14 These attacks began in "A Pleasant Quiz," *Albion*, n.s. 14 (8 September 1855), 429. The *Saturday Review* strove to expose Whitman for violating literary etiquette: "Not only does the donor send us the book, but he favours us with hints—pretty broad hints—towards a favourable review of it. He has pasted in the first page a number of notices extracted with the scissors from American newspapers, and all magnificently eulogistic of *Leaves of Grass*."

15 New York *Daily Times*, 13 November 1856, p. 2.

16 "Walt. Whitman's New Poem," Cincinnati *Daily Commercial*, 28 December 1859, reprinted in Thomas Ollive Mabbott and Rollo G. Silver, *A Child's Reminiscence by Walt Whitman* (Seattle: University of Washington Book Store, 1930), pp. 37–40.

17 A significant exception is "Walt Whitman and His Critics," *Leader and Saturday Analyst*, 30 June 1860, 614–5. This piece was one of the earliest to differentiate the biographical Whitman from the poet's persona. The reviewer complained of other "critics, who treated the new author as one self-educated, yet in the rough, unpolished, and owing nothing to instruction. Fudge! The authority for so treating the author was derived from himself." In addition, a careful distinction is drawn between "the individual writer, and . . . the subjective-hero supposed to be writing."

18 "*Leaves of Grass*," *Saturday Review*, 10 (7 July 1860), 19–20; *Westminster Review*, 74, n.s. 18 (1 October 1860), 590; and *Spectator*, 33 (14 July 1860), 669–70.

19 "New Publications: The New Poets," New York *Times*, 19 May 1860 Supplement, p. 1; "Literature," Boston *Banner of Light*, 7 (2 June 1860), 4.

20 [Moncure Conway], *Dial* (Cincinnati), 1 (August 1860), 519 and 517; and "Walt Whitman—*Leaves of Grass*," New York *Saturday Press*, 19 May 1860, p. 2.

21 [A. S. Hill], *North American Review*, 104 (January 1867), 301.

22 Specifically, *Watson's Weekly Art Journal* of 4 November 1865 found "greater regularity of rhythm, and more unity of conception in the grouping of details" (35).

23 "*Drum-Taps*—Walt Whitman," *Watson's Weekly Art Journal*, 4 November 1865, p. 34; "Walt Whitman's *Drum-Taps*," *The Radical*, 1 (March 1866), 311; John Burroughs, "Walt Whitman and His '*Drum-Taps*,'" *Galaxy*, 2 (1 December 1866), 612.

24 "Walt Whitman's *Drum Taps*," New York *Times*, 22 November 1865, p. 4; W[illiam] D[ean] H[owells], "*Drum-Taps*," *Round Table*, 2 (11 November 1865), 147–8; [Henry James], "Mr. Walt Whitman," *Nation*, 1 (16 November 1865), 625.

25 Robert Buchanan, "Walt Whitman," *Broadway Magazine*, 1 (November 1867), 188–95, and J[ohn] B[urroughs], "Literary Review," Boston *Commonwealth*, 10 November 1867, pp. 1–2.

26 With the exception of Edward Dowden's long article in the *Westminster Review* (July 1871), the only item that could be construed to be a review of *Democratic Vistas* did not appear until 30 June 1888. The latter item, by Walter Lewin, is a review of an anthology entitled *Democratic Vistas and Other Papers*, a reprinting intended for the British public.

27 For a discussion of Whitman's publishing practices, see Joel Myerson, "Whitman: Bibliography as Biography," in *Walt Whitman: The Centennial Essays*, ed. Ed Folsom (Iowa City: University of Iowa Press, 1994), pp. 19–29.

28 London *Sunday Times*, 29 March 1868, p. 7; *Lloyd's Weekly London Newspaper*, 19 April 1868, p. 8; "Walt Whitman's Poems," London *Sun*, 17 April 1868, p. 31490.

29 *Saturday Review*, 25 (2 May 1868), 590.

30 "Walt Whitman's Poems," *Saturday Review*, 25 (2 May 1868), 590; "Walt Whitman," *Chambers's Journal of Popular Literature, Science, and Art*, 45 (4 July 1868), 420.

31 Edmund W. Gosse, "Walt Whitman's New Book," *Academy*, 9 (24 June 1876), 602–3; J. H. McCarthy, "Songs Overseas," *Examiner*, 3586 (21 October 1876), 1192; W. Hale White, "The Genius of Walt Whitman," *Secular Review*, 20 March 1880, p. 180.

32 "Walt Whitman and the Poetry of the Future," New York *Sun*, 19 November 1881, p. 2; "*Leaves of Grass*," *Liberty*, 1 (26 November 1881), 3; "Whitman's '*Leaves of Grass*,'" *Critic* [New York], 1 (5 November 1881), 302–3.

33 [Francis F. Browne], "Briefs on New Books," *The Dial* [Chicago], 2 (January 1882), 218–19; "Walt Whitman's Poems," *Literary World*, 12 (19 November 1881), 411–12.

34 "New Publications," Detroit *Free Press*, 7 January 1882, p. 3; "The Poetry of the Future," New York *Examiner*, 19 January 1882, p. 1; [T. W. Higginson], "Recent Poetry," *Nation*, 33 (15 December 1881), 476–7; "*Leaves of Grass*," *Catholic World*, 34 (February 1882), 720; "Walt Whitman's Claim to be Considered a Great Poet," Chicago *Tribune*, 26 November 1881, p. 9.

35 T. Francis Gordon, "Walt Whitman's Complete Volume," *American*, 2 (12 August 1882), 282; [Lafcadio Hearn], "*Leaves of Grass*!" New Orleans *Times-Democrat*, 30 July 1882, p. 4; Boston *Commonwealth*, 2 September 1882, p. 1.

36 "New Publications," New York *Tribune*, 14 October 1882, p. 6; "Whitman's New Book," Boston *Sunday Herald*, 15 October 1882, p. 9; "New Publications: Walt Whitman's Prose," New York *Times*, 18 December 1882, p. 2; "All About Walt Whitman," *Literary World*, 13 (4 November 1882), 372; "Walt Whitman's New Book," *Critic* [New York], 3 (13 January 1883), 2–3.

37 *Westminster Review*, n.s. 64 (July 1883), 291; Edward Dowden, *Academy*, 22 (18 November 1882), 357–9; "Walt Whitman's Prose Works," *Spectator*, 21 July 1883, p. 934.

38 [Sylvester Baxter], "Whitman's Complete Works," Boston *Herald*, 3 January 1889, p. 4.

39 [Oscar Wilde], "The Gospel According to Walt Whitman," *Pall Mall Gazette*, 25 January 1889, p. 3; Hamlin Garland, "Whitman's *November Boughs*," Boston *Evening Transcript*, 15 November 1888, p. 6; [William Dean Howells], "Editor's Study," *Harper's New Monthly Magazine*, 78 (February 1889), 488.

40 "*November Boughs*," *Saturday Review*, 67 (2 March 1889), 260–1; W. Harrison, "Walt Whitman's '*November Boughs*,'" *Critic* [New York], n.s. 11 (19 January 1889), 25; *Scottish Review*, 14 (July 1889), 212; "Whitman's *November Boughs*," *Literary World*, 19 (8 December 1888), 446; "*November Boughs*," San Francisco *Chronicle*, 13 January 1889, p. 7.

41 "Whitman's Farewell: A Melancholy Book," New York *Tribune*, 16 August 1891, p. 14; *Independent*, 43 (10 September 1891), 1355; Sidney Morse, "The Second Annex to *Leaves of Grass*," *Conservator*, 2 (September 1891), 51–2; "*Good-Bye My Fancy*!" *Critic* [New York], n.s. 16 (5 September 1891), 114; *Literary News*, n.s. 12 (September 1891), 282; "*Good-Bye My Fancy*," *Literary World*, 22 (12 September 1891), 305.

42 The book was bound at four different times.

43 Whitman, who saved many press clippings about *Leaves* all his life, employed these reviews again when he coordinated (anonymously) Appendix II of Richard Maurice Bucke's *Walt Whitman*, entitled "Contemporaneous Notices, 1855 to 1883." For Whitman's review of "*Leaves of Grass* Imprints," see "A Brooklynite Criticised," Brooklyn *City News*, 10 October 1860, reprinted in facsimile in *Walt Whitman's Autograph Revision of the Analysis of Leaves of Grass*, ed. Stephen Railton (New York: New York University Press, 1974), p. 144.

44 "Walt Whitman and the Poetry of the Future," New York *Sun*, 19 November 1881, p. 2.

Editorial Note and Acknowledgments

This volume reprints most of the contemporary reviews of Walt Whitman's works. These reviews, a good window for viewing his immediate critical reception, are generally reproduced in full. In those cases where part of a review has been omitted, the ellipsis has been marked within square brackets. Unbracketed ellipsis dots appear in the original reviews. For clarity's sake, I identify Whitman's poems by using his familiar final titles, as is conventional in Whitman studies.

I thank Joel Myerson of the University of South Carolina for help in procuring illustrations for this volume. Most of the illustrations are drawn from his *Walt Whitman: A Descriptive Bibliography* and are reproduced by courtesy of the University of Pittsburgh Press. Thanks also go to the Tracy W. McGregor Library, Rare Books Department, University of Virginia Library, and to the William D. Bayley Walt Whitman Collection, Ohio Wesleyan University, for photographs of *Poems by Walt Whitman* (1868) and *Complete Poems & Prose of Walt Whitman* (1888), respectively.
   I owe much to Bruce A. White, Randall Waldron, Geoffrey Sill and Guiyou Huang for help in obtaining various photographs and reviews, and to Jerome Loving, M. Thomas Inge, and Ezra Greenspan for assistance with the Introduction.

LEAVES OF GRASS (1855)

Leaves

of

Grass.

—•—

Brooklyn, New York:
1855.

[Charles A. Dana]. "New Publications: *Leaves of Grass*." New York *Daily Tribune*, 23 July 1855, p. 3.

From the unique effigies of the anonymous author of this volume which graces the frontispiece, we may infer that he belongs to the exemplary class of society sometimes irreverently styled "loafers." He is therein represented in a garb, half sailor's, half workman's, with no superfluous appendage of coat or waistcoat, a "wide-awake" perched jauntily on his head, one hand in his pocket and the other on his hip, with a certain air of mild defiance, and an expression of pensive insolence in his face which seems to betoken a consciousness of his mission as the "coming man." This view of the author is confirmed in the preface. He vouchsafes, before introducing us to his poetry, to enlighten our benighted minds as to the true function of the American poet. Evidently the original, which is embodied in the most extraordinary prose since the "Sayings" of the modern Orpheus, was found in the "interior consciousness" of the writer. Of the materials afforded by this country for the operations of poetic art we have a lucid account.

> The Americans of all nations at any time upon the earth have probably the fullest poetical nature. The United States themselves are essentially the greatest poem. In the history of the earth hitherto the largest and most stirring appear tame and orderly to their ampler largeness and stir. Here at last is something in the doings of man that corresponds with the broadcast doings of the day and night. Here is not merely a nation but a teeming nation of nations. Here is action untied from strings, necessarily blind to particulars and details magnificently moving in vast masses. Here is the hospitality which forever indicates heroes ... Here are the roughs and beards and space and ruggedness and nonchalance that the soul loves. Here the performance disdaining the trivial unapproached in the tremendous audacity of its crowds and groupings and the push of its perspective spreads with crampless and flowing breadth and showers its prolific and splendid extravagance. One sees it must indeed own the riches of the Summer and Winter, and need never be bankrupt while corn grows from the ground or the orchards drop apples or the bays contain fish or men beget children upon women.

With veins full of such poetical stuff, the United States, as we are kindly informed, "of all nations most needs poets, and will doubtless have the greatest and use them the greatest." Here is a full-length figure of the true poet:

> Of all mankind the great poet is the equable man. Not in him but off from him things are grotesque or eccentric or fail of their sanity. Nothing out of its place is good and nothing in its place is bad. He bestows on every object or quality its fit proportions, neither more nor less. He is the arbiter of the diverse and he is the key. He is the equalizer of his age and land. ... he supplies what wants supplying and checks what wants checking. If peace is the routine out of him speaks the spirit of peace, large, rich, thrifty, building vast and populous cities, encouraging agriculture and the arts and commerce—lighting the study of man, the soul, immortality—federal, state

3

or municipal government, marriage, health, freetrade, intertravel by land and sea. . . . nothing too close, nothing too far off . . . the stars not too far off. In war he is the most deadly force of the war. Who recruits him recruits horse and foot. . . . he fetches parks of artillery the best that engineer ever knew. If the time becomes slothful and heavy he knows how to arouse it. . . . he can make every word he speaks draw blood. Whatever stagnates in the flat of custom or obedience or legislation, he never stagnates. Obedience does not master him, he masters it. High up out of reach he stands turning a concentrated light. . . . he turns the pivot with his finger. . . . he baffles the swiftest runners as he stands and easily overtakes and envelops them. The time straying toward infidelity and confections and persiflage he withholds by his steady faith. . . . he spreads out his dishes. . . . he offers the sweet firm-fibred meat that grows men and women. His brain is the ultimate brain. He is no arguer . . . he is judgment. He judges not as the judge judges but as the sun falling around a helpless thing. As he sees the farthest he has the most faith. His thoughts are the hymns of the praise of things. In the talk on the soul and eternity and God off of his equal plane he is silent. He sees eternity less like a play with a prologue and denouement . . . he sees eternity in men and women . . . he does not see men and women as dreams or dots.

Of the nature of poetry the writer discourses in a somewhat too oracular strain, especially as he has been anticipated in his "utterances" by Emerson and other modern "prophets of the soul":

The poetic quality is not marshaled in rhyme or uniformity or abstract addresses to things, nor in melancholy complaints or good precepts, but is the life of these and much else and is in the soul. The profit of rhyme is that it drops seeds of a sweeter and more luxuriant rhyme, and of uniformity that it conveys itself into its own roots in the ground out of sight. The rhyme and uniformity of perfect poems show the free growth of metrical laws and bud from them as unerringly and loosely as lilacs or roses on a bush, and take shapes as compact as the shapes of chestnuts and oranges and melons and pears, and shed the perfume impalpable to form. The fluency and ornaments of the finest poems or music or orations or recitations are not independent but dependent. All beauty comes from beautiful blood and a beautiful brain. If the greatnesses are in conjunction in a man or woman it is enough. . . . the fact will prevail through the universe. . . . but the gaggery and gilt of a million years will not prevail. Who troubles himself about his ornaments or fluency is lost. This is what you shall do: Love the earth and sun and the animals, despise riches, give alms to every one that asks, stand up for the stupid and crazy, devote your income and labor to others, hate tyrants, argue not concerning God, have patience and indulgence toward the people, take off your hat to nothing known or unknown or to any man or number of men, go freely with powerful uneducated persons and with the young and with the mothers of families, read these leaves in the open air every season of every year of your life, reexamine all you have been told at school or church or in any book, dismiss whatever insults your own soul, and your very flesh shall be a great poem and have the richest fluency not only in its words

4

but in the silent lines of its lips and face and between the lashes of your eyes and in every motion and joint of your body.

Such is the poetic theory of our name-less bard. He furnishes a severe standard for the estimate of his own productions. His *Leaves of Grass* are doubtless in-tended as an illustration of the natural poet. They are certainly original in their external form, have been shaped on no pre-existent model out of the author's own brain. Indeed, his independence of-ten becomes coarse and defiant. His lan-guage is too frequently reckless and inde-cent though this appears to arise from a naive unconsciousness rather than from an impure mind. His words might have passed between Adam and Eve in Para-dise, before the want of fig-leaves brought no shame; but they are quite out of place amid the decorum of modern society, and will justly prevent his volume from free circulation in scrupulous circles. With these glaring faults, the *Leaves of Grass* are not destitute of peculiar poetic merits, which will awaken an interest in the lov-ers of literary curiosities. They are full of bold, stirring thoughts—with occasional passages of effective description, betray-ing a genuine intimacy with Nature and a keen appreciation of beauty—often pre-senting a rare felicity of diction, but so disfigured with eccentric fancies as to prevent a consecutive perusal without of-fense, though no impartial reader can fail to be impressed with the vigor and quaint beauty of isolated portions. A few speci-mens will suffice to give an idea of this odd genius.

THE LOVER OF NATURE.

I am he that walks with the tender
   and growing night;
I call to the earth and sea half-held
   by the night.

Press close barebosomed night! Press
   close magnetic nourishing night!
Night of south winds! Night of the
   large few stars!
Still nodding night! Mad naked
   summer night!
Smile O voluptuous coolbreathed
   earth!
Earth of the slumbering and liquid
   trees!
Earth of departed sunset! Earth of the
   mountains misty-topt!
Earth of the vitreous pour of the full
   moon just tinged with blue!
Earth of shine and dark mottling the
   tide of the river!
Earth of the limpid gray of clouds
   brighter and clearer for my sake!
Far-swooping elbowed earth! Rich
   apple-blossomed earth!
Smile, for your lover comes!

Prodigal! you have given me
   love!. . . . therefore I to you give
   love!
O unspeakable passionate love!
You sea! I resign myself to you
   also. . . . I guess what you mean,
I behold from the beach your
   crooked inviting fingers,
I believe you refuse to go back
   without feeling of me;
We must have a turn together. . . . I
   undress. . . . hurry me out of sight
   of the land,
Cushion me soft. . . . rock me in
   billowy drowse,
Dash me with amorous wet. . . . I can
   repay you.

Sea of stretched ground-swells!
Sea breathing broad and convulsive
   breaths!
Sea of the brine of life! Sea of
   unshoveled and always-ready
   graves!
Howler and scooper of storms!
   Capricious and dainty sea!

I am integral with you. . . . I too am
of one phase and of all phases.

AFTER A SEA-FIGHT.

Stretched and still lay the midnight,
Two great hulls motionless on the
   breast of the darkness,
Our vessel riddled and slowly
   sinking . . . preparations to pass to
   the one we had conquered,
The captain on the quarter-deck
   coldly giving his orders through a
   countenance white as a sheet,
Near by the corpse of the child that
   served in the cabin,
The dead face of an old salt with
   long white hair and carefully curled
   whiskers,
The flames spite of all that could be
   done flickering aloft and below,
The husky voices of the two or three
   officers yet fit for duty,
Formless stacks of bodies and bodies
   by themselves . . . dabs of flesh
   upon the mass and spars,
The cut of cordage and dangle of
   rigging. . . . the slight shock of the
   soothe of waves,
Black and impassive guns, and litter
   of powder parcels, and the strong
   scent,
Delicate sniffs of the seabreeze. . . .
   smells of sedgy grass and fields by
   the shore. . . . death messages given
   in charge to survivors,
The hiss of the surgeon's knife and
   the gnawing teeth of his saw,
The wheeze, the cluck, the swash of
   falling blood. . . . the short wild
   scream, the long dull tapering
   groan,
These so. . . . these irretrievable!

NATURAL IDEALISM.

All doctrines, all politics and
   civilization exurge from you,
All scripture and monuments and
anything inscribed anywhere are
   tallied in you,
The gist of histories and statistics as
   far back as the records reach is in
   you this hour—and myths and tales
   the same;
If you were not breathing and
   walking here where would they all
   be?
The most renowned poems would be
   ashes . . . orations and plays would
   be vacuums.
All architecture is what you do to it
   when you look upon it;
Did you think it was in the white or
   gray stone? or the lines of the
   arches and cornices?
All music is what awakens from you
   when you are reminded by the
   instruments,
It is not the violins and the
   cornets. . . . it is not the oboe nor
   the beating drums—nor the notes
   of the baritone singer singing his
   sweet romanza. . . . nor those of
   the men's chorus, nor those of the
   women's chorus,
It is nearer and further than they.

THE LAST OF EARTH.

When the dull nights are over, and
   the dull days also,
When the soreness of lying so much
   in bed is over,
When the physician, after long
   putting off, gives the silent and
   terrible look for an answer,
When the children come hurried and
   weeping, and the brothers and
   sisters have been sent for,
When medicines stand unused on the
   shelf, and the camphor-smell has
   pervaded the rooms,
When the faithful hand of the living
   does not desert the hand of the
   dying,
When the twitching lips press lightly

on the forehead of the dying,
When the breath ceases and the pulse
of the heart ceases,
Then the corpse-limbs stretch on the
bed, and the living look upon
them.
They are palpable as the living are
palpable.

The living look upon the corpse with
their eyesight.
But without eyesight lingers a
different living and looks curiously
on the corpse.

THE HUMAN FACE DIVINE.

Sauntering the pavement or riding the
country by-road here then are
faces,
Faces of friendship, precision,
caution, suavity, ideality,
The spiritual prescient face, the
always welcome common
benevolent face,
The face of the singing of music, the
grand faces of natural lawyers and
judges broad at the backtop,
The faces of hunters and fishers,
bulged at the brows. . . . the shaved
blanched faces of orthodox
citizens,
The pure extravagant yearning
questioning artist's face,
The welcome ugly face of some
beautiful soul. . . . the handsome
detested or despised face,
The sacred faces of infants . . . the
illuminated face of the mother of
many children,
The face of an amour . . . the face of
veneration,
The face as of a dream . . . the face of
an immobile rock,
The face withdrawn of its good and
bad . . . a castrated face,
A wild hawk . . . his wings clipped by
the clipper.

Sauntering the pavement or crossing
the ceaseless ferry, here then are
faces;
I see them and complain not and am
content with all.
Do you suppose I could be content
with all if I thought them their
own finale?
This now is too lamentable a face for
a man:
Some abject louse asking leave to
be . . . cringing for it,
Some milk-nosed maggot blessing
what lets it wrig to its hole.

This face is a dog's snout sniffing for
garbage;
Snakes nest in that mouth . . . I hear
the sibilant threat.
This face is a haze more chill than
the Arctic Sea,
Its sleepy and wobbling icebergs
crunch as they go.
This is a face of bitter herbs . . . this
an emetic . . . they need no label,
And more of the drug-shelf . . .
laudanum, caoutchouc, or hog's
lard.

This face is an epilepsy advertising
and doing business. . . . its wordless
tongue gives out the unearthly cry,
Its veins down the neck distend. . . .
its eyes roll till they show nothing
but their whites,
Its teeth grit . . . the palms of the
hands are cut by the turned-in
nails,
The man falls struggling and foaming
to the ground while he speculates
well.
This face is bitten by vermin and
worms,
And this is some murderer's knife
with a half-pulled scabbard.

This face owes to the sexton his
dismalest fee,
As unceasing death-bell tolls there.

The volume contains many more "Leaves of Grass" of similar quality, as well as others which cannot be especially commended either for fragrance or form. Whatever severity of criticism they may challenge for their rude ingenuousness, and their frequent divergence into the domain of the fantastic, the taste of not over dainty fastidiousness will discern much of the essential spirit of poetry beneath an uncouth and grotesque embodiment.

Life Illustrated, 28 July 1855 [page number unknown].

A curious title; but the book itself is a hundred times more curious. It is like no other book that ever was written, and therefore, the language usually employed in notices of new publications is unavailable in describing it.

It is a thin volume of 95 pages, shaped like a small atlas. On the first page is a portrait of the unknown author. He stands in a careless attitude, without coat or vest, with a rough felt hat on his head, one hand thurst [sic.] lazily into his pocket and the other resting on his hip. He is the picture of a *perfect loafer;* yet a thoughtful loafer, an amiable loafer, an able loafer. Then follows a long preface, which most steadygoing, respectable people would pronounce perfect nonsense, but which free-souled persons, here and there, will read and *chuckle over* with real delight, as the expression of their own best feelings. This remarkable preface is something in the Emersonian manner—that is, it is a succession of independent sentences, many of which are of striking truth and beauty. The body of the vol-

ume is filled with 'Leaves of Grass,' which are lines of rhythmical prose, or a series of *utterances* (we know not what else to call them), unconnected, curious, and original. The book, perhaps, might be called, *American Life, from a Poetical Loafer's Point of View.*

The discerning reader will find in this singular book much that will please him, and we advise all who are fond of new and peculiar things to procure it. We may add that the book was printed by the author's own hands, and that he is philosophically indifferent as to its sale. It pleased him to write *so,* and the public may take it or let it alone, just as they prefer.

[Walt Whitman]. "Walt Whitman and His Poems." *United States Review* 5 (September 1855), 205–12.

An American bard at last! One of the roughs, large, proud, affectionate, eating, drinking, and breeding, his costume manly and free, his face sunburnt and bearded, his posture strong and erect, his voice bringing hope and prophecy to the generous races of young and old. We shall cease shamming and be what we really are. We shall start an athletic and defiant literature. We realize now how it is, and what was most lacking. The interior American republic shall also be declared free and independent.

For all our intellectual people, followed by their books, poems, novels, essays, editorials, lectures, tuitions, and criticism, dress by London and Paris modes, receive what is received there, obey the authorities, settle disputes by the old tests, keep out of rain and sun, retreat to the shelter of houses and schools, trim their hair, shave, touch not the earth barefoot, and enter not the sea except in a complete bathing-dress. One sees unmistakably genteel persons, travelled, college-learned, used to be served by servants, conversing without heat or vulgarity, supported on chairs, or walking through handsomely-carpeted parlors, or along shelves bearing well-bound volumes, and walls adorned with curtained and collared portraits, and china things, and nick-nacks. But where in American literature is the first show of America? Where are the gristle and beards, and broad breasts, and space and ruggedness and nonchalance that the souls of the people love? Where is the tremendous outdoors of these States? Where is the majesty of the federal mother, seated with more than antique grace, calm, just, indulgent to her brood of children, calling them around her regarding the little and the large and the younger and the older with perfect impartiality? Where is the vehement growth of our cities? Where is the spirit of the strong rich life of the American mechanic, farmer, sailor, hunter, and miner? Where is the huge composite of all other nations, cast in a fresher and brawnier matrix, passing adolescence, and needed this day, live and arrogant, to lead the marches of the world?

Self-reliant, with haughty eyes, assuming to himself all the attributes of his country, steps Walt Whitman into literature, talking like a man unaware that there was ever hitherto such a production as a book, or such a being as a writer. Every move of him has the free play of the muscle of one who never knew what it was to feel that he stood in the presence of a superior. Every word that falls from his mouth shows silent disdain and defiance of the old theories and forms.

Every phrase announces new laws; not once do his lips unclose except in conformity with them. With light and rapid touch he first indicates in prose the principles of the foundation of a race of poets so deeply to spring from the American people, and become ingrained through them, that their Presidents shall not be the common referees so much as that great race of poets shall. He proceeds himself to exemplify this new school, and set models for their expression and range of subjects. He makes audacious and native use of his own body and soul. He must re-create poetry with the elements always at hand. He must imbue it with himself as he is, disorderly, fleshy, and sensual, a lover of things, yet a lover of men and women above the whole of the other objects of the universe. His work is to be achieved by unusual methods. Neither classic or romantic is he, nor a materialist any more than a spiritualist. Not a whisper comes out of him of the old stock talk and rhyme of poetry—not the first recognition of gods or goddesses, or Greece or Rome. No breath of Europe, or her monarchies, or priestly conventions, or her notions of gentlemen and ladies founded on the idea of caste, seems ever to have fanned his face or been inhaled into his lungs. But in their stead pour vast and fluid the fresh mentality of this mighty age, and the realities of this mighty continent, and the sciences and inventions and discoveries of the present world. Not geology, nor mathematics, nor chemistry, nor navigation, nor astronomy, nor anatomy, nor physiology, nor engineering, is more true to itself than Walt Whitman is true to them. They and the other sciences underlie his whole superstructure. In the beauty of the work of the poet, he affirms, are the tuft and final applause of science.

Affairs then are this man's poems. He will still inject nature through civilization.

The movement of his verses is the sweeping movement of great currents of living people, with a general government, and state and municipal governments, courts, commerce, manufactures, arsenals, steamships, railroads, telegraphs, cities with paved streets, and aqueducts, and police and gas—myriads of travellers arriving and departing—newspapers, music, elections and all the features and processes of the nineteenth century in the wholesomest race and the only stable form of politics at present upon the earth. Along his words spread the broad impartialities of the United States. No innovations must be permitted on the stern severities of our liberty and equality. Undecked also is this poet with sentimentalism, or jingle, or nice conceits or flowery similes. He appears in his poems surrounded by women and children, and by young men, and by common objects and qualities. He gives to each just what belongs to it, neither more or less. The person nearest him, that person he ushers hand in hand with himself. Duly take places in his flowing procession, and step to the sounds of the newer and larger music, the essences of American things, and past and present events—the enormous diversity of temperature and agriculture and mines—the tribes of red aborigines—the weatherbeaten vessels entering new ports, or making landings on rocky coasts—the first settlements north and south—the rapid stature and impatience of outside control—the sturdy defiance of '76, and the war and peace, and the leadership of Washington, and the formation of the Constitution—the Union always calm and impregnable—the perpetual coming of immigrants—the wharf-hemmed cities and superior marine—the unsurveyed interior—the log-house, and clearings, and wild animals, and hunters, and trappers—the fisheries, and whaling, and golddigging—the endless gestation of new states—the convening of Congress every December, the members coming up from all climates, and from the uttermost parts—the noble character of the free American workman and workwoman—the fierceness of the people when well-roused—the ardor of their friendships—the large amativeness—the Yankee swap—the New York fireman, and the target excursion—the southern plantation life—the character of the north-east, and of the north-west and south-west—and the character of America and the American people everywhere. For these the old usages of poets afford Walt Whitman no means sufficiently fit and free, and he rejects the old usages. The style of the bard that is waited for is to be transcendent and new. It is to be indirect and not direct or descriptive or epic. Its quality is to go through these to much more. Let the age and wars (he says) of other nations be chanted, and their eras and characters be illustrated, and that finish the verse. Not so (he continues) the great psalm of the republic. Here the theme is creative and has vista. Here comes one among the well-beloved stonecutters, and announces himself, and plans with decision and science, and sees the solid and beautiful forms of the future where there are now no solid forms.

The style of these poems, therefore, is simply their own style, new-born and red. Nature may have given the hint to the author of the *Leaves of Grass*, but there exists no book or fragment of a book, which can have given the hint to them. All beauty, he says, comes from beautiful blood and a beautiful brain. His rhythm and uniformity he will conceal in the roots of his verses, not to be seen of themselves, but to break forth loosely as lilies on a bush, and take shapes compact as the shapes of melons, or chestnuts, or pears.

The poems of the *Leaves of Grass* are twelve in number. Walt Whitman at first proceeds to put his own body and soul into the new versification:

"I celebrate myself,
And what I assume you shall assume,
For every atom belonging to me, as good belongs to you."

He leaves houses and their shuttered rooms, for the open air. He drops disguise and ceremony, and walks forth with the confidence and gayety of a child. For the old decorums of writing he substitutes new decorums. The first glance out of his eyes electrifies him with love and delight. He will have the earth receive and return his affection; he will stay with it as the bride-groom stays with the bride. The cool-breathed ground, the slumbering and liquid trees, the just-gone sunset, the vitreous pour of the full moon, the tender and growing night, he salutes and touches, and they touch him. The sea supports him, and hurries him off with its powerful and crooked fingers. Dash me with amorous wet! then he says, I can repay you.

By this writer the rules of polite circles are dismissed with scorn. Your stale modesties, he says, are filthy to such a man as I.

"I believe in the flesh and the appetites,
Seeing, hearing, and feeling are miracles, and each part and tag of me is a miracle.
I do not press my finger across my mouth,
I keep as delicate around the bowels as around the head and heart."

No sniveller, or tea-drinking poet, no puny clawback or prude, is Walt Whitman. He will bring poems fit to fill the days and nights—fit for men and women with the attributes of throbbing blood and flesh. The body, he teaches, is beautiful. Sex is also beautiful. Are you to be put down, he seems to ask, to that shallow level of literature and conversation that stops a man's recognizing the delicious pleasure of his sex, or a woman hers? Nature he proclaims inherently pure. Sex will not be put aside; it is a great ordination of the universe. He works the muscle of the male and the teeming fibre of the female throughout his writings, as wholesome realities, impure only by deliberate intention and effort. To men and women he says: You can have healthy and powerful breeds of children on no less terms than these of mine. Follow me and there shall be taller and nobler crops of humanity on the earth.

In the *Leaves of Grass* are the facts of eternity and immortality, largely treated. Happiness is no dream, and perfection is no dream. Amelioration is my lesson, he says with calm voice, and progress is my lesson and the lesson of all things. Then his persuasion becomes a taunt, and his love bitter and compulsory. With strong and steady call he addresses men. Come, he seems to say, from the midst of all that you have been your whole life surrounding yourself with. Leave all the preaching and teaching of others, and mind only these words of mine.

"Long enough have you dreamed contemptible dreams,
Now I wash the gum from your eyes,
You must habit yourself to the dazzle of the light and of every moment of your life.

Long have you timidly waded, holding a plank by the shore,
Now I will you to be a bold swimmer,

11

To jump off in the midst of the sea,
and rise again and nod to me and
shout, and laughingly dash with
your hair.
I am the teacher of athletes,
He that by me spreads a wider
breast than my own proves the
width of my own,
He most honors my style who learns
under it to destroy the teacher.
The boy I love, the same becomes a
man not through derived power
but in his own right,
Wicked, rather than virtuous out of
conformity or fear,
Fond of his sweetheart, relishing
well his steak,
Unrequited love or a slight cutting
him worse than a wound cuts,
First rate to ride, to fight, to hit the
bull's eye, to sail a skiff; to sing a
song, or play on the banjo,
Preferring scars and faces pitted
with small-pox over all latherers
and those that keep out of the
sun.
I teach straying from me, yet who
can stray from me?
I follow you whoever you are from
the present hour;
My words itch at your ears till you
understand them.

I do not say these things for a
dollar, or to fill up the time while
I wait for a boat;
It is you talking just as much as
myself—I act as the tongue of
you.
It was tied in your mouth—in mine
it begins to be loosened.
I swear I will never mention love or
death inside a house,
And I swear I never will translate
myself at all, only to him or her
who privately stays with me in
the open air."

The eleven other poems have each distinct purposes, curiously veiled. Theirs is
no writer to be gone through with in a
day or a month. Rather it is his pleasure
to elude you and provoke you for deliberate purposes of his own.

Doubtless in the scheme this man has
built for himself the writing of poems is
but a proportionate part of the whole. It
is plain that public and private performance, politics, love, friendship, behav-
ior, the art of conversation, science, society, the American people, the reception of
the great novelties of city and country, all
have their equal call upon him and receive equal attention. In politics he could
enter with the freedom and reality he
shows in poetry. His scope of life is the
amplest of any yet in philosophy. He is
the true spiritualist. He recognizes no annihilation, or death, or loss of identity.
He is the largest lover and sympathizer
that has appeared in literature. He loves
the earth and sun, and the animals. He
does not separate the learned from the
unlearned, the Northerner from the Southerner, the white from the black, or the
native from the immigrant just landed at
the wharf. Every one, he seems to say,
appears excellent to me, every employment is adorned, and every male and female glorious.

"The press of my foot to the earth
springs a hundred affections,
They scorn the best I can do to
relate them.

I am enamored of growing outdoors,
Of men that live among cattle or
taste of the ocean or woods,
Of the builders and steerers of ships,
of the wielders of axes and mauls,
of the drivers of horses,
I can eat and sleep with them, week
in and week out.

What is commonest and cheapest

12

and nearest and easiest is Me,
Me going in for my chances,
    spending for vast returns,
Adorning myself to bestow myself
    on the first that will take me,
Not asking the sky to come down to
    my good will.
Scattering it freely for ever."

If health were not his distinguishing
attribute, this poet would be the very har-
lot of persons. Right and left he flings his
arms, drawing men and women with undeniable love to his close embrace, loving
the clasp of their hands, the touch of
their necks and breasts, and the sound of
their voice. All else seems to burn up under his fierce affection for persons. Politics, religion, institutions, art, quickly fall
aside before them. In the whole universe,
he says, I see nothing more divine than
human souls.

"When the psalm sings instead of
    singer,
When the script preaches instead of
    the preacher,
When the pulpit descends and goes
    instead of the carver that carved
    the supporting desk,
When the sacred vessels or the bits
    of the eucharist, or the lath and
    plast, procreate as effectually as
    the young silversmiths or bakers,
    or the masons in their overalls,
When a university course convinces
    like a slumbering woman and
    child convince,
When the minted gold in the vault
    smiles like the night-watchman's
    daughter,
When warrantee deeds loafe in
    chairs opposite, and are my
    friendly companions,
I intend to reach them my hand and
    make as much of them as I make
    of men and women."

Who then is that insolent unknown?
Who is it, praising himself as if others
were not fit to do it, and coming rough
and unbidden among writers to unsettle
what was settled, and to revolutionize, in
fact, our modern civilization? Walt Whitman was born on Long-Island, on the
hills about thirty miles from the greatest
American city, on the last day of May,
1819, and has grown up in Brooklyn and
New York to be thirty-six years old, to
enjoy perfect health, and to understand
his country and its spirit.

Interrogations more than this, and that
will not be put off unanswered, spring
continually through the perusal of these
Leaves of Grass:

If there were to be selected, out of the
incalculable volumes of printed matter in
existence, any single work to stand for
America and her times, should this be the
work?

Must not the true American poet indeed absorb all others, and present a new
and far more ample and vigorous type?

Has not the time arrived for a school
of live writing and tuition consistent with
the principles of these poems? consistent
with the free spirit of this age, and with
the American truths of politics? consistent with geology, and astronomy, and all
science and human physiology? consistent with the sublimity of immortality and
the directness of common-sense?

If in this poem the United States have
found their poetic voice, and taken measure and form, is it any more than a beginning? Walt Whitman himself disclaims
singularity in his work, and announces
the coming after him of great successions
of poets, and that he but lifts his finger to
give the signal.

Was he not needed? Has not literature
been bred in and in long enough? Has it
not become unbearably artificial?

Shall a man of faith and practice in
the simplicity of real things be called

13

eccentric, while the disciple of the fictitious school writes without question?

Shall it still be the amazement of the light and dark that freshness of expression is the rarest quality of all?

You have come in good time, Walt Whitman! In opinions, in manners, in costumes, in books, in the aims and occupancy of life, in associates, in poems, conformity to all unnatural and tainted customs passes without remark, while perfect naturalness, health, faith, self-reliance, and all primal expressions of the manliest love and friendship, subject one to the stare and controversy of the world.

[Charles Eliot Norton]. "Whitman's *Leaves of Grass.*" *Putnam's Monthly: A Magazine of Literature, Science, and Art* 6 (September 1855), 321–3.

Our account of the last month's literature would be incomplete without some notice of a curious and lawless collection of poems, called *Leaves of Grass*, and issued in a thin quarto without the name of publisher or author. The poems, twelve in number, are neither in rhyme nor blank verse, but in a sort of excited prose broken into lines without any attempt at measure or regularity, and, as many readers will perhaps think, without any idea of sense or reason. The writer's scorn for the wonted usages of good writing; extends to the vocabulary he adopts; words usually banished from polite society are here employed without reserve and with perfect indifference to their effect on the reader's mind; and not only is the book one not to be read aloud to a mixed audience, but the introduction of terms, never before heard or seen, and of slang expressions, often renders an otherwise striking passage altogether laughable. But, as the writer is a new light in poetry, it is only fair to let him state his theory for himself. We extract from the preface:—

"The art of art, the glory of expression, is simplicity. Nothing is better than simplicity, and the sunlight of letters is simplicity. Nothing is better than simplicity—nothing can make up for excess, or for the lack of definiteness ... To speak in literature, with the perfect rectitude and the insouciance of the movements of animals and the unimpeachableness of the sentiment of trees in the woods, is the flawless triumph of art ... The greatest poet has less a marked style, and is more the channel of thought and things, without increase or diminution, and is the free channel of himself. He swears to his art, I will not be meddlesome, I will not have in my writing any elegance, or effect, or originality to hang in the way between me and the rest, like curtains. What I feel, I feel for precisely what it is. Let who may exalt, or startle, or fascinate, or soothe, I will have purposes, as health, or heat, or snow has, and be as regardless of observation. What I experience or portray shall go from my composition without a shred of my composition. You shall stand by my side to look in the mirror with me."

The application of these principles, and of many others equally peculiar, which are expounded in a style equally oracular throughout the long preface,— is made *passim*, and often with comical

14

success, in the poems themselves, which may briefly be described as a compound of the New England transcendentalist and New York rowdy. A fireman or omnibus driver, who had intelligence enough to absorb the speculations of that school of thought which culminated at Boston some fifteen or eighteen years ago, and resources of expression to put them forth again in a form of his own, with sufficient self-conceit and contempt for public taste to affront all usual propriety of diction, might have written this gross yet elevated, this superficial yet profound, this preposterous yet somehow fascinating book. As we say, it is a mixture of Yankee transcendentalism and New York rowdyism, and, what must be surprising to both these elements, they here seem to fuse and combine with the most perfect harmony. The vast and vague conceptions of the one, lose nothing of their quality in passing through the coarse and odd intellectual medium of the other; while there is an original perception of nature, a manly brawn, and an epic directness in our new poet, which belong to no other adept of the transcendental school. But we have no intention of regularly criticising this very irregular production; our aim is rather to cull, from the rough and ragged thicket of its pages, a few passages equally remarkable in point of thought and expression. Of course we do not select those which are the most transcendental or the most bold:—

> "I play not a march for victors
>   only. . . . I play great marches for
>   conquered and slain persons.
>   Have you heard that it was good to
>   gain the day?
>   I also say it is good to fall . . .
>   battles are lost in the same spirit
>   in which they are won.
>   I sound triumphal drums for the
>   dead. . . .

> I fling through my embouchures the
>   loudest and gayest music to them—
> Vivas to those who have failed, and
>   to those whose war-vessels sank
>   in the sea, and to those
>   themselves who sank in the sea.
> And to all generals that lost
>   engagements, and to all overcome
>   heroes, and the numberless
>   unknown heroes equal to the
>   greatest heroes known."

> "I am the mashed fireman, with
>   breast-bone broken. . . . tumbling
>   walls buried me in their debris—
> Heat and smoke, I respired. . . . I
>   heard the yelling shouts of my
>   comrades—
> I heard the distant click of their
>   picks and shovels.
> They have cleared the beams
>   away. . . . they tenderly lift me
>   forth.
> I lie in the night air in my red
>   shirt. . . . the pervading hush is for
>   my sake.
> Painless after all I lie, exhausted, but
>   not so unhappy.
> White and beautiful are the faces
>   around me. . . . the heads are
>   bared of their firecaps—
> The kneeling crowd fades with the
>   light of the torches."

> ———

> "I tell not the fall of Alamo. . . . not
>   one escaped to tell the fall of
>   Alamo:
> The hundred and fifty are dumb yet
>   at Alamo.
>   .   .   .   .

> They were the glory of the race of
>   rangers,
> Matchless with a horse, a rifle, a
>   song, a supper, or a courtship:
> Large, turbulent, brave, handsome,
>   generous, proud and
>   affectionate—

Bearded, sun-burnt, dressed in the
free costume of hunters."

———

"Did you read in the books of the
old-fashioned frigate fight?
Did you learn who won by the light
of the moon and stars?
Our foe was no skulk in his ship, I
tell you,
His was the English pluck, and there
is no tougher or truer, and never
was, and never will be:
Along the lowered eve he came,
terribly raking us.

We close with him: the yards
entangled . . . the masts touched:
My captain lashed fast with his own
hands.
We had received some eighteen-
pound shots under the water—
On our lower gun-deck two large
pieces had burst at the first fire,
killing all around and blowing up,
overhead.
Ten o'clock at night and the full
moon shining, and the leaks on
the gain, and five feet of water
reported;
The master-at-arms loosing the
prisoners in the after-hold, to give
them a chance for themselves.
The transit to and from the
magazine was now stopped by the
sentinels—
They saw so many strange faces,
they did not know whom to trust.

Our frigate was a-fire—the other
asked if we demanded quarters? if
our colors were struck and the
fighting done?
I laughed content when I heard the
voice of my little captain—
'We have not struck,' he composedly
cried. 'We have just begun our
part of the fighting.'
Only three guns were in use.

One was directed by the captain
himself, against the enemy's
mainmast:
Two, well served with grape and
canister, silenced his musketry and
cleared his decks.

.   .   .   .   .

Not a moment's cease—
The leaks gained fast on the
pumps. . . . the fire eat toward the
powder magazine:
One of the pumps was shot away; it
was generally thought we were
sinking.
Serene stood the little captain:
He was not hurried. . . . his voice
was neither high nor low—
His eyes gave more light to us than
our battle-lanterns.
Toward twelve at night, there in the
beams of the moon, they
surrendered to us."

———

"As to you, life, I reckon you are the
leavings of many deaths:
No doubt I have died myself ten
thousand times before.
I hear you whispering there, O stars
of heaven—
O suns! O grave of graves! O
perpetual transfers and
promotions, if you do not say
anything, how can I say anything,
Of the turbid pool that lies in the
autumn forest—
Of the moon that descends the
steeps of the soughing twilight?
Toss, sparkles of day and dusk—
toss on the black stems that decay
in the muck—
Toss to the moaning gibberish of the
dry limbs!"

———

"A slave at auction!
I help the auctioneer. . . . the sloven
does not half know his business.

16

'Gentlemen, look on this curious
   creature:
Whatever the bids of the bidders,
   they cannot be high enough for
   him—
For him, the globe lay preparing
   quintillions of years, without one
   animal or plant—
For him the revolving cycles truly
   and steadily rolled:
In that head, the all-baffling brain—
In it, and below it, the making of
   heroes.
Examine these limbs, red, black, or
   white . . . they are very cunning in
   tendon and nerve;
They shall be stript, that you may
   see them.

.   .   .   .

Within there runs his blood. . . . the
   same old blood. . . . . the same
   red-running blood—
There, swells and jets his heart. . . .
   there all passions and desires. . . .
   all reachings and aspirations;
Do you think they are not there,
   because they are not expressed in
   parlors and lecture rooms?
This is not only one man. . . . he is
   the father of those who shall be
   fathers in their turns:
In him the start of populous states
   and rich republics;
Of him, countless immortal lives,
   with countless embodiments and
   enjoyments.
How do you know who shall come
   from the offspring of his
   offspring, through the centuries?

.   .   .   .   .

A woman at auction!
She, too, is not only herself . . . she
   is the teeming mother of mothers:
She is the bearer of them who shall
   grow and be mates to the
   mothers.
Her daughters, or their daughters'

daughters . . . who knows who
   shall mate with them?
Who knows, through the centuries,
   what heroes may come from
   them?
In them, and of them, natal love . . .
   in them the divine mystery . . . the
   same old, beautiful mystery."

————

"Behold a woman!
She looks out from her Quaker
   cap. . . . her face is clearer and
   more beautiful than the sky,
She sits in an arm-chair, under the
   shaded porch of the farm house—
The sun just shines on her old white
   head.
Her ample gown is of cream-hued
   linen:
Her grandsons raised the flax, and
   her granddaughters spun it with
   the distaff and the wheel.
The melodious character of the
   earth!
The finish, beyond which
   philosophy cannot go, and does
   not wish to go!
The justified mother of men!"

————

"Old age superbly rising! Ineffable
   grace of dying days."

————

"Day, full-blown and splendid. . . .
   day of the immense sun, and
   action, and ambition, and
   laughter:
The night follows close, with
   millions of suns, and sleep, and
   restoring darkness."

As seems very proper in a book of
transcendental poetry, the author withholds his name from the title page, and
presents his portrait, neatly engraved on
steel, instead. This, no doubt, is upon the

principle that the name is merely accidental; while the portrait affords an idea of the essential being from whom these utterances proceed. We must add, however, that this significant reticence does not prevail throughout the volume, for we learn on p. 29, that our poet is "Walt Whitman, an American, one of the roughs, a kosmos." That he was an American, we knew before, for, aside from America, there is no quarter of the universe where such a production could have had a genesis. That he was one of the roughs was also tolerably plain; but that he was a kosmos, is a piece of news we were hardly prepared for. Precisely what a kosmos is, we trust Mr. Whitman will take an early occasion to inform the impatient public.

"*Leaves of Grass*—an Extraordinary Book." Brooklyn *Daily Eagle*, 15 September 1855, p. 2.

Here we have a book which fairly staggers us. It sets all the ordinary rules of criticism at defiance. It is one of the strangest compounds of transcendentalism, bombast, philosophy, folly, wisdom, wit and dullness which it ever catered into the heart of man to conceive. Its author is Walter Whitman, and the book is a reproduction of the author. His name is not on the frontispiece, but his portrait, half length, is. The contents of the book form a daguerreotype of his inner being, and the title page bears a representation of its physical tabernacle. It is a poem; but it conforms to none of the rules by which poetry has ever been judged. It is not an epic nor an ode, nor a lyric; nor does its verses move with the measured pace of poetical feet—of Iambic, Trochaic or Anapaestic, nor seek the aid of Amphibrach, of dactyl or Spondee, nor of final or cesural pause, except by accident. But we had better give Walt's own conception of what a poet of the age and country should be. We quote from the preface:

"Other States indicate themselves in their deputies, but the genius of the United States is not best or most in executives or legislatures, nor in its ambassadors or authors, or colleges, or churches, or parlors, nor even in its newspapers or inventors; but always most in the common people, their manners, speech, dress, friendship— the friendship and candor of their physiognomy—the picturesque looseness of their carriage—their deathless attachment to freedom—their aversion to anything indecorous, or soft or mean, the practical acknowledgment of the citizens of all other States—the fierceness of their roused resentments— their curiosity and welcome of novelty—their self-esteem and wonderful sympathy—their susceptibility of a slight—the air they have of persons who never knew how it felt to stand in the presence of superiors—the fluency of their speech—their delight in music, the sure symptom of manly tenderness and native elegance of soul— their good temper and open handedness—the terrible significance of their elections—the President's taking off his hat to them, not they to him— these too are unrhymed poetry."

But the poetry which the author contemplates must reflect the nation as well as the people themselves.

"His spirit responds to his country's spirit; he incarnates its geography and natural life, and rivers and lakes. Mississippi with annual freshets and changing chutes, Missouri, and Columbia, and Ohio, and the beautiful masculine Hudson, do not embouchure where they spend themselves more than they embouchure into him. The blue breadth over the inland sea of Virginia and Maryland, and the sea of Massachusetts and Maine, over Manhattan Bay, and over Champlain and Erie, and over Ontario and Huron, and Michigan and Superior, and over the Texan, and Mexican, and Floridian and Cuban seas, and over the seas of California and Oregon, is not tallied by the blue breadth of the waters below more than the breadth of above and below is tallied by him.

... "To him enter the essence of the real things, and past and present events—of the enormous diversity of temperature, and agriculture, and mines—the tribes of red aborigines—the weather-beaten vessels entering new ports or making landings on rocky coasts—the first settlement North and South—the rapid stature and muscle—the haughty defiance of '76, and the war, and peace, and formation of the constitution—the union surrounded by blatherers, and always impregnable—the perpetual coming of immigrants—the wharf-hemmed cities and superior marine—the unsurveyed interior—the log houses, and clearings, and wild animals, and hunters, and trappers—the free commerce, the fishing, and whaling, and gold digging—the endless gestation of new States—the convening of Congress every December, the members duly coming up from all climates and the uttermost parts—the noble character of the young mechanics, and of all free American workmen and workwomen—the general ardor, and friendliness, and enterprise—the perfect equality of the female with the male—the large amativeness—the fluid movement of the population," &c. . . .

"For such the expression of the American poet is to be transcendent and new."

And the poem seems to accord with the ideas here laid down. No drawing room poet is the author of the *Leaves of Grass*; he prates not of guitar thrumming under ladies' windows, nor deals in the extravagances of sentimentalism; no pretty conceits or polished fancies are tacked together "like orient pearls at random strung;" but we have the free utterance of an untramelled spirit without the slightest regard to established models or fixed standards of taste. His scenery presents no shaven lawns or neatly trimmed arbors; no hot house conservatory, where delicate exotics odorise the air and enchant the eye. If we follow the poet we must scale unknown precipices and climb untrodden mountains; or we boat on nameless lakes, encountering probably rapids and waterfalls, and start wild fowls never classified by Wilson or Audubon; or we wander among primeval forests, now pressing the yielding surface of velvet moss, and anon caught among thickets and brambles. He believes in the ancient philosophy that there is no more real beauty or merit in one particle of matter than another; he appreciates all; everything is right that is in its place, and everything is wrong that is not in its place. He is guilty, not only of breaches of conventional decorum but treats with nonchalant defiance what goes by the name of refinement and delicacy of feeling and expression. Whatever is natural he takes to his heart; whatever is artificial (in the frivolous sense) he makes of no account. The following description of himself is more truthful than many self-drawn pictures:

19

"Apart from the pulling and hauling,
    stands what I am,
Stands amused, complacent,
    compassionating, idle, unitary,
Looks down, is erect, bends an arm
    on an impalpable certain rest,
Looks with its side-curved head
    curious, what will come next,
Both in and out of the game, and
    watching and wondering at it."

As a poetic interpretation of nature, we believe the following is not surpassed in the range of poetry:

"A child said, What is grass! fetching
    it to me with full hands;
How could I answer the child! I do
    not know any more than he.
I guess it is the handkerchief of the
    Lord;
A scented gift and remembrancer,
    designedly dropped,
Bearing the owner's name someway
    on the corners, that we may see,
    and remark, and say, Whose?"

We are afforded glimpses of half-formed pictures to tease and tantalize with their indistinctness: like a crimson cheek and flashing eye looking on us through the leaves of an arbor—mocking us for a moment, but vanishing before we can reach them. Here is an example:

"Twenty-eight young men bathe by
    the shore;
Twenty-eight young men, and all so
    friendly.
Twenty-eight years of womanly life
    and all so lonesome.
She owns the fine house by the rise
    of the bank;
She hides handsome and richly drest
    aft the blinds of the window.
Which of the young men does she
    like the best?

Ah, the homeliest of them is
    beautiful to her.
Dancing and laughing along the
    beach came the twenty-ninth
    bather;
The rest did not see her, but she saw
    them, &c."

Well, did the lady fall in love with the twenty-ninth bather, or *vice versa*? Our author scorns to gratify such puerile curiosity; the denouement which novel readers would expect is not hinted at.

In his philosophy justice attains its proper dimensions:

"I play not a march for victors only:
    I play great marches for
    conquered and slain persons.
Have you heard that it was good to
    gain the day?
I also say that it is good to fall—
    battles are lost in the same spirit
    in which they are won.
I sound triumphal drums for the
    dead—I fling thro' my
    embouchures the loudest and
    gayest music for them.
Vivas to those who have failed and
    to those whose war vessels sank
    in the sea.
And to those themselves who sank
    into the sea.
And to all generals that lost
    engagements, and all overcome
    heroes and the numberless
    unknown heroes equal to the
    greatest heroes known."

The triumphs of victors had been duly celebrated, but surely a poet was needed to sing the praises of the defeated whose cause was righteous, and the heroes who have been trampled under the hoofs of iniquity's onward march.

He does not pick and choose senti-ments and expressions fit for general cir-

20

culation—he gives a voice to whatever *is*, whatever we see, and hear, and think, and feel. He descends to grossness, which debars the poem from being read aloud in any mixed circle. We have said that the work defies criticism; we pronounce no judgment upon it; it is a work that will satisfy few upon a first perusal; it must be read again and again, and then it will be to many unaccountable. All who read it will agree that it is an extraordinary book, full of beauties and blemishes, such as nature is to those who have only a half formed acquaintance with her mysteries.

[Walt Whitman].
"Walt Whitman, a
Brooklyn Boy."
Brooklyn *Daily Times*,
29 September 1855, p. 2.

To give judgment on real poems, one needs an account of the poet himself. Very devilish to some, and very divine to some, will appear these new poems, the *Leaves of Grass*: an attempt, as they are, of a live, naive, masculine, tenderly affectionate, rowdyish, contemplative, sensual, moral, susceptible and imperious person, to cast into literature not only his own grit and arrogance, but his own flesh and form, undraped, regardless of foreign models, regardless of modesty or law, and ignorant or silently scornful, as at first appears, of all except his own presence and experience, and all outside of the fiercely loved land of his birth and the birth of his parents, and their parents for several generations before him. Politeness this man has none, and regulation he has none. The effects he produces are no effects of artists or the arts, but effects of

the original eye or arm, or the actual atmosphere of grass or brute or bird. You may feel the unconscious teaching of the presence of some fine animal, but will never feel the teaching of the fine writer or speaker.

Other poets celebrate great events, personages, romances, wars, loves, passions, the victories and power of their country, or some real or imagined incident—and polish their work, and come to conclusions, and satisfy the reader. This poet celebrates himself: and that is the way he celebrates all. He comes to no conclusions, and does not satisfy the reader. He certainly leaves him what the serpent left the woman and the man, the taste of the tree of the knowledge of good and evil, never to be erased again.

What good is it to argue about egotism? There can be no two thoughts on Walt Whitman's egotism. That is what he steps out of the crowd and turns and faces them for. Mark, critics! for otherwise is not used for you the key that leads to the use of the other keys to this well enveloped yet terribly in earnest man. His whole work, his life, manners, friendships, writing, all have among their leading purposes, an evident purpose, as strong and avowed as any of the rest, to stamp a new type of character, namely his own, and indelibly fix it and publish it, not for a model but an illustration, for the present and future of American letters and American young men, for the south the same as the north, and for the Pacific and Mississippi country, and Wisconsin and Texas and Canada and Havana, just as much as New York and Boston. Whatever is needed toward this achievement he puts his hand to, and lets imputations take their time to die.

First be yourself what you would show in your poem—such seems to be this man's example and inferred rebuke to the schools of poets. He makes no allusions to books or writers; their spirits do not seem to have touched him; he has not a word to say for or against them, or their theories or ways. He never offers others; what he continually offers is the man whom our Brooklynites know so well. Of pure American breed, of reckless health, his body perfect, free from taint top to toe, free forever from headache and dyspepsia, full-blooded, six feet high, a good feeder, never once using medicine, drinking water only—a swimmer in the river or bay or by the seashore—of straight attitude and slow movement of foot—an indescribable style evincing indifference and disdain—ample limbed, weight one hundred and eighty-five pounds, age thirty-six years (1855)—never dressed in black, always dressed freely and clean in strong clothes, neck open, shirt-collar flat and broad, countenance of swarthy, transparent red, beard short and well mottled with white hair like hay after it has been mowed in the field and lies tossed and streaked—face not refined or intellectual, but calm and wholesome—a face of an unaffected animal—a face that absorbs the sunshine and meets savage or gentleman on equal terms—a face of one who eats and drinks and is a brawny lover and embracer—a face of undying friendship and indulgence toward men and women, and of one who finds the same returned many fold—a face with two grey eyes where passion and hauteur sleep, and melancholy stands behind them—a spirit that mixes cheerfully with the world—a person singularly beloved and welcomed, especially by young men and mechanics—one who has firm attachments there, and associates there—one who does not associate with literary and elegant people—one of the two men sauntering along the street with their arms over each other's shoulders, his companions some boatman or ship joiner, or from the hunting-tent or lumber-raft—

one who has that quality of attracting the best out of people that they present to him, none of their meaner and stingier traits, but always their sweetest and most generous traits—a man never called upon to make speeches at public dinners, never on platforms amid the crowds of clergymen or professors or aldermen or congressmen—rather down in the bay with pilots in their pilot boats—or off on a cruise with fishers in a fishing smack—or with a band of laughers and roughs in the streets of the city or the open grounds of the country—fond of New York and Brooklyn—fond of the life of the wharves and great ferries, or along Broadway, observing the endless wonders of that thoroughfare of the world—one whom, if you would meet, you need not expect to meet an extraordinary person—one in whom you will see the singularity which consists in no singularity—whose contact is no dazzling fascination, nor require any difference, but has the easy fascination of what is homely and accustomed—of something you knew before, and was waiting for—of natural pleasures, and well-known places, and welcome familiar faces—perhaps of a remembrance of your brother or mother, or friend away or dead—there you have Walt Whitman, the begetter of a new offspring out of literature, taking with easy nonchalance the chances of its present reception, and, through all misunderstandings and distrusts, the chances of its future reception.

[Walt Whitman]. "An English and American Poet" [review of Alfred Tennyson, *Maud, and other Poems* and *Leaves of Grass*]. *American Phrenological Journal* 22, no. 4 (October 1855), 90–1.

It is always reserved for second-rate poems immediately to gratify. As first-rate or natural objects, in their perfect simplicity and proportion, do not startle or strike, but appear no more than matters of course, so probably natural poetry does not, for all its being the rarest, and telling of the longest and largest work. The artist or writer whose talent is to please the connoisseurs of his time, may obey the laws of his time, and achieve the intense and elaborated beauty of parts. The perfect poet cannot afford any special beauty of parts, or to limit himself by any laws less than those universal ones of the great masters, which include all times, and all men and women, and the living and the dead. For from the study of the universe is drawn this irrefragable truth, that the law of the requisites of a grand poem, or any other complete workmanship, is originality, and the average and superb beauty of the ensemble. Possessed with this law, the fitness of aim, time, persons, places, surely follows. Possessed with this law, and doing justice to it, no poet or any one else will make anything ungraceful or mean, any more than any emanation of nature is.

The poetry of England, by the many rich geniuses of that wonderful little island, has grown out of the facts of the English race, the monarchy and aristocracy prominent over the rest, and conforms to the spirit of them. No nation ever did or ever will receive with national affection any poets except those born of its national blood. Of these, the writings express the finest infusions of government, traditions, faith, and the dependence or independence of a people, and even the good or bad physiognomy, and the ample or small geography. Thus what very properly fits a subject of the British crown may fit very ill an American freeman. No fine romance, no inimitable delineation of character, no grace of delicate illustrations, no rare picture of shore or mountain or sky, no deep thought of the intellect, is so important to a man as his opinion of himself is; everything receives its tinge from that. In the verse of all those undoubtedly great writers, Shakspeare just as much as the rest, there is the air which to America is the air of death. The mass of the people, the laborers and all who serve, are slag, refuse. The countenances of kings and great lords are beautiful; the countenances of mechanics are ridiculous and deformed. What play of Shakspeare, represented in America, is not an insult to America, to the marrow in its bones? How can the tone never silent in their plots and characters be applauded, unless Washington should have been caught and hung, and Jefferson was the most enormous of liars, and common persons, north and south, should bow low to their betters, and to organic superiority of blood? Sure as the heavens envelop the earth, if the Americans want a race of bards worthy of 1855, and of the stern reality of this republic, they must cast around for men essentially different from the old poets, and from the modern successions of jinglers and snivellers and fops.

23

English versification is full of these danglers, and America follows after them. Every body writes poetry, and yet there is not a single poet. An age greater than the proudest of the past is swiftly slipping away, without one lyric voice to seize its greatness, and speak it as an encouragement and onward lesson. We have heard, by many grand announcements, that he was to come, but will he come?

A mighty Poet whom this age shall
    choose
To be its spokesman to all coming
    times.
In the ripe full-blown season of his
    soul,
He shall go forward in his spirit's
    strength,
And grapple with the questions of all
    time,
And wring from them their meanings.
    As King Saul
Called up the buried prophet from
    his grave
To speak his doom, so shall this
    Poet-king
Call up the dread past from its awful
    grave
To tell him of our future. As the air
Doth sphere the world, so shall his
    heart of love—
Loving mankind, not peoples. As the
    lake
Reflects the flower, tree, rock, and
    bending heaven,
Shall he reflect our great humanity;
And as the young Spring breathes
    with living breath
On a dead branch, till it sprouts
    fragrantly
Green leaves and sunny flowers, shall
    he breathe life
Through every theme he touch,
    making all Beauty
And Poetry forever like the stars.
    (*Alexander Smith*.)

The best of the school of poets at present received in Great Britain and America is Alfred Tennyson. He is the bard of ennui and of the aristocracy, and their combination into love. This love is the old stock love of playwrights and romancers, Shakspeare the same as the rest. It is possessed of the same unnatural and shocking passion for some girl or woman, that wrenches it from its manhood, emasculated and impotent, without strength to hold the rest of the objects and goods of life in their proper positions. It seeks nature for sickly uses. It goes screaming and weeping after the facts of the universe, in their calm beauty and equanimity, to note the occurrence of itself, and to sound the news, in connection with the charms of the neck, hair, or complexion of a particular female.

Poetry, to Tennyson and his British and American eleves, is a gentleman of the first degree, boating, fishing, and shooting genteelly through nature, admiring the ladies, and talking to them, in company, with that elaborate half-choked deference that is to be made up by the terrible license of men among themselves. The spirit of the burnished society of upper-class England fills this writer and his effusions from top to toe. Like that, he does not ignore courage and the superior qualities of men, but all is to show forth through dandified forms. He meets the nobility and gentry half-way. The models are the same both to the poet and the parlors. Both have the same supercilious elegance, both love the reminiscences which extol caste, both agree on the topics proper for mention and discussion, both hold the same undertone of church and state, both have the same languishing melancholy and irony, both indulge largely in persiflage, both are marked by the contour of high blood and a constitutional aversion to anything cowardly and mean, both accept the love

24

depicted in romances as the great business of a life as a poem, both seem unconscious of the mighty truths of eternity and immortality, both are silent on the presumptions of liberty and equality, and both devour themselves in solitary lassitude. Whatever may be said of all this, it harmonizes and represents facts. The present phases of high-life in Great Britain are as natural a growth there, as Tennyson and his poems are a natural growth of those phases. It remains to be distinctly admitted that this man is a real first-class poet, infused amid all that ennui and aristocracy.

Meanwhile a strange voice parts others aside and demands for its owner that position that is only allowed after the seal of many returning years has stamped with approving stamp the claims of the loftiest leading genius. Do you think the best honors of the earth are won so easily, Walt Whitman? Do you think city and country are to fall before the vehement egotism of your recitative of yourself?

I am the poet of the body,
And I am the poet of the soul.

The pleasures of heaven are with me,
   and the pains of hell are with me,
The first I graft and increase upon
   myself, the latter I translate into a
   new tongue.

I am the poet of the woman the same
   as the man,
And I say it is as great to be a
   woman as to be a man,
And I say there is nothing greater
   than the mother of men.

I chant a new chant of dilation or
   pride,
We have had ducking and
   deprecating about enough.
I show that size is only development.

It is indeed a strange voice! Critics and lovers and readers of poetry as hitherto written, may well be excused the chilly and unpleasant shudders which will assuredly run through them, to their very blood and bones, when they first read Walt Whitman's poems. If this is poetry, where must its foregoers stand? And what is at once to become of the ranks of rhymesters, melancholy and swallow-tailed, and of all the confectioners and upholsterers of verse, if the tan-faced man here advancing and claiming to speak for America and the nineteenth hundred of the Christian list of years, typifies indeed the natural and proper bard?

The theory and practice of poets have hitherto been to select certain ideas or events or personages, and then describe them in the best manner they could, always with as much ornament as the case allowed. Such are not the theory and practice of the new poet. He never presents for perusal a poem ready-made on the old models, and ending when you come to the end of it; but every sentence and every passage tells of an interior not always seen, and exudes an impalpable something which sticks to him that reads, and pervades and provokes him to tread the half-invisible road where the poet, like an apparition, is striding fearlessly before. If Walt Whitman's premises are true, then there is a subtler range of poetry than that of the grandeur of acts and events, as in Homer, or of characters, as in Shakspeare—poetry to which all other writing is subservient, and which confronts the very meanings of the works of nature and competes with them. It is the direct bringing of occurrences and persons and things to bear on the listener or beholder, to re-appear through him or her; and it offers the best way of making them a part of him and her as the right aim of the greatest poet.

Of the spirit of life in visible forms— of the spirit of the seed growing out of

25

the ground—of the spirit of the resistless motion of the globe passing unsuspected but quick as lightning along its orbit—of them is the spirit of this man's poetry. Like them it eludes and mocks criticism, and appears unerringly in results. Things, facts, events, persons, days, ages, qualities, tumble pell-mell, exhaustless and copious, with what appear to be the same disregard of parts, and the same absence of special purpose, as in nature. But the voice of the few rare and controlling critics, and the voice of more than one generation of men, or two generations of men, must speak for the inexpressible purposes of nature, and for this haughtiest of writers that has ever yet written and printed a book. He is to prove either the most lamentable of failures or the most glorious of triumphs, in the known history of literature. And after all we have written we confess our brain-felt and heart-felt inability to decide which we think it is likely to be.

[Rufus W. Griswold].
Criterion 1
(10 November 1855), 24.

An unconsidered letter of introduction has oftentimes procured the admittance of a scurvy fellow into good society, and our apology for permitting any allusion to the above volume in our columns is, that it has been unworthily recommended by a gentleman of wide repute, and might, on that account, obtain access to respectable people, unless its real character were exposed.

Mr. Ralph Waldo Emerson either recognises and accepts these 'leaves,' as the gratifying results of his own peculiar doctrines, or else he has hastily endorsed them, after a partial and superficial reading. If it is of any importance, he may extricate himself from the dilemma. We, however, believe that this book does express the bolder results of a certain transcendental kind of thinking, which some have styled philosophy.

As to the volume itself, we have only to remark, that it strongly fortifies the doctrines of the Metempsychosists, for it is impossible to imagine how any man's fancy could have conceived such a mass of stupid filth, unless he were possessed of the soul of a sentimental donkey that had died of disappointed love. This *poet* (?) without wit, but with a certain vagrant wildness, just serves to show the energy which natural imbecility is occasionally capable of under strong excitement.

There are too many persons, who imagine they demonstrate their superiority to their fellows, by disregarding all the politenesses and decencies of life, and, therefore, justify themselves in indulging the vilest imaginings and shamefullest license. But nature, abhorring the abuse of the capacities she has given to man, retaliates upon him, by rendering extravagant indulgence in any direction followed by an insatiable, ever-consuming, and never to be appeased passion.

Thus, to these pitiful beings, virtue and honor are but names. Bloated with self-conceit, they strut abroad unabashed in the daylight, and expose to the world the festering sores that overlay them like a garment. Unless we admit this exhibition to be beautiful, we are at once set down for non-progressive conservatives, destitute of the "inner light," the far-seeingness which, of course, characterize those gifted individuals. Now, any one who has noticed the tendency of thought in these later years, must be aware that a quantity of this kind of nonsense is being constantly displayed. The immodesty of presumption exhibited by these *seers*; their arrogant pretentiousness; the complacent smile with which they listen to the echo of their own braying, should be, and we believe is, enough to disgust the great majority of sensible folks; but, unfortunately, there is a class that, mistaking sound for sense, attach some importance to all this rant and cant. These candid, these ingenuous, these honest "progressionists;" these human diamonds without flaws; these men that have *come*, detest furiously all shams; "to the pure, all things are pure;" they are pure, and, consequently, must thrust their reeking presence under every man's nose.

They seem to think that man has no instinctive delicacy; is not imbued with a conservative and preservative modesty, that acts as a restraint upon the violence of passions, which, for a wise purpose, have been made so strong. No! these fellows have no secrets, no disguises; no, indeed! But they do have, conceal it by whatever language they choose, a degrading, beastly sensuality, that is fast rotting the healthy core of all the social virtues.

There was a time when licentiousness laughed at reproval; now it writes essays and delivers lectures. Once it shunned the light; now it courts attention, writes books showing how grand and pure it is, and prophesies from its lecherous lips its own ultimate triumph.

Shall we argue with such men? Shall we admit them into our houses, that they may leave a foul odor, contaminate the pure, healthful air? Or shall they be placed in the same category with the comparatively innocent slave of poverty, ignorance and passion, that skulks along in the shadows of by-ways; even in her deep degradation possessing some sparks of the Divine light, the germ of good that reveals itself by a sense of shame?

Thus, then, we leave this gathering of muck to the laws which, certainly, if they fulfil their intent, must have power to suppress such gross obscenity. As it is entirely destitute of wit, there is no probability that any one would, after this exposure, read it in the hope of finding that; and we trust no one will require further evidence—for, indeed, we do not believe there is a newspaper so vile that would print confirmatory extracts.

In our allusions to this book, we have found it impossible to convey any, even the most faint idea of its style and contents, and of our disgust and detestation of them, without employing language that cannot be pleasing to ears polite; but it does seem that some one should, under circumstances like these, undertake a most disagreeable, yet stern duty. The records of crime show that many monsters have gone on in impunity, because the exposure of their vileness was attended with too great indelicacy. "*Peccatum illud horribile, inter Christianos non nominandum.*"

"Studies among the Leaves: The Assembly of Extremes" [Review of *Leaves of Grass* and Tennyson's *Maud*]. *Crayon* 3 (January 1856), 30–2.

A subtle old proverb says, "extremes meet," and science, Art, and even morality, sometimes testify to the truth of the proverb; and there are some curious problems involved in the demonstration of it. The loftiest attainment of the wisdom and worth of age only reaches to the simplicity and fervor of childhood, from which we all start, and returning to which we are blessed. Art makes the same voyage round its sphere, holding ever westward its way into new and unexplored regions, until it does what Columbus would have done, had his faith and self-denial been greater, reaches the east again. If the individual, Columbus, failed to accomplish the destiny, the class, Columbus, fails never. And so in Art, what no one does, the many accomplish, and finally the cycle is filled.

We see this most forcibly in the comparison of two late poems, as unlike, at first thought, as two could be, and yet in which the most striking likenesses prevail, *Maud*, and *Leaves of Grass*; the one as refined in its Art as the most refined, delicate in its structure, and consummate in its subtlety of expression, the other rude and rough, and heedless in its forms—*nonchalant* in everything but its essential ideas. The one comes from the last stage of cultivation of the Old World, and shows evidence of morbid, luxurious waste of power, and contempt of mental wealth, from inability longer to appreciate the propriety of subjects on which to expend it; as, to one who has overlived, all values are the same, because nothing, and indifferent; while the other, from among the "roughs," is morbid from overgrowth, and likewise prodigal of its thought-treasure, because it has so much that it can afford to throw it away on everything, and considers all things that are, as equally worth gilding. The subject of *Maud* is nothing—a mere commonplace incident, but artistically dealt with—a blanched, decayed sea-shell, around which the amber has gathered; and that of the newer poem is equally nothing, blades of sea-grass amber-cemented. Both are characterized by the extreme of affectation of suggestiveness—piers of thought being given, over which the reader must throw his own arches. Both are bold, de-fiant of laws which attempt to regulate forms, and of those which *should* regulate essences. Maud is irreligious through mental disease, produced by excess of sentimental action—*Leaves of Grass*, through irregularly-developed mental action and insufficiency of sentiment. A calmer perception of Nature would have corrected in Tennyson that feeling which looks upon sorrow as the only thing poetic, and serenity and holy trust, as things to which Love has no alliance, while a higher seeing of Nature would have shown Walt Whitman that all things in Nature are not alike beautiful, or to be loved and honored by song.

Although it is mainly with the Art of the two poems that we have to deal, the form rather than the motive, yet so entirely does the former arise from the latter that the criticism passed on the one must lie upon the other. In the mere versification, for instance, of both, see what indifference to the dignity of verse (while there is still the extorted homage to its forms), arising in both cases, it would seem, from an overweening confidence in the value of what is said, as in the following passages:

"Long have I sighed for a calm; God
  grant I may find it at last!
It will never be broken by Maud,
  she has neither savor nor salt,
But a cold, clear, cut face, as I found
  when her carriage past,
Perfectly beautiful: let it be granted
  her: where is the fault?"
          Maud, Sec. ii., St. 1.

"Do you suspect death? If I were to
  suspect death, I should die now.
Do you think I could walk
  pleasantly and well-suited toward
  annihilation?
Pleasantly and well-suited I walk,
Whither I walk I cannot define, but
  I know it is good.

28

The whole universe indicates that it
   is good.
The past and present indicates that
   it is good."
                    Leaves of Grass, p. 69.

All Tennyson's exquisite care over his
lines produces no other impression than
that which Whitman's carelessness ar-
rives at; viz., nonchalance with regard to
forms. In either case, it is an imperfection, we are bold to say, since we do not
love beauty and perfection of form for
nothing, nor can the measure of poetic
feeling be full when we do not care for
the highest grace and symmetry of construction. It is an impertinence which
says to us, "my ideas are so fine that they
need no dressing up," even greater than
that which says, "mine are so fine that
they cannot be dressed as well as they
deserve." The childlike instinct demands
perfect melody as an essential to perfect
poetry, and more than that, the melodious thought will work out its just and
adequate form by the essential law of its
spiritual organization—when the heart
sings, the feet will move to its music. An
unjust measure in verse is *prima facie* evidence of a jarring note in the soul of the
poem, and studied or permitted irregular-
ity of form proves an arrogant self-
estimation or irreverence in the poet; and
both these poems are irreverent, irreligious, in fact. Maud commences, singularly enough, with the words, "I hate,"
and the whole sentiment of the poem
ignores the nobler and purer feelings of
humanity—it is full of hatred and morbid feeling, diseased from pure worldli-
ness. This is well enough for one whom
the world calls a laureate, but the true
poet seeks a laurel that the world cannot
gather, growing on mountains where its
feet never tread, he lives with beauty and
things holy, or, if evil things come to him,
it is that they may be commanded behind

him. *Maud* rambles and raves through
human love and human hate, and the
hero lives his life of selfish desire and
selfish enjoyment, and then through the
bitterness of selfish regret and despair,
without one thought of anything better,
nobler than himself—the summit of creation. He worships nothing, even reverences nothing, his love is only passion,
and his only thought of God one of fear.
In his happiness, he is a cynic, in his un-
happiness, a madman.

For the drift of the Maker is dark, an
   Isis hid by the veil.
Who knows the ways of the world,
   how God will bring them about?
Our planet is one, the suns are many,
   the world is wide.
Shall I weep if a Poland fail? shall I
   shriek if a Hungary fail?
Or an infant civilization be ruled
   with rod or with knout?
I have not made the world, and He
   that made it will guide.

Be mine a philosopher's life in the
   quiet woodland ways,
Where if I cannot be gay let a
   passionless peace be my lot,
Far off from the clamor of liars belied
   in the hubbub of lies;
From the long-neck'd geese of the
   world that are ever hissing
   dispraise
Because their natures are little, and,
   whether he heed it or not,
Where each man walks with his head
   in a cloud of poisonous flies.
.   .   .   .

Dead, long dead,
Long dead!
And my heart is a handful of dust,
And the wheels go over my head,
And my bones are shaken with pain,
For into a shallow grave they are
   thrust,
Only a yard beneath the street,

And the hoofs of the horses beat,
beat,
The hoofs of the horses beat,
Beat into my scalp and my brain,
With never an end to the stream of
passing feet,
Driving, hurrying, marrying, burying,
Clamor and rumble, and ringing and
clatter,
And here beneath it is all as bad,
For I thought the dead had peace, but
it is not so;
To have no peace in the grave, is that
not sad?
But up and down and to and fro,
Ever about me the dead men go;
And then to hear a dead man chatter
Is enough to drive one mad.

Wretchedest age, since Time began,
They cannot even bury a man;
And tho' we paid our tithes in the
days that are gone,
Not a bell was rung, not a prayer
was read;
It is that which makes us loud in the
world of the dead;
There is none that does his work, not
one;
A touch of their office might have
sufficed,
But the churchmen fain would kill
their church,
As the churches have kill'd their
Christ.

See, there is one of us sobbing,
No limit to his distress;
And another, a lord of all things,
praying
To his own great self, as I guess;
And another, a statesman there,
betraying
His party-secret, fool, to the press;
And yonder a vile physician, blabbing
The case of his patient—all for what?
To tickle the maggot born in an
empty head,

And wheedle a world that loves him
not,
For it is but a world of the dead.

Leaves of Grass is irreligious, because
it springs from a low recognition of the
nature of Deity, not, perhaps, so in
intent, but really so in its result. To
Whitman, all things are alike good—
no thing is better than another, and
thence there is no ideal, no aspiration, no
progress to things better. It is not enough
that all things are good, all things are
equally good, and, therefore, there is no
order in creation; no better, no worse—
but all is a democratic level from which
can come no symmetry, in which there is
no head, no subordination, no system,
and, of course, no result. With a wonderful vigor of thought and intensity of perception, a power, indeed, not often
found, *Leaves of Grass* has no ideality,
no concentration, no purpose—it is bar-
barous, undisciplined, like the poetry of a
half-civilized people, and, as a whole,
useless, save to those miners of thought
who prefer the metal in its unworked
state. The preface of the book contains
an inestimable wealth of this unworked
ore—it is a creed of the material, not
denying the ideal, but ignorant of it.

"The greatest poet hardly knows pettiness or triviality. If he breathes into
anything that was before thought
small, it dilates with the grandeur and
life of the universe. He is a seer . . . he
is individual . . . he is complete in himself . . . the others are as good as he,
only he sees it and they do not. He is
not one of the chorus . . . he does not
stop for any regulation: he is the president of regulation. What the eyesight
does to the rest he does to the rest.
Who knows the curious mystery of
the eyesight? The other senses cor-
roborate themselves, but this is re-

moved from any proof but its own, and foreruns the identities of the spiritual world. A single glance of it mocks all the investigations of man, and all the instruments and books of the earth, and all reasoning. What is marvellous? what is unlikely? what is impossible, or baseless, or vague? after you have once just opened the space of a peachpit, and given audience to far and near, and to the sunset, and had all things enter with electric swiftness, softly and duly, without confusion, or jostling, or jam.

"The land and sea, the animals, fishes, and birds, the sky of heaven and the orbs, the forests, mountains, and rivers, are not small themes... but folks expect of the poet to indicate more than the beauty and dignity which always attach to dumb, real objects... they expect him to indicate the path between reality and their souls. Men and women perceive the beauty well enough... probably as well as he. The passionate tenacity of hunters, woodmen, early risers, cultivators of gardens, and orchards, and fields, the love of healthy women for the manly form, sea-faring persons, drivers of horses, the passion for light and the open air, all is an old varied sign of the unfailing perception of beauty, and of a residence of the poetic in out-door people. They can never be assisted by poets to perceive.... some may, but they never can. The poetic quality is not marshalled in rhyme, or uniformity, or abstract addresses to things, nor in melancholy complaints or good precepts, but is the life of these and much else, and is in the soul. The profit of rhyme is that it drops seeds of a sweeter and more luxuriant rhyme, and of uniformity, that it conveys itself into its own roots in the ground out of sight. The rhyme and uniformity of perfect poems show the free growth of metrical laws, and bud from them as unerringly and loosely as lilacs or roses on a bush, and take shapes as compact as the shapes of chestnuts, and oranges, and melons, and pears, and shed the perfume impalpable to form. The fluency and ornaments of the finest poems, or music, or orations, or recitations, are not independent, but dependent. All beauty comes from beautiful blood and a beautiful brain. If the greatnesses are in conjunction in a man or woman it is enough... the fact will prevail through the universe... but the gaggery and gilt of a million years will not prevail. Who troubles himself about his ornaments or fluency is lost.

"The greatest poet has less a marked style, and is more the channel of thoughts and things without increase or diminution, and is the free channel of himself. He swears to his art, I will not be meddlesome, I will not have in my writing any elegance, or effect, or originality, to hang in the way between me and the rest like curtains. I will have nothing hang in the way, not the richest curtains. What I tell I tell for precisely what it is. Let who may exalt, or startle, or fascinate, or sooth, I will have purposes as health, or heat, or snow, has, and be as regardless of observation. What I experience or portray shall go from my composition without a shred of my composition. You shall stand by my side, and look in the mirror with me."

"I am of old and young, of the
    foolish as much as the wise,
Regardless of others, ever regardful
    of others,
Maternal as well as paternal, a child
    as well as a man,

31

Stuffed with the stuff that is coarse,
and stuffed with the stuff that is
fine,
One of the great nation, the nation
of many nations—the smallest the
same and the largest the same,
A southerner soon as a northerner, a
planter nonchalant and
hospitable,
A Yankee bound my own way . . . .
ready for trade . . . . my joints the
limberest joints on earth and the
sternest joints on earth,
A Kentuckian walking the vale of
the Elkhorn in my deerskin
leggings,
A boatman over the lakes or bays or
along coasts . . . a Hoosier, a
Badger, a Buckeye,
A Louisianian or Georgian, a poke-
easy from sandhills and pines,
At home on Canadian snow-shoes
or up in the bush, or with
fishermen off Newfoundland,
At home in the fleet of ice-boats,
sailing with the rest and tacking,
At home on the hills of Vermont or
in the woods of Maine or the
Texan ranch,
Comrade of Californians . . . .
comrade of free north-westerns,
loving their big proportions,
Comrade of raftsmen and
coalmen—comrade of all who
shake hands and welcome to
drink and meat;
A learner with the simplest, a
teacher of the thoughtfullest,
A novice beginning experient of
myriads of seasons,
Of every hue and trade and rank, of
every caste and religion.
Not merely of the New World but
of Africa, Europe or Asia . . . . a
wandering savage,
A farmer, mechanic, or artist . . . . a
gentleman, sailor, lover or quaker,

A prisoner, fancy-man, rowdy,
lawyer, physician or priest.
.   .   .   .   .   .

I am he attesting sympathy;
Shall I make my list of things in the
house and skip the house that
supports them?

I am the poet of common sense and
of the demonstrable and of
immortality;
And am not the poet of goodness
only . . . . I do not decline to be
the poet of wickedness also.
Washes and razors for foofoos . . . .
for me freckles and a bristling
beard.

What blurt is it about virtue and
about vice?
Evil propels me, and reform of evil
propels me . . . . I stand indifferent,
My gait is no fault-finder's or
rejecter's gait,
I moisten the roots of all that has
grown.

In other words, according to Whitman's
theory, the greatest poet is he who per-
forms the office of camera to the world,
merely reflecting what he sees—art is
merely reproduction.

Yet it cannot be denied that he has felt
the beauty of the material in full measure, and sometimes most felicitously.

A child said, What is the grass?
fetching it to me with full hands;
How could I answer the child?. . . . I
do not know what it is any more
than he.

I guess it must be the flag of my
disposition, out of hopeful green
stuff woven.

Or I guess it is the handkerchief of
the Lord,
A scented gift and remembrancer
designedly dropped,

32

Bearing the owner's name someway
    in the corners, that we may see and
    remark, and say Whose?
Or I guess the grass itself is a
    child . . . . the produced babe of the
    vegetation.
Or I guess it is a uniform
    hieroglyphic,
And it means, Sprouting alike in
    broad zones and narrow zones,
Growing among black folks as
    among white,
Kanuck, Tuckahoe, Congressman,
    Cuff, I give them the same, I
    receive them the same.
And now it seems to me the beautiful
    uncut hair of graves.

.   .   .   .

The big doors of the country-barn
    stand open and ready,
The dried grass of the harvest-time
    loads the slow-drawn wagon,
The clear light plays on the brown
    gray and green intertinged,
The armfuls are packed to the
    sagging mow;
I am there . . . . I help . . . . I came
    stretched atop of the load,
I felt its soft jolts . . . . one leg
    reclined on the other,
I jump from the crossbeams, and
    seize the clover and timothy,
And roll head over heels, and tangle
    my hair full of wisps.

.   .   .   .

I think I could turn and live awhile
    with the animals . . . . they are so
    placid and self-contained,
I stand and look at them sometimes
    half the day long.
They do not sweat and whine about
    their condition,
They do not lie awake in the dark
    and weep for their sins,
They do not make me sick discussing
    their duty to God,

Not one is dissatisfied . . . . not one is
    demented with the mania of
    owning things,
Not one kneels to another nor to his
    kind that lived thousands of years
    ago,
Not one is respectable or industrious
    over the whole earth.

So they show their relations to me
    and I accept them;
They bring me tokens of myself . . . .
    they evince them plainly in their
    possession.

.   .   .   .   .

When the dull nights are over, and
    the dull days also,
When the soreness of lying so much
    in bed is over,
When the physician, after long
    putting off, gives the silent and
    terrible look for an answer,
When the children come hurried and
    weeping, and the brothers and
    sisters have been sent for,
When medicines stand unused on the
    shelf, and the camphor-smell has
    pervaded the rooms,
When the faithful hand of the living
    does not desert the hand of the
    dying,
When the twitching lips press lightly
    on the forehead of the dying,
When the breath ceases and the pulse
    of the heart ceases,
Then the corpse-limbs stretch on the
    bed, and the living look upon
    them,
They are palpable as the living are
    palpable.
The living look upon the corpse with
    their eyesight,
But without eyesight lingers a
    different living and looks curiously
    on the corpse.

.   .   .   .   .

I knew a man . . . . he was a common
farmer . . . . . he was the father of
five sons . . . . and in them were the
fathers of sons . . . . and in them
were the fathers of sons.

This man was of wonderful vigor and
calmness and beauty of person;

The shape of his head, the richness
and breadth of his manners, the
pale yellow and white of his hair
and beard, the immeasurable
meaning of his black eyes,

These I used to go and visit him to
see . . . . He was wise also,

He was six feet tall . . . . he was over
eighty years old . . . . his sons were
massive, clean-bearded, tanfaced
and handsome,

They and his daughters loved
him . . . . all who saw him loved
him . . . . they did not love him by
allowance . . . . they loved him with
personal love;

He drank water only . . . . the blood
showed like scarlet through the
clear brown skin of his face;

He was a frequent gunner and
fisher . . . . he sailed his boat
himself . . . . he had a fine one
presented to him by a
shipjoiner . . . . he had fowling
pieces, presented to him by men
that loved him;

When he went with his five sons and
many grandsons to hunt or fish
you would pick him out as the
most beautiful and vigorous of the
gang,

You would wish long and long to be
with him . . . you would wish to sit
by him in the boat that you and he
might touch each other.

It is not possible to compare the feverish, dying sentiment of Tennyson, dying
from false indulgence, to the rude,
vigorous, and grand if chaotic thought of

Whitman, imperfect only from want
of development—the poems are alike
maimed, but one from loss of parts, the
other from not yet having attained its
parts. But still they are the extremes—
truth lies between *them* always. What if
Columbus had sailed round the world,
and made its extremes meet! He would
only have been back in Spain again—the
true end of his voyage was midway.

Edward Everett Hale.
North American Review 83 (January 1856), 275–7.

Everything about the external arrangement of this book was odd and out of the
way. The author printed it himself, and it
seems to have been left to the winds of
heaven to publish it. So it happened that
we had not discovered it before our last
number, although we believe the sheets
had then passed the press. It bears no
publisher's name, and, if the reader goes
to a bookstore for it, he may expect to be
told at first, as we were, that there is no
such book, and has not been. Nevertheless, there is such a book, and it is well
worth going twice to the bookstore to
buy it. Walter Whitman, an American,—
one of the roughs,—no sentimentalist,—
no stander above men and women, or
apart from them,—no more modest than
immodest,—has tried to write down here,
in a sort of prose poetry, a good deal of
what he has seen, felt, and guessed at in
a pilgrimage of some thirty-five years. He
has a horror of conventional language of
any kind. His theory of expression is,
that, "to speak in literature with the perfect rectitude and *insouciance* of the

movements of animals, is the flawless triumph of art." Now a great many men have said this before. But generally it is the introduction to something more artistic than ever,—more conventional and strained. Antony began by saying he was no orator, but none the less did an oration follow. In this book, however, the prophecy is fairly fulfilled in the accomplishment. "What I experience or portray shall go from my composition without a shred of my composition. You shall stand by my side and look in the mirror with me."

So truly accomplished is this promise,—which anywhere else would be a flourish of trumpets,—that this thin quarto deserves its name. That is to say, one reads and enjoys the freshness, simplicity, and reality of what he reads, just as the tired man, lying on the hill-side in summer, enjoys the leaves of grass around him,—enjoys the shadow,—enjoys the flecks of sunshine,—not for what they "suggest to him," but for what they are.

So completely does the author's remarkable power rest in his simplicity, that the preface to the book—which does not even have large letters at the beginning of the lines, as the rest has—is perhaps the very best thing in it. We find more to the point in the following analysis of the "genius of the United States," than we have found in many more pretentious studies of it.

"Other states indicate themselves in their deputies, but the genius of the United States is not best or most in its executives or legislatures, nor in its ambassadors or authors or colleges or churches or parlors, nor even in its newspapers or inventors;—but always most in the common people. Their manners, speech, dress, friendships;—the freshness and candor of their physiognomy, the picturesque looseness of their carriage, their deathless attachment to freedom,

their aversion to everything indecorous or soft or mean, the practical acknowledgment of the citizens of one State by the citizens of all other States, the fierceness of their roused resentment, their curiosity and welcome of novelty, their self-esteem and wonderful sympathy, their susceptibility to a slight, the air they have of persons who never knew how it felt to stand in the presence of superiors, the fluency of their speech, their delight in music (the sure symptom of manly tenderness and native elegance of soul), their good temper and open-handedness, the terrible significance of their elections, the President's taking off his hat to them, not they to him,—these too are unrhymed poetry. It awaits the gigantic and generous treatment worthy of it."

The book is divided into a dozen or more sections, and in each one of these some thread of connection may be traced, now with ease, now with difficulty,—each being a string of verses, which claim to be written without effort and with entire *abandon*. So the book is a collection of observations, speculations, memories, and prophecies, clad in the simplest, truest, and often the most nervous English,—in the midst of which the reader comes upon something as much out of place as a piece of rotten wood would be among leaves of grass in the meadow, if the meadow had no object but to furnish a child's couch. So slender is the connection, that we hardly injure the following scraps by extracting them.

"I am the teacher of Athletes;
He that by me spreads a wider breast
   than my own, proves the width of
   my own;
He most honors my style who learns
   under it to destroy the teacher;
The boy I love, the same becomes a
   man, not through derived power,
   but in his own right,

Wicked rather than virtuous out of
    conformity or fear,
Fond of his sweetheart, relishing well
    his steak,
Unrequited love, or a slight, cutting
    him worse than a wound cuts,
First-rate to ride, to fight, to hit the
    bull's-eye, to sail a skiff, to sing a
    song, or to play on the banjo,
Preferring scars, and faces pitted with
    small-pox, over all latherers and
    those that keep out of the sun."

Here is the story of the gallant seaman
who rescued the passengers on the San
Francisco:—

"I understand the large heart of
    heroes,
The courage of present times and all
    times;
How the skipper saw the crowded
    and rudderless wreck of the
    steamship, and death chasing it
    up and down the storm,
How he knuckled tight, and gave
    not back one inch, and was
    faithful of days and faithful of
    nights,
And chalked in large letters on a
    board, 'Be of good cheer, we will
    not desert you';
How he saved the drifting company
    at last,
How the lank, loose-gowned women
    looked when boated from the side
    of their prepared graves,
How the silent old-faced infants,
    and the lifted sick, and the sharp-
    lipped, unshaved men;
All this I swallowed, and it tastes
    good; I like it well, and it
    becomes mine:
I am the man, I suffered, I was
    there."

Claiming in this way a personal interest in every thing that has ever happened

in the world, and, by the wonderful sharpness and distinctness of his imagination,
making the claim effective and reasonable, Mr. "Walt Whitman" leaves it a
matter of doubt where he has been in this
world, and where not. It is very clear,
that with him, as with most other effective writers, a keen, absolute memory,
which takes in and holds every detail of
the past,—as they say the exaggerated
power of the memory does when a man
is drowning,—is a gift of his organization
as remarkable as his vivid imagination.
What he has seen once, he has seen for
ever. And thus there are in this curious
book little thumb-nail sketches of life in
the prairie, life in California, life at
school, life in the nursery,—life, indeed,
we know not where not,—which, as they
are unfolded one after another, strike us
as real,—so real that we wonder how
they came on paper.

For the purpose of showing that he is
above every conventionalism, Mr. Whitman puts into the book one or two lines
which he would not address to a woman
nor to a company of men. There is not
anything, perhaps, which modern usage
would stamp as more indelicate than are
some passages in Homer. There is not
a word in it meant to attract readers by
its grossness, as there is in half the literature of the last century, which holds its
place unchallenged on the tables of our
drawing-rooms. For all that, it is a pity
that a book where everything else is natural should go out of the way to avoid the
suspicion of being prudish.

"Notes on New Books." Washington *Daily National Intelligencer*, 18 February 1856, p. 2.

Such is the curt and undescriptive title of a prose poem which has created some remark in certain literary circles. It is in every way a singular volume: singular in its form, singular in its arrangement, singular in its style, and most singular of all in its rhapsodical fancies. Its title-page, as will be seen, bears upon it the name of no author, and the book is ushered into the world without the patronage of any publisher to give it currency and protection. Of "complimentary copies" for the press, none, so far as we are aware, have been vouchsafed by the writer. Ostrich-like, he has laid his egg in the sand and left it to quicken or not, according to that time and chance which, as the wise man says, happen to all things. We are not left, however, in the body of the work, wholly ignorant of the writer's name, profession, or age—"Walt Whitman, an American, one of the roughs, a kosmos, disorderly, fleshly, and sensual, no sentimentalist, no stander above men or women or apart from them, no more modest than immodest," is the odd fish who avows himself as the father of this odd volume. Walt Whitman is a printer by trade, whose punctuation is as loose as his morality, and who no more minds his *ems* than his p's and q's. He tells us that he was born on the last day of May, and "passed from a babe in the creeping trance of three summers and three winters to articulate and walk," all which he thinks "wonderful;" while that he "grew six feet high and became a man thirty-six years old in 1855, and that he is [I am] here any how," are facts which he pronounces equally "wonderful" in the wonderworld of his philosophy.

Though Walt Whitman has modestly withheld his name from the title-page of his production, he has favored us with his likeness by way of frontispiece to the volume. If the artist has faithfully depicted his effigy, Walt is indeed "one of the roughs;" for his picture would answer equally well for a "Bowery boy," one of the "killers," "Mose" in the play, "Bill Sykes after the murder of Nancy," or the "B'hoy that runs with the engine," much as we have known certain "portraits taken from life" compelled to do duty in pictorial newspapers as the true likeness of half a dozen celebrated criminals. Walt Whitman is evidently the "representative-man" of the "roughs."

The avowed object of Walter in the loose quarto before us is to "celebrate" himself; and as the pastoral muse of Virgil "meditated" on a slender oat straw, so Mr. Whitman "leans and loafes" at his ease, "observing a spear of summer grass." Holy Writ informs us that "all flesh is grass," which, according to quaint old Sir Thomas Browne, is just as true literally as metaphorically; for all the adipose matter deposited in the human body from roast beef and mutton is, after all, at the bottom of the account only grass taking upon itself a coat of flesh, for grass forms the ox and roast beef forms the physical man; ergo, the most carnivorous gastronome, no less than the most immaculate vegetarian, is nothing but grass at the last chemical analysis of his constituents. Hence it will be seen that "grass" is what Mr. Whitman calls a "uniform hieroglyphic" of the whole human family, and as such deserves to be scanned by the minute philosopher.

A handful of grass fetched by a child to Walter Whitman inspires him with mysterious thoughts which he vainly essays to grasp, and hints intrusive questionings which he vainly endeavors to answer. At first he guesses that blades of grass "must be the flag of his disposition, out of hopeful green stuff woven," and anon he guesses they are the "handkerchief of the Lord," designedly dropped from above "as scented gifts and remembrancers." He next guesses that "the grass itself is a child, the produced babe of the vegetation," and now he exclaims, in the next breath, "it seems to me the beautiful uncut hair of graves," and hence he feels like caressing it, and breaks out in the following address to the "curling grass:"

"It may be you transpire from the
    breasts of young men;
It may be that if I had known them
    I would have loved them;
It may be that you are from old
    people and from women, and
    from offspring taken soon out of
    their mothers' laps,
And here you are the mother's lap.
.   .   .   .

What do you think has become of
    the young and old men?
And what do you think has become
    of the women and children?

They are alive and well somewhere.
The smallest sprout shows there is
    really no death;
All goes onward and outward....
    and nothing collapses,
And to die is different from what
    any one supposed and luckier.
Has any one supposed it lucky to be
    born?
I hasten to inform him or her that it
    is just as lucky to die, and I know
    it."

The reader who has proceeded only thus far begins already to discover that Walter Whitman is a pantheist. Without, perhaps, ever having read Spinoza, he is a Spinozist. Without, perhaps, much deep insight into Plato the divine, he is a Platonist "in the rough," and believes profoundly in the "immanence of all in each," without ever once mouthing that grand phrase of the Greek philosopher. Without knowing how to chop the formal logic of the schools, he is a necessitarian and fatalist, with whom "whatever is is right." The world as he finds it, and man as he is, good or bad, high or low, ignorant or learned, holy or vicious, are all alike good enough for Walter Whitman, who is in himself a "kosmos," and whose emotional nature is at once the sensorium of humanity and the sounding board which catches up and intones each note of joy or sorrow in the "gamut of human feeling."

He represents himself as being alike of the old and the young, of the foolish as much as the wise; maternal in his instincts as well as paternal; a child as well as a man; a Southerner as soon as a Northerner; a planter, nonchalant and hospitable; a Yankee, bound his own way and ever ready for a swap; a Kentuckian, walking the trail of the Elkhorn with deerskin leggings; a boatman over the lakes or bays or along coasts; a Hoosier, a Badger, a Wolverine, a Buckeye, a Louisianian, a "poke-easy" from sandhills and pines: at home equally on the hills of Vermont, or in the woods of Maine, or the Texas ranch; a learner with the simplest, a teacher of the thoughtfulest, a farmer, mechanic, or artist, a gentleman, sailor, lover, or quaker, a prisoner, fancy-man, rowdy, lawyer, physician, or priest. He rejoices to feel that he is "not stuck up and is in his place," for

"The moth and the fish eggs are in
    their place:
The suns I see and the suns I cannot
    see are in their place;
The palpable is in its place and the
    impalpable is in its place."

38

So fully has the world-spirit possessed the soul of Walter that he thinks he could turn and live awhile with the animals; "they are so placid and self-contained" that he sometimes "stands and looks at them half the day long."

> They do not sweat and whine about
>   their condition;
> They do not lie awake in the dark
>   and weep for their sins;
> They do not make me sick discussing
>   their duty to God.

Mr. Whitman's philosophy, it will be seen, is somewhat different from Blaise Pascal's, and we hope we shall not hurt Mr. W's feelings if we venture to give to the devout Jansenist a slight precedence over him. Pascal, the poor man, having no better guides than his own august reason and the oracles of divine inspiration, in his profound speculations on the greatness and misery of man, came to the conclusion that man's consciousness of his misery was one of the most signal and primary proofs of his greatness. These anxious longings of the soul as for an unknown good were to his mind the indication of slumbering capacities not yet developed, and revealed that power of introspection and self-scrutiny which is at once the attribute of consciousness and the attestation of human responsibility. The man who degrades himself to the level of the brutes, or sinks even lower than they, does yet by his very nature rise above them in that he is conscious of his degradation. At least so thought Pascal, and so think still all those who find in man's consciousness the proof of his dignity and of his elevation above the brute creation.

Mr. Whitman thinks, however, he would like to turn and live awhile with the animals. Well, one's associates should certainly be determined according to one's tastes. Every one to his liking, as remarked the venerable dame in the proverb when she kissed her cow. *De gustibus*, &c. Mr. Whitman, it is true, can plead royal example and ancient precedent in defence of his "passional attraction" towards the dumb animals. King Nebuchadnezzar, many years before him, consorted with the oxen of the field and went to graze after the most approved style of the bovine quadruped. We do not read, however, that his majesty greatly relished this species of out door life [. . .] because, "unlike one of the roughs," he failed to remark how "placid and self-contained" were his companions of the herd. Nebuchadnezzar too, it is to be feared, lacked the proper pantheistic instincts to permit his entering fully into the sublime mysteries of Serapis and Anubis. If his life-experiences had been the same as "Walt Whitman's" before undergoing his change, he might have managed better to enjoy his new society.

In the "Golden Ass" of Apuleius we have also another record of life among the animals. We need not repeat the story of Fotis's ill-starred lover and his magical transformation into an ass, with the long series of misfortunes, the cudgellings and flayings which, sad to tell, befell him in that condition. Are they not all written in the "golden" book aforesaid?—a book which Mr. Whitman, we are sure, would find very much after his own heart in its freedom from anything like sentimental refinement or prudish delicacy, while it is to be hoped that its faithful portraiture of life among the *graminivors* [grass eaters] would cure him of his disposition to herd awhile with the quadrupeds, and render him willing to content himself with his present advantages in the privilege of "standing and looking at them half the day long." It behooves him also to bear in mind that according to all accounts the condition of the Irish peasantry is not greatly elevated over "the rest of mankind" by their hereditary custom of assigning to the "placid" porker and domestic cow a cozy corner in the cabin along with its other inmates. If much good was to be expected from turning and living with the animals, Ireland would have convinced the world of it long before Mr. Whitman's day, and if he had properly studied her history we question whether he would have considered it a matter worth boasting of that he feels himself—

> "Stucco'd with quadrupeds and birds all over."

As we do not wish, however, to press Mr. Whitman too hard upon this point, and seek to exhibit rather the philosophy of his teachings than his *petits ridicules*, we append in this same connection the following lyrical outburst of the true pantheistic spirit:

> How beautiful and perfect are the
>   animals! How perfect is my soul!
> How perfect the earth and the
>   minutest thing upon it!
> What is called good is perfect, and
>   what is called sin is just as perfect.
> The vegetables and minerals are all
>   perfect, and imponderable fluids
>   are perfect.
> Oh, my soul! If I realize you I have
>   satisfaction. Laws of the earth and
>   air! If I realize you I have
>   satisfaction.
> I swear I see now that every thing has
>   a living soul!
> The trees have, rooted in the ground;
>   the weeds of the sea have; the
>   animals!

It is quite possible that, owing to some radical and congenital defect of our mental organization, we have never been able to penetrate "within the veil" in the Pantheon of the transcendentalists and of the Emersonian school in general. Mr. Emerson, we understand, greatly admires the present work; indeed, we have read a published letter of his in which he tenders to Mr. Whitman his thanks for the *Leaves of Grass*. When we read that eulogy we were satisfied that this volume would prove to us a sealed book, and that its hieroglyphs would be as unintelligible to our ken as was the inscription around the sacred ibex to the erudite Mr. [George Robins] Gliddon. Still we determined to read it, in the humble but earnest hope of endeavoring occasionally to catch its esoteric meaning in a few at least of those passages, which we are assured from Mr. Emerson's enjoyment of them must contain a hidden significance which nothing less potent than the magic salve of the dervise of Balsora can open our eyes to behold; and in default of which we must be content with such a poor comprehension of these Sibylline leaves as falls to the lot of common readers.

No one, we may say, however, in all candor, can read this singular prose-poem without being struck by the writer's wonderful powers of description and of word-painting. His memory seems as retentive of its treasures as his imagination is opulent in its creations. He writes like one who has but to prick his mind and forthwith it gushes out in a perennial flow of "thoughts which have tarried in its inner chambers." It is only when we are balked in our attempt to trail his transcendental sinuosities of thought that we feel ourselves at fault, and then we are reminded of Longfellow's description of the Emersonian philosophy, which he likened to some of the roads in our great West, which at first open very fair and wide, and are shaded on both sides by the towering giants of the primeval forest, but which before long become narrower and narrower and at last dwindle to a squirrel path and run up a tree.

[William Howitt? or William J. Fox?]. London *Weekly Dispatch*, 9 March 1856, p. 6.

We have before us one of the most extraordinary specimens of Yankee intelligence and American eccentricity in authorship, it is possible to conceive. It is of a *genus* so peculiar as to embarrass us, and has an air at once so novel, so audacious, and so strange as to verge upon absurdity, and yet it would be an injustice to pronounce it so, as the work is saved from this extreme by a certain mastery over diction not very easy of definition. What Emerson has pronounced to be good must not be lightly treated, and before we pronounce upon the merits of this performance it is but right to examine them. We have, then, a series of pithy prose sentences strung together—forming twelve grand divisions in all, but which, having a rude rhythmical cadence about them admit of the designation poetical being applied. They are destitute of rhyme, measure of feet, and the like, every condition under which poetry is generally understood to exist being absent; but in their strength of expression, their fervor, hearty wholesomeness, their originality, mannerism, and freshness, one finds in them a singular harmony and flow, as if by reading, they gradually formed themselves into melody, and adopted characteristics peculiar and appropriate to themselves alone. If, however, some sentences be fine, there are others altogether laughable; nevertheless, in the bare strength, the unhesitating frankness of a man who "believes in the flesh and the appetites," and who dares to call simplest things by their plainest names, conveying also a large sense of the beautiful, and with an emphasis which gives a clearer conception of what manly modesty really is than any thing we have, in all conventional forms of word, deed, or act so far known of, that we rid ourselves, little by little, of the strangeness with which we greet this bluff newcomer, and, beginning to understand him better, appreciate him in proportion as he becomes more known. He will soon make his way into the confidence of his readers, and his poems in time will become a pregnant text-book, out of which quotation as sterling as the minted gold will be taken and applied to every form and phase of the "inner" or the "outer" life; and we express our pleasure in making the acquaintance of Walt Whitman, hoping to know more of him in time to come.

Examiner 2512 (22 March 1856), 180–1.

We have too long overlooked in this country the great poet who has recently arisen in America, of whom some of his countrymen speak in connection with Bacon and Shakespeare, whom others compare with Tennyson,—much to the disadvantage of our excellent laureate,—and to whom Mr Emerson writes that he finds in his book "incomparable things, said incomparably well." The book he pronounces "the most extraordinary piece of wit and wisdom that America has yet contributed;" at which, indeed, says Mr Emerson in the printed letter sent to us,—"I rubbed my eyes a little, to see if this sunbeam were no illusion."

No illusion truly is Walt Whitman, the new American prodigy, who, as he is himself candid enough to intimate, sounds his barbaric yawp over the roofs of the world. He is described by one of his own local papers as "a tenderly affectionate, rowdyish, contemplative, sensual, moral, susceptible, and imperious person," who aspires to cast some of his own grit, whatever that may be, into literature. We have ourselves been disposed to think there is in literature grit enough, according to the ordinary sense, but decidedly Walt Whitman tosses in some more. The author describes himself as "one of the roughs, a kosmos;" indeed, he seems to be very much impressed with the fact that he is a kosmos, and repeats it frequently. A kosmos we may define, from the portrait of it on the front of the book, as a gentleman in his shirt-sleeves, with one hand in a pocket of his pantaloons, and his wide-awake cocked with a dammee-sir air over his forehead.

On the other hand, according to an American review that flatters Mr Whitman, this kosmos is "a compound of the New England transcendentalist and New York rowdy."

But as such terms of compliment may not be quite clear to English readers, we must be content, in simpler fashion, to describe to them this Brooklyn boy as a wild Tupper of the West. We can describe him perfectly by a few suppositions. Suppose that Mr Tupper had been brought up to the business of an auctioneer, then banished to the backwoods, compelled to live for a long time as a backwoodsman, and thus contracting a passion for the reading of Emerson and Carlyle? Suppose him maddened by this course of reading, and fancying himself not only an Emerson but a Carlyle and an American Shakespeare to boot when the fits come on, and putting forth his notion of that combination in his own self-satisfied way, and in his own wonderful cadences? In

that state he would write a book exactly like Walt Whitman's *Leaves of Grass*.

[four extracts from "Song of Myself" totaling sixty-seven lines]

We must be just to Mr Whitman in allowing that he has one positive merit. His verse has a purpose. He desires to assert the pleasure that a man has in himself, his body and its sympathies, his mind (in a lesser degree, however) and its sympathies. He asserts man's right to express his delight in animal enjoyment, and the harmony in which he should stand, body and soul, with fellow men and the whole universe. To express this, and to declare that the poet is the highest manifestation of this, generally also to suppress shams, is the purport of these *Leaves of Grass*. Perhaps it might have been done as well, however, without being always so purposely obscene, and intentionally foul-mouthed, as Mr Whitman is.

[ten-line extract from "Song of Myself"]

The fit being very strong indeed upon him, our Wild Tupper of the West thus puts into words his pleasure at the hearing of an overture:

[fifteen-line extract from "Song of Myself"]

In the construction of our artificial Whitman, we began with the requirement that a certain philosopher should have been bred to the business of an auctioneer. We must add now, to complete the imitation of Walt Whitman, that the wild philosopher and poet, as conceived by us, should be perpetually haunted by the delusion that he has a catalogue to make. Three-fourths of Walt Whitman's book is poetry as catalogues of auctioneers are poems. Whenever any general term is used, off the mind wanders on this fatal track, and an attempt is made to specify all lots included under it. Does Mr Whitman speak of a town, he is at once ready with pages of town lots. Does he mention the American country, he feels bound thereupon to draw up a list of barns, waggons, wilds, mountains, animals, trees, people, "a Hoosier, a Badger, a Backeye, a Lousianian, or Georgian, a poke-easy from sandhills and pines," &c. &c. We will give an illustration of this form of lunacy. The subject from which the patient starts off is equivalent to things in general, and we can spare room only for half the catalogue. It will be enough, however, to show how there arises catalogue within catalogue, and how sorely the paroxysm is aggravated by the incidental mention of any one particular that is itself again capable of sub-division into lots.

[thirty-one–line extract from "A Song for Occupations"]

Now let us compare with this a real auctioneer's catalogue. We will take that of Goldsmith's chambers, by way of departing as little as we can from the poetical. For, as Mr Whitman would say (and here we quote quite literally, prefixing only a verse of our own, from "A Catalogue of the Household Furniture with the select collection of scarce, curious, and valuable books of Dr Goldsmith, deceased, which, by order of the adm^r, will be sold by auction, &c., &c.)"—

[. . .]

After all, we are not sure whether the poetry of that excellent Mr Good, the auctioneer who, at his Great Room, No. 121 Fleet street, sold the household furniture of Oliver Goldsmith in the summer of 1774, does not transcend in wisdom and in wit "the most extraordinary piece of wit and wisdom that" (according to Mr Emerson) "America has yet contributed."

Critic [London] 15 (1 April 1856), 170–1.

We had ceased, we imagined, to be surprised at anything that America could produce. We had become stoically indifferent to her Woolly Horses, her Mermaids, her Sea Serpents, her Barnums, and her Fanny Ferns; but the last monstrous importation from Brooklyn, New York, has scattered our indifference to the winds. Here is a thin quarto volume without an author's name on the title-page; but to atone for which we have a portrait engraved on steel of the notorious individual who is the poet presumptive. This portrait expresses all the features of the hard democrat, and none of the flexile delicacy of the civilised poet. The damaged hat, the rough beard, the naked throat, the shirt exposed to the waist, are each and all presented to show that the man to whom those articles belong scorns the delicate arts of civilisation. The man is the true impersonation of his book—rough, uncouth, vulgar. It was by the merest accident that we discovered the name of this erratic and newest wonder; but at page 29 we find that he is—

Walt Whitman, an American, one of
   the roughs, a Kosmos,
Disorderly, fleshly, and sensual.

The words 'an American' are a surplusage, 'one of the roughs' too painfully apparent; but what is intended to be conveyed by 'a Kosmos' we cannot tell, unless

43

it means a man who thinks that the fine essence of poetry consists in writing a book which an American reviewer is compelled to declare is 'not to be read aloud to a mixed audience.' We should have passed over this book, *Leaves of Grass,* with indignant contempt, had not some few Transatlantic critics attempted to 'fix' this Walt Whitman as the poet who shall give a new and independent literature to America—who shall form a race of poets as Banquo's issue formed a line of kings. Is it possible that the most prudish nation in the world will adopt a poet whose indecencies stink in the nostrils? We hope not; and yet there is a probability, and we will show why, that this Walt Whitman will not meet with the stern rebuke which he so richly deserves. America has felt, oftener perhaps than we have declared, that she has no national poet—that each one of her children of song has relied too much on European inspiration, and clung too fervently to the old conventionalities. It is therefore not unlikely that she may believe in the dawn of a thoroughly original literature, now there has arisen a man who scorns the Hellenic deities, who has no belief in, perhaps because he has no knowledge of, Homer and Shakspere; who relies on his own rugged nature, and trusts to his own rugged language, being himself what he shows in his poems. Once transfix him as the genesis of a new era, and the manner of the man may be forgiven or forgotten. But what claim has this Walt Whitman to be thus considered, or to be considered a poet at all? We grant freely enough that he has a strong relish for nature and freedom, just as an animal has; nay, further, that his crude mind is capable of appreciating some of nature's beauties; but it by no means follows that, because nature is excellent, therefore art is contemptible. Walt Whitman is, as unacquainted with art, as a hog is with mathematics. His

poems—we must call them so for convenience—twelve in number, are innocent of rhythm, and resemble nothing so much as the war-cry of the Red Indians. Indeed, Walt Whitman has had near and ample opportunities of studying the vociferations of a few amiable savages. Or rather perhaps, this Walt Whitman reminds us of Caliban flinging down his logs, and setting himself to write a poem. In fact Caliban, and not Walt Whitman, might have written this:

> I too am not a bit tamed—I too am
>   untranslatable.
> I sound my *barbaric yawp* over the
>   roofs of the world.

Is this man with the 'barbaric yawp' to push Longfellow into the shade, and he meanwhile to stand and 'make mouths' at the sun? The chance of this might be formidable were it not ridiculous. That object or that act which most develops the ridiculous element carries in its bosom the seeds of decay, and is wholly powerless to trample out of God's universe one spark of the beautiful. We do not, then, fear this Walt Whitman, who gives us slang in the place of melody, and rowdyism in the place of regularity. The depth of his indecencies will be the grave of his fame, or ought to be if all proper feeling is not extinct. The very nature of this man's compositions excludes us from proving by extracts the truth of our remarks; but we, who are not prudish, emphatically declare that the man who wrote page 79 of the *Leaves of Grass* deserves nothing so richly as the public executioner's whip. Walt Whitman libels the highest type of humanity, and calls his free speech the true utterance of *a man*: we, who may have been misdirected by civilisation, call it the expression of *a beast*.

The leading idea of Walt Whitman's poems is as old as the hills. It is the doctrine of universal sympathy which the first poet maintained, and which the last on earth will maintain also. He says:

> Not a mutineer walks handcuffed to
>   the jail but I am handcuffed to him
>   and walk by his side,
> Not a cholera patient lies at the last
>   gasp but I also lie at the last gasp.

To show this sympathy he instances a thousand paltry, frivolous, and obscene circumstances. Herein we may behold the difference between a great and a contemptible poet. What Shakspere—mighty shade of the mightiest bard, forgive us the comparison!—expressed in a single line,

> One touch of nature makes the whole
>   world kin,

this Walt Whitman has tortured into scores of pages. A single extract will show what we mean. This miserable spinner of words declares that the earth has 'no themes, or hints, or provokers,' and never had, if you cannot find such themes, or hints, or provokers in

[eighteen-line extract from "A Song for Occupations"]

Can it be possible that its author intended this as a portion of a poem? Is it not more reasonable to suppose that Walt Whitman has been learning to write, and that the compositor has got hold of his copy-book? The American critics are, in the main, pleased with this man because he is self-reliant, and because he assumes all the attributes of his country. If Walt Whitman has really assumed those attributes, America should hasten to repudiate them, be they what they may. The critics are pleased also because he talks like a man unaware that

there was ever such a production as a book, or ever such a being as a writer. This in the present day is a qualification exceedingly rare, and *may* be valuable, so we wish those gentlemen joy of their GREAT UNTAMED.

We must not neglect to quote an unusual passage, which may be suggestive to writers of the Old World. To silence our incredulous readers, we assure them that the passage may be found at page 92:—

> Is it wonderful that I should be
>   immortal? As every one is
>   immortal, I know it is wonderful;
>   but my eyesight is equally
>   wonderful, and how I was
>   conceived in my mother's womb is
>   equally wonderful.
> And how I was not palpable once but
>   am now, and was born on the last
>   day of May 1819, and passed from
>   a babe in the creeping trance of
>   three summers and three winters to
>   articulate and walk, are all equally
>   wonderful.
> And that I grew six feet high, and
>   that I have become a man thirty-six
>   years old in 1855, and that I am
>   here anyhow, are all equally
>   wonderful.

The transformation and the ethereal nature of Walt Whitman is marvellous to us, but perhaps not so to a nation from which the spirit-rappers sprung.

> I depart as air, I shake my white
>   locks at the runaway sun;
> I effuse my flesh in eddies, and drift it
>   in lacy jags;
> I bequeath myself to the dirt, to grow
>   from the grass I love.
> If you want me again, look for me
>   under your boot-soles.

Here is also a sample of the man's slang and vulgarity:

45

[ten-line extract from "Song of My-self"]

And here a spice of his republican inso-lence, his rank Yankeedom, and his auda-cious trifling with death:

[eleven-line extract from "A Boston Ballad"]

We will neither weary nor insult our readers with more extracts from this no-table book. Emerson *has praised it*, and called it the 'most extraordinary piece of wit and wisdom America has yet contrib-uted.' Because Emerson has grasped sub-stantial fame, he can afford to be gener-ous; but Emerson's generosity must not be mistaken for justice. If this work is re-ally a work of genius—if the principles of those poems, their free language, their amazing and audacious egotism, their animal vigour, be real poetry and the divinest evidence of the true poet—then our studies have been in vain, and vainer still the homage which we have paid the monarchs of Saxon intellect, Shak-spere, and Milton, and Byron. This Walt Whitman holds that his claim to be a poet lies in his robust and rude health. He is, in fact, as he declares, 'the poet of the body.' Adopt this theory, and Walt Whitman is a Titan; Shelley and Keats the merest pigmies. If we had commenced a notice of *Leaves of Grass* in anger, we could not but dismiss it in grief, for its author, we have just discovered, is conscious of his affliction. He says, at page 33,

I am given up by traitors;
I talk wildly, I am mad.

Fanny Fern.
"Fresh Fern Leaves:
Leaves of Grass."
New York Ledger,
10 May 1856, p. 4.

Well baptized: fresh, hardy, and grown for the masses. Not more welcome is their natural type to the winter-bound, bed-ridden, and spring-emancipated invalid. *Leaves of Grass* thou art unspeakably de-licious, after the forced, stiff, Parnassian exotics for which our admiration has been vainly challenged.

Walt Whitman, the effeminate world needed thee. The timidest soul whose wings ever drooped with discouragement, could not choose but rise on thy strong pinions.

"Undrape—you are not guilty to me,
    nor stale nor discarded;
  I see through the broadcloth and
    gingham whether or no."

"O despairer, here is my neck,
  You shall *not* go down! Hang your
    whole weight upon me."

Walt Whitman, the world needed a "Native American" of thorough, out and out breed—enamored of *women* not *ladies*, *men* not *gentlemen*; something beside a mere Catholic-hating Know-Nothing; it needed a man who dared speak out his strong, honest thoughts, in the face of pusillanimous, toadeying, republican aristocracy; dictionary-men, hypocrites, cliques and creeds; it needed a large-hearted, untainted, self-reliant, fear-less son of the Stars and Stripes, who dis-dains to sell his birthright for a mess of pottage; who does

46

"Not call one greater or one smaller,
  That which fills its period and place
  being equal to any;"

who will

"Accept nothing which all cannot
  have their counterpart of on the
  same terms."

Fresh *Leaves of Grass*! not submitted by the self-reliant author to the fingering of any publisher's critic, to be arranged, rearranged and disarranged to his circumscribed liking, till they hung limp, tame, spiritless, and scentless. No. It were a spectacle worth seeing, this glorious Native American, who, when the daily labor of chisel and plane was over, himself, with toil-hardened fingers, handled the types to print the pages which wise and good men have since delighted to endorse and to honor. Small critics, whose contracted vision could see no beauty, strength, or grace, in these *Leaves*, have long ago repented that they so hastily wrote themselves down shallow by such a premature confession. Where an Emerson, and a Howitt have commended, my woman's voice of praise may not avail; but happiness was born a twin, and so I would fain share with others the unmingled delight which these "Leaves" have given me.

I say unmingled; I am not unaware that the charge of coarseness and sensuality has been affixed to them. My moral constitution may be hopelessly tainted or—too sound to be tainted, as the critic wills, but I confess that I extract no poison from these *Leaves*—to me they have brought only healing. Let him who can do so, shroud the eyes of the nursing babe lest it should see its mother's breast. Let him look carefully between the gilded covers of books, backed by high-sounding names, and endorsed by parson and priest, lying unrebuked upon his own family table; where the asp of sensuality lies coiled amid rhetorical flowers. Let him examine well the paper dropped weekly at his door, in which virtue and religion are rendered disgusting, save when they walk in satin slippers, or, clothed in purple and fine linen, kneel on a damask *"prie-dieu."*

Sensual!—No—the moral assassin looks you not boldly in the eye by broad daylight; but Borgia-like takes you treacherously by the hand, while from the glittering ring on his finger he distils through your veins the subtle and deadly poison.

Sensual? The artist who would inflame, paints you not nude Nature, but stealing Virtue's veil, with artful artlessness now conceals, now exposes, the ripe and swelling proportions.

Sensual? Let him who would affix this stigma upon *Leaves of Grass*, write upon his heart, in letters of fire, these noble words of its author:

"In woman I see the bearer of the
  great fruit, which is
  immortality. . . . the good thereof
  is not tasted by *roues*, and never
  can be.
  ·   ·   ·   ·   ·   ·   ·   ·   ·   ·
  Who degrades or defiles the living
  human body is cursed,
  Who degrades or defiles the body of
  the dead is not more cursed."

Were I an artist I would like no more suggestive subjects for my easel than Walt Whitman's pen has furnished.

"The little one sleeps in its cradle,
  I lift the gauze and look a long time,
  and silently brush away flies with
  my hand.
  The farmer stops by the bars of a
  Sunday and looks at the oats
  and rye.

47

Earth of the slumbering and liquid
   trees!
Earth of departed Sunset,
Earth of the mountain's misty topt!
Earth of the vitreous pour of the full
   moon just tinged with blue!
Earth of shine and dark mottling the
   tide of the river!
Earth of the limpid grey of clouds
   brighter and clearer for my sake!
Far swooping elbowed earth! Rich
   apple-blossomed earth!
Smile, for your lover comes!"

I quote at random, the following passages which appeal to me:

"A morning glory at my window,
   satisfies me more than the
   metaphysics of books.
.   .   .   .
Logic and sermons never convince.
The damp of the night drives deeper
   into my soul."

Speaking of animals, he says:

"I stand and look at them sometimes
   half the day long.
They do not make me sick,
   discussing their duty to God.
.   .   .   .
—Whoever walks a furlong without
   sympathy, walks to his own
   funeral dressed in his shroud.
.   .   .   .
I hate him that oppresses me,
I will either destroy him, or he shall
   release me.
.   .   .   .
I find letters from God dropped in
   the street, and every one is signed
   by God's name,
And I leave them where they are,
   for I know that others will
   punctually come forever and ever.

————Under Niagara, *the cataract
falling like a veil over my
countenance.*"

Of the grass he says:

"It seems to me *the beautiful uncut
hair of graves.*"

I close the extracts from these *Leaves*,
which it were easy to multiply, for one is
more puzzled what to leave unculled, than
what to gather, with the following sentiments; for which, and for all the good
things included between the covers of his
book Mr. Whitman will please accept the
cordial grasp of a woman's hand:

"The wife—and she is not one jot
   less than the husband,
The daughter—and she is just as
   good as the son,
The mother—and she is every bit as
   much as the father."

"Transatlantic Latter-Day Poetry."
Leader 7 (7 June 1856), 547–2 [*sic*, should be 548].

—"Latter-day poetry" in America is of a
very different character from the same
manifestation in the old country. Here, it
is occupied for the most part with dreams
of the middle ages, of the old knightly
and religious times: in America, it is employed chiefly with the present, except
when it travels out into the undiscovered
future. Here, our latter-day poets are apt
to whine over the times, as if Heaven

were perpetually betraying the earth with a show of progress that is in fact retrogression, like the backward advance of crabs: there, the minstrels of the stars and stripes blow a loud note of exultation before the grand new epoch, and think the Greeks and Romans, the early Oriental races, and the later men of the middle centuries, of small account before the onward tramping of these present generations. Of this latter sect is a certain phenomenon who has recently started up in Brooklyn, New York—one Walt Whitman, author of *Leaves of Grass*, who has been received by a section of his countrymen as a sort of prophet, and by Englishmen as a kind of fool. For ourselves, we are not disposed to accept him as the one, having less faith in latter-day prophets than in latter-day poets; but assuredly we cannot regard him as the other. Walt is one of the most amazing, one of the most startling, one of the most perplexing, creations of the modern American mind; but he is no fool, though abundantly eccentric, nor is his book mere food for laughter, though undoubtedly containing much that may most easily and fairly be turned into ridicule.

The singularity of the author's mind—his utter disregard of ordinary forms and modes—appears in the very title-page and frontispiece of his work. Not only is there no author's name (which in itself would not be singular), but there is no publisher's name—that of the English bookseller being a London addition. Fronting the title is the portrait of a bearded gentleman in his shirt-sleeves and a Spanish hat, with an all-pervading atmosphere of Yankee-doodle about him; but again there is no patronymic, and we can only infer that this roystering blade is the author of the book. Then follows a long prose treatise by way of Preface (and here once more the anonymous system is carried out, the treatise having no heading whatever); and after that we have the poem, in the course of which, a short autobiographical discourse reveals to us the name of the author.

A passage from the Preface, if it may be so called, will give some insight into the character and objects of the work. The dots do not indicate any abbreviation by us, but are part of the author's singular system of punctuation:—

Other states indicate themselves in their deputies . . . but the genius of the United States is not best or most in its executives or legislatures, nor in its ambassadors or authors or colleges or churches or parlors, nor even in its newspapers or inventors . . . but always most in the common people. Their manners speech dress friendships—the freshness and candour of their physiognomy—the picturesque looseness of their carriage . . . their deathless attachment to freedom—their aversion to anything indecorous, or soft, or mean—the practical acknowledgment of the citizens of one state by the citizens of all other states—the fierceness of their roused resentment—their curiosity and welcome of novelty—their self-esteem and wonderful sympathy—their susceptibility to a slight—the air they have of persons who never knew how it felt to stand in the presence of superiors—the fluency of their speech—their delight in music, the sure symptom of manly tenderness and native elegance of soul . . . their good temper and open-handedness—the terrible significance of their elections—the President's taking off his hat to them not they to him—these too are unrhymed poetry. It awaits the gigantic and generous treatment worthy of it.

This "gigantic and generous treatment," we presume, is offered in the pages which ensue. The poem is written in wild, irregular, unrhymed, almost unmetrical "lengths," like the measured prose of Mr. Martin Farquhar Tupper's *Proverbial Philosophy*, or of some of the Oriental writings. The external form, therefore, is startling, and by no means seductive, to English ears, accustomed to the sumptuous music of ordinary metres; and the central principle of the poem is equally staggering. It seems to resolve itself into an all-attracting egotism—an eternal presence of the individual soul of Walt Whitman in all things, yet in such wise that this one soul shall be presented as a type of all human souls whatsoever. He goes forth into the world, this rough, devil-may-care Yankee; passionately identifies himself with all forms of being, sentient or inanimate; sympathizes deeply with humanity; riots with a kind of Bacchanal fury in the force and fervour of his own sensations; will not have the most vicious or abandoned shut out from final comfort and reconciliation; is delighted with Broadway, New York, and equally in love with the desolate backwoods, and the long stretch of the uninhabited prairie, where the wild beasts wallow in the reeds, and the wilder birds start upwards from their nests among the grass; perceives a divine mystery wherever his feet conduct or his thoughts transport him; and beholds all beings tending towards the central and sovereign Me. Such, as we conceive, is the key to this strange, grotesque, and bewildering book; yet we are far from saying that the key will unlock all the quirks and oddities of the volume. Much remains of which we confess we can make nothing; much that seems to us purely fantastical and preposterous; much that appears to our muddy vision gratuitously prosaic, needlessly plain-speaking, disgusting without purpose, and singular without result. There are so many evidences of a noble soul in

Whitman's pages that we regret these aberrations, which only have the effect of discrediting what is genuine by the show of something false; and especially do we deplore the unnecessary openness with which Walt reveals to us matters which ought rather to remain in a sacred silence. It is good not to be ashamed of Nature; it is good to have an all-inclusive charity; but it is also good, sometimes, to leave the veil across the Temple.

That the reader may be made acquainted with the vividness with which Walt can paint the unhackneyed scenery of his native land, we subjoin a panorama:—

[twenty-four–line extract from "Song of Myself"]

D.W.
[from review of W. Edmondstoune Aytoun, *Bothwell: A Poem in Six Parts* and *Leaves of Grass*].
Canadian Journal n.s. 1 (November 1856), 541–51.

In the works named above we have two not unmete representatives of the extremes of the Old and of the New World poetic ideal: *Bothwell*, the product of the severely critical, refined, and ultra-conservative author of the *Lays of the Scottish Cavaliers*; and *Leaves of Grass*, the wild, exuberant, lawless offspring of Walt Whitman, a Brooklyn Boy, "One of the Roughs!"

[. . .]

In contrast with this we have named the effusions of the Brooklyn Bard. If the accredited author of "Firmilian" has now shown us what a poem ought to be, assuredly Walt Whitman is wide of the mark. Externally and internally he sets all law, decorum, prosody and propriety at defiance. A tall, lean, sallow, most republican, and Yankee-looking volume, is his *Leaves of Grass*; full of egotism, extravagance, and spasmodic eccentricities of all sorts; and heralded by a sheaf of double-columned extracts from Reviews—not always the least curious of its singular contents. Here, for example, is a protest against the intrusion of the British muse on the free soil of the States of the Union, which must surely satisfy the most clamant demand for native poetics and republican egotism:

"What very properly fits a subject of the British crown, may fit very ill an American freeman. No fine romance, no inimitable delineation of character, no grace of delicate illustrations, no rare picture of shore or mountain or sky, no deep thought of the intellect, is so important to a man as his opinion of himself is; everything receives its tinge from that. In the verse of all those undoubtedly great writers, *Shakespeare, just as much as the rest*, there is the air which to America is the air of death. The mass of the people, the laborers and all who serve, are slag, refuse. The countenances of kings and great lords are beautiful; the countenances of mechanics are ridiculous and deformed. What play of Shakespeare represented in America, is not an insult to America, to the marrow in its bones? How can the tone—never silent in their plots and characters—be applauded, unless Washington should have been caught and hung, and Jefferson was the most enormous of liars, and common persons, North and South, should bow low to their betters, and to organic superiority of blood? Sure as the heavens envelop the earth, if the Americans want a race of bards worthy of 1855, and of the stern reality of this republic, they must cast around for men essentially different from the old poets, and from the modern successions of jinglers and snivellers and fops."—and here accordingly is something essentially different from all poets, both old and new.

The poet, unnamed on his title page, figures on his frontispiece, and unmistakeably utters his own poem:

"I celebrate myself,
 And what I assume, you shall
  assume;
 For every atom belonging to me as
  good belongs to you.
 I loafe, and invite my soul;
 I lean and loafe at my ease—
 Observing a spear of Summer
  grass."

Such is the starting point of this most eccentric and republican of poets; of whom the republican critic above quoted, after contrasting with him Tennyson, as "The bard of ennui, and the aristocracy and their combination into love, the old stock love of playwrights and romancers, Shakespeare, the same as the rest."—concludes by confessing his inability to decide whether Walt Whitman is "to prove the most lamentable of failures, or the most glorious of triumphs, in the known history of literature."

Assuredly, the Brooklyn poet is no commonplace writer. That he is startling and *outré*, no one who opens his volume will doubt. The conventionalities, and proprieties, and modesties, of thought, as well as of language, hold him in no restraint; and hence he has a vantage ground from which he may claim such credit as its licence deserves. But, apart from this, there are unmistakeable freshness, originality,

and true poetic gleams of thought, mingled with the strange incoherencies of his
boastful rhapsody. To call his *Leaves* poems, would be a mistake; they resemble
rather the poet's first jottings, out of
which the poem is to be formed; the ore
out of which the metal is to be smelted;
and, in its present form, with more of
dross than sterling metal in the mass.

To find an extractable passage is no
easy task. Here a fine suggestive fancy
ends in some offensive pruriency; there it
dwindles into incomprehensible aggrega-
tions of words and terms, which—
unless Machiavelli was right in teaching
that words were given us to conceal our
thoughts,—are mere clotted nonsense!
Were we disposed to ridicule: our selections would be easy enough; or gravely
to censure: abundant justification is at
hand. We rather cull—not without needful omissions—the thoughts that seem to
have suggested the quaint title of *Leaves
of Grass.*

> "Loafe with me on the grass . . . . . .
>   loose the stop from your throat,
> Not words, not music or rhyme I
>   want: not custom or lecture, not
>   even the best,
> Only the lull I like, the hum of your
>   valved voice.
> .   .   .   .
> I know that the hand of God is the
>   elderhand of my own,
> And I know that the spirit of God is
>   the eldest brother of my own,
> And that all the men ever born are
>   also my brothers . . . . and the
>   women my sisters and lovers,
> And that a kelson of the Creation is
>   love;
> And limitless are leaves, stiff or
>   drooping in the fields.
> A child said, what is the Grass?
>   fetching it to me with full hands;
> How could I answer the child? I

> do not know what it is any more
>   than he.
> I guess it must be the flag of my
>   disposition, out of hopeful green
>   stuff woven.
> Or I guess it is the handkerchief of
>   the Lord,
> A scented gift and remembrancer
>   designedly dropped,
> Bearing the owner's name some way
>   in the corners, that we may see
>   and remark, and say Whose?
> Or I guess the grass is itself a
>   child . . . the produced babe of the
>   vegetation.
> Or I guess it is a uniform
>   hieroglyphic,
> And it means, Sprouting, alike in
>   broad zones and narrow zones,
> Growing among black folks as
>   among white,
> Kanuck, Tuckahoe, Congressmen,
>   Cuff,
> I give them the same, I receive them
>   the same.
> And now it seems to me the
>   beautiful uncut hair of graves.
> .   .   .   .
> .   .   .   .
> All truths wait in all things,
> They neither hasten their own
>   delivery nor resist it,
> They do not need the obstetric
>   forceps of the surgeon,
> The insignificant is as big to me as
>   any,
> What is less or more than a touch?
> Logic and sermons never convince,
> The damp of the night drives deeper
>   into my soul.
> .   .   .   .
> I believe a leaf of grass is no less
>   than the journeywork of the stars,
> And the pismire is equally perfect,
>   and a grain of sand, and the egg
>   of the wren,
> And the tree-toad is a chef-d'œuvre

52

for the highest,
And the running blackberry would
adorn the parlors of heaven,
And the narrowest hinge in my
hand puts to scorn all machinery,
And the cow crunching with
depressed head surpasses any
statue,
And a mouse is miracle enough to
stagger sextillions of infidels."

This passage is far from being the most characteristic of the poem, and even in it we have stopped abruptly for one line more, and . . . . Yet this will show that the punctuation is as odd as any other feature of the work; for the whole is full of conceits which speak fully as much of coarse vain-glorious egotism as of originality of genius. Any man may be an original, whether in the fopperies of the dress he puts on himself or on his poem. We are not, therefore, disposed to rate such very high, or to reckon Walt Whitman's typographical whims any more indicative of special genius, than the shirt-sleeves and unshaven chin of his frontispiece. If they indicate any thing specially, we should infer that he is a compositor by trade, and, for all his affectations of independence, could not keep "the shop" out of his verse. But that he sets all the ordinary rules of men and poets at defiance is visible on every page of his lank volume; and if readers judge thereby that he thinks himself wiser than all previous men and poets—we have no authority to contradict them. That some of his thoughts are far from vain or commonplace, however, a few gleanings may suffice to prove; culled in the form, not of detached passages but of isolated ideas—line, or fragments of lines:—

"The friendly and flowing savage . . . .
Who is he?
Is he waiting for civilization or past
it and mastering it?"

"The welcome ugly face of some
beautiful soul."
"The clock indicates the moment . . . .
but what does eternity indicate?"

"Afar down I see the huge first
Nothing, the vapor from the
nostrils of death,
I know I was even there I
waited unseen and always,
And slept while God carried me
through the lethargic mist,
And took my time . . . . and took no
hurt from the fœtid carbon."

"See ever so far . . . . there is limitless
space outside of that,
Count ever so much . . . . there is
limitless time around that.
Our rendezvous is fitly
appointed . . . . God will be there
and wait till we come."

These doubled and quadrupled points, let us add, pertain to the original, whatever their precise significance may be. Here again is a grand idea, not altogether new; and rough in its present setting, as the native gold still buried in Californian beds of quartz and debris. Nevertheless it is full of suggestive thought, and like much else in the volume—though less than most,—only requires the hand of the artist to cut, and polish, and set, that it may gleam and sparkle with true poetic lustre:—

"A slave at auction!
I help the auctioneer . . . . the sloven
does not half know his business.
Gentlemen look on this curious
creature,
Whatever the bids of the bidders
they cannot be high enough for
him,
For him the globe lay preparing
quintillions of years without one
animal or plant,

For him the revolving cycles truly
  and steadily rolled.
In that head the allbaffling brain,
In it and below it the making of the
  attributes of heroes.
Examine these limbs, red, black or
  white . . . . they are very cunning
  in tendon and nerve;
They shall be stript that you may
  see them.
Exquisite senses, lifelit eyes, pluck,
  volition,
Flakes of breastmuscle, pliant
  backbone and neck, flesh not
  flabby, good sized arms and legs,
And wonders within there yet.
Within there runs his blood . . the
  same old blood . . the same red
  running blood
There swells and jets his heart . . . .
  There all passions and desires . . . .
  all reachings and aspirations:
Do you think they are not there
  because they are not expressed in
  parlors and lecture-rooms?
This is not only one man . . . . he is
  the father of those who shall be
  fathers in their turns,
 In him the start of populous states
  and rich republics,
Of him countless immortal lives
  with countless embodiments and
  enjoyments.
How do you know who shall come
  from the offspring of his offspring
  through the centuries?
Who might you find you have come
  from yourself?"

"Great is life . . and real and
  mystical . . wherever and whoever,
Great is death . . . . sure as life holds
  all parts together, death holds all
  parts together;
Sure as the stars return again after
  they merge in the light, death is
  greater than life."

Such are some of the "Leaves of Grass,"
of the Brooklyn poet who describes himself in one of them as:

  "Walt Whitman, an American, one of
    the roughs, a Kosmos!"

But if the reader—recognising true poetry
in some of these,—should assume such a
likeness running through the whole as
pertains to the blades of Nature's Grass,
we disclaim all responsibility if he find
reason to revise his fancy.

  In the two very diverse volumes under
review it seems to us that we have in the
one the polish of the artist, which can accomplish so much when applied to the
gem or rich ore; in the other we discern
the ore, but overlaid with the valueless
matrix and foul rubbish of the mine, and
devoid of all the unveiling beauties of art.
Viewed in such aspects these poems are
characteristic of the age. From each we
have striven to select what appeared most
worthy of the space at command, and
best calculated to present them to the
reader in the most favorable point of
view consistent with truth. And so we
leave the reader to his own judgment, between the old-world stickler for authority, precedent, and poetical respectability,
and the new-world contemner of all authorities, laws, and respectabilities whatsoever. Happily for us, all choice is not
necessarily limited to these. The golden
mean of poesie does not, we imagine, lie
between such extremes. There are not a
few left, both in England and in America,
for whom old Shakspeare is still respectable enough, and poetical enough,—aye
and free enough too, in spite of all the
freedom which has budded and bloomed
since that year 1616, when his sacred
ashes were laid beneath the chancel stone
whose curse still guards them from impious hands. Nevertheless we have faith
in the future. We doubt not even the

present. When a greater poet than Shakespeare does arrive we shall not count him an impossibility.

Checklist of Additional Reviews

Christian Spiritualist, 1856.
Bibliographic information missing; listed in Scott Giantvalley, *Walt Whitman: A Reference Guide, 1838–1939* (Boston: G. K. Hall, 1981), p. 7; reprinted in Whitman, *Leaves of Grass Imprints* (Boston: Thayer & Eldridge, 1860), 32–6 and in Milton Hindus, *Walt Whitman: The Critical Heritage* (London: Routledge & Kegan Paul, 1971), pp. 80–4.

Monthly Trade Gazette, 1856.
Bibliographic information missing; listed in Giantvalley; reprinted in Hindus.

"*Leaves of Grass*," *Saturday Review* 1 (March 1856), 393–4.

Boston *Intelligencer*, 3 May 1856 [page number unknown].

LEAVES OF GRASS (1856)

Leaves

of

Grass.

———~~~———

BROOKLYN, NEW YORK,

1856.

Christian Examiner 60
[also numbered as 4th
series, 26, no. 3]
(November 1856), 471–3.

So, then, these rank *Leaves* have sprouted afresh, and in still greater abundance. We hoped that they had dropped, and we should hear no more of them. But since they thrust themselves upon us again, with a pertinacity that is proverbial of noxious weeds, and since these thirty-two poems (!) threaten to become 'several hundred,—perhaps a thousand,'—we can no longer refrain from speaking of them as we think they deserve. For here is not a question of literary opinion principally, but of the very essence of religion and morality. The book might pass for merely hectoring and ludicrous, if it were not something a great deal more offensive. We are bound in conscience to call it impious and obscene. *Punch* made sarcastic allusion to it some time ago, as a specimen of American literature. We regard it as one of its worst disgraces. Whether or not the author really bears the name he assumes,—whether or not the strange figure opposite the title-page resembles him, or is even intended for his likeness—whether or not he is considered among his friends to be of a sane mind,—whether he is in earnest, or only playing off some disgusting burlesque,—we are hardly sure yet. We know only, that, in point of style, the book is an impertinence towards the English language; and in point of sentiment, an affront upon the recognized morality of respectable people. Both its language and thought seem to have just broken out of Bedlam. It sets off upon a sort of distracted philosophy, and openly deifies the bodily organs, senses, and appetites, in terms that admit of no double sense. To its pantheism and libidinousness it adds the most ridiculous swell of self-applause; for the author is 'one of the roughs, a kosmos, disorderly, fleshy, sensual, divine inside and out. This head more than churches or bibles or creeds. The scent of these arm-pits an aroma finer than prayer. If I worship any particular thing, it shall be some of the spread of my body.' He leaves 'washes and razors for foofoos;' thinks the talk 'about virtue and about vice' only 'blurt,' he being above and indifferent to both of them; and he himself, 'speaking the password primeval, By God! will accept nothing which all cannot have the counterpart of on the same terms.' These quotations are made with cautious delicacy. We pick our way as cleanly as we can between other passages which are more detestable.

A friend whispers as we write, that there is nevertheless a vein of benevolence running through all this vagabondism and riot. Yes; there is plenty of that philanthropy, which cares as little for social rights as for the laws of God. This Titan in his own esteem is perfectly willing that all the rest of the world should be as frantic as himself. In fact, he has no objection to any persons whatever, unless they wear good clothes, or keep themselves tidy. Perhaps it is not judicious to call any attention to such a prodigious impudence. Dante's guide through the infernal regions bade him, on one occasion, Look and pass on. It would be a still better direction sometimes, when in neighborhoods of defilement and death, to pass on without looking. Indeed, we should even now hardly be tempted to make the slightest allusion to this crazy outbreak of conceit and vulgarity, if a sister Review had not praised it, and even undertaken to set up a plea in apology for its indecencies. We must be allowed to say, that it is not good to confound the blots upon great compositions with the compositions that are nothing but a blot. It is not good to confound the occasional ebullitions of too loose a fancy or too wanton a wit, with a profession and 'illustrated' doctrine of licentiousness. And furthermore, it is specially desirable to be able to discern the difference between the nudity of a statue and the gestures of a satyr; between the plain language of a simple state of society, and the lewd talk of the opposite state, which a worse than heathen lawlessness has corrupted; between the 'εὐνῇ καὶ φιλότητι,' or 'φιλότητι καὶ εὐνῇ μιγῆναι,' of the *Iliad* and *Odyssey*, and an ithyphallic audacity that insults what is most sacred and decent among men.

There is one feature connected with the second edition of this foul work to which we cannot feel that we do otherwise than right in making a marked reference, because it involves the grossest violation of literary comity and courtesy that ever passed under our notice. Mr. Emerson had written a letter of greeting to the author on the perusal of the first edition, the warmth and eulogium of which amaze us. But 'Walt Whitman' has taken the most emphatic sentence of praise from this letter, and had it stamped in gold, signed 'R. W. Emerson,' upon the back of his *second* edition. This *second* edition contains some additional pieces, which in their loathsomeness exceed any of the contents of the first. Thus the honored name of Emerson, which has never before been associated with anything save refinement and delicacy in speech and writing, is made to indorse a work that teems with abominations.

New York *Daily Times*, 13 November 1856, p. 2.

What Centaur have we here, half man, half beast, neighing shrill defiance to all the world? What conglomerate of thought is this before us, with insolence, philosophy, tenderness, blasphemy, beauty and gross indecency tumbling in drunken confusion through the pages? Who is this arrogant young man who proclaims himself the Poet of the Time, and who roots like a pig among a rotten garbage of licentious thoughts? Who is this flushed and full-blooded lover of Nature who studies her so affectionately, and who sometimes utters her teachings with a lofty tongue? This mass of extraordinary contradictions, this fool and this wise man, this lover of beauty and this sunken sensualist, this original thinker and blind egotist, is Mr. WALT WHITMAN, author of *Leaves of Grass*, and, according to his own account, 'a Kosmos.'

Some time since there was left at the office of this paper a thin quarto volume bound in green and gold. On opening the book we first beheld, as a frontispiece, the picture of a man in his shirt sleeves, wearing an expression of settled arrogance upon his countenance. We next arrived at a title page of magnificent proportions, with letter-press at least an inch and a half in length. From this title page we learned that the book was entitled *Leaves of Grass*, and was printed at Brooklyn in the year 1855. This inspected, we passed on to what seemed to be a sort of preface, only that it had no beginning, was remarkable for a singular sparseness in the punctuation, and was broken up in a confusing manner by frequent rows of dots separating the paragraphs. To this succeeded eighty-two pages of what appeared at the first glance to be a number of prose sentences printed somewhat after a biblical fashion. Almost at the first page we opened we lighted upon the confession that the author was

> WALT WHITMAN, an American, one of
> the roughs, a Kosmos,
> Disorderly, fleshy and sensual. . . .

This was sufficient basis for a theory. We accordingly arrived at the conclusion that the insolent-looking young man on the frontispiece was this same WALT WHITMAN, and author of the *Leaves of Grass*.

Then returning to the fore-part of the book, we found proof slips of certain review articles about the *Leaves of Grass*. One of these purported to be extracted from a periodical entitled the *United States Review*, the other was headed 'From the *American Phrenological Journal*.' These were accompanied by a printed copy of an extravagant letter of praise addressed by Mr. RALPH WALDO EMERSON to Mr. WALT WHITMAN, complimenting him on the benefaction conferred on society in the present volume. On subsequently comparing the critiques from the *United States Review* and the *Phrenological Journal* with the preface of the *Leaves of Grass*, we discovered unmistakable internal evidence that Mr. WALT WHITMAN, true to his character, of a Kosmos, was not content with writing a book, but was also determined to review it; so Mr. WALT WHITMAN, had concocted both those criticisms of his own work, treating it we need not say how favorably. This little discovery of our 'disorderly' acquaintance's mode of proceeding rather damped any enthusiasm with which Mr. EMERSON's exravagant letter may have inspired us. We reflected, here is a man who sets himself up as the poet and teacher of his time; who professes a scorn of everything mean and dastardly and

double-faced, who hisses with scorn as he passes one in the street whom he suspects of the taint, hypocrisy—yet this self-contained teacher, this rough-and-ready scorner of dishonesty, this rowdy knight-errant who tilts against all lies and shams, himself perpetrates a lie and a sham at the very outset of his career. It is a lie to write a review of one's own book, then extract it from the work in which it appeared and send it out to the world as an impartial editorial utterance. It is an act that the most degraded helot of literature might blush to commit. It is a dishonesty committed against one's own nature, and all the world. Mr. WALT WHITMAN in one of his candid rhapsodies announces that he is 'no more modest than immodest.' Perhaps in literary matters he carries the theory farther, and is no more honest than dishonest. He likewise says in his preface: 'The great poets are known by the absence in them of tricks, and by the justification of perfect personal candor.' Where, then, can we place Mr. WALT WHITMAN's claims upon immortality?

We confess we turn from Mr. WHITMAN as Critic, to Mr. WHITMAN as Poet, with considerable pleasure. We prefer occupying that independent position which Mr. WHITMAN claims for man, and forming our own opinions, rather than swallowing those ready-made. This gentleman begins his poetic life with a coarse and bitter scorn of the past. We have been living stale and unprofitable lives; we have been surfeited with luxury and high living, and are grown lethargic and dull; the age is fast decaying, when, lo! the trump of the Angel Whitman brings the dead to life, and animates the slumbering world. If we obey the dictates of that trumpet, we will do many strange things. We will fling off all moral clothing and walk naked over the earth. We will disembarrass our language of all the proprieties of speech, and talk indecency broadcast. We will act in short as if the Millennium were arrived in this our present day, when the absence of all vice would no longer necessitate a virtuous discretion. We fear much, Mr. WALT WHITMAN, that the time is not yet come for the nakedness of purity. We are not yet virtuous enough to be able to read your poetry aloud to our children and our wives. What might be pastoral simplicity five hundred years hence, would perhaps be stigmatized as the coarsest indecency now, and—we regret to think that you have spoken too soon.

The adoration of the 'Me,' the 'Ego,' the 'eternal and universal I,' to use the jargon of the Boston *Oracle*, is the prevailing motive of *Leaves of Grass*. Man embraces and comprehends the whole. He is everything, and everything is him. All nature ebbs and flows through him in ceaseless tides. He is 'his own God and his own Devil,' and everything that he does is good. He rejoices with all who rejoice; suffers with all who suffer. This doctrine is exemplified in the book by a panorama as it were of pictures, each of which is shared in by the author, who belongs to the universe, as the universe belongs to him. In detailing these pictures he hangs here and there shreds and tassels of his wild philosophy, till his work, like a maniac's robe, is bedizened with fluttering tags of a thousand colors. With all his follies, insolence, and indecency, no modern poet that we know of has presented finer descriptive passages than Mr. WALT WHITMAN. His phrasing, and the strength and completeness of his epithets, are truly wonderful. He paints in a single line with marvellous power and comprehensiveness. The following rhapsody will illustrate his fulness of epithet:

I am he that walks with the tender
and growing night;

I call to the earth and sea, half held
by the night.

Press close bare-bosomed night! Press
close magnetic, nourishing night!
Night of South winds! Night of the
large few stars!
Still nodding night! Mad, naked,
Summer night!

Smile, O voluptuous cool-breathed
earth!
Earth of the slumbering and liquid
trees!
Earth of departed sunset! Earth of the
mountains misty-topt!
Earth of the vitreous pour of the full
moon just tinged with blue!
Earth of shine and dark, mottling the
tide of the river!
Earth of the limpid gray of clouds
brighter and clearer for my sake!
Far-swooping elbowed earth! Rich
apple-blossomed earth!
Smile, for your lover comes!

You sea! I resign myself to you
also. . . . I guess what you mean,
I behold from the beach your
crooked inviting fingers,
I believe you refuse to go back
without feeling of me;
We must have a turn together . . . I
undress . . . hurry me out of sight
of the land.
Cushion me soft. . . . rock me in
billowy drowse,
Dash me with amorous wet. . . . I can
repay you.

Sea of stretched ground-swells!
Sea, breathing broad and convulsive
breaths!
Sea of the brine of life! Sea of
unshovelled and always-ready
graves!
Howler and scooper of storms!
Capricious and dainty sea!
I am integral with you . . . I too am
of one phase and of all phases.

62

Here are fine expressions well placed. Mr. WHITMAN's study of nature has been close and intense. He has expressed certain things better than any other man who has gone before him. He talks well, and largely, and tenderly of sea and sky, and men and trees, and women and children. His observation and his imagination are both large and well-developed. Take this picture; how pathetic, how tenderly touched!

Agonies are one of my changes of
    garments;
I do not ask the wounded person
    how he feels. . . . I myself become
    the wounded person,
My hurt turns livid upon me as I lean
    on a cane and observe.

I am the mashed fireman with breast-
    bone broken. . . . tumbling walls
    buried me in their debris.
Heat and smoke I inspired. . . . I
    heard the yelling shouts of my
    comrades,
I heard the distant click of their picks
    and shovels;
They have cleared the beams
    away . . . they tenderly lift me
    forth.

I lie in the night air in my red
    shirt. . . . the pervading hush is for
    my sake,
Painless after all I lie, exhausted but
    not so unhappy.
White and beautiful are the faces
    around me. . . . the heads are bared
    of their fire-caps.
The kneeling crowd fades with the
    light of the torches.

If it were permitted to us to outrage all precedent, and print that which should not be printed, we could cull some passages from the *Leaves of Grass*, and place them in strange contrast with the extracts we have already made. If being a Kosmos is to set no limits to one's imagination; to use coarse epithets when coarseness is not needful; to roam like a drunken satyr, with inflamed blood, through every field of lascivious thought; to return time after time with a seemingly exhaustless prurient pleasure to the same licentious phrases and ideas, and to jumble all this up with bits of marvellously beautiful description, exquisite touches of nature, fragments of savagely uttered truth, shreds of unleavened philosophy; if to do all this is to be a Kosmos, then indeed we cede to Mr. WALT WHITMAN his arrogated title. Yet it seems to us that one may be profound without being beastly; one may teach philosophy without clothing it in slang; one may be a great poet without using a language which shall outlaw the minstrel from every decent hearth. Mr. WALT WHITMAN does not think so. He tears the veil from all that society by a well-ordered law shrouds in a decent mystery. He is proud of his nakedness of speech; he glories in his savage scorn of decorum. Like the priests of Belus, he wreathes around his brow the emblems of the Phallic worship.

With all this muck of abomination soiling the pages, there is a wondrous, unaccountable fascination about the *Leaves of Grass*. As we read it again and again, and we will confess that we have returned to it often, a singular order seems to arise out of its chaotic verses. Out of the mire and slough edged thoughts and keen philosophy start suddenly, as the men of Cadmus sprang from the muddy loam. A lofty purpose still dominates the uncleanness and the ridiculous self-conceit in which the author, led astray by ignorance, indulges. He gives token everywhere that he is a huge uncultivated thinker. No country save this could have given birth to the man. His mind is Western—brawny, rough, and original. Wholly uncultivated, and beyond his associates, he has begotten within him the egotism of intellectual solitude. Had he mingled with scholars and men of intellect, those effete beings whom he so despises, he would have learned much that would have been beneficial. When we have none of our own size to measure ourselves with, we are apt to fancy ourselves broader and taller and stronger than we are. The poet of the little country town, who has reigned for years the Virgil or Anacreon of fifty square miles, finds, when he comes into the great metropolis, that he has not had all the thinking to himself. There he finds hundreds of men who have thought the same things as himself, and uttered them more fully. He is astonished to discover that his intellectual language is limited, when he thought that he had fathomed expression. He finds his verse unpolished, his structure defective, his best thoughts said before. He enters into the strife, clashes with his fellows, measures swords with this one, gives thrust for thrust with the other, until his muscles harden and his frame swells. He looks back upon his provincial intellectual existence with a smile; he laughs at his country arrogance and ignorant faith in himself. Now we gather from Mr. WHITMAN's own admissions—admissions that assume the form of boasts—that he has mingled but little with intellectual men. The love of the physical—which is the key-note of his entire book—has as yet altogether satisfied him. To mix with large-limbed, clean-skinned men, to look on ruddy, fair-proportioned women, is his highest social gratification. This love of the beautiful is by him largely and superbly expressed in many places, and it does one good to read those passages pulsating with the pure blood of animal life. But those associates, though manly and handsome, help but little to a man's inner appreciation of himself. Perhaps our author among his comrades had no equal in intellectual force. He reigned triumphantly in an unquestioning circle of admirers. How easy, then, to fancy one's self a wonderful being! How easy to look around and say, 'There are none like me here. I am the coming man!' It may be said that books will teach such a man the existence of other powerful minds, but this will not do. Such communion is abstract, and has but little force. It is only in the actual combat of mind striving with mind that a man comes properly to estimate himself. Mr. WHITMAN has grown up in an intellectual isolation which has fully developed all the eccentricities of his nature. He has made some foolish theory that to be rough is to be original. Now, external softness of manner is in no degree incompatible with muscularity of intellect; and one thinks no more of a man's brains for his treading on one's toes without an apology, or his swearing in the presence of women. When Mr. WHITMAN shall have learned that a proper worship of the individual man need not be expressed so as to seem insolence, and that men are not to be bullied into receiving as a Messiah every man who sneers at them in his portrait, and disgusts them in his writings, we have no doubt that in some chastened mood of mind he will produce moving and powerful books. We select some passages exhibiting the different phases of Mr. WHITMAN's character. We do so more readily as, from the many indecencies contained in *Leaves of Grass*, we do not believe it will find its way into many families.

A MODEST PROFESSION OF
FAITH.

Nothing, not God, is greater to one
   than one's self is,
And whoever walks a furlong
   without sympathy, walks to his
   own funeral,
Dressed in his shroud.

A FINE LANDSCAPE.

The turbid pool that lies in the
    Autumn forest.
The moon that descends the steeps of
    the soughing twilight,
Toss, sparkles of day and dusk . . . .
    toss on the black stems that decay
    in the muck;
Toss to the moaning gibberish of the
    dry limbs.

A TRUTH.

I, too, am not a bit tamed . . . . I, too,
    am untranslatable;
I sound my barbaric yawp over the
    roofs of the world.

A DEATH-BED.

When the dull nights are over, and
    the dull days also;
When the soreness of lying so much
    in bed is over,
When the physician, after long
    putting off, gives the silent and
    terrible look for an answer;
When the children come hurried and
    weeping, and the brothers and
    sisters have been sent for;
When medicines stand unused on the
    shelf, and the camphor-smell has
    pervaded the rooms;
When the faithful hand of the living
    does not desert the hand of the
    dying,
When the twitching lips press lightly
    on the forehead of the dying,
When the breath ceases, and the
    pulse of the heart ceases,
Then the corpse limbs stretch on the
    bed, and the living look upon
    them,
They are palpable as the living are
    palpable.
The living look upon the corpse with
    their eye-sight,
But without eye-sight lingers a

different living and looks curiously
on the corpse.

IMMORTALITY.

If maggots and rats ended us, then
    suspicion, and treachery and death.
Do you suspect death? If I were to
    suspect death I should die now.
Do you think I could walk pleasantly
    and well-suited towards
    annihilation?

THE REVOLUTION OF 1848.

Yet behind all, lo, a Shape,
Vague as the night, draped
    interminably, head, front and form
    in scarlet folds,
Whose face and eyes none may see,
Out of its robes only this . . . . the red
    robes, lifted by the arm,
One finger pointed high over the top,
    like the head of a snake appears.

Meanwhile corpses lie in new-made
    graves . . . . bloody corpses of
    young men:
The rope of the gibbet, hangs
    heavily . . . . the bullets of princes
    are flying . . . . the creatures of
    power laugh aloud,
And all these things bear fruits . . . .
    and they are good.

Those corpses of young men,
Those martyrs that hang from the
    gibbets . . . those hearts pierced by
    the gray lead,
Cold and motionless as they seem . .
    live elsewhere with unslaughter'd
    vitality.

They live in other young men, O
    Kings,
They live in brothers again ready to
    defy you:
They were purified by death . . . .
    They were taught and exalted.

Not a grave of the murdered for

freedom but sows seed for
freedom . . . . in its turn to bear
seed,
Which the winds carry afar and re-
sow, and the rains and the snows
nourish.
Not a disembodied spirit can the
weapons of tyrants let loose,
But it stalks invisibly o'er the
earth . . . whispering, counselling,
cautioning.

Since the foregoing was written—and
it has been awaiting its turn at the printing press some months—Mr. WALT WHIT-
MAN has published an enlarged edition of
his works, from which it is fair to infer
that his first has had a ready sale. From
twelve poems, of which the original book
was composed, he has brought the number up to thirty, all characterized by the
same wonderful amalgamation of beauty
and indecency. He has, however, been in
his new edition guilty of a fresh immodesty. He has not alone printed Mr.
EMERSON's private letter in an appendix,
but he has absolutely printed a passage of
that gentleman's note, 'I greet you at the
beginning of a great career,' in gold letters on the back, and affixed the name of
the writer. Now, Mr. EMERSON wrote a
not very wise letter to Mr. WHITMAN on
the publication of the first twelve poems—indorsing them, and so there might
be some excuse for the poet's anxiety to
let the public know that his first edition
was commended from such a quarter. But
with the additional poems, Mr. EMERSON
has certainly nothing whatever to do;
nevertheless, the same note that indorsed
the twelve is used by Mr. WHITMAN in the
coolest manner to indorse the thirty-two.
This is making a private letter go very far
indeed. It is as if after a man signed a
deed, the person interested should introduce a number of additional clauses,
making the original signature still cover

them. It is a literary fraud, and Mr. WHIT-
MAN ought to be ashamed of himself.

Still, this man has brave stuff in him.
He is truly astonishing. The originality of
his philosophy is of little account, for if
it is truth, it must be ever the same,
whether uttered by his lips or PLATO's. In
manner only can we be novel, and truly
Mr. WHITMAN is novelty itself. Since the
greater portion of this review was written, we confess to having been attracted
again and again to *Leaves of Grass*. It
has a singular electric attraction. Its manly vigor, its brawny health, seem to incite
and satisfy. We look forward with curious anticipation to Mr. WALT WHITMAN's
future works. We are much mistaken if,
after all, he does not yet contribute something to American literature which shall
awaken wonder.

"New Publications." Brooklyn *Daily Times*, 17 December 1856, p. 1.

This is a new, enlarged and stereotyped
edition of that singular production of
"WALT WHITMAN," whose first appearance in '55 created such an extraordinary
sensation in the literary world on both
sides of the Atlantic. The first edition—
which was duly noticed in these columns—
contained twelve poems. In the present
edition those poems are revised, and
twenty others are added. The form of the
book has been changed from 4 to 16mo,
and the typography is much improved.

The work, in its singular character, we
understand to be an assertion of a two-
fold individuality for the author: of himself personally, and of himself nationally;
and the author, by example at least, to be
an advocate of as much for all of his na-

tion. A bold example he sets. The titles of the poems are various, and the poems under them present differences; yet through them all, with whatever else, runs one vital view; one ontological lesson in the same idiosyncratic strain.

Fanciful, fertile, and free in words, yet often, conventionally speaking, inelegant, and sometimes downright low; simple, abrupt, and detached sentences; frequently aphoristic, yet diffuse and uniform, sometimes to tediousness; at times strikingly clear and forcible, and again impenetrably obscure; a meeting of the extremes of literalness and metaleptic figures—of tiresome superficial details and comprehensive subtle generalities, oddities, ruggedness and strength; these are the chief characteristics of his style. There occur frequent instances of all-important and majestic thought, and so fitly expressed that the dissonance to the unaccustomed ears of the reader cannot prevent his stopping to admire. The matter is characterized by thought rather than by sentiment. The right and duty of man with the passions are enjoined and celebrated, rather than the passions themselves. There are speculative philosophies advanced, upon which readers will differ with the author and with each other; and some of these to intolerant conventionalists will give offense. We are not prepared to endorse them all ourselves. And there are practical philosophies of which he treats, destined to encounter fiercer repugnance. But the book is not one that warrants its dismissal with disgust or contempt. There is a deep substratum of observant and contemplative wisdom as broad as the foundation of society, running through it all; and whatever else there is of questionable good, so much at least is a genuine pearl that we cannot afford to trample it under our feet. The poems contain some lessons of the highest importance, and possess a further value in their strong suggestiveness. We accord to the leading idea of the work alone, personal with national individuality, exemplified and recommended as it is, an incalculable value. The poems improve upon a second reading, and they may commonly require a repetition in order to [gain] a deserved appreciation, like a strange piece of music with subtle harmonies.

The work is altogether *sui generis*, unless we may call it Emersonian. That name is ample enough to cover a multitude of oddities and excellencies; but that it is not shaped to all the radiations of the unbridled muse of the author under notice we think a single extract from his first poem will show:

[thirty-seven–line extract from "Song of Myself"]

A CHILD'S REMINISCENCE (1859)

The New-

VOL. II.—NO. 52.

A Child's Reminiscence.

PRE-VERSE.

Out of the rocked cradle,
Out of the mocking-bird's throat, the musical shuttle,
Out of the boys's mother's womb, and from the nipples
of her breasts,
Out of the Ninth-Month midnight,
Over the sterile sea-sands, and the fields beyond, where
the child, leaving his bed, wandered alone, bare-
headed, barefoot,
Down from the showered halo and the moonbeams,
Up from the mystic play of shadows twining and
twisting as if they were alive,
Out from the patches of briars and blackberries,
From the memories of the bird that chanted to me,
From your memories, sad brother—from the fitful
risings and fallings I heard,
From that night, infantile, under the yellow half-
moon, late-risen, and swollen as if with tears,
From those beginning notes of sickness and love, there
in the mist,
From the thousand responses in my heart, never to
cease,
From the myriad thence-aroused words,
From the word stronger and more delicious than any,
From such, as now they start, the scene revisiting,
As a flock, twittering, rising, or overhead passing,
Borne hither—ere all eludes me, hurriedly,
A man—yet by these tears a little boy again,
Throwing myself on the sand, I,
Confronting the waves, sing.

REMINISCENCE.

I.

Once, Paumanok,
Up this sea-shore, in some briars,
Two guests from Alabama—two together,
And their nest, and four light-green eggs, spotted with
brown,
And every day the he-bird, to and fro, near at hand,
And every day the she-bird, crouched on her nest, si-
lent, with bright eyes,
And every day I, a curious boy, never too close, never
disturbing them,
Cautiously peering, absorbing, translating.

Pierce the woods—the earth,
Somewhere listening to catch you must be the one I want.

XX.

Shake out, carols !
Solitary here—the night's carols !
Carols of lonesome love ! Death's carols !
Carols under that lagging, yellow, waning moon !
O, under that moon, where she droops almost down into the sea!
O reckless, despairing carols !

XXI.

But soft !
Sink low—soft !
Soft ! Let me just murmur,
And do you hush and wait a moment, you sea,
For somewhere I believe I heard my mate responding to me,
So faint—I must be still to listen,
But not altogether still, for then she might not come immediately
to me.

XXII.

Hither, my love !
Here I am ! Here !
With this just-sustained note I announce myself to you,
This gentle call is for you, my love.

XXIII.

Do not be decoyed elsewhere !
That is the whistle of the wind—it is not my voice,
That is the fluttering of the spray,
Those are the shadows of leaves.

XXIV.

O darkness ! O in vain !
O I am very sick and sorrowful !

XXV.

O brown halo in the sky, near the moon, drooping upon the
sea !
O troubled reflection in the sea !
O throat ! O throbbing heart !
O all—and I singing uselessly all the night.

XXVI.

Murmur ! Murmur on !
O murmurs—you yourselves make me continue to sing, I know
not why.

XXVII.

O past ! O joy !
In the air—in the woods—over fields,
Loved ! Loved ! Loved ! Loved ! Loved !
Loved—but no more with me.

"Walt Whitman's New Poem."
Cincinnati *Daily Commercial*, 28 December 1859, p. 2.

The author of *Leaves of Grass* has perpetrated another "poem." The N. Y. *Saturday Press*, in whose columns, we regret to say, it appears, calls it "a curious warble." Curious, it may be; but warble it is not, in any sense of that mellifluous word. It is a shade less heavy and vulgar than the *Leaves of Grass*, whose unmitigated badness seemed to cap the climax of poetic nuisances. But the present performance has all the emptiness, without half the grossness, of the author's former efforts.

How in the name of all the Muses this so-called "poem" ever got into the columns of the *Saturday Press*, passes our poor comprehension. We had come to look upon that journal as the prince of literary weeklies, the *arbiter elegantiarum* of dramatic and poetic taste, into whose well filled columns nothing stupid or inferior could intrude. The numerous delicious poems; the sparkling *bons mots*; the puns, juicy and classical, which almost redeemed that vicious practice, and raised it to the rank of a fine art; the crisp criticisms, and delicate dramatic humors of "Personne," and the charming piquancies of the *spirituelle* Ada Clare—all united to make up a paper of rare excellence. And it is into this gentle garden of the Muses that that unclean cub of the wilderness, Walt Whitman, has been suffered to intrude, trampling with his vulgar and profane hoofs among the delicate flowers which bloom there, and soiling the spotless white of its fair columns with lines of stupid and meaningless twaddle.

Perhaps our readers are blissfully ignorant of the history and achievements of Mr. Walt Whitman. Be it known, then, that he is a native and resident of Brooklyn, Long Island, born and bred in an obscurity from which it were well that he never had emerged. A person of coarse nature, and strong, rude passions, he has passed his life in cultivating, not the amenities, but the rudeness of character; and instead of tempering his native ferocity with the delicate influences of art and refined literature, he has studied to exaggerate his deformities, and to thrust into his composition all the brute force he could muster from a capacity not naturally sterile in the elements of strength. He has undertaken to be an artist, without learning the first principle of art, and has presumed to put forth "poems," without possessing a spark of the poetic faculty. He affects swagger and independence, and blurts out his vulgar impertinence under a full assurance of "originality."

In his very first performance, this truculent tone was manifested. He exaggerated every sentiment, and piled up with endless repetition every epithet, till the reader grew weary, even to nausea, of his unmeaning rant. He announced himself to the world as a new and striking thinker, who had something to reveal. His *Leaves of Grass* were a revelation from the Kingdom of Nature. Thus he screams to a gaping universe:

I, Walt Whitman, an American, one of the roughs, a kosmos; I shout my voice high and clear over the waves; I send my barbaric yawp over the roofs of the world!

Such was the style of his performance, only it was disfigured by far worse sins of

71

morality than of taste. Never, since the days of Rabelais was there such literature of uncleanness as some portions of this volume exhibited. All that is beautiful and sacred in love was dragged down to the brutal plane of animal passion, and the writer appeared to revel in language fit only for the lips of the Priapus of the old mythology.

We had hoped that the small reception accorded to his first performance had deterred Mr. Whitman from fresh trespasses in the realms of literature. Several years had passed away, his worse than worthless book had been forgotten, and we hoped that this Apollo of the Brooklyn marshes had returned to his native mud. But we grieve to say he revived last week, and although somewhat changed, changed very little for the better. We do not find so much that is offensive, but we do find a vast amount of irreclaimable drivel and inexplicable nonsense.

We have searched this "poem" through with a serious and deliberate endeavor to find out the reason of its being written; to discover some clue to the mystery of so vast an expenditure of words. But we honestly confess our utter inability to solve the problem. It is destitute of all the elements which are commonly desiderated in poetical composition; it has neither rhythm nor melody, rhyme nor reason, metre nor sense. We do solemnly assert, that there is not to be discovered, throughout the whole performance, so much as the glimmering ghost of an idea. Here is the poem, which the author, out of his characteristic perversity, insists upon calling the *Pre-verse*:

"Out of the rocked cradle.
  Out of the mocking bird's throat,
  The musical shuttle,
  Out of the boy's mother's womb,
    and from the nipples of her breasts,
  Out of the Ninth-Month midnight,

Over the sterile sea-sands, and the
  field beyond, where the child,
  leaving his bed, wandered alone,
  bareheaded, barefoot,
Down from the showered halo and
  the moonbeams,
Up from the mystic play of shadows
  twining and twisting as if they
  were alive,
Out from the patches of briars and
  blackberries,
From the memories of the bird that
  chanted to me,
From your memories, sad brother—
  from the fitful risings and fallings
  I heard,
From that night, infantile, under the
  yellow half-moon, late risen, and
  swollen as if with tears,
From those beginning notes of
  sickness and love, there in the mist,
From the thousand responses in my
  heart, never to cease,
From the myriad thence-aroused
  words,
From the word stronger and more
  delicious than any,
From such, as now they start, the
  scene revisiting,
As a flock, twittering, rising, or
  overhead passing,
Borne hither—ere all eludes me,
  hurriedly,
A man—yet by these tears a little
  boy again,
Throwing myself on the sand, I,
Confronting the waves, sing."

This is like nothing we ever heard of in literature, unless it be the following lucid and entertaining composition:

"Once there was an old woman went into the garden to get some cabbage to make an apple pie. Just then a great she-bear comes up and pops his head into the shop. 'What, no soap!' So he

72

died, and she married the barber; and there was present at the wedding the Jicaninies and the Picaninies, and the Grand Panjandrum himself, with a little round button at the top; and they all fell to playing the game of catch as catch can, till the gun powder ran out of the heels of their boots."

The "poem" goes on, after the same maudlin manner, for a hundred lines or more, in which the interjection "O" is employed above five-and-thirty times, until we reach the following gem:

"Never again leave me to be the
    peaceful child I was before; what
    there, in the night,
By the sea, under the yellow and
    sagging moon,
The dusky demon aroused, the fire,
    the sweet hell within
The unknown want, the destiny of
    me."
    O, but this is bitter bad!
"O give me some clue!
O if I am to have so much, let me
    have more!
O a word! O what is my
    destination?
O I fear it is henceforth chaos!"

There is not a doubt of it, we do assure you! And what is more, it never was anything else. Now, what earthly object can there be in writing and printing such unmixed and hopeless drivel as that? If there were any relief to the unmeaning monotony, some glimpse of fine fancy, some oasis of sense, some spark of "the vision and the faculty divine," we would not say a word. But we do protest, in the name of the sanity of the human intellect, against being invited to read such stuff as this, by its publication in the columns of a highly respectable literary journal. What is the comment of the *Saturday Press* itself on the "poem"? It says:

"Like the *Leaves of Grass*, the purport of this wild and plaintive song, well enveloped, and eluding definition, is positive and unquestionable, like the effect of music. The piece will bear reading many times—perhaps, indeed, only comes forth, as from recesses, by many repetitions."

Well, Heaven help us, then, for as we are a living man, we would not read that poem "many times" for all the poetry that was ever perpetrated since the morning stars sang together. "Well enveloped, and eluding definition." Indeed! We should think so. For our part, we hope it will remain "well enveloped" till doomsday; and as for "definition," all we can do in that direction is to declare that either that "poem" is nonsense, or we are a lunatic.

If any of the tuneful Nine have ever descended upon Mr. Walt Whitman, it must have been long before that gentleman reached the present sphere of existence. His amorphous productions clearly belong to that school which it [is] said that neither gods nor men can endure. There is no meaning discoverable in his writings, and if there were, it would most certainly not be worth the finding out. He is the laureate of the empty deep of the incomprehensible; over that immortal limbo described by Milton, he has stretched the drag-net of his genius; and as he has no precedent and no rival, so we venture to hope that he will never have an imitator.

[Walt Whitman]. "All about a Mocking-Bird."
New York *Saturday Press*, 7 January 1860, p. 3.

What is the reason-why of Walt Whitman's lyric utterances, as soon as any of them is heard, rousing up such vehement intellectual censures and contumely from some persons, and their equally determined bravos from other persons?

Passing by certain of the latter, the complimentary sort, with which the journals, welcoming Walt's reappearance and recovery of his singing-voice after an obstinate three years' dumbness, have accepted that Mocking-Bird Chant printed by us in the SATURDAY PRESS, of Dec. 24, preceding, we seize upon and give to our readers, in another part of the paper, a specimen of the sort of censure alluded to—a tip-top cutting-and-slashing criticism from the *Cincinnati Daily Commercial*, which we have conned with unfeigned pleasure. All of which is respectfully submitted as outset for something else made way to be said, namely:

We feel authorized to announce, for certain, that the Mocking-Bird, having come to his throat again, his cantabile, is not going to give cause to his admirers for complaining that he idles, mute, any more, up and down the world. His songs, in one and another direction, will, he promises us, after this date, profusely appear.

We are able to declare that there will also soon crop out the true *LEAVES OF GRASS*, the fuller-grown work of which the former two issues were the inchoates—this forthcoming one, far, very far ahead of them in quality, quantity, and in supple lyric exuberance.

Those former issues, published by the author himself in little pittance-editions, on trial, have just dropped the book enough to ripple the inner first-circles of literary agitation, in immediate contact with it. The outer, vast, extending, and ever-wider-extending circles, of the general supply, perusal, and discussion of such a work, have still to come. The market needs to-day to be supplied—the great West especially—with copious thousands of copies.

Indeed, *LEAVES OF GRASS* has not yet been really published at all. Walt Whitman, for his own purposes, slowly trying his hand at the edifice, the structure he has undertaken, has lazily loafed on, letting each part have time to set—evidently building not so much with reference to any part itself, considered alone, but more with reference to the ensemble—always bearing in mind the combination of the whole, to fully justify the parts when finished.

Of course the ordinary critic, even of good eye, high intellectual calibre, and well accomplished, grasps not, sees not, any such ideal ensemble—likely sees not the only valuable part of these mystic leaves, namely, not what they state, but what they infer—scornfully wants to know what the Mocking-Bird means, who can tell?—gives credit only for what is proved to the surface-ear—and makes up a very fine criticism, not out of the soul, to which these poems altogether appeal, and by which only they can be interpreted, but out of the intellect, to which Walt Whitman has not, as far as we remember, addressed one single word in the whole course of his writings.

Then the workmanship, the art-statement and argument of the question. Is this man really any artist at all? Or not plainly a sort of naked and hairy savage, come among us, with yelps and howls, disregarding all our lovely metrical laws? How can it be that he offends so many and so much?

Quite after the same token as the Italian Opera, to most bold Americans, and all new persons, even of latent proclivities that very way, only accustomed to tunes, piano-noises and the performances of the negro bands—satisfied, (or rather fancying they are satisfied), with each and several thereof, from association and habit, until they pass utterly beyond them—which comes in good time, and cannot be deferred much longer, either, in such a race as yours, O bold American of the West!

Walt Whitman's method in the construction of his songs is strictly the method of the Italian Opera, which, when heard, confounds the new person aforesaid, and, as far as he can then see, showing no purport for him, nor on the surface, nor any analogy to his previous-accustomed tunes, impresses him as if all the sounds of earth and hell were tumbled promiscuously together. Whereupon he says what he candidly thinks (or supposes he thinks), and is very likely a first-rate fellow—with room to grow, in certain directions.

Then, in view of the latter words, bold American! in the ardor of youth, commit not yourself, too irretrievably, that there is nothing in the Italian composers, and nothing in the Mocking-Bird's chants. But pursue them awhile—listen—yield yourself—persevere. Strange as the shape of the suggestion may be, perhaps such free strains are to give to these United States, or commence giving them, the especial nourishments which, though all solid and mental and moral things are in boundless profusion provided, have hardly yet begun to be provided for them—hardly yet the idea of that kind of

nourishment thought of, or the need of it suspected. Though it is the sweetest, strongest meat—pabulum of a race of giants—true pabulum of the children of the prairies.

You, bold American! and ye future two hundred millions of bold Americans, can surely never live, for instance, entirely satisfied and grow to your full stature, on what the importations hither of foreign bards, dead or alive, provide—nor on what is echoing here the letter and the spirit of the foreign bards. No, bold American! not even on what is provided, printed from Shakespeare or Milton—not even of the Hebrew canticles—certainly not of Pope, Byron, or Wordsworth—nor of any German or French singer, nor any foreigner at all.

We are to accept those and every other literary and poetic thing from beyond the seas, thankfully, as studies, exercises. We go back—we pause long with the old, ever-modern one, the Homer, the only chanting mouth that approaches our case near enough to raise a vibration, an echo. We then listen with accumulated eagerness for those mouths that can make the vaults of America ring here to-day—those who will not only touch our case, but embody it and all that belongs to it—sing it with varied and powerful idioms, and in the modern spirit, at least as capable, as loud and proud as the best spirit that has ever preceded us.

Our own song, free, joyous, and masterful. Our own music, raised on the soil, carrying with it all the subtle analogies of our own associations—broad with the broad continental scale of the New World and full of the varied products of its varied soils—composite—comprehensively Religious—Democratic —the red life-blood of Love, warming, running through every line, every word. Ah, if this Walt Whitman, as he keeps on, should ever succeed in presenting *such* music, *such* a poem, an identity, emblematic, in the regions of creative art, of the wondrous all-America, material and moral, he would indeed do something.

And if he don't, the Mocking-Bird may at least have the satisfaction of dying in a good cause. But then again he looks so little like dying, anyhow.

LEAVES OF GRASS (1860–1)

Leaves of GRASS.

Boston,
Thayer and Eldridge,
Year 85 of The States.
(1860-61)

[Henry Clapp? or Walt Whitman?].
"Walt Whitman: *Leaves of Grass.*"
New York *Saturday Press*, 19 May 1860, p. 2.

We announce a great Philosopher—perhaps a great Poet—in every way an original man. It is Walt Whitman. The proof of his greatness is in his book; and there is proof enough.

The intellectual attitude expressed in these *Leaves of Grass*, is grand with the grandeur of independent strength, and beautiful with the beauty of serene repose. It is the attitude of a proud, noble, vigorous life. A human heart is here in these pages—large, wild, comprehensive—beating with all throbs of passion—enjoying all of bliss—suffering all of sorrow that is possible to humanity. "This is no book," it says; "whoever touches this, touches a man." It is the electrical contact of a great nature.

[eighteen-line extract from "Song of Myself"]

Such is the intellectual attitude of the *Leaves of Grass*; such the position and purpose of their author. To accept everything as liberally as Nature accepts everything; to rightly appreciate all laws and all things, each thing in its place; to realize, reflect, and reproduce the emotions of every heart and the experiences of every person; to recognize and assert the universal harmony of creation; to know the beautiful union of Body and Soul in the individual, sublime in the present, and with a sublime destiny for the future; to repose in the certainty of infinite development and progression; to assert the individual above all things, knowing that 'nothing endures but personal quality'; to express for all mankind what all mankind feel without the power of expressing; to live the comprehensive life of the Philosopher, of the Poet, broad and vigorous, all lives in one,—reaching up into heaven, reaching down into hell, stretching backward over all the Past to gather up its results, throbbing with all the vital activity of the Present, making the Future glorious with more than hope,—this is the aim and the mission of Walt Whitman, this the felicity of his life as expressed in his poems. No man could utter himself more fully and truly. No book exists anywhere more beautifully in earnest than this. To the intelligent, sympathetic mind, none can explain itself with keener accuracy.

[twenty-one–line extract from "Starting from Paumanok"]

The leading idea in the philosophy of the *Leaves of Grass* is the idea of grandeur and supremacy in the Individual. It asserts that there is nothing more divine than the human soul, and impels to a knowledge of living motive behind each thing and every action. It will have the singer and not the psalm, the preacher and not the script he preaches. It will not ignore the Body, but asserts its beauty and the divine harmony of Body and Soul.

... "I believe in you, my Soul—the
    other I am must not abase itself to
    you,
And you must not be abased to the
    other....
Welcome is every organ and attribute
    of me, and of any man hearty and
    clean,

Not an inch, nor a particle of an
   inch, is vile, and none shall be less
   familiar than the rest. . . . .
I believe in the flesh and the
   appetites,
Seeing, hearing, and feeling are
   miracles, and each tag and part of
   me is a miracle.—

It finds all things embraced and comprehended in the individual, to whom indeed the universe belongs and who belongs
to the universe. It recognizes the common
brotherhood of mankind, and the same
human nature repeated in every person.
Its aspiration is for a noble race of human creatures, healthy and beautiful, living delightfully, in sympathy with Nature, their perfect lives in a perfect world.

Perhaps the scope and significance of
Walt Whitman's poetry may be more clearly indicated by contrasting its character
with that of the poetry ordinarily accepted and popular at the present time.
The latter is rhymed and measured. It is
sometimes powerful with passion and
sometimes stately with thought. It is
generally sweet and graceful—expressing
mild and monotonous sentiments in a
thousand respectable ways. It is gay for a
feast and sorry for a funeral. It is sweet
as to Spring-time, and thoughtful as to
sober Autumn days. It rhymes 'kisses'
with 'blisses,' and expresses its writer's
willingness to partake of the same. It
mourns persistently for dead infants, for
those who are snatched away in beauty's
bloom, and for blighted blossoms generally. It has an amatory tendency, of a sentimental description, and wastes a good
deal of miscellaneous sweetness. It presents
its author as one who desires burial under a sweet-apple tree, and will not have
a decent graveyard on any terms; it affects
to ignore and despise the human body; it
dwells fondly upon the sublime nature
and destiny of the soul; and passing

smoothly over all that is significant in
this actual present life, it hints lugubrious-
ly at another and a better world. On the
other hand these poems of Walt Whitman concern themselves alike with the
largest and with the pettiest topics. They
are free as the wandering wind that
sweeps over great oceans and inland seas,
over the continents of the world, over
mountains, forests, rivers, plains, and cities; free as the sunshine are they, and like
the sunshine ardent and fierce. Nothing
in the creation is too sacred or too distant for the lightning glance of their aspiration; nothing that in any way concerns
the souls and the bodies of the human
race is too trivial for their comprehension. Everywhere they evince the philo-
sophic mind, deeply seeking, reasoning,
feeling its way toward a clear knowledge
of the system of the universe.

[nineteen-line extract from "Song of
Myself" and "Starting from Paumanok"]

In this liberal scope of vision and purpose are indicated the insight and the
earnestness characteristic of a poetic nature. Other elements of that poetic nature
are evident in the vigor of imagination
and splendor of imagery which make certain of these poems so truly remarkable.
In the 'Salut au Monde'; in the poem
called 'A Word Out of the Sea'—which,
under the title of 'A Child's Reminiscence,' was printed in this paper last December; in the poem of 'Brooklyn Ferry';
in that of 'Sleep Chasings,' and that of
'Burial';—in these, and in others, such
qualities largely and beautifully appear.

Some reflections may properly be submitted here, relative to the form in which
Walt Whitman's poems are embodied and
expressed. It is a form so rough and rugged—so careless, variable, and peculiar—
that perhaps it is very natural the poetry
should sometimes degenerate into prose.

Something is to be said, however, in defence of this system of versification. It is at least original. The theory would seem to be, as Walt has variously indicated, that always the thought or the passion of the poet should determine itself in natural, congenial expression. It is assumed in this theory, and indeed it is very true, that much of the verse ordinarily written, is written without a sincere motive, and has therefore neither power nor value. It is further assumed that the styles of versification generally accredited and employed are inadequate to the utterance of earnest thought and feeling. Consequently, Walt Whitman, who presents himself as the Poet of the American Republic in the Present Age, who is actuated by a sincere motive, and has earnest thought and feeling to express, refuses to confine and cripple himself within the laws of what to him is inefficient art. Reverencing the spirit of poetry above the form, he submits that the one shall determine the other. That his volume is poetic in spirit cannot rationally be denied; and, whatever the eccentricities of its form, no critical reader can fail to perceive that the expression seems always the suitable and natural result of the thought. It is indeed tame and prosy in the conveyance of any commonplace idea or feeling, but it rises and melts into sweet and thrilling music whenever impelled by the beautiful impulse of a grand thought or emotion.

A fine example of this felicity of style occurs in the following beautiful passage, which also delightfully illustrates the poet's ardent and profound love of Nature:

> "I am He that walks with the tender
>   and growing Night,
> I call to the earth and sea, half-held
>   by the Night.

[twenty-six additional lines extracted from "Song of Myself" and "To Think of Time"]

Of the defects in this book something also may properly be said. They are not trivial and they are not few. It is the law of a great nature to err greatly as well as to be greatly wise. Walt Whitman has exemplified that law. There are, as it seems to us, defects alike in his philosophy, art, taste, and style. It is fair to say there is much in his book that, like the peace of God, passeth all understanding, and that it does not lack passages which should never have been published at all. We may have occasion to refer to this book again, and to explain ourselves more fully in these regards. Meantime we submit, as appropriate in this connection, the following critical remarks from the *North American Review*:

"For the purpose of showing that he is above every conventionalism, Mr. Whitman puts into the book one or two lines which he would not address to a woman nor to a company of men. There is not anything, perhaps, which modern usage would stamp as more indelicate than are some passages in Homer. There is not a word in it meant to attract readers by its grossness, as there is in half the literature of the last century, which holds its place unchallenged on the tables of our drawing-rooms. For all that, it is a pity that a book where everything else is natural, should go out of the way to avoid the suspicion of being prudish."

We should not conclude our notice of the *Leaves of Grass* without expressing our very great delight at the sumptuous elegance of the style in which Messrs. Thayer & Eldridge have published Walt Whitman's poetry. The volume presents one of the richest specimens of taste and skill in book-making, that has ever been afforded to the public by either an English or an American publisher.

"New Publications: The New Poets."
New York *Times*, 19 May 1860, Supplement, p. 1.

Five years ago a new poet appeared, styling himself the representative of America, the mouthpiece of free institutions, the personification of all that men had waited for. His writings were neither poetry nor prose, but a curious medley, a mixture of quaint utterances and gross indecencies, a remarkable compound of fine thoughts and sentiment of the pot-house. It was not an easy task to winnow the chaff from the wheat, the tares came up in such heavy luxuriance that they stunted the chance kernels of the grain, and nothing but the most vigorous of threshing was adequate to the elimination of one pure thought. That first edition of the *Leaves of Grass* was the earliest appearance of Mr. Walt Whitman as an author. For a *debutant*, he was sufficiently egotistic and assuming. He announced, with a degree of confidence which could only have been the natural result of unparalleled self-conceit, that his mission lay in the reformation of the public taste, that the American people were to be enlightened and civilized and cultivated up to the proper standard, by virtue of his superior endowments, and that, being "a Kosmos," and inclined to "loafe" at his ease, and "invite his soul," he could afford to wait for the public's warm appreciation of his self-sacrifice, and to recline in a comfortable attitude until the world saw fit to come round to him. Two years after the publication of the first thin and unprepossessing volume of the *Leaves,* a larger edition appeared, and that again is followed by a third and still more pretentious book, the present issue from the Boston house of Thayer & Eldridge.

Mr. Whitman has added to this volume a large collection of his writings which have never been given to the public. If possible, he is more reckless and vulgar than in his two former publications. He seems to delight in the contemplation of scenes that ordinary men do not love, or which they are content to regard as irremediable evils, about which it is needless to repine. Mr. Whitman sees nothing vulgar in that which is commonly regarded as the grossest obscenity; rejects the laws of conventionality so completely as to become repulsive; gloats over coarse images with the gusto of a Rabelais, but lacks the genius or the grace of Rabelais to vivify or adorn that which, when said at all, should be said as delicately as possible.

Yet it would be unjust to deny the evidences of remarkable power which are presented in this work. In his hearty human sympathy, his wonderful intensity, his fullness of epithet, the author shows that he is a man of strong passion, vigorous in thought and earnest in purpose. He is uncultured, rude, defiant and arrogant, but these are faults of his nature which have not been tempered by severe training. Occasionally, a gleam of the true poetic fire shines out of the mass of his rubbish, and there are tender and beautiful touches in the midst of his most objectionable and disagreeable writings. A rough diamond, much in need of cutting and grinding and polishing, he has great intrinsic worth, but the impurities which cling about him must keep him out of the refined company he desires to enter. To be an agent for the civilization of men, he must first himself become civilized. He can do no manner of good by throwing filth, even though a handful of pure gold be sometimes mingled with a cast from his moral cesspool.

Nearly two hundred poems, of all sizes and qualities, are contained in this edition. Two dozens of these are properly the *Leaves of Grass,* grouped under that title, and mainly published in former editions. "Chants Democratic and Native American" comprise twenty-one curious specimens of composition, which are neither metrical nor harmonious. Fifteen others are collected under the comprehensive heading of "Enfans d'Adam," and are humanitary. Fifteen others are "Messenger Leaves." Four hundred and fifty pages of these productions establish the industry of the writer; and the fact that a respectable house has undertaken their publication, illustrates a lively faith in the eagerness of the public for the reception of novelties.

Some of the finer passages in this intricate maze of incongruous materials occur in the first hundred pages. Take the following weird conceit:

A child said: What is the grass? fetching it to me with full hands.
How could I answer the child? I do not know what it is, any more than he.
. . . . . I guess it is the handkerchief of the Lord,
A scented gift and remembrancer, designedly dropped,
Bearing the owner's name someway in the corners, that we may see and remark, and say, Whose?
. . . . . Or I guess the grass is itself a child, the produced babe of the vegetation:
. . . . . And now it seems to me the beautiful uncut hair of graves.

In "Chants Democratic," the poet discourses of strong wills, and mirrors the image of the reformer.

How beggarly appear poems, arguments, orations, before an electric deed!
How the floridness of the materials of cities shrivels before a man's or woman's look!
All waits, or goes by default, till a strong being appears;
A strong being is the proof of the race, and of the ability of the universe;
When he or she appears, materials are overawed,
The dispute on the Soul stops,
The old customs and phrases are confronted, turned back, or laid away.

Again, he studies faces, and draws sharply-lined portraits:

This face is a life-boat;
This is the face commanding and bearded; it asks no odds of the rest;
This face is flavored fruit, ready for eating;
This face of a healthy, honest boy, is the programme of all good.

Yet the tendency to fall into the vulgar, apparently ineradicable in Mr. Whitman's composition, leads him to interlard with these such expressions as "abject louse, asking leave to be"—"milk-nosed maggot, blessing what lets it wrig to its hole"—"dog's snout, sniffing for garbage." He will be gross, and there is no help for it.

The egotism of the book is amusing. Mr. Whitman is not only "a man-myself, typical before all," but he is "a man thirty-six years old in the year 79 of America, and is here anyhow"—but, being here, lies in libraries "as one dumb, a gawk, or unborn, or dead," thereby evincing a hearty contempt for scholastic culture; but nevertheless avowing a stern determination to:

..... make a song for these States,
..... and a shrill song of curses on
    him who would dissever the Union.

It is fair to presume that this "song of curses," should it ever come to be sung, will be "shrill," and loud, not to say foul and abusive. Mr. Whitman is master of the art.

A better passage is that in which he describes the effect of music upon himself:

The orchestra wrenches such ardors
    from me, I did not know I
    possessed them,
It throbs me to gulps of the farthest
    down horror;
It sails me—I dab with bare feet—
    they are licked by the indolent waves,
I am exposed, cut by bitter and
    poisoned hail,
Steeped amid honeyed morphine, my
    windpipe throttled in fakes of
    death,
At length let up again to feel the
    puzzle of puzzles,
And that we call Being.

There is great power in this passage—rude strength, unpolished but vigorous.

A lover of nature, he sees all natural things through a pleasant medium. Trees, birds, fish alike delight him; he loves:

The cheerful voice of the public
    road—the gay fresh sentiment of
    the road.

He sees Deity in everything:

..... finds letters from God dropped
    in the street—and every one is
    signed by God's name.

He loves the stillness of night, and apostrophizes it with passionate vehemence;

Press close, bare-bosomed Night!
    Press close, magnetic, nourishing
    Night!
Night of south winds! Night of the
    large, few stars!
Still, nodding Night! Mad, naked,
    Summer Night!

It is needless to multiply extracts from these extraordinary productions. We make room for one more passage—a description of the close of a sea-battle, which is strongly tinted;

Toward twelve at night, there, in the
    beams of the moon, they
    surrendered to us.
Stretched and still lay the midnight;
Two great hulls motionless on the
    breast of the darkness,
Our vessel riddled and slowly
    sinking—preparations to pass to
    the one we had conquered—
The captain on the quarter-deck,
    coldly giving his orders through a
    countenance white as a sheet;
Near by, the corpse of the child that
    served in the cabin,
The dead face of an old salt, with
    long white hair and carefully curled
    whiskers;
The flames, spite of all that could be
    done, flickering aloft and below,
The husky voices of the two or three
    officers yet fit for duty—
Formless stacks of bodies, and bodies
    by themselves; dabs of flesh upon
    the masts and spars—
Cut of cordage, dangle of rigging,
    slight shock of the soothe of waves,
Black and impassive guns, litter of
    powder parcels, strong scent,
Delicate sniffs of sea-breeze, smells of
    sedgy grass and fields by the shore,
    death-messages given in charge to
    survivors,
The hiss of the surgeon's knife, the
    gnawing teeth of his saw,

Wheeze, cluck, swash of falling
  blood, short wild scream, and long,
  dull, tapering groan—
These so—these irretrievable.

We infer that this is not the last of Mr. Walt Whitman. In point of fact, he gravely tells us that he is "around, tenacious, acquisitive, tireless and can never be shaken away;" he sings "from the irresistible impulses of me;" purposes to make "the Poem of the New World;" and "invites defiance to make himself superseded," avowing his cheerful willingness to be "trod under foot, if it might only be the soil of superior poems,"—from which latter confession it is clear that he regards himself as the fertilizing agent of American Poetry; perhaps all the better for fertilizing purposes that the rains and snows of a rough life have caused it to fester in a premature and unwholesome decay.

"Literature."
Boston *Banner of Light* 7
(2 June 1860), 4.

The people who have not yet heard of Walt Whitman are few indeed. This last enlarged collection of his poems makes a stout volume, to which the bold and tasteful publishers have given a dress altogether striking, unique and original. All sorts of things—hard and soft—have been said by the literary critics about this same Walt Whitman and his writings. One paper, in commenting upon another's indiscriminate praise of him, remarks that it is "into this gentle garden of the Muses that that unclean cub of the wilderness, Walt Whitman, has been suffered to intrude, trampling with his vulgar and profane hoofs among the delicate flowers which bloom there," &c.

Nobody who has read Whitman's poems, can question his originality. He betrays high culture, even when he seems almost swinishly to spurn it. We think that few writers of our day, if any, whether in prose or verse, have so seized hold of the *spirit* of things—no matter what, where found, or intertwisted with whatever associations—as this one before us. And the best proof of it is just that free habit of expression which all the literary poodles are happy to style "barbaric." It is time their snobbery was supplanted by strength of some sort even if it be barbaric. We have had soft flute-blowing long enough; now let us bear the jarring screech of a fife. Our poet they call *nasty*, because he scorns to be *knavish*; he has the right of it, beyond a question, calling a spade a spade, and a meat-axe a meat-axe; and in exercising his elephantine strength and motions, he doubtless takes a secret delight in the mere act of exercising them, and holding all napper-tandy forms and by-laws in scorn; he proudly refuses to so much as appease the prejudices of critics by respecting the commonly received statutes of the great Literary Republic.

This man's verse—wild, rapid, Ossianic, wailing, grand, humble, innocent, defiant, irregular, defective, overfull, and altogether inflexible as it is—forms, after all, the truest illustration, if not representative, of the real American Age that is, and is to be. He has searched all truth, all knowledge, all science. Even when his expression torments you, the great, surcharged soul that throbs and plays underneath, looks forth serious and awful, refusing to be satisfied with itself, unsettling all things, breaking up the heavens into new and sometimes terrific forms, and pointing down to abysmal deeps in human experience, to which even the most powerful sight of spirit has never penetrated. Above all other singers of songs—rude or rhyming—Whitman hints to you of your capacity; if you have not yet awakened to the possession of any, you cannot understand him, of course. Neither can you understand him wholly, at best; for his own writings prove that he does not, and never will entirely, understand himself. And this is the mystery that gives Life its deep meaning.

The whole body of these Poems—spiritually considered—is alive with power, throbbing and beating behind and between the lines. There is more here than mere oddity, and barbaric indifference to elegant forms of speech; there is a *living soul*—no matter whether its owner drove an omnibus once, or stands on State street and chaffers greedily every day for gold—and that soul insists on giving itself to its fellows, even if it has to rend the most sacred rules of speech to achieve its larger liberty. Carlyle did so, and triumphed; Whitman's way is as much his own, too. It is no way at all, to make up even literary judgment by examining the colors, and not the warp and woof. It is the texture of the stuff that tells, because it is that which is going to endure.

Thus much of the Poet Whitman; we leave our readers to examine his wonderful productions—so bizarre, so fine, so entirely out of and beyond all rule—and know for themselves, as they would know a familiar friend, the spirit that lives in them. The *disjecta membra* of the man's speech we throw to the hungry critics, who are ever delighted to snap up such meaty morsels; of the soul that burns through—nay, *burns up*—all the mere words, consuming the verbiage as fire licks up dried grass, we are but too eager to speak as it deserves; and with that soul all other growing souls will hasten to make themselves acquainted. Whitman comes to us—perhaps not a

discoverer, but certainly a grand interpreter. One-sided and all sided—intense and indifferent—lazy and lashed into fury-spouting words and pouring out streams of rubies and diamonds—he is nothing more than the very child of nature, to whom accidentally has been given the name, Walt Whitman.

"Walt Whitman." New York *Illustrated News* 2 (2 June 1860), 60.

"Walt Whitman." New York *Illustrated News* 2 (2 June 1860), 60.

In pursuance of our plan to give the patrons of the ILLUSTRATED NEWS illustrated information in regard to all the new sensations of the day, whether in politics, art or literature, we present here a finely-executed portrait of WALT WHITMAN, the new American poet, the recent publication of a superb edition of whose poems *Leaves of Grass* is bringing him permanently before the American people as one of the most remarkable men of this day and generation.

WALT WHITMAN was born in Brooklyn, Long Island, May 31, 1819, and is yet a resident of the "City of Churches." He is a printer by trade, as many other men distinguished in the annals of this country have been; and, by the force of his own native genius, has risen from the case to become one of the great lights and leaders of literature—a poet whose broad and vigorous power and uncommon felicity of illustration is acknowledged wherever the English language is spoken. His first appearance before the public was in 1855, when he issued a small and unprepossessing edition of his *Leaves of Grass*, previous to which however, he had contributed some poems to the press, which attracted attention by their power and originality. On sending a copy of the first edition of his poems to Ralph Waldo Emerson, who is acknowledged to be the foremost man in modern literature, he received the following letter in reply:

CONCORD, Mass.,
July 21, 1855.

DEAR SIR:—I am not blind to the worth of the wonderful gift of "Leaves of Grass." I find it the most extraordinary piece of wit and wisdom that America has yet contributed. I am very happy in reading it, as great power makes us happy. It meets the demand I am always making of what seemed the sterile and stingy nature, as if too much handiwork, or too much lymph in the temperament, were making our western wits fat and mean.

I give you joy of your free and brave thought. I have great joy in it. I find incomparable things said incomparably well, as they must be. I find the courage of treatment which so delights us, and which large perception only can inspire.

I greet you at the beginning of a great career, which yet must have had a long foreground somewhere, for such a start. I rubbed my eyes a little to see if this sunbeam were no illusion; but the solid sense of the book is a sober certainty. It has the best merits, namely, of fortifying and encouraging.

I did not know, until I last night saw the book advertised in a newspaper, that I could trust the name as real and available for a post-office. I wish to see my benefactor, and have felt much like striking my tasks and visiting New York to pay you my respects.

R. W. EMERSON.

WALT WHITMAN.

This letter of the highest praise, from one of the greatest minds in the world, called the attention of many literary people to these new poems, and they were largely bought up. In 1856 he issued another and somewhat enlarged edition, which were speedily disposed of. An interim of four years has elapsed, and having had ample leisure in the meantime for composition of new pieces, he now comes before the public with a superb edition of his work, containing about twice as much matter as the first edition, the success of which has already been great, and must be enormous.

There is a great career in store for Walt Whitman, and we shall watch his future with interest. An interesting review of his work was given in the last number of the ILLUSTRATED NEWS.

The *Leaves of Grass* is published by Thayer & Eldridge, of Boston, and the book—take it altogether—is, perhaps, the most magnificent specimen of typography ever issued by the American Press.

C.C.P.
"Walt Whitman's New Volume."
New York *Saturday Press*, 23 June 1860, p. 1.

—I do not ask a place for this letter in your columns because I feel that Mr. Whitman's poems need any justification; they justify themselves, and I have full faith that they will continue to do so long after the swarm of attacking critics are gone; nor do I hope to give more generous or appreciative praise to *Leaves of Grass* than you have given in your notice of the work, but because, being a woman, and having read the uncharitable and bitter attacks upon the book, I wish to give my own view of it.

I have read it carefully, and in reading, have found no page which made me blush, and no sentiment which might not be expressed by a pure man.

In humanity or art I consider that coarse and licentious wherein the soul is made subservient to the body. I am not shocked when I read the stories of the Old Testament: I see behind the apparently gross form, great meanings. Yet I find in the novels and the versification of modern literature, a subtle sensuality which, under the semblance of virtue, destroys all that is pure and elevated in the mind, leaving it enslaved by sensation and petty circumstance.

In Mr. Whitman's poetry, I see a breadth of view which overlooks distinctions. To him, nothing is base when used for a great purpose; he makes all things subservient to thought, and thus dignifies by his touch.

I find there an admirable courage. While we truckle to our bodies, trying to cheat ourselves and one another into oblivion of the potent physical facts, while we feed with exciting novels and amorous poetry those passions we dare not own, we are shocked, for sooth, when a great, earnest, sorrowful man gives us the facts which, gilded over with poor art, we accept readily enough: and when, with manly courage, he owns that he has sinned with prostitutes and felons, (and who has not?) we despise him. Was it not Christ who said of old, "Let him who is without blame among you cast the first stone"?

I find in these poems great ideas, large, cheerful, healthy views of life. No sentimentality, no weak or misplaced passion, but a wisdom which looks through all, behind all, beyond all, which sees the tendency of things, and rests content that all is well. I find a reverence so great and tender as not to despise the meanest thing, knowing that Nature has fashioned everything through ages of patient toil; a reverence which sees in the mud and slime of the pond the same fitness and beauty as in the dainty lily floating above it; which holds the 'woman just as great as the man;' and a mother. 'The melodious character of the earth, the finish beyond which philosophy cannot go and does not wish to go;' a reverence which recognizes in the distinction of sex, that great principle which asserts itself from the lowest to the highest forms of vegetable and animal life, a mystery equally holy with the mystery of birth, the mystery of death.

I find there a generosity, giving without stint. Nothing is too precious, nothing too great, nothing too holy to be bestowed. The experiences which most men in their selfishness hug close, which they call 'too sacred for the eyes of the world,' Mr. Whitman, like a true poet, deals out largely.

And I find more than all these: I find a wonderful knowledge of history, of philosophy, of mythology, of language, of mechanics and geography, of the customs of all peoples at all times; a knowledge which could have been acquired only by hard and long-continued study.

I find the highest artistic merits. A measure at once original and melodious, into which the words form themselves so naturally that we forget it is measure, and are awake of the thought alone. It is like the sound of the wind or the sea, a fitting measure for the first distinctive American bard who speaks for our large-scaled nature, for the red men who are gone, for our vigorous young population.

Yet grand, wild, free, and natural, as is Mr. Whitman's poetry, it is not careless or hap-hazard, anymore than Niagara, the Mississippi, the prairies, or the great

Western cities, are hap-hazard; it is the result of patient labor, of intense thought; for it is the highest art which most closely imitates nature. Here we see not only boldness of conception, but finish of detail. What is there so graphic in the English language that Mr. Whitman should be ashamed to place beside it the pictures of the 'Fall of Alamo,' 'The Mashed Fireman,' 'The Sinking Ship,' or any other of the hundreds of pictures scattered throughout the book. What so exquisitely delicate as to eclipse 'A Word out of the Sea.'

There are few poems which I can read with so intense a thrill of exultation at the greatness of my destiny, at the exquisite harmony and balance of the universe, at the boundless love brooding over mankind; that fill me with so strong a faith in the working together of all things for good, so great forbearance toward error —yet nerve me so resolutely to action, as these poems of Walt Whitman.

"Walt Whitman and His Critics."
Leader and Saturday Analyst [London], 30 June 1860, pp. 614–15.

There is a tendency in the critical mind of America, and, for that matter, of other countries too, to create wonders where in the natural course of things, no wonder, or a very small wonder exists. Among American authors there is one named Walt Whitman, who, in 1855, first issued a small quarto volume of ninety-five pages, under the title of *Leaves of Grass*. In appearance and mode of publication it

was an oddity, this same small volume, which, it appears, the author had printed himself, and then 'left to the winds of heaven to publish.' By the booksellers of the United States generally the book was ignored, but it *could* be obtained by the persevering applicant. Walt Whitman was then about thirty-six years of age, a native of Long Island, born on the hills about thirty miles from the greatest American city, and brought up in Brooklyn and in New York. Mr. R. W. Emerson, it seems, recognized the first issue of the *Leaves* and hastened to welcome the author, then totally unknown. Among other things, said Emerson to the new avatar,

> I greet you at the beginning of a great career, which yet *must have had a long foreground somewhere for such a start.*

This last clause was, however, overlooked entirely by the critics, who treated the new author as one self-educated, yet in the rough, unpolished, and owing nothing to instruction. Fudge! The authority for so treating the author was derived from himself, who thus described, in one of his poems, his person, character, and name, having omitted the last from his title-page:

> "Walt Whitman, an American, one of the roughs, a Kosmos,
> Disorderly, fleshly, and sensual,"—

and in various other passages confessed to all the vices, as well as the virtues of man. All this, with intentional wrongheadedness, was attributed by the sapient reviewers to the individual writer, and not to the subjective-hero supposed to be writing. Notwithstanding the word 'Kosmos,' the writer was taken to be an ignorant man. Emerson perceived at once that

89

there had been 'a long foreground some-where' or somehow—not so they. *Every page teems with knowledge, with information,*—but they saw it not, because it did not answer their purpose to see it.

The poem in which the word *Kosmos* appears explains in fact the whole mystery—nay the word itself explains it. The poem is nominally upon himself, but really includes everybody. It begins,

> "I celebrate myself,
> And what I assume you shall
>   assume,
> For every atom belonging to me, as
>   good belongs to you."

In a word WALT WHITMAN *represents the Kosmical man—he is the* ADAMUS *of the 19th century—not an Individual, but* MANKIND. As such, in celebrating himself, he proceeds to celebrate universal humanity in its attributes, and accordingly commences his dithyramb with the five senses, beginning with that of smell. Afterwards, he deals with the intellectual, rational, and moral powers; showing throughout his treatment an intimate acquaintance with Kant's transcendental method, and perhaps including in his development the whole of the German school, down to Hegel; at any rate as interpreted by Cousin and others in France, and Emerson in the United States. He certainly includes Fichte, for he mentions the Egotist as the only true philosopher; and consistently identifies himself not only with every man, but with the Universe and its Maker;—and it is in doing so that the strength of his description consists. It is from such an ideal elevation that he looks down on Good and Evil, regards them as equal, and extends to them the like measure of equity.

Instead therefore of regarding these *Leaves of Grass* as a marvel, they seem to us as the most natural product of the American soil. *They are certainly filled with an American spirit, breathe the American air, and assert the fullest American freedom.* Nay it may be said also that they assert the fullest Yankee license. Respecting the latter feature, his American puffers, in the disguise of critics, charge the author with irreligion and indecency; and these charges are unblushingly reprinted by his publishers, among the critical recommendations of his performances, as if thereby they would attract a numerous class of prurient readers.

All this is undoubtedly an unworthy trade-trick, to be thoroughly denounced, condemned, and punished. That class of readers, however, will be disappointed, as the passages intended are only so many instances adduced in support of a philosophical principle; *not meant for obscenity, but for scientific examples, introduced as they might be in any legal, medical, or physiological book, for the purpose of instruction.* They chiefly relate to the sense of *touch*, and might be found in substance in any Cyclopedic article on the specific topic.

So much for the matter of the book. As to the manner, it is the same as that with which Mr. Martin Tupper has made us familiar in his *Proverbial Philosophy*, and Mr. Warren in his *Lily and the Bee*. There is nothing that we can see miraculous in such an imitation. The result is a rhapsody, somewhat Oriental in appearance, prose in form, but rhythmical in its effect on the ear, producing a disjointed impression, such as might be produced by a bold prose-translation of Klopstock's famous odes, which would then present so many unconnected assertions, expressed in extravagant diction. The style of the work is therefore anything but attractive—calculated rather to puzzle than to please. It is however, as a printed book, got up in a splendid manner, and is electrotyped for the sake of cheapness, the publishers evidently designing to sell it by millions, if possible.

Notwithstanding all its drawbacks, we have little hesitation in saying that *they will probably succeed,*—on the principle, perhaps, of the quack, who calculated there were many more fools than wise men in the world. No matter, if the fools are all made wise, by the perusal of these *Leaves.* They may be; it is not utterly impossible; but we doubt it.

Crayon 7 (July 1860), 211.

It seems as if the author of *Leaves of Grass* had converted his mind into a mental reservoir by tumbling into it pélemêle all the floating conceits his brain ever gave birth to. He manifests no other sign of mental capacity; for we find no trace of judgment, taste, or healthy sensibility in the work. It is a book of poetry such as may well please twenty-one year old statesmen and philosophers, and people who pride themselves more in being able to read and write than able to think. Such poetry(!) is characteristic of a country like ours, where there is abundance of everything to eat and drink, and to wear, and good pay for labor.

"*Leaves of Grass.*" *Literary Gazette* n.s. 4 (7 July 1860), 798–9.

Not the least surprising thing about this book is its title. Had it been called "Stenches from the Sewer," "Garbage from the Gutter," or "Squeals from the Sty," we could have discerned the application. But "leaves"—which, we take it, is the Transatlantic for blades—"of grass" have nothing of irreligion or indecency about them. Mr. Walt Whitman—for it is with that choice spirit we are now dealing—might as well let them alone.

It is, for reasons we shall presently specify, rather a difficult matter to give the class of readers for whom we write, any adequate notion of this remarkable volume. Let them, however, imagine a Mormon, a medical student, and Miss Eugenie Plummer combining to draw up a treatise in the style of "Proverbial Philosophy," and they will have a faint idea of the last production of Mr. Walt Whitman.

The folly of the work is its least defect. The gregarious qualities of birds of a feather furnish matter for a very common aphorism, and we therefore see no reason to question the correctness of the subjoined assertion:—

> The wild gander leads his flock
>   through the cool night,
> *Ya-honk!* he says, and sounds it
>   down to me like an invitation;
> The pert may suppose it meaningless,
>   but I listen close,
> I find its purpose and place up there
>   toward the wintry sky.

The following forms the conclusion of a pretty long rhapsody of the author concerning himself. We extract it because it is more decent and not more foolish than the rest of the volume:—

> I too am not a bit tamed—I too am
>   untranslatable,
> I sound my barbaric yawp over the
>   roofs of the world.
>
> The last scud of day holds back for
>   me,

91

It flings my likeness, after the rest,
    and true as any, on the shadowed
    wilds,
It coaxes me to the vapor and the
    dusk.

I depart as air—I shake my white
    locks at the run-away sun,
I effuse my flesh in eddies, and drift it
    in lacy jags.

I bequeath myself to the dirt to grow
    from the grass I love,
If you want me again, look for me
    under your boot-soles.

You will hardly know who I am, or
    what I mean,
But I shall be good health to you
    nevertheless,
And filter and fibre your blood.

Failing to fetch me at first, keep
    encouraged,
Missing me one place, search another,
I stop somewhere waiting for you.

It is related of poor crazy Nat Lee that when a small poet asked him if it was not very easy to write like a madman, he replied, "No; but it is very easy indeed to write like a fool, as you do." Doubtless Mr. Walt Whitman imagines he is writing like a madman, when, as a matter of fact, he is only writing like—Nat Lee's friend.

He tells us that the world is not devout enough—that he understands "Him who was crucified;" and in general tries to impress upon us that he is an apostle of no mean pretensions. But his creed, so far as we understand it, consists in a peculiarly coarse materialism. He tells us pretty roundly that he worships his own body, and people who would like to learn a great number of particulars about Mr. Walt Whitman's body, may find them in Mr. Walt Whitman's book.

Throughout the work there is a tone of consistent impurity which reaches its climax in some compositions entitled "En-fans d'Adam"—a designation which we can only explain by imagining it to contain some allusion to the Adamites, of which interesting, though as we had supposed, extinct sect, Mr. Walt Whitman is a very fair representative. For the downright foulness of some of these passages we do not believe that a parallel could be found even by ransacking the worst classical poets from Aristophanes to Ausonius, and we are rather surprised that with John Lord Campbell on the woolsack, and a certain act of his still unrepealed on the statute-book, Mr. Walt Whitman should have found a London vendor for his uncleanly work.

This is more decided language than we generally employ, and our readers may ask us for some justification of it. Let us remind them of Lord Macaulay's description of Wycherley, which we can certainly apply to Walt Whitman. "His indecency is protected against the critics as a skunk is protected against the hunters. It is safe because it is too filthy to handle, and too noisome even to approach." There are certain criminals whom even literary judges must try with closed doors, and our readers must deduce from our verdict that "the evidence is unfit for publication." We say, then, deliberately, that of all the writers we have ever perused, Mr. Walt Whitman is the most silly, the most blasphemous, and the most disgusting; if we can think of any stronger epithets, we will print them in a second edition.

"Leaves of Grass." *Saturday Review* 10 (7 July 1860), 19–21.

It is now four or five years since we reviewed Mr. Whitman's *Leaves of Grass.*

On that occasion we were spared the trouble of setting forth the new poet's merits, as he or his publisher was good enough to paste into his presentation-copy a number of criticisms from American periodicals, which we were satisfied to reprint along with a few extracts illustrative of the volume they recommended. We cannot treat a new edition of *Leaves of Grass* in the same way. It is, we believe, the sixth or seventh which has appeared in the United States, and shows, both externally and internally, that Mr. Whitman is now much too confident in his own popularity and influence to care for directing English reviewers in the way they should go. The volume itself is splendid. The type is magnificent, the paper is as thick as cardboard, and the covers, ornamented with an intaglio of the earth moving through space and displaying only the American hemisphere, are almost as massive as the house-tiles which, according to Mr. Gladstone, are produceable from rags boiled to pulp. It is a book evidently intended to lie on the tables of the wealthy. No poor man could afford it, and it is too bulky for its possessor to get it into his pocket or to hide it away in a corner.

This is simply astonishing to us, for Mr. Whitman reappears with all his characteristics. He is still

Walt Whitman, an American, one of
  the roughs, a kosmos,
Disorderly, fleshy, sensual, eating,
  drinking, breeding;
No sentimentalist—no stander above
  men or women or apart from
  them,
No more modest than immodest—

in short, one of the most indecent writers who ever raked out filth into sentences. Such books as this have occasionally been printed in the guise of a

scrofulous French novel,
On grey paper with blunt type,

but this, we verily believe, is the first time that one of them has been decorated with all the art of the binder and the pressman. The odd thing is, that it irresistibly suggests its being intended for the luxurious and cultivated of both sexes. We are almost ashamed to ask the question—but do American ladies read Mr. Whitman? At all events, it is startling to find such a poet acquiring popularity in the country where piano-legs wear frilled trousers, where slices are cut from turkeys' bosoms, and where the male of the gallinaceous tribe is called a "rooster." The theory that the affectation of an artistic object will justify any conceivable mode of treatment has never been carried farther.

Poetry of so singular a kind deserves some degree of analysis. Mr. Whitman's first characteristic is, that he is an Emersonian. It is curious to observe the effect of the secondary Carlylism of Emerson on a thorough American rowdy. It is generally the weak through over-refinement who are imposed on by that philosophy which pre-eminently affects to disdain conventionalities; but here is a "disorderly, fleshy, sensual" nature, which takes the disease in quite a new form. Mr. Whitman is a professed Pantheist, but he draws from his Pantheism some conclusions not dreamed of by his teachers. From the principle that all things are divine, he derives the inference that all things are equally beautiful and equally fitted for poetical treatment, and this is his justification for writing with the utmost minuteness on subjects on which Nature herself has sometimes been thought to command silence to everybody except doctors. Mr. Whitman's philosophy seems also to deny that man has any personality distinct from the rest of the universe. A very large part of his poetry is taken up with assertions that he is everything else, and everything else is he; nor do we remember to have come across a doctrine more convenient for a poet. It relieves one from the necessity of doing more than enumerating the various elements of which the moral and material worlds are composed, the various scenes of which they are the theatre, or the various passions they include, and then the enumeration may be closed with the remark that all these things are equally godlike, or are equally dear to the poet, or are equally part of him, or have an equal claim on him as a part of themselves. We take, almost at random, the following passage, to give a notion of Emersonianism done into verse by Mr. Whitman:—

Good in all,
In the satisfaction and aplomb of
    animals,
In the annual return of the seasons,
In the hilarity of youth;
In the strength and flush of manhood,
In the grandeur and exquisiteness of
    old age,
In the superb vistas of Death.
Wonderful to depart!
Wonderful to be here!
The heart, to jet the all-alike and
    innocent blood,
To breathe the air, how delicious!
To speak! to walk! to seize something
    by the hand!
To prepare for sleep, for bed—to
    look on my rose-coloured flesh,
To be conscious of my body, so
    amorous, so large.
To be this incredible God I am,
To have gone forth among other
    Gods—those men and women I
    love.
.   .   .   .
I sing the Equalities,
I sing the endless finales of things,

I say Nature continues—Glory
    continues,
I praise with electric voice,
For I do not see one imperfection in
    the universe,
And I do not see one cause or result
    lamentable at last in the universe.

These lines will show that Mr. Whitman has adopted a metre which, like his philosophy, is calculated to make the labour of writing poetry much slighter than it has been usually considered. He has a better ear than Mr. Tupper, and his versification has occasionally a vague rhythm about it, but it is evidently the free and easy Tupperian pseud-hexameter which he has taken for his model. The elasticity of the rules by which this peculiar metre is governed here and there receives startling illustration in *Leaves of Grass*, as in the last two verses of the following extract:—

Who are you, indeed, who would
    talk or sing in America?
Have you studied out MY LAND, its
    idioms and men?
Have you learned the physiology,
    phrenology, politics, geography,
    pride, freedom, friendship, of my
    land? its substratums and objects?
Have you considered the organic
    compact of the first day of the first
    year of the independence of The
    States, signed by the
    Commissioners, ratified by The
    States, and read by Washington at
    the head of the army?

The same metrical oddities appear in another passage, which we quote because it gives us Mr. Whitman's description—doubtless a faithful one—of himself and his habits:—

His shape arises,
    Arrogant, masculine, naïve, rowdyish,

94

Laugher, weeper, worker, idler,
citizen, countryman,
Saunterer of woods, stander upon
hills, summer swimmer in rivers or
by the sea,
Of pure American breed, of reckless
health, his body perfect, free from
taint from top to toe, free forever
from headache and dyspepsia,
clean-breathed,
Ample-limbed, a good feeder, weight
a hundred and eighty pounds, full-
blooded, six feet high, forty inches
round the breast and back,
Countenance sun-burnt, bearded,
calm, unrefined,
Reminder of animals, meeter of
savage and gentleman on equal
terms,
.   .   .   .
Never offering others, always offering
himself, corroborating his
phrenology,
Voluptuous, inhabitive, combative,
conscientious, alimentive, intuitive,
of copious friendship, sublimity,
firmness, self-esteem, comparison,
individuality, form, locality,
eventuality,
Avowing by life, manners, works, to
contribute illustrations of results of
The States,
Teacher of the unquenchable creed,
namely, egotism,
Inviter of others continually
henceforth to try their strength
against his.

It will be seen that Mr. Whitman calls
himself "naïve," in the feminine. One of
his peculiarities is that he mixes up
French words, generally much misspelt
and otherwise abused, with the English
or American of his verses. In one poem,
each stanza begins with "Allons." In another, the words "Accouche; accouchez"
form a whole line; and elsewhere he calls

upon the world to "respondez." But if his
French is a new ingredient in poetry, still
newer is his American slang, particularly
journalistic and debating slang, with
which he sometimes fills entire pages.
Nothing can be absurder than the way
in which the commonplaces of public
speaking are occasionally intruded, as in
this couplet:—

I say, nourish a great intellect, a great
brain;
*If I have said anything to the
contrary, I hereby retract it.*

Or in the following:—

I, an habitué of the Alleghenies, treat
man as he is in the influences of
Nature, in himself, in his
inalienable rights.
I do not tell the usual facts, proved
by records and documents;
What I tell (talking to every born
American) requires no further
proof than he or she who hears me
will furnish, by silently meditating
alone.

The extracts we have given will perhaps lead the reader to wonder by what
extraordinary hallucination as to the
character of poetry Americans have been
led to regard Mr. Whitman as a poet. Yet
we are far from saying that he has nothing of the poetical fibre. He is certainly
an unredeemed New York rowdy of the
lowest stamp. He is absolutely without
sense of decency. He has obviously no
sort of acquaintance with the masters of
his art, and his studies have been apparently confined to Mr. Tupper, his newspaper, and the semi-lyrical rhapsodies of
the Boston transcendentalists. But his
taste, now hopelessly perverted, seems to
have been naturally delicate, and he has a
very vivid imagination. When his pictures

happen (as is rarely the case) to be neither befouled with filth nor defaced by vulgarity, they are, for the most part, strikingly presented. A sort of catalogue of scenes of American life, which, according to Mr. Whitman's easy method, is continued for half-a-dozen pages and results in nothing particular, gives a good idea of his descriptive power. We can only quote the beginning:—

Over the growing sugar—over the
cotton plant—over the rice in its
low moist field,
Over the sharp-peaked farm house,
with its scalloped scum and slender
shoots from the gutters,
Over the western persimmon—over
the long-leaved corn—over the
delicate blue-flowered flax,
Over the white and brown
buckwheat, a hummer and buzzer
there with the rest,
Over the dusky green of the rye as it
ripples and shades in the breeze,
Scaling mountains, pulling myself
cautiously up, holding on by low
scragged limbs,
Walking the path worn in the grass
and beat through the leaves of the
brush,
Where the quail is whistling betwixt
the woods and the wheat-lot,
Where the bat flies in the Seventh
Month eve—Where the great gold
bug drops through the dark,
Where the flails keep time on the
barn floor,
Where the brook puts out of the
roots of the old tree and flows to
the meadow,
Where cattle stand and shake away
flies with the tremulous shuddering
of their hides,
Where the cheese-cloth hangs in the
kitchen—Where andirons straddle
the hearth-slab—Where cob-webs

fall in festoons from the rafters,
Where trip-hammers crash—Where
the press is whirling its cylinders,
Wherever the human heart beats with
terrible throes out of its ribs—

there, and everywhere else, is Mr. Whitman.

We conclude with some lines which are more like true poetry than anything else in the volume. They are fished out from the very midst of a sea of foul impurities:—

Press close, bare-bosomed Night Press
close, magnetic, nourishing Night!
Night of south winds! Night of the
large few stars!
Still, nodding night! Mad, naked,
summer night.

Smile, O voluptuous, cool-breathed
Earth!
Earth of the slumbering and liquid
trees!
Earth of departed sunset! Earth of the
mountains, misty-topt!
Earth of the vitreous pour of the full
moon, just tinged with blue!
Earth of shine and dark, mottling the
tide of the river!
Earth of the limpid grey of clouds,
brighter and clearer for my sake!
Far-swooping elbowed Earth! Rich,
apple-blossomed Earth!
Smile, for your lover comes!

Prodigal, you have given me love!
Therefore I to you give love!
O unspeakable passionate love!

Critic [London] 21 (14 July 1860), 43–4.

Every one recollects the story of the Scotch dramatic author who, when Garrick assured him his genius lay neither for comedy nor tragedy, asked him "Where the de'il it did lie?" Now Mr. Walt Whitman's *Leaves of Grass* puzzle us nearly as much as the Scotsman's query did the great actor. Are we criticising in these *Leaves* prose or poetry? or rather something of an epicene gender, which unites in itself the bad qualities of both one and the other? So far as our perusal of the handsome volume before us has extended—and we must admit that nothing can be more tasteful than its paper and typography—we have scarcely been able to find a single consecutive sentence or expression out of which a meaning can be cudgelled. Taking an odd line here and there, and sometimes even as many as half a dozen, we can extract some hazy nonsense out of them; but what they have to do with those which go before or follow, or why they should be styled "Chants Democratic," or "A Leaf of Faces," or "Calamus," or anything else but "sheer nonsense," we have in vain tried to find out. Nor are we, that we know of, dealing with the productions of a lunatic. Mr. Walt Whitman is sane enough to do the poetry for an American newspaper or two: from whose columns these Leaves are reprints. In this degenerate land of Britain the only persons who nowadays keep a poet are, we believe, the members of an eminent Jewish clothing firm; and though we do not profess to be well versed in the lays of the bard in question, our impression is that they are quite as musical, and at least ten times as intelligible, as these *Leaves of Grass*. After all, a horrible idea strikes us that our native land is not entirely guiltless of the paternity of this production. Can it be possible that Mr. Tupper's *Proverbial Philosophy* has inspired Mr. Walt Whitman with the idea of his Leaves? We have most of us probably heard and read of persons who solved mathematical problems or composed poetry while asleep; and we think it just possible that the author of *Proverbial Philosophy* may unconsciously, while suffering from a fit of the nightmare, have had something to do with the composition of these American Leaves. At least we trace in them some wild fantastic resemblance to his style; such as to make us pretty sure that Mr. Whitman has occasionally "tasted the simple store and rested one soothing hour" with the English poetaster whose words we quote.

We give the five opening paragraphs or stanzas of a lucubration headed simply "Walt Whitman."

I celebrate myself,
And what I assume you shall assume,
For every atom belonging to me, as
    good belongs to you.
I loafe and invite my Soul,
I lean and loafe at my ease, observing
    a spear of summer grass.
Houses and rooms are full of
    perfumes—the shelves are crowded
    with perfumes,
I breathe the fragrance myself, and
    know it and like it,
The distillation would intoxicate me
    also, but I shall not let it.
The atmosphere is not a perfume—it
    has no taste of the distillation, it is
    odourless,
It is for my mouth forever—I am in
    love with it,
I will go to the bank by the wood,
    and become undisguised and
    naked,
I am mad for it to be in contact with
    me.
The smoke of my own breath,
Echoes, ripples, buzzed whispers,
    love-root, silk-thread, crotch and
    vine,
My respiration and inspiration, the
    beating of my heart, the passing of

blood and air through my lungs,
The sniff of green leaves and dry
leaves, and of the shore, and dark-
coloured sea-rocks, and of hay in
the barn.
The sound of the belched words of
my voice, words loosed to the
eddies of the wind,
A few light kisses, a few embraces, a
reaching around of arms,
The play of shine and shade on the
trees as the supple boughs wag,
The delight alone, or in the rush of
the streets, or along the fields and
hill-sides,
The feeling of health, the full-noon
trill, the song of me rising from
bed and meeting the sun.

Now we assure our readers that these
"belched words," to speak à la Walt
Whitman, are a perfectly fair, honest
specimen of the four hundred and fifty-
six pages of the volume before us.

"Walt Whitman" extends over eighty
pages, and contains three hundred and
seventy-two paragraphs and stanzas. We
are particular in stating these items; and
lest our readers should suppose we are
unfairly mutilating this production, we
assure them that we give each paragraph
in full in making the following extracts,
and that, so far as we can make out, each
is perfect in itself.

In the ninety-sixth stanza we are
asked
What is man anyhow? What am I?
What are you?

Possibly the four following paragraphs
which we quote may be supposed to answer this question:

All I mark as my own, you shall
offset it with your own,
Else it were time lost listening to me.

I do not snivel that snivel the world
over.
That months are vacuums, and the
ground but wallow and filth,
That life is a suck and a sell, and
nothing remains at the end but
threadbare crape, and tears.
Whimpering and truckling fold with
powders for invalids—conformity
goes to the fourth-removed,
I cock my hat as I please, indoors or
out.
Why should I pray? Why should I
venerate and be ceremonious?

Our poet goes on to say (105):

I know I am august,
I do not trouble my spirit to vindicate
itself or be understood,
I see that the elementary laws never
apologise,
I reckon I behave no prouder than
the level I plant my house by, after
all.

And again (109):

I am the poet of the body,
And I am the poet of the soul.

Presently he dissects his own individuality a little more closely:

Walt Whitman, an American, one of
the roughs, a kosmos,
Disorderly, fleshy, sensual, eating,
drinking, breeding,
No sentimentalist—no stander above
men and women, or apart from
them,
No more modest than immodest.
Unscrew the locks from the doors!
Unscrew the doors themselves from
their jambs!
Whoever degrades another degrades
me,

And whatever is done or said returns
at last to me,
And whatever I do or say, I also
return.
Through me the afflatus surging and
surging—through me the current
and index.
I speak the pass-word primeval—I
give the sign of democracy,
By God! I will accept nothing which
all cannot have their counterpart of
on the same terms.

The succeeding "voices," though, as
the writer tells us, they are "voices indecent, by me clarified and transfigured,"
strike us, so far as they can be conjectured to mean anything, as retaining all
their pristine indecency.

And in this way our American non-
sense-verse writer maunders on for some
hundred pages, sometimes "doting on
himself—there is that lot of me, and all
is so luscious;" now "snuffing the sidle
of evening," whatever that may be; or
asking—

Do I contradict myself?
Very well, then, I contradict myself;
I am large—I contain multitudes.

Verily we for once agree with him
when he says:

I am untranslatable:
I sound my barbaric yawp over the
roofs of the world.

One of the most curious whims of Mr.
Walt Whitman is to give his readers from
time to time inventories of the various
component parts of some thing or person. Thus (in pages 300–2) we might for
a brief moment fancy ourselves poring
over a manual of surgery. The mention of
the word "body" enables him to write
down about one hundred and fifty differ-

ent items which belong, or may be supposed by poetical licence to belong, to
the human form divine. Some of the
terms, as "neck-slue," "man-balls," "in-
ward and outward rounds," "the flex of
the mouth," are to us rather vague; and
we scarcely wonder at their exciting "the
curious sympathy one feels, when feeling
with the hand the naked meat of his own
body or another person's body." So again
we have lists, extending over more than a
page, or an iron-monger's and carpenter's
shop or store, &c. &c., interspersed with
such lyric strophes as the following:

Because you are greasy or pimpled,
or that you was once drunk, or a
thief, or diseased, or rheumatic, or
a prostitute, or are so now, or from
frivolity or impotence, or that you
are no scholar, and never saw your
name in print, do you give in that
you are any less immortal?

There are some other specimens of
Mr. Walt Whitman's muse—for we have
now discovered that this amazing rubbish is meant for poetry—which we had
rather not quote, for decency's sake; and
we fancy our readers will by this time
one and all be inclined to cry, *Ohe jam
satis*! Nevertheless we have not altogether wasted their time. They ought to
know that this pure unmitigated trash is
read and admired by not a few persons in
America; and that what would go far in
England to stamp its inditer as a lunatic
has earned in America for its writer a
poet's crown.

Me quoque vatem
Pastores dicunt; sed non ego credulus
illis,

says Virgil's modest swain. Not so, however, with Walt Whitman. He tells us
many times over that he is a son of song;

99

and that the "daughter of the lands" (which we suppose means America) has been "waiting for a poet with a flowing mouth and indicative hand"—a vision realised doubtless in himself.

We shall conclude with saying that one of the most curious traits of this volume is the crazy earnestness with which the writer believes in his own poetical infallibility. He is not only a poet, but *the* poet; not only a teacher, but *the* teacher. To be sure, it follows that if Mr. Walt Whitman really be a poet, and if the contents of this book really be poetry, what Shakespeare and Milton have written must be styled by some new name. Sense, grammar, and metre are but very minor parts in the composition of poetry; but nevertheless, *pace* Walt Whitman, poetry cannot exist without this humble triad.

"*Leaves of Grass.*" Spectator 33 (14 July 1860), 669–70.

America is unreasonably impatient to possess a great national poet as intrinsically her own as Shakespeare is English, Burns Scotch, Goethe German, and Dante Italian. She may have an emperor sooner—ubsit omen! Young as she is, the land of the stars and stripes has within her plenty of the stuff of which emperors can be made; but poets are a choicer growth, and need more years than the Union numbers from its birth to acclimatize their race in a new country. Of the few poets born in America, not one is distinctively American in his poetry; all are exotics, and their roots are nurtured by pabulum imported from the old country. In process of time, the foreign stock will ac-commodate itself to the new conditions by which it is surrounded; it will gradually undergo a transformation of species and become racy of the soil, but the soil itself must meanwhile pass through a corresponding change. It is still too crude; there is in it, as Oliver Wendell Holmes avows, "no sufficient flavour of humanity," such as inheres in every inch of ground belonging to some of the ancient seats of civilization. These truths are plainly discerned by the most cultivated minds in the States, and by them only; others believe that a great poet has actually arisen amongst them, and they hail his appearance with the more rapture because there has certainly never been anything like him in the guise of a poet since the world began. In the year 1855, this prodigy, this "compound of the New England transcendentalist and the New York rowdy," as a friendly critic calls him with literal truth, put forth the first issue of his *Leaves of Grass*—videlicet Scurvy grass—twelve poems, or rather bundles, in ninety-five pages, small quarto. The book was immediately pronounced by Ralph Waldo Emerson to be "the most extraordinary piece of wit and wisdom that America has yet contributed." Other critics followed suit, and Walt Whitman became as famous as the author of the Book of Mormon. A second edition of his *Leaves of Grass*, with twenty additional bundles, making together 384 pages, was published within a year after the first; and now there lies before us a new, enlarged, and glorified edition, for which the publishers "confidently claim recognition as one of the finest specimens of modern bookmaking." The paper, print, and binding are indeed superb; but one thing these gentlemen have forgotten: where are the phallic emblems, and the figures of Priapus and the Satyrs that should have adorned the covers and the pages of this new gospel of lewdness and obscenity? Its frontispiece should have been, not the head and shoulders of the author, but a full-length portrait drawn as he loves to depict himself in his "poems"—naked as an Anabaptist of Munster, or making love like Diogenes coram populo—with his own lines for inscription:—

> "Walt Whitman, an American, one of
> the roughs, a kosmos,
> Disorderly, fleshy, sensual, eating,
> drinking, breeding,
> No sentimentalist—no stander
> above men and women, or apart
> from them,
> No more modest than immodest.
>
> .   .   .   .
>
> Arrogant, masculine, naïve,
> rowdyish,
> Laugher, weeper, worker, idler,
> citizen, countryman,
> Saunterer of the woods, stander
> upon hills, summer swimmer in
> rivers or by the sea,
> Of pure American breed, of reckless
> health, his body perfect, free from
> taint from top to toe, free for ever
> from headache and dyspepsia,
> clean-breathed,
> Ample limbed, a good feeder, weight
> a hundred and eighty pounds,
> full-blooded, six feet high, forty
> inches round the breast and back,
>
> .   .   .   .
>
> Countenance sunburnt, bearded,
> calm, unrefined,
> Reminder of animals, meeter of
> savage and gentleman on equal
> terms.
> Never offering others, always
> offering himself, corroborating his
> phrenology,
> Voluptuous, inhabitive, combative,
> conscientious, alimentive,
> intuitive, of copious friendship,
> firmness, self esteem, comparison,
> individuality, form, locality,
> eventuality.
> Avowing by life, manners, works, to
> contribute illustrations of the
> results of the States,
> Teacher of the unquenchable creed,
> namely, egotism,
> Inviter of others continually
> henceforth to try their strength
> against his."
>
> .   .   .   .
>
> I too am not a bit tamed—I too am
> untranslatable,
> I sound my barbaric yawp over the
> roofs of the world."

Such is the man, and such the sort of poetry, which have inaugurated "an athletic and defiant literature," destined, it is said, to supersede for the great republic the effete theories and forms that still amuse the senile decrepitude of the old country. Vast beyond comparison are the immunities enjoyed by the new school of poetry; it needs no intellectual capital to work with, disdains all submission to the laws of art as well as to the restraints of common decency, and may yawp away to its heart's content, never bothering itself about such trifles as rhythm or melody, rhyme or reason, metre or sense. Never was there so free and easy a school, and surely its founder, who announces himself as a "teacher of the unquenchable creed, namely, egotism," will not find it a very hard task to teach the young American idea how to shoot in that direction. Walt Whitman's egotism is twofold—swaggering and brutish by virtue of his rowdyism, all conglomerating and incomprehensible by virtue of his pantheistic transcendentalism. As a rowdy, he asks, "Why should I venerate and be ceremonious?" since, after the closest inquiry, "I find no sweeter fat than sticks to my own bones." Presently rising into a pantheistic strain he exclaims:—

101

"Divine am I inside and out, and I
    make holy whatever I touch or am
    touched from,
The scent of these arm pits, aroma
    finer than prayer,
This head more than churches, bibles,
    and all the creeds.
If I worship any particular thing, it
    shall be some of the spread of my
    own body."

A perfectly logical deduction from the
premises. Since all things are divine, Walt
Whitman's body, with each several part
and function of it, is divine, and it becomes him to sing hymns to them all. To
refrain from celebrating their praises
would be rank impiety. Another corollary
from the same principle is that there is
not a pin's point to choose between good
and evil:—

"What blurt is this about virtue, and
    about vice?
Evil propels me and reform of evil
    propels me—I stand indifferent,
My gait is no fault-finder's or
    rejecter's gait,
I moisten the roots of all that has
    grown."

All things being good, and equally
good, all are alike fit for the poet's use,
and he may jot them down pell-mell,
without regard to order, proportion, or
perspective. If he wish to cram as much
poetry into his pages as they can hold, he
has only to fill them with compendious
inventories of all sorts of things. Pages by
the score of Walt Whitman's poetry are
made up of simple enumeration:—

Sunday, Monday, Tuesday,
    Wednesday, Thursday, Friday,
    Saturday,

is almost as rich a line as any among
them, and so is—

Moses, Homer, Neptune, Hercules,
    Wat Tyler, and Tycho Brahe.

According to the Emersonian jargon,
the Ego and the Non Ego are one. The
"eternal and universal I" embraces and
comprehends all nature. Walt Whitman is
everything, and everything is Walt Whitman. He is here, there, and everywhere
at the same moment. He is not born yet;
he is dead and buried, alive and kicking.
He is his own father and mother, brothers and sisters, uncles and aunts, lots of
cousins, and all their progenitors; likewise his own children, nephews, and
nieces, and all their posterity, for ever
and ever. He is you and I, and the beef
we eat, and the butcher that kills it, and
the fire that cooks it; and he got drunk
upon himself tomorrow, and will wake
with a headache yesterday. Our own
heads ache in trying to make head or tail
of some of the polyphone utterances of
this Protean, ubiquitous, and multitudinous person. Here is a whole poem of
his, hers, its, or theirs, printed in dupli-
cate, the [first version of each numbered
section] being by Walt Whitman's Ego,
and the other by his Non Ego, a writer in
the New York *Saturday Press*:—

"1. With antecedents,
With my fathers and mothers, and
    the accumulations of past ages,
With all which, had it not been, I
    would not now be here, as I am,
With Egypt, India, Phenicia, Greece,
    and Rome,
With the Celt, the Scandinavian, the
    Alb, and the Saxon,
With antique maritime ventures—
    with laws, artisanship, wars, and
    journeys,
With the poet, the skald, the saga,
    the myth, and the oracle,
With the sale of slaves—with
    enthusiasts—with the troubadour,
    the crusader, and the monk,

With those old continents whence
we have come to this new
continent,
With the fading kingdoms and kings
over there,
With the fading religions and
priests,
With the small shores we look back
to, from our own large and
present shores,
With countless years drawing
themselves onward, and arrived at
these years,
You and Me arrived—America
arrived, and making this year,
This year! sending itself ahead
countless years to come.

"1. With antecedents and
consequents,
With our fathers, mothers, aunts,
uncles, and the family at large
accumulated by past ages,
With all which would have been
nothing if anything were not
something which everything is,
With Europe, Asia, Africa, America,
Peoria, and New Jersey,
With the Pre-Adamite, the Yarab,
the Guebre, the Hottentot, the
Esquimaux, the Gorilla, and the
Nondescriptian,
With antique powwowing—with
laws, jaws, wars, and three-tailed
bashaws,
With the butcher, the baker, the
candlestick-maker, and Ralph
Waldo Carlyle,
With the sale of Long Island railway
stock,—with spiritualists, with the
yawper, with the organ-grinder
and monkey,
With everybody and everything in
general and nothing and nobody
in particular, besides otherbodies
and things too numerous to
mention,
Yourn and Mine arrived,—the

Arrival arrove, and making this
Nonsense:
This Nonsense! sending itself ahead
of any sane comprehension this
side of Jordan.

2. O but it is not the years—it is I—
it is You,
We touch all laws, and tally all
antecedents,
We are the skald, the oracle, the
monk, and the knight—we easily
include them, and more,
We stand amid time, beginningless
and endless—we stand amid evil
and good,
All swings around us—there is as
much darkness as light,
The very sun swings itself and its
system of planets around us,
Its sun, and its again, all swing
around us.

2. O, but it is not the Nonsense—it
is Mine,—it is Yourn,
We touch all 'effects,' and tally all
bread-sticks,
We are the Etceteras and Soforths,—
we easily include them, and more;
All obfusticates around us,—there is
as much as possible of a
muchness;
The entire system of the universe
discomboborates around us with
a perfect looseness.

3. As for me,
I have the idea of all, and am all,
and believe in all;
I believe materialism is true, and
spiritualism is true—I reject no
part.

3. As for Mine,
Mine has the idea of my own, and
what's Mine is my own, and my
own is all Mine and believes in it
all,
Mine believes meum is true, and
rejects nix.

4. Have I forgotten any part?
Come to me, whoever and whatever,
   till I give you recognition.

4. Has Mine forgotten to grab any
   part?
Fork over then whoever and
   whatever is worth having, till
   Mine gives a receipt in full.

5. I respect Assyria, China,
   Teutonia, and the Hebrews,
I adopt each theory, myth, god, and
   demi-god,
I see that the old accounts, bibles,
   geneaologies, are true, without
   exception.
I assert that all past days were what
   they should have been,
And that they could no how have
   been better than they were,
And that today is what it should
   be—and that America is,
And that today and America could
   no how be better than they are.

5. Mine respects Brahma, Vishnu,
   Mumbo-Jumbo, and the great
   Panjandrum,
Mine adopts things generally which
   are claimed by Yourn,
Mine asserts that these should have
   been my own in all past days,
And that they could not no how
   have been nobody else's,
And that today is neither yesterday
   nor tomorrow,—and that I-S is is.

6. In the name of These States, and
   in your and my name, the Past,
And in the name of These States,
   and in your and my name, the
   Present time.

6. In the name of Dogberry,—and in
   Mine and Yourn,—Bosh!
And in the name of Bombastes
   Furioso,—and in Yourn and
   Mine,—Gas!

7. I know that the past was great,

and the future will be great,
And I know that both curiously
   conjoint in the present time,
(For the sake of him I typify—for
   the common average man's sake—
   your sake, if you are he;)
And that where I am, or you are,
   this present day, there is the
   centre of all days, all races,
And there is the meaning, to us, of
   all that has ever come of races
   and days, or ever will come."

7. Mine knows that Dogberry was
   an Ass and Bombastes Furioso a
   likewise,
And that both curiously conjoint in
   the present time, in Yourn and
   Mine,
And that where Mine is, or Yourn
   is, this present day, there is the
   centre of all Asininities,
And there is the meaning to us, of
   all that has ever come of Yourn
   and Mine, or ever will come."

We must not leave our readers under the
impression that there is nothing in Walt
Whitman's book but nonsense, coarseness, and filth. He has strong perceptive
faculties and a vivid imagination, and he
can express his human sympathies in language that becomes a man. Look on this
picture:—

"Agonies are one of my changes of
   garments,
I do not ask the wounded person
   how he feels—I myself become
   the wounded person,
My hurt turns livid upon me as I
   lean on a cane and observe,
I am the mashed fireman with
   breastbone broken,
Tumbling walls buried me in their
   debris,
Heat and smoke I inspired—I heard
   the yelling shouts of my
   comrades,

104

I heard the distant click of their
   picks and shovels,
They have cleared the beams
   away—they tenderly lift me forth.
I lie in the night air in my red
   shirt—the pervading hush is for
   my sake,
Painless after all I lie, exhausted but
   not so unhappy,
White and beautiful are the faces
   around me—the heads are bared
   of their fire-caps,
The kneeling crowd fades with the
   light of the torches."

[Moncure D. Conway]. *Dial* [Cincinnati] 1 (August 1860), 517–19.

Better dressed than we ever expected to see him, Walt Whitman again makes his bow, but with purpose unabated to "sound his barbaric yawp over the roofs of the world." The sensations of the roofs under this process are, as may be imagined, various and strong. "Some said that it thundered, others that an angel spoke." The *Christian Examiner*, with the unctuous air of one who has just read without blinking the accounts of Joseph and Potiphar, Judah and Tamar, pronounces it "impious and obscene." Mr. Emerson sends word, "I greet you at the beginning of a great career." When doctors, etc. Well, we have gone to the book itself for a decision. The *Leaves of Grass* has been our companion out in the wild outlooks of Newport and Nahant, we have read it at night after following the throngs of New York by day, we have conversed with its music when the obligato was the whizz and scream of the locomotive which bore us across the con-

tinent, and have turned to it from the calm rush of the Father of Waters, from the loading here and there on its shores by the glare of pine-knot fires, from the eager crowd of men and women chatting, singing, gaming in the saloon, and we confidently announce that Walt Whitman has set the pulses of America to music. Here are the incomplete but real utterances of New York city, of the prairies, of the Ohio and Mississippi,—the volume of American autographs. To these formidable eyes the goddess Yoganidra, who veils the world in illusion, surrenders; to them there are no walls, nor fences, nor dress-coats, no sheaths of faces and eyes. All are catalogued by names, appraised, and his relentless hammer comes down on the right value of each.

We can not dwell on this remarkable work as much as we would like, because we wish to place here some extracts.

"O truth of the earth! O truth of
   things, I am determined to press
   my way toward you; Sound your
   voice! I scale mountains, or dive
   in the sea after you."

"I do not doubt but the majesty and
   beauty of the world are latent in
   any iota of the world."

VOICES.

"Oh, what is it in me that makes me
   tremble so at Voices?
Surely whoever speaks to me in the
   right voice, him or her I shall
   follow, as the waters follow the
   moon, silently, with fluid steps,
   anywhere around the globe.
Now I believe that all waits for the
   right voices;
Where is the practiced and perfect
   organ? Where is the developed
   soul?
For I see every word uttered thence
   has deeper, sweeter new sounds,

impossible on less terms.
I see brains and lips closed—I see
tympans and temples unstruck,
Until that comes which has the
quality to strike and to unclose."

TO A COMMON PROSTITUTE.

"Not till the sun excludes you, do I
exclude you;
Not till the waters refuse to glisten
for you, and the leaves to rustle
for you, do my words refuse to
glisten and rustle for you."

THE CHILD.

"There was a child went forth every
day,
And the first object he looked upon
and received with wonder, pity,
love or dread, that object he
became,
And that object became part of him
for the day, or a certain part of
the day, or for many years, or
stretching cycles of years.
The early lilacs became part of this
child;
And grass, and white and red
morning-glories, and white and
red clover, and the song of the
phœbe-bird,
And the Third-Month lambs, and
the sow's pink-faint litter, and the
mare's foal, and the cow's calf,
And the noisy brood of the barnyard, or by the mire of the pond-
side,
And the fish suspending themselves
so curiously below there, and the
beautiful curious liquid,
And the water-plants with their
graceful flat-heads—all became
part of him.
The strata of colored clouds, the
long bar of maroon-tint, away by
itself—the spread of purity it lies
motionless in,

The horizon's edge, the flying sea-
crow, the fragrance of salt-marsh
and shore-mud—
These became part of that child who
went forth every day, and who
now goes, and will always go
forth every day."

A friend of ours told us that once,
when he was visiting Lizst, a fine gentleman from Boston was announced, and
during the conversation the latter spoke
with great contempt of Wagner (the new
light) and his music. Lizst did not say
anything, but went to the open piano and
struck with grandeur the opening chords
of the *Tannhaüser* overture; having
played it through, he turned and quietly
remarked, "The man who doesn't call
that good music is a fool." It is the only
reply which can be made to those who do
not find that quintessence of things which
we call Poetry in many passages of this
work.

We can not, nor do we wish to deny
that biblical plainness of speech which
characterizes these poems; we or nature
are in some regards so untranslateable
that in some of these pages one must
hold his nose whilst he reads; the writer
does not hesitate to bring the slop-bucket
into the parlor to show you that therein
also the chemic laws are at work; but to
lose the great utterances which are in this
work because of these, is as if one should
commit suicide, refusing to dwell on the
planet because it was not all an English
Park, but had here and there a Dismal
Swamp or a dreary desert. This Poet,
though "one of the roughs," as he calls
himself, is never frivolous, his profanity
is reverently meant, and he speaks what
is unspeakable with the simple unreserve
of a child.

Westminster Review 74, n.s. 18 (1 October 1860), 590.

If Mr. Walt Whitman's *Leaves of Grass* had been printed on paper as dirty as his favourite topics,—if the book itself had presented the general aspect of that literature which usually falls under no other criticism than that of the police office, we should have passed it by without notice, as addressing only such a public as we have no concern with; but when a volume containing more obscenity and profanity than is perhaps elsewhere to be found within the same compass, presents itself in all the glories of hot-pressed paper, costly binding, and stereotype printing, and we believe as a fourth edition, it is manifest that it not only addresses, but has found a public of a much wider class, and it becomes a question how such a book can have acquired a vogue and popularity that could induce an American publisher to spend so much upon its outward setting-forth.

Perhaps loose thinking and tall talk are nowhere so efficacious in attracting notice as in the United States, and Mr. Whitman, by pretentiously assuming to be the exponent of Hegelian morality, by offering himself as the high-priest of that religion, whose sole dogma is comprised in the proposition *Homo sibi deus*, attracts and perplexes readers, whose natural good sense would otherwise soon cast aside his frightful fustian. That he has any direct acquaintance with those forms of German speculation on which he falls back for the justification of the language he makes use of, we think may be confidently denied, not only from the manner in which he conceives its problems, but from the absence of any German catch words with which he would otherwise have infallibly adorned his motley, for even an ignorance of its grammar does not daunt him when the French language offers a term to his taste. Mr. Emerson has much to answer for, and will in reputation dearly pay for the fervid encomium with which he introduced the Author to the American public. That to the public defence of polygamy and slavery, should now be added that of the emancipation of the flesh, is an indication of a moral disorganization in the States, which is of every evil promise. That a drunken Helot should display himself without shame in the market place, speaks sad reproach to the public that does not scourge him back to his cellar.

In form these poems, if poems they can be called, are composed in irregular rhythmical lines, after the manner of Tupper, and in fact they may be described by the following equation,—as Tupper is to English Humdrum, so is Walt Whitman to the American Rowdy. They have been praised as containing many poetical passages; in this opinion we cannot concur. That sometimes a poetical expression occurs among a dreary waste of rhetorical verbiage may be allowed, but this might have been expected—a naked savage has often a wild grace of movement that a civilized man can hardly possess, but certainly not display.

These *Leaves of Grass* are the symptoms of a moral fermentation in America, which no doubt will result in a broader and clearer life—but the progress is painful and the yeast nauseous.

[Review of *Leaves of Grass* (1860) and William Douglas O'Connor's *Harrington*].
Boston *Wide World*, 8 December 1860 [page number unknown].

'Sensation books,' or what are so called, are now the rage, and each successive production of this kind is more mysterious or murderous than its predecessor. Sir Rohan's Ghost, Households of Bouveries, Gold Bricks, and the like, are thrust down our throats whether we will or not. Their authors for the most part belong to the foggy or to the flippant schools of book-makers; for the former Emerson and his 'set' are partly responsible. These scribblers seem to fancy that it is a mark of genius to be mysterious; they hide one grain of thought in a bushel of chaff and have the assurance to ask us to look for it. Oh! for the days and works of Goldsmith, Addison and Irving, who drew from pure wells of English undefiled, and charmed us by their simplicity. The other day we noticed a commendatory notice (save the mark!) of Walt Whitman's Poems, by Emerson, and we looked over the volume of one who has been declared about 'to inaugurate a new era in American poetry.' Why, these 'poems' (prose run crazy) are the veriest trash ever written, and vulgar and disgusting to the last degree. There never was more unblushing obscenity presented to the public eye than is to be found in these prurient pages and how any respectable House could publish the volume is beyond my powers to comprehend. But enough of the 'nasty' school.

And now we have another 'sensation' book—an anti-slavery affair—one of the brood spawned by 'Uncle Tom.' It is called 'Harrington'; but it ought to be styled, 'A Glorification of Wendell Phillips, William Lloyd Garrison, Theodore Parker, C. Burleigh and other gentlemen of their peculiar way of thinking.' Burleigh is said to look like the portraits of Jesus Christ. Parker resembles Socrates, Phillips, Cicero; and Garrison, Jove himself. And then the female characters are marvels of beauty and virtue. The house of Muriel, the heroine, is a perfect paradise of upholstery. But the hero, Harrington, is one of those

'faultless monsters, whom the world
ne'er saw,'

whose 'mission' it is to comfort the sable population of 'Nigger Hill.' It is absolutely sickening to read the manworship to be found in this volume, the only powerful writing in which is the description of Anthony's escape. As a work of art it will be as ephemeral as most books of its class.

Checklist of Additional Reviews

New Orleans *Weekly Mirror*, 9 June 1860, [page numbers unknown].
Boston *Cosmopolite*, 4 August 1860, [page numbers unknown].

DRUM-TAPS (1865)

WALT   WHITMAN'S

DRUM-TAPS.

New-York.

—

1865.

"*Drum Taps*—Walt Whitman."
Watson's Weekly Art Journal, 4 November 1865, pp. 34–5.

The appearance of Walt Whitman's new book of poems, conjointly with Ward's "Indian Hunter," is not without significance. Both Whitman and Ward are representative men. In them, for the first time, the full strength of our American life receives expression—receives assertion. We have had in our Poetry and Art idealizations of loftier aspiration—imaginations of finer conceit—but they were not grounded in our soil; even though American in their reference, they were foreign to our New World; they belonged rather to some modern school of *thought*, than to our modern and American *life*—they were not the outgrowth of that new movement in civilization which America inaugurates.

In all human organizations, whether those of personal or of national life, there is the moment of consciousness as self, as individual—a moment full of original force.

This "I Am" of youth, may include more or less of meaning according to the status of organic development. The youthful self-assertion of one age implies more than the assertion of an anterior epoch. Life is an ever on-flowing tide; each successive wave strands the human consciousness upon a higher look-out. The earlier ages expressed their consciousness of life, through the imagination, by mythical rites and symbols. America now first in the world's history experiences this life as superior to all forms—as ever forming—itself never bounded by form—

as the common life, common as the "leaves of grass"—as the great fraternizing element—as the all-sufficient—the vast, indomitable, sole Fact. In literature—Whitman, in art—Ward, are they who come forward to express this New-World self-assertion of ours, in all its boundless and fierce strength. Both fling aside the buskin and come down to the common ground; they state that which is, and thereby give the fact—the thing—its truest and highest idealization; for the fact—the thing—thus simply and absolutely given, is at once spiritual and material—is ideal.

As an artist—that is, as one who gives a complete and harmonious externalization to his feeling—Mr. Whitman is much inferior to Mr. Ward. Still the poet may be said to be more truly artistic than if he were more ostensibly so. He sets out to assert himself—the conscious American life as superior to restrictions of time and place, as all-containing, all-sanctifying. His inartistic looseness of style and expression is quite consistent with this mood. The poet, in consequence, presents himself to the mind as a more congruous and artistic whole than if he had modeled his verse in accordance with all the unities of Art.

In Whitman's last collection, we observe a much greater regard for beauty of form than the *Leaves of Grass* displayed. The latter work was full of the ungoverned vigor of life-consciousness; the present exhibits a tendency to define this vigor by lines of beauty. We accordingly discover greater regularity of rhythm, and more unity of conception in the grouping of details.

But our present object is to introduce an extract from *Drum Taps*, which may, we hope, incite the reader to a serious study of the works of its author—the most remarkable outgrowths of our New-World life. As the earlier poems were not a bouquet of garden flowers, but leaves of grass plucked by the handful from the bosom of nature, with here and there a wild blossom, fresh, juicy, wet with the dews of morning, so the recent ones—referring to that upheaving of the Great Life in human action which has marked our times—are not the elaborate martial strains of the parade-ground, but the vigorous "drums taps" of the column in march.

["Pioneers! O Pioneers!" quoted in full]

Modern verse has nowhere a nobler ring. This is our American war-song, good not only for the battle-field, but for the labor-field—the present, still more than the past; for ours are not the "*piping times of peace;*" our American life is on the march, filing through the passes of outgrown formalism, outflanking the hosts of slavery, gaining the mountain heights of an all-comprehending vision.

"Pioneers! O Pioneers!"

In our next number we shall give some extracts from *Drum Taps*, illustrative of the author's great power of word-picture-making, in which, as might be expected from his close hold upon the fact of life, he stands preëminent among the poets of the times.

W. D. H[owells].
"*Drum-Taps.*"
Round Table 2
(11 November 1865),
147–8.

Will saltpeter explode? Is Walt Whitman a true poet? Doubts to be solved by the

wise futurity which shall pay off our national debt. Poet or not, however, there was that in Walt Whitman's first book which compels attention to his second. There are obvious differences between the two: this is much smaller than that; and whereas you had at times to hold your nose (as a great sage observed) in reading *Leaves of Grass*, there is not an indecent thing in *Drum-Taps*. The artistic method of the poet remains, however, the same, and we must think it mistaken. The trouble about it is that it does not give you sensation in a portable shape; the thought is as intangible as aroma; it is no more put up than the atmosphere.

We are to suppose that Mr. Whitman first adopted his method as something that came to him of its own motion. This is the best possible reason, and only possible excuse, for it. In its way, it is quite as artificial as that of any other poet, while it is unspeakably inartistic. On this account it is a failure. The method of talking to one's self in rhythmic and ecstatic prose is one that surprises at first, but, in the end, the talker can only have the devil for a listener, as happens in other cases when people address their own individualities; not, however, the devil of the proverb, but the devil of reasonless, hopeless, all-defying egotism. An ingenious French critic said very acutely of Mr. Whitman that he made you partner of the poetical enterprise, which is perfectly true; but no one wants to share the enterprise. We want its effect, its success; we do not want to plant corn, to hoe it, to drive the crows away, to gather it, husk it, grind it, sift it, bake it, and butter it, before eating it, and then take the risk of its being at last moldy in our mouths. And this is what you have to do in reading Mr. Whitman's rhythm.

At first, a favorable impression is made by the lawlessness of this poet, and one asks himself if this is not the form which the unconscious poetry of American life would take, if it could find a general utterance. But there is really no evidence that such is the case. It is certain that among the rudest peoples the lurking sublimity of nature has always sought expression in artistic form, and there is no good reason to believe that the sentiment of a people with our high average culture would seek expression more rude and formless than that of the savagest tribes. Is it not more probable that, if the passional principle of American life could find utterance, it would choose the highest, least dubious, most articulate speech? Could the finest, most shapely expression be too good for it?

If we are to judge the worth of Mr. Whitman's poetic theory (or impulse, or possession) by its popular success, we must confess that he is wrong. It is already many years since he first appeared with his claim of poet, and in that time he has employed criticism as much as any literary man in our country, and he has enjoyed the fructifying extremes of blame and praise. Yet he is, perhaps, less known to the popular mind, to which he has attempted to give an utterance, than the newest growth of the magazines and the newspaper notices. The people fairly rejected his former revelation, letter and spirit, and those who enjoyed it were readers with a cultivated taste for the quaint and the outlandish. The time to denounce or to ridicule Mr. Whitman for his first book is past. The case of *Leaves of Grass* was long ago taken out [of] the hands of counsel and referred to the great jury. They have pronounced no audible verdict; but what does their silence mean? There were reasons in the preponderant beastliness of that book why a decent public should reject it; but now the poet has cleansed the old channels of their filth, and pours through them a stream of blameless purity, and the public

has again to decide, and this time more directly, on the question of his poethood. As we said, his method remains the same, and he himself declares that, so far as concerns it, he has not changed nor grown in any way since we saw him last.

"Beginning my studies, the first step
    pleased me so much,
The mere fact, consciousness—these
    forms—the power of motion.
The least insect or animal—the
    senses—eye-sight;
The first step, I say, aw'd me and
    pleas'd me so much,
I have never gone, and never wish'd
    to go, any further,
But stop and loiter all my life to
    sing it in ecstatic songs."

Mr. Whitman has summed up his own poetical theory so well in these lines, that no criticism could possibly have done it better. It makes us doubt, indeed, if all we have said in consideration of him has not been said idly, and certainly releases us from further explanation of his method.

In *Drum-Taps*, there is far more equality than in *Leaves of Grass*, and though the poet is not the least changed in purpose, he is certainly changed in fact. The pieces of the new book are nearly all very brief, but generally his expression is freer and fuller than ever before. The reader understands, doubtless, from the title, that nearly all these pieces relate to the war; and they celebrate many of the experiences of the author in the noble part he took in the war. One imagines that burly tenderness of the man who went to supply the

"———lack of woman's nursing"

that there was in the hospitals of the field, and woman's tears creep unconsciously to the eyes as the pity of his heart communicates itself to his reader's. No doubt the pathos of many of the poems gains something from the quaintness of the poet's speech. One is touched in reading them by the same inarticulate feeling as that which dwells in music; and is sensible that the poet conveys to the heart certain emotions which the brain cannot analyze, and only remotely perceives. This is especially true of his inspirations from nature; memories and yearnings come to you folded, mute, and motionless in his verse, as they come in the breath of a familiar perfume. They give a strange, shadowy sort of pleasure, but they do not satisfy, and you rise from the perusal of this man's book as you issue from the presence of one whose personal magnetism is very subtle and strong, but who has not added to this tacit attraction the charm of spoken ideas. We must not mistake this fascination for a higher quality. In the tender eyes of an ox lurks a melancholy, soft and pleasing to the glance as the pensive sweetness of a woman's eyes; but in the orb of the brute there is no hope of expression, and in the woman's look there is the endless delight of history, the heavenly possibility of utterance.

Art cannot greatly employ itself with things in embryo. The instinct of the beast may interest science; but poetry, which is nobler than science, must concern itself with natural instincts only as they can be developed into the sentiments and ideas of the soul of man. The mind will absorb from nature all that is speechless in her influences: and it will demand from kindred mind those higher things which can be spoken. Let us say our say here against the nonsense, long current, that there is, or can be, poetry *between the lines*, as is often sillily asserted. *Expression* will always suggest; but mere *suggestion* in art is unworthy of existence, vexes the heart, and shall not live. Every man has tender, and beautiful, and lofty emotions; but the poet was sent into this world to give these a tangible utterance, and if he do not this, but only give us back dumb emotion for dumb emotion, he is a cumberer of the earth. There is a yearning, almost to agony at times, in the human heart, to throw off the burden of inarticulate feeling, and if the poet will not help it in this effort, if, on the contrary, he shall seek to weigh it and sink it down under heavier burdens, he has not any reason to be.

So long, then, as Mr. Whitman chooses to stop at mere consciousness, he cannot be called a true poet. We all have consciousness; but we ask of art an utterance. We do not so much care in what way we get this expression; we will take it in ecstatic prose, though we think it is better subjected to the laws of prosody, since every good thing is subject to some law; but the expression we must have. Often, in spite of himself, Mr. Whitman grants it in this volume, and there is some hope that he will hereafter grant it more and more. There are such rich possibilities in the man that it is lamentable to contemplate his error of theory. He has truly and thoroughly absorbed the idea of our American life, and we say to him as he says to himself, "You've got enough in you, Walt; why don't you get it out?" A man's greatness is good for nothing folded up in him, and if emitted in barbaric yawps, it is not more filling than Ossian or the east wind.

[Henry James]. "Mr. Walt Whitman." *Nation* 1 (16 November 1865), 625–6.

It has been a melancholy task to read this book; and it is a still more melancholy one to write about it. Perhaps since the day of Mr. Tupper's *Philosophy* there has been no more difficult reading of the poetic sort. It exhibits the effort of an essentially prosaic mind to lift itself, by a prolonged muscular strain, into poetry. Like hundreds of other good patriots, during the last four years, Mr. Walt Whitman has imagined that a certain amount of violent sympathy with the great deeds and sufferings of our soldiers, and of admiration for our national energy, together with a ready command of picturesque language, are sufficient inspiration for a poet. If this were the case, we had been a nation of poets. The constant developments of the war moved us continually to strong feeling and to strong expression of it. But in those cases in which these expressions were written out and printed with all due regard to prosody, they failed to make poetry, as any one may see by consulting now in cold blood the back volumes of the *Rebellion Record*. *Of course* the city of Manhattan, as Mr. Whitman delights to call it, when regiments poured through it in the first months of the war, and its own sole god, to borrow the words of a real poet, ceased for a while to be the millionaire, was a noble spectacle, and a poetical statement to this effect is possible. *Of course* the tumult of a battle is grand, the results of a battle tragic, and the untimely deaths of young men a theme for elegies. But he is not a poet who merely reiterates these plain facts *ore rotundo*. He only sings them worthily who views them from a height. Every tragic event collects about it a number of persons who delight to dwell upon its superficial points—of minds which are bullied by the *accidents* of the affair. The temper of such minds seems to us to be the reverse of the poetic temper; for the poet, although he incidentally masters, grasps, and uses the superficial traits of his theme, is really a poet only in so far as he extracts its latent meaning and holds it up to common eyes. And yet from such minds most of our war-verses have come, and Mr. Whitman's utterances, much as the assertion may surprise his friends, are in this respect no exception to general fashion. They are an exception, however, in that they openly pretend to be something better; and this it is that makes them melancholy reading. Mr. Whitman is very fond of blowing his own trumpet, and he has made very explicit claims for his book. "Shut not your doors," he exclaims at the outset—

> "Shut not your doors to me, proud libraries,
> For that which was lacking among you all, yet needed most, I bring;
> A book I have made for your dear sake, O soldiers,
> And for you, O soul of man, and you, love of comrades;
> The words of my book nothing, the life of it everything;
> A book separate, not link'd with the rest, nor felt by the intellect;
> But you will feel every word, O Libertad! arm'd Libertad!
> It shall pass by the intellect to swim the sea, the air,
> With joy with you, O soul of man."

These are great pretensions, but it seems to us that the following are even greater:

"From Paumanok starting, I fly like a
     bird,
Around and around to soar, to sing
     the idea of all;
To the north betaking myself, to
     sing there arctic songs,
To Kanada, 'till I absorb Kanada in
     myself—to Michigan then,
To Wisconsin, Iowa, Minnesota, to
     sing their songs (they are
     inimitable);
Then to Ohio and Indiana, to sing
     theirs—to Missouri and Kansas
     and Arkansas to sing theirs,
To Tennessee and Kentucky—to the
     Carolinas and Georgia, to sing
     theirs,
To Texas, and so along up toward
     California, to roam accepted
     everywhere;
To sing first (to the tap of the war-
     drum, if need be)
The idea of all—of the western
     world, one and inseparable,
And then the song of each member
     of these States."

Mr. Whitman's primary purpose is to
celebrate the greatness of our armies; his
secondary purpose is to celebrate the greatness of the city of New York. He pursues
these objects through a hundred pages
of matter which remind us irresistibly of
the story of the college professor who, on
a venturesome youth's bringing him a
theme done in blank verse, reminded him
that it was not customary in writing
prose to begin each line with a capital.
The frequent capitals are the only marks
of verse in Mr. Whitman's writing. There
is, fortunately, but one attempt at rhyme.
We say fortunately, for if the inequality
of Mr. Whitman's lines were self-reg-
istering, as it would be in the case of an
anticipated syllable at their close, the effect would be painful in the extreme. As
the case stands, each line starts off by it-

self, in resolute independence of its companions, without a visible goal. But if Mr.
Whitman does not write verse, he does
not write ordinary prose. The reader has
seen that liberty is "libertad." In like
manner, comrade is "camerado;" Americans are "Americanos;" a pavement is a
"trottoir," and Mr. Whitman himself is
a "chansonnier." If there is one thing that
Mr. Whitman is not, it is this, for Béranger was a *chansonnier*. To appreciate
the force of our conjunction, the reader
should compare his military lyrics with
Mr. Whitman's declamations. Our author's
novelty, however, is not in his words, but
in the form of his writing. As we have
said, it begins for all the world like verse
and turns out to be arrant prose. It is
more like Mr. Tupper's proverbs than
anything we have met. But what if, in
form, it *is* prose? it may be asked. Very
good poetry has come out of prose before
this. To this we would reply that it must
first have gone into it. Prose, in order to
be good poetry, must first be good prose.
As a general principle, we know of no
circumstance more likely to impugn a
writer's earnestness than the adoption of
an anomalous style. He must have something very original to say if none of the
old vehicles will carry his thoughts. Of
course he *may* be surprisingly original.
Still, presumption is against him. If on
examination the matter of his discourse
proves very valuable, it justifies, or at any
rate excuses, his literary innovation.

But if, on the other hand, it is of a
common quality, with nothing new about
it but its manners, the public will judge
the writer harshly. The most that can be
said of Mr. Whitman's vaticinations is,
that, cast in a fluent and familiar manner,
the average substance of them might escape unchallenged. But we have seen that
Mr. Whitman prides himself especially on
the substance—the life—of his poetry. It
may be rough, it may be grim, it may be

clumsy—such we take to be the author's argument—but it is sincere, it is sublime, it appeals to the soul of man, it is the voice of a people. He tells us, in the lines quoted, that the words of his book are nothing. To our perception they are everything, and very little at that. A great deal of verse that is nothing but words has, during the war, been sympathetically sighed over and cut out of newspaper corners, because it has possessed a certain simple melody. But Mr. Whitman's verse, we are confident, would have failed even of this triumph, for the simple reason that no triumph, however small, is won but through the exercise of art, and that this volume is an offense against art. It is not enough to be grim and rough and careless; common sense is also necessary, for it is by common sense that we are judged. There exists in even the commonest minds, in literary matters, a certain precise instinct of conservatism, which is very shrewd in detecting wanton eccentricities. To this instinct Mr. Whitman's attitude seems monstrous. It is monstrous because it pretends to persuade the soul while it slights the intellect; because it pretends to gratify the feelings while it outrages the taste. The point is that it does this *on theory*, wilfully, consciously, arrogantly. It is the little nursery game of "open your mouth and shut your eyes." Our hearts are often touched through a compromise with the artistic sense, but never in direct violation of it. Mr. Whitman sits down at the outset and counts out the intelligence. This were indeed a wise precaution on his part if the intelligence were only submissive! But when she is deliberately insulted, she takes her revenge by simply standing erect and open-eyed. This is assuredly the best she can do. And if she could find a voice she would probably address Mr. Whitman as follows: "You came to woo my sister, the human soul. Instead of giving me a kick as you approach, you should either greet me courteously, or, at least, steal in unobserved. But now you have me on your hands. Your chances are poor. What the human heart desires above all is sincerity, and you do not appear to me sincere. For a lover you talk entirely too much about yourself. In one place you threaten to absorb Kanada. In another you call upon the city of New York to incarnate you, as you have incarnated it. In another you inform us that neither youth pertains to you nor 'delicatesse,' that you are awkward in the parlor, that you do not dance, and that you have neither bearing, beauty, knowledge, nor fortune. In another place, by an allusion to your 'little songs,' you seem to identify yourself with the third person of the Trinity. For a poet who claims to sing 'the idea of all,' this is tolerably egotistical. We look in vain, however, through your book for a single idea. We find nothing but flashy imitations of ideas. We find a medley of extravagances and commonplaces. We find art, measure, grace, sense sneered at on every page, and nothing positive given us in their stead. To be positive one must have something to say; to be positive requires reason, labor, and art; and art requires, above all things, a suppression of one's self, a subordination of one's self to an idea. This will never do for you, whose plan is to adapt the scheme of the universe to your own limitations. You cannot entertain and exhibit ideas; but, as we have seen, you are prepared to incarnate them. It is for this reason, doubtless, that when once you have planted yourself squarely before the public, and in view of the great service you have done to the ideal, have become, as you say, 'accepted everywhere,' you can afford to deal exclusively in words. What would be bald nonsense and dreary platitudes in any one else becomes sublimity in you. But all this is a mistake. To become adopted as a national poet, it is not enough to discard everything in particular and to accept everything in general, to amass crudity upon crudity, to discharge the undigested contents of your blotting-book into the lap of the public. You must respect the public which you address; for it has taste, if you have not. It delights in the grand, the heroic, and the masculine; but it delights to see these conceptions cast into worthy form. It is indifferent to brute sublimity. It will never do for you to thrust your hands into your pockets and cry out that, as the research of form is an intolerable bore, the shortest and most economical way for the public to embrace its idols—for the nation to realize its genius—is in your own person. This democratic, liberty-loving, American populace, this stern and war-tried people, is a great civilizer. It is devoted to refinement. If it has sustained a monstrous war, and practised human nature's best in so many ways for the last five years, it is not to put up with spurious poetry afterwards. To sing aright our battles and our glories it is not enough to have served in a hospital (however praiseworthy the task in itself), to be aggressively careless, inelegant, and ignorant, and to be constantly preoccupied with yourself. It is not enough to be rude, lugubrious, and grim. You must also be serious. You must forget yourself in your ideas. Your personal qualities—the vigor of your temperament, the manly independence of your nature, the tenderness of your heart— these facts are impertinent. You must be *possessed*, and you must strive to possess your possession. If in your striving you break into divine eloquence, then you are a poet. If the idea which possesses you is the idea of your country's greatness, then you are a national poet; and not otherwise."

New York *Times*, 22 November 1865, p. 4.

Mr. WHITMAN has strong aspirations toward poetry, but he is wanting entirely in the qualities that Praed possessed in such large measure. He has no ear, no sense of the melody of verse. His poems only differ from prose in the lines being cut into length, instead of continuously pointed. As prose, they must be gauged by the sense they contain, the mechanism of verse being either despised by, or out of the reach of the writer. Considered as prose, then, we find in them a poverty of thought, paraded forth with a hubbub of stray words, and accompanied with a vehement self-assertion in the author, that betrays an absence of true and calm confidence in himself and his impulses. Mr. WHITMAN has fortunately better claims on the gratitude of his countrymen than any he will ever derive from his vocation as a poet. What a man *does*, is of far greater consequence than what he *says* or *prints*, and his devotion to the most painful of duties in the hospitals at Washington during the war, will confer honor on his memory when *Leaves of Grass* are withered and *Drum Taps* have ceased to vibrate.

F. "*Drum-Taps.*" New York *Saturday Press*, 27 January 1866, p. 3.

Few persons, we imagine, have read the much over-praised, as well as greatly underrated writings of Walt Whitman, without a conviction that their author is a genuine poet, although they may not agree with his more enthusiastic critics in ranking him above all of the moderns, and finding his true place beside Isaiah, Ezekiel and Job. It is impossible to sympathize heartily with the greatest thoughts that have found utterance in literature, and not to admire him. The two ideas which have him in their possession,—the omnipresence of the soul, and the sacredness of the individual—lie at the roots of poetry and civilization; and he chants them with an invincible faith, which is, of itself, sufficient to place him on a plane beyond that of the poets who believe in art as a finality.

But to be a Pantheist and a Democrat, does not constitute a claim sufficient to entitle any man to the distinction of being a great poet; and Walt Whitman has no other, save a picturesqueness of phrase unsurpassed in literature, and a powerful rhythm, whose long musical roll is like that of the waves of the sea. For he is not a man of ideas. What is called his sanity, his tenacious grasp on realities, is, after all, the monomania of a man whom a great thought has robbed of his self-possession. The unity of the soul is a key that unlocks all doors, but Walt Whitman stopped at the first one to which he applied it. He celebrates the divinity of matter, and worships the shells of things with such fervor that he almost persuades us that there is no substance behind them. It is a dangerous error. The sphinx, Matter, stands in her terrible beauty before every soul, and no answer to her riddle is more fatal than this. Whisper to her that she is divine, and her smiling lips open surely for your destruction. The idea which led Oriental thinkers to the life of contemplation, and which gives Emerson a serenity like that of the unclouded summer sky, leads this poet to

materialism. His songs, though beautiful and inspiring, smack too strongly of the earth. His suggestions are sometimes vast, but himself is chaotic and fragmentary. The truth is that the two ideas which find expression through him are antagonistic. *Because* the soul is one and all mighty, the individual is nothing. "I want no masses at all," says Emerson; but in Whitman the passion for individuals is so strong that it continually wrestles with and overthrows his belief in the universal. Democracy is a good thought to found a state upon, but it is not the profoundest basis for a poem.

Jefferson may claim that "all men are born free and equal," and Whitman may "accept nothing which all cannot have the counterpart of on the same terms;" but the soul, which does not divide itself impartially through the whole universe, but incarnates itself wholly in each atom, is an aristocrat—does not whiffle about rights and duties—claims all and will not be hindered of its own. Mr. Gradgrind's facts, Walt Whitman's patriotism, the vilest man, the purest saint, are equally sacred, and equally valueless, for they are the stepping-stones only, to the unattainable beyond. Let any man assume the attitude of adoration, no matter how fair the shrine, and his shell instantly hardens around him. And porous as this poet thinks himself to all the influences of the universe, he is prostrated, deaf, dumb and blind, before an idol from which the god has departed.

And yet, as Thoreau said, he suggests at times something more than human. In his latest volume there are a few passages which contain the very essence of poetry, and are inexpressibly pathetic, moreover, with the yearning humanity that breathes through them. Setting aside his war chants, which are remarkable for nothing but the startling vividness of their pictures, there are certain poems which make one doubt

119

the correctness of the impression made by the whole man. Such, for instance, are the invocation to Death in the poem called "When last in the dooryard the lilacs bloomed [*sic*]," "Chanting the Square Deific," and "As I lay with my head in your lap." If his faith in the unseen were more of a prophetic fury, and less a premeditated and coolly considered belief; if he clung closer to realities and less tenaciously to appearances, he would be the greatest poet of our day. But he hesitates, as he says, with a rare self-appreciation, at the first step in his progress. He shuts himself from hearty sympathy on all sides. His music, his picturesque force avail him little with the poets, while he so persistently produces poetical effects outside of the accepted rules of their art; and his vast ideas fail of half their force to those who, believing in them as faithfully as he, feel that his application of them is limited and material.

"Literary Review." Boston *Commonwealth*, 24 February 1866, p. 1.

Such is the title of the latest volume of poems by a man of singular genius, Mr. Walter Whitman, of Brooklyn, N. Y. lately displaced from a humble clerkship in Washington by the husband of Mrs. Harlan. In it is included also a smaller collection of verses, called "Sequel to Drum Taps," and containing chiefly poems which relate to the death of President Lincoln and the close of the war. The poems called *Drum Taps*, as the name indicates, relate mostly to the beginning and the progress of the war. Before noticing at any length either these poems or

their author, let us make a little comparison which is not without significance.

Mr. Whitman is a native of New York, a staunch patriot, and through the war, by his services to our soldiers in camp and hospital, has earned the gratitude of tens of thousands of the men who fought and died for their country. He has tenderly cared for the wounded, nursed the sick, consoled the dying and buried the dead. This he did not for pay or for glory—for he got neither—but for love of the sacred cause of freedom and of mankind. He had previously been known to many of his countrymen as a poet of original powers, occupied with the most important themes, which he did not always treat in conformity to the preconceived opinions of the multitude. Having served in his chosen work through the war, both before and after his appointment and dismissal from a clerkship at Washington, he sought in his native city a publisher for his patriotic verses, but he found none willing to put his name to the volume. Messrs. Bunce & Huntington finally printed it, but without their name, and without taking any of customary steps to introduce the book to the reading public. It is scarcely to be got at a bookstore, has hardly been noticed by a newspaper, and, though full of the noblest verses, is utterly unknown to the mass of readers.

Now, look at another fact. Mr. John Esten Cooke is a Virginian, who early joined the rebellion, in which his State played so prominent a part. He served in the army, and did his noble best to destroy the government and kill our brave soldiers. Being a writer, too, he aided his sword by his pen; and by what passes in Virginia for fine writing, he encouraged his fellow-traitors to prolong their treason. He had been known at the North, too, before the war, as a writer of trashy verses and sensational fiction.

Whether Mr. Cooke was pardoned by President Johnson at the urgency of Mrs. Cobb, or whether he is still unpardoned, (if he ever rose to the rank which made a pardon necessary,) we do not know. But he has had the effrontery to come to New York with a fourth-rate novel, written in the style of Mrs. Henry Wood, but full of the rankest treason and laudation of traitors, and he, too, has needed a publisher. But he did not wait long. Messrs. Bunce & Huntington, the same who treat Mr. Whitman so cavalierly, are eager to put his trash into the market. They announce it months in advance; they advertise it in all the newspapers; they send advance copies and secure long notices in the leading journals. The *Advertiser* devotes nearly a column to it; the *Evening Post* notices it at some length; the *Round Table* blows a trumpet before and behind it; and other journals pay it the courtesy of a serious review. Yet neither the author nor the book have any merit to be compared with Tupper and the Country Parson, while both are full of the vilest political heresy and bad taste.

This is the way we encourage poets and patriots; this is the way we reward them, and make treason odious!

Yet this displaced and slighted poet has written the most touching dirge for Abraham Lincoln of all that have appeared. Here it is copied from [the] volume before us:—

["O Captain! My Captain!" quoted in full]
[. . .]

B.
"Walt Whitman's *Drum-Taps*."
Radical 1 (March 1866), 311–12.

Said Thoreau: "The wisest definition of poetry the poet will instantly prove false by setting aside its requisitions." This acute observation has never been more strikingly proved than by the author of the volume before us. The curious and the metaphysical have frequently essayed a complete and accurate definition of the word *poetry*; but it would be impossible to locate within any of their survey-bills, the strange pastures into which Walt Whitman leads his flocks. And yet the author of *Leaves of Grass*, is as unquestionably a true poet, as the greatest of his contemporaries. He seems to us more purely permeated with the subtile essence of poetry than almost any other. It is the air he breathes: the very blood of his arteries. With others there are wide vistas of unmitigated prose in their view of life; to this poet, everything in the world is glowing with poetic beauty. Objects which seem so insignificant—so homely and common-place to most of us, he weaves into his poems. We would not, of course, be understood to say that a simple photography of whatever objects pass before us answers the ends of art. The hand which holds the pencil is everything; and all must be so portrayed that we view them from the poet's own high stand-point. This answers the artistic end; and it is vain to deny artistic treatment in Walt Whitman's poems because they are not constructed in accordance with canons previously laid down. The true poet discovers new and unsuspected laws of art, and makes his own rules. If he touches the secret chords of poetry in our soul, that is the only test, whether we can explain it to our own understanding or not.

Drum-Taps contains but few strikingly different characteristics from the author's former volume. We are pleased to find that certain features of that are not introduced in this; for we are compelled to confess that there were certain pages of the *Leaves of Grass* which we regretted had been written. We have written upon the fly-leaf of our copy this passage from *The Essays*: "Osmand had a humanity so broad and deep, that although his speech was so bold and free with the Koran as to disgust all the dervishes, yet was there never a poor outcast, eccentric or insane man, some fool who had cut off his beard, or who had been mutilated under a vow, or had a pet madness in his brain, but fled at once to him: *that great heart lay there so sunny and hospitable in the centre of the country*, that it seemed as if the instinct of all sufferers drew them to his side."

On looking through the pages of *Drum-Taps*, and catching the soft and sweet strains of a sublime tenderness, much more than the martial music which the title indicates, certain scenes in Washington in the winter of '63 and '64 recur very vividly to memory; his meeting soldiers on the street whom he had nursed and tended—

"Many a soldier's loving arms about
    this neck have crossed and rested—
Many a soldier's kiss dwells on these
    bearded lips,"—

walks with him through some of the hospitals, where he came a ministering spirit, daily. It was very affecting to witness the adoration which this divine love kindled. And it was somewhat amusing, too, to discover certain little myths which were afloat from bed to bed concerning him, for he was not known among them as writer or poet, and there seemed to be some mystery attached to his mission.

In this brief notice we have left little space for some extracts which we proposed to give. How striking a trope, for instance, is this!—

"One doubt, nauseous, undulating
    like a snake, crawl'd on the
    ground before me,
Continually preceding my steps,
    turning upon me oft, ironically
    hissing low."

In vivid word-painting our poet has few equals, as these scattered lines, from "The Veteran's Vision" show:

"The skirmishers begin—they crawl
    cautiously ahead—I hear the
    irregular snap! snap!
I hear the sounds of the different
    missiles—the short *t-h-t! t-h-t!* of
    the rifle balls;"
... "I hear the great shells shrieking
    as they pass;
The grape like the hum and whirr of
    wind through the trees." ...
"And ever the sound of the cannon,
    far and near, (rousing, even in
    dreams, a devilish exultation, and
    all the old mad joy, in the depths
    of my soul.)"

John Burroughs.
"Walt Whitman and His *Drum-Taps*."
Galaxy 2
(1 December 1866),
606–15.

Considering the amount of adverse criticism that has been aimed at Walt Whitman for the last ten years, and the apparent security with which the public rests in the justness of its verdict concerning him, it certainly cannot be damaging to the cause of literature in America, where discussion and agitation in all things are the need of every hour, for us to set up a claim, in a mild way, illustrated by his recent publication called *Drum Taps*, more favorable to this rejected and misinterpreted poet.

Moreover, the beautiful benevolence he has shown during the war in nourishing the sick and wounded soldiers, and his great love and humanity as exhibited in this little volume, entitle him, on grounds of justice alone, to more respect and consideration than he has hitherto received at the hands of his countrymen. He has been sneered at and mocked and ridiculed; he has been cursed and caricatured and persecuted, and instead of retorting in a like strain, or growing embittered and misanthropic, he has preserved his serenity and good nature under all, and illustrated the doctrine of charity he has preached by acts of the most pure and disinterested benevolence.

Walt Whitman was born on Long Island, N. Y., in the Spring of 1819, and boasts that his tongue and every atom of his blood was formed from this soil, this air. "Born here of parents born here, from parents the same and their parents' parents the same," and hence, physiologically, is American to the very marrow of his bones.

On his father's side, his stock is English; on his mother's, Holland Dutch. From his father he inherits his large frame and muscular build—his antecedents here being a race of farmers and mechanics, silent, good-natured, playing no high part in society, politics or the church, and noted chiefly for strength and size. His early life was passed partly in Brooklyn and partly in the country about forty miles east of Brooklyn, where he lived much in presence of the sea. Between the ages of seventeen and twenty he seems to have been mostly engaged in teaching country schools in his native town and vicinity. It was about this time that he began writing for the press. His first productions, mostly sketches, appeared in the *Democratic Review*, from which they were copied into some of the newspapers. Between the ages of twenty and thirty, he was variously occupied as writer and editor on the press of New York and Brooklyn, sometimes going into the country and delivering political addresses. During this period he was on familiar terms of acquaintance with William Cullen Bryant, and the two were in the habit of taking long walks, which, of course, were equivalent to long talks, in and about Brooklyn. In 1850 he went to New Orleans in the capacity of editor, where he remained a year. On his trip to and from that city he made it a point to penetrate various parts of the West and Southwest, particularly to explore the Mississippi and its tributaries, searching, one might say, for hints and models to be used in the making of his poems.

He does not seem to have conceived the idea of writing *Leaves of Grass* till after his thirtieth year. How he was led to adopt this style of expression, thoroughly versed as he was in the literature of the day, is uncertain. The most probable explanation is, that he felt hampered by the old forms and measures, and saw that if America ever came to possess a style of her own it would be in the direction of more freedom and scope—a feeling in which many of his contemporaries are beginning to share. For three or four years before he began to write in this vein, and while his loaf was leavening, as it were, he was a diligent student of the critical literature of the age, delving into foreign magazines and quarterly reviews, and collecting together a vast amount of matter, bearing upon poetry and literature generally, for further use and study. It is quite probable that this course of reading had some influence in determining his own course as a poet, and that he knew well beforehand wherein the head and front of his offending would lie. It has not been with his eyes shut that he set himself squarely against the popular taste and standards, and wrote for an audience of which he did not count upon the present existence of a single member. It cannot be said with the same force of any other writer, living or dead, that he must "wait to be understood by the growth of the taste of himself."

When *Leaves of Grass* was written and published, the author was engaged in putting up small frame houses in the suburbs of Brooklyn, partly with his own hands and partly with hired help. The book was still-born. To a small job printing office in that city belongs the honor, if such, of bringing it to light. Some three score copies were deposited in a neighboring book store, and as many more in another book store in New York. Weeks elapsed and not one was sold. Presently there issued requests from both the stores that the thin quarto, for such it was, should be forthwith removed. The copies found refuge in a well-known phreno-

logical publishing house in Broadway, whose proprietors advertised it and sent specimen copies to the journals and to some distinguished persons. The journals remained silent, and several of the volumes sent to the distinguished persons were returned with ironical and insulting notes. The only attention the book received was, for instance, the use of it by the collected *attachés* of a leading daily paper of New York, when at leisure, as a butt and burlesque—its perusal aloud by one of the party being equivalent to peals of ironical laughter from the rest.

A small but important occurrence seems to have turned the tide. This was the appearance of a letter from the most illustrious literary man in America, brief, but containing a magnificent eulogium of the book. A demand arose, and before many months all the copies of the thin quarto were sold. At the present date, a curious person, poring over the shelves of second-hand book stalls in side places of the city, may light upon a copy of this quarto, for which the stall-keeper will ask him treble its first price. *Leaves of Grass*, considerably added to, and printed in the new shape of a handy 16mo. of about 350 pages, again appeared in 1857. This edition also sold. The newspaper notices of it both here and in Great Britain were numerous, and nearly all of them scoffing, bitter and condemnatory. The most general charge made was that it had passages of serious indelicacy.

For the third time, now much enlarged and in a really beautiful typography and accompaniments, these *Leaves* were issued in Boston as a 12mo. of 456 pages, in 1860. This is their last appearance. An edition of several thousand was taken up, but the business panic of the year, joined with the war, broke down the publishing house that had the book in hand, and the stereotype plates were locked up in chancery. We understand,

124

however, that a new edition is now (August) in the hands of the printer and will shortly be given to the public. This edition will include *Drum Taps*, and show many changes, both in the text and arrangement of the other poems, and indicate much more clearly the purpose or idea of the poet than any edition heretofore published. The entire carrying out of his plan, however, still contemplates the addition of a series of short pieces, like those called "Calamus," expressive of the religious sentiment and aspiration of man.

The full history of the book, if it could ever be written, would be a very curious one. No American work has ever before excited at once such diametrically opposite judgments, some seeing in it only matter for ridicule and contempt; others, eminent in the walks of literature, regarding it as a great American poem. Its most enthusiastic champions are young men, and students and lovers of nature; though the most pertinent and suggestive criticism of it we have ever seen, and one that accepted it as a whole, was by a lady— one whose name stands high on the list of our poets. Some of the poet's warmest personal friends, also, are women of this mould. On the other hand, the most bitter and vindictive critic of him of whom we have heard was a Catholic priest, who evoked no very mild degree of damnation upon his soul; if, indeed, we except the priestly official at the seat of government who, in administering the affairs of his department, on what he had the complacency to call Christian principles, took occasion, for reason of the poet's literary heresies alone, to expel him from a position in his office. Of much more weight than the opinion of either of these Christian gentlemen is the admiration of that Union soldier we chanced to hear of, who by accident came into possession of the book, and without any previous knowledge of it or its author, and by the aid of his mother wit alone, came to regard it with feelings akin to those which personal friendship and intercourse alone awaken; carrying it in his knapsack through three years of campaigning on the Potomac, and guarding it with a sort of jealous affection from the hands of his comrades.

It certainly is an astounding book; but if one will face it fairly, it is by no means so hopeless as it would seem. If the book as a whole means anything, it means power, health, freedom, democracy, self-esteem, a full life in the open air, an escape from the old forms and standards, and a declaration for new and enlarged modes, not only in letters, but in life. In other words, *Leaves of Grass* is the expression in literature of a perfectly healthy, unconventional man; not an abstract, or an intellectual statement of him merely, but the full rendering of a human personality for better or for worse. The poet celebrates himself, that is, uses himself, as an illustration of the character upon which his book is predicated, and which he believes to be typical of the American of the future. This character he has mapped out in bold, strong lines, and in its interest has written his poems. Hence it is not for the man of to-day he has spoken; he has discarded the man of to-day as effete—has rejected his models and standards, and spoken for what he believes to be the man of the future. He must, therefore, have been well prepared for the reception he has met with. Is it to be expected that current conventionalities will endorse him who seeks their overthrow? If we see correctly, the book is also a terrible reaction against the petty, dainty, drivelling ways into which literature has fallen.

But to return to our account of the poet himself. Contrary to the hasty opinions of the critics, who mistook the personal element in his poems and their unliterary spirit (the spirit of nature and life is always unliterary) as evidence of the want of culture in their author, he is a man deeply learned in all the great literatures of the world. The Greek dramatists he has read as few moderns have, and knows Homer to his finger ends. The sects and commentators have not spoilt for him that greatest of books, the Bible, which he always has near. And his mastery of the German metaphysicians has not barred his mind to the enjoyment of the other extreme of literature; the stores of ballad poetry, as the Spanish songs of the *Cid*, and Walter Scott's *Border Minstrelsy*, which last is a source of never-failing delight to him. Considering how the critics have fathered him on Emerson, it is valuable to know that he did not make the acquaintance of Emerson's mind till after the publication of the first edition of his poems. Going, as was his wont, to spend a long Summer day by the sea-shore on Coney Island, in those years a place entirely uninhabited, he carried with him in the basket that contained his dinner, three volumes of "Emerson's Essays," which a friend had recommended to him. There, on that solitary beach fronting the sea, he that day, for the first time, read Emerson.

But he has been a reader of men and of things, and a student of America, much more than of books. Fond of cities, he has gone persistently into all their haunts and by-places, not as a modern missionary and reformer, but as a student and lover of men, finding beneath all forms of vice and degradation the same old delicious, yearning creatures, after all.

Lethargic during an interview, passive and receptive, an admirable listener, never in a hurry, with the air of one who has plenty of leisure, always in perfect repose, simple and direct in manners, a lover of plain, common people, "meeter of savage and gentleman on equal terms,"

temperate, chaste, sweet-breathed, tender and affectionate, of copious friendship, preferring always to meet as flesh and blood, and with a large, summery, motherly soul that shines in all his ways and looks, he is by no means the "rough" people have been so willing to believe. Fastidious as a high caste Brahmin in his food and personal neatness and cleanliness, well dressed, with a gray, open throat, a deep, sympathetic voice, a kind, genial look, the impression he makes upon you is that of the best blood and breeding. He reminds one of the first men—the beginners; has a primitive, outdoor look—not so much from being in the open air as from the texture and quality of his make—a look as of the earth, the sea, or the mountains, and "is usually taken," says a late champion of his cause, "for some great mechanic, or stevedore, or seaman, or grand laborer of one kind or another." His physiognomy presents very marked features—features of the true antique pattern, almost obsolete in modern faces—seen in the strong, square bridge of his nose, his high arching brows, and the absence of all bulging in his forehead, a face approximating in type to the statued Greek. He does not mean intellect merely, but life; and one feels that he must arrive at his results rather by sympathy and absorption than by hard intellectual processes; by the effluence of power rather than by direct and total application of it. In keeping with this, his poems do not have the character of carefully elaborated specimens—of gems cut and polished by the intellect, but are warm and vascular, like living organisms.

In the matter of health he is an exception to most known instances. He presents the rare phenomenon of a man giving himself to intellectual labor without suffering the slightest detriment to his physical powers; never knowing dyspepsia, nervousness, ennui, and an entire stranger to headache until his presence in the army hospitals, and his stopping too long consecutively after the battles of the Wilderness, with a collection of gangrened wounds, had inoculated his system with a malignant virus. And this robust bodily health, as we have said, is one key to his poems. The peculiar quality of them—a quality as of the open air, the woods, the shore, we believe to be more or less attributable to this source. The absence of all pettiness, dallying and sentimentalism, follows from a like cause.

We need not praise him for his patriotism, yet was there ever such a lover of country? He has trailed its entire geography through his poems, courteously saluted every city, great and small, celebrated every phase of its life, the habits of its people, their trades, tools, employments, etc.; has tallied in his poems its vast mass movements, and has not merely predicted, but unhesitatingly counted upon, a future greatness for it absolutely unparalleled in the history of the world.

Soon after the breaking out of the Rebellion, he was drawn to the seat of war to look after a wounded brother—a captain in one of the New York regiments—and since that time has been engaged in field and hospital in nourishing the sick and wounded soldiers. Up to a very recent date he was still quietly but steadily occupied in the same ministrations among the few worst specimens that lingered in the hospitals about Washington.

His theory seems to have been that what the soldiers—many of them becoming worse, and even dying of sheer homesickness—most needed, was a fresh, cheerful countenance, a strong, hopeful voice, and the atmosphere and presence of a loving and healthy friend. Hence he went among them purely in the spirit of love, distributing small gifts—sometimes of money, books, or papers, sometimes of fruits, delicacies, or special food—now reading aloud to a listening group, now soothing by his presence the worst, and, may be, last moments of some poor sufferer. Many soldiers can be found who aver that he saved their lives out and out. His mere presence was tonic and invigorating.

The book called *Drum Taps*, which is the result of the poet's experience in the army and in the hospitals, and to which we propose to devote the remainder of this article, is a little volume of less than a hundred pages, full of warlike passion, singularly blended with as much sadness, perhaps, as was ever printed in a like space.

Those who know Walt Whitman will not be surprised at his calmness and good nature under the treatment awarded to his previous book, and that he should still display the same confidence in himself, and determination to "fight it out on that line" that he evinced at first.

> I am more resolute because all have denied me that I could ever have been had all accepted me; I heed not, and have never heeded, either experience, cautions, majorities, nor ridicule.

Yet, on the whole, the sadness and solemnity of *Drum Taps* contrasts strongly with the flushed, exultant, arrogant, forenoon spirit of *Leaves of Grass*. Here the thought is of death and suffering, and of the desolation of hearts.

Though his themes are mostly suggested by our recent war, yet it is evidently not the purpose of the poet to give descriptions of battles and of great campaigns, or to celebrate great leaders and brilliant achievements; but rather to give the human aspects of anguish that follow in the train of war. He has looked deeper into the matter than the critics are willing to believe. He perhaps feels that the permanent condition of modern society is that of peace; that war, as a business, as a means of growth, has served its time, and that, notwithstanding the vast difference between ancient and modern warfare, both in the spirit and in the means, Homer's pictures are essentially true yet, and no additions to them can be made. War can never be to us what it was to Greece, Rome, and, indeed, to the nations of all ages down to the present; never the main fact—the paramount condition, tyrannizing over all the affairs of national and individual life; but only an episode, a passing interruption; and the poet who in our day would be as true to his nation and times as Homer was to his, must treat of it from the standpoint of peace and progress, and even benevolence. Vast armies rise up in a night and disappear in a day—half a million of men, inured to battle and to blood, go back to the avocations of peace without a moment's confusion or delay—indicating clearly the tendency that prevails.

Also, in obedience to the true democratic spirit, which is the spirit of the times, the attention of the poet is not drawn to the army as a unit—as a tremendous power wielded by a single will, but to the private soldier, the man in the ranks, from the farm, the shop, the mill, the mine, still a citizen engaged in the sacred warfare of peace. Always and always the individual, this is the modern doctrine, as opposed to slavery and caste and the results of the feudal world.

Hence those of the poet's friends who expected to find in this little volume all the "pomp and circumstance of glorious war" have been disappointed. Apostrophizing the genius of America, he says:

No poem proud I chanting bring to
    thee—nor mastery's rapturous
    verse;
But a little book containing night's

darkness and blood-dripping
    wounds,
And psalms of the dead.

His aim does not permit of the slightest expression of partisan or sectional feeling, or any exultation over a fallen foe. Under the head of "Reconciliation" are these lines:

[six-line extract]

The following lines express with great vividness and force the feeling in which all true patriots shared during the second year of the war:

[six-line extract from "Year that Trembled and Reel'd Beneath Me"]

The poem on page 71 is so full of an overmastering pathos; and displays so well the poet's peculiar method and spirit, that we give it entire:

["Pensive on Her Dead Gazing" quoted in full]

Or again in this:

Look down, fair moon, and bathe
    this scene;
Pour softly down night's nimbus
    floods, on faces ghastly, swollen,
    purple;
On the dead, on their backs, with
    their arms toss'd wide,
Pour down your unstinted nimbus,
    sacred moon.

The following exquisite stanza illustrates the poet's power to give a human interest to inanimate objects, and his biblical largeness and freedom in the use of metaphors:

[six-line extract from "Bath'd in War's Perfume"]

128

We invite the reader's careful consideration of one more piece, in which the poet's subtle art and large range of sympathies are perhaps best seen—the poem commemorating the death of Lincoln, beginning, "When lilacs last in the dooryard bloomed." This poem must not be dismissed with a single perusal—a caution, indeed, which may well be observed in reference to the whole book. For, let it be understood, we are dealing with one of the most tyrannical and exacting of bards—one who steadfastly refuses to be read in any but his own spirit. It is only after repeated readings and turning to him again and again, that the atmosphere he breathes is reached. "You must Summer and Winter with people to know them," says an old proverb, which is especially true of this poet. The piece referred to is like intricate and involved music, with subtle, far-reaching harmonies. By that curious indirect method which is always the method of nature, the poet makes no reference to the mere facts of Lincoln's death—neither describes it, or laments it, or dwells upon its unprovoked atrocity, or its political aspects, but quite beyond the possibilities of the art of the ordinary versifier, he seizes upon three beautiful facts of nature which he weaves into a wreath for the dead President's tomb. The central thought is of death, but around this he curiously twines, first the early blooming lilacs which the poet may have plucked the day the dark shadow came; next the song of the hermit thrush, the most sweet and solemn of all our songsters, heard at twilight in the dusky cedars; and with these the evening star, which, as many may remember, night after night in the early part of that eventful Spring, hung low in the west with unusual lustre and brightness. These are the premises whence he starts his solemn chant.

The poem may disappoint on the first perusal. The treatment of the subject is so unusual—so unlike the direct and prosy style to which our ears have been educated—that it seems to want method and purpose. It eludes one; it hovers and hovers and will not be seized by the mind, though the soul feels it. But it presently appears that this is precisely the end contemplated by the poet. He would give as far as possible the analogy of music, knowing that in that exalted condition of the sentiments at the presence of death in a manner so overwhelming, the mere facts or statistics of the matter are lost sight of, and that it is not a narrative of the great man's death, done into rhyme, however faultless, or an eulogy upon his character, however just and discriminating, that offers an opportunity for the display of the highest poetic art, or that would be the most fitting performance on an occasion so august and solemn. Hence the piece has little or none of the character of the usual productions on such occasions. It is dramatic, yet there is no procession of events or development of plot, but a constant interplay—a turning and re-turning of images and sentiments, so that the section in which is narrated how the great shadow fell upon the land occurs far along in the piece. It is a poem that may be slow in making admirers, yet it is well worth the careful study of every student of literature.

[sixty-four–line extract from "When Lilacs Last in the Dooryard Bloom'd"]

The gravity and seriousness of this book and its primitive untaught ways are entirely new in modern literature. With all our profuse sentimentalism, there is no deep human solemnity—the solemnity of a strong, earnest affectionate, unconventional man—in our literature. There are pathos and tears and weeds of mourning; but we would indicate an attitude or

129

habit of the soul which is not expressed by melancholy—which is no sudden burst, or fit, or spasm—which is not inconsistent with cheerfulness and good nature, but which is always coupled with these—a state or condition induced by large perceptions, faith, and deep human sympathies. It may be further characterized as impatient of trifles and dallyings, tires even of wit and smartness, dislikes garrulity and fiction and all play upon words, and is but one remove from silence itself. The plainness and simplicity of the biblical writers afford the best example.

Contemplation, without love or sympathy, of the foibles, follies, and fashions of men and women and of their weaknesses and oddities begets the punning, scoffing, caricaturing habit we deprecate; contemplation of the laws and movements of society, the shows and processes of nature and issues of life and death, begets the rugged faith and sweet solemnity we would describe in *Drum Taps*.

The reader perceives that the quality of these poems is not in any word, or epithet, or metaphor, or verbal and labial felicity whatever; but in the several atmospheres they breathe and exhale. The poet does not aim to load his pages with sweets—he makes no bouquets, distils no perfumes—whatever flower-scents there are, are lost in a smell as of the earth, the shore, the woods. Fine writing, with him, goes for naught. He seeks neither to please nor startle, nor even convince any more than nature does; and beauty follows, if at all, never as the aim, always as the result. There are none of the generally sought for, and, when found, much applauded, delicate fancies or poetical themes—but a large and loving absorption of whatever the earth holds. And this leads us to our final remark upon this subject, in making which we mean discredit to none.

It seems to us that Walt Whitman possesses almost in excess, a quality in which every current poet is lacking. We mean the faculty of being in entire sympathy with nature, and the objects and shows of nature, and of rude, abysmal man; and appalling directness of utterance therefrom, without any intermediate agency or modification.

The influence of books and works of art upon an author may be seen in all respectable writers. If knowledge alone made literature, or culture genius, there would be no dearth of these things among the moderns. But we feel bound to say that there is something higher and deeper than the influence or perusal of any or all books, or all other productions of genius—a quality of information which the masters can never impart, and which all the libraries do not hold. This is the absorption by an author, previous to becoming so, of the spirit of nature, through the visible objects of the universe, and his affiliation with them subjectively and objectively. The calm, all-permitting, wordless spirit of nature yet so eloquent to him who hath ears to hear! The sunrise, the heaving sea, the woods and mountains, the storm and the whistling winds, the gentle Summer day, the Winter sights and sounds, the night and the high dome of stars—to have really perused these, especially from childhood onward, till what there is in them so impossible to define finds its full mate and echo in the mind—his only is the lore which breathes the breath of life into all the rest. Without it, literary productions may have the superb beauty of statues, but with it only can they have the beauty of life.

[A. S. Hill].
[Review of *Drum-Taps* and *Sequel to Drum-Taps*].
North American Review 104 (January 1867), 301–3.

It is fortunate that Walt Whitman's *Drum-Taps*, unlike his *Leaves of Grass*, is in point of propriety unexceptionable, so that it can be judged on its intrinsic merits.

The pieces of which *Drum-Taps* consists are in form, like those in *Leaves of Grass*, neither blank verse nor rhythmical prose. A poet of genuine artistic power would suffer from the absence of those restraints which are to genius what its banks are to a river,—limitations that aid in the development of beauty and of force; and Mr. Whitman is so far from being an artist, that he boasts of his lack of culture, after the fashion of "self-made" men. Yet it is precisely this deficiency which disguises his real excellence, and stands between him and the fame he predicts for himself. A writer whose works are to live must have taste to discriminate between what is worth saying in a given poem, and what is not worth saying, and must have courage to excise the latter. The business of cataloguing the works of creation should be left to the auctioneer.

Poets of vastly more genius and culture than Mr. Whitman possesses have committed the error of thinking all objects and fancies equally worthy of a poem. Wordsworth, for example, patched his shining robes with homespun; but Wordsworth had the manners and speech of a gentleman, while Whitman has the characteristics, good and bad, of a Bowery boy. His love of New York City has more in common with Gavroche's love for Paris than with that of Victor Hugo, and more in common with Tony Weller's love for London than with that of Dr. Johnson, Lamb, or even Dickens. His glorification of America smacks of the "We can lick all creation" of Tammany Hall. But with the extravagance, coarseness, and general "loudness" of Bowery boys, Mr. Whitman possesses in an unusual degree their better traits. He is not ashamed of the body he lives in, and he calls all things by plain names. His compositions, without being sentimental or pretty, show genuine sensibility to the beauty of nature and of man. His braggart patriotism evinced its genuineness during the war.

> "Beauty, knowledge, fortune, inure
>   not to me, yet there are two
>   things inure to me.
> I have nourished the wounded and
>   soothed many a dying soldier;
> And at intervals I have strung
>   together a few songs,
> Fit for war and the life of a camp."

The fact that the "songs" in *Drum-Taps* were written under such circumstances ought to have rebutted in the most fastidious minds whatever presumption may have been raised against the volume by previous publications.

But the claims of these productions to consideration rest upon a more solid basis than the author's personal services in the hospital. Mr. Whitman not only possesses an almost photographic accuracy of observation, a masculine directness of expression, and real tenderness of feeling, but he sometimes hits upon an original epithet which illuminates a page of prosaic details. He speaks of "the *sturdy* artillery.... soon, unlimbered to begin the *red business*"; "the hurrying, crashing, sad, distracted, *robust* year" (1861); the "*hinged* knees and steady hand" of the dresser of wounds; the "elderly (sick) man, so gaunt and grim, with *well-grayed hair and flesh all sunken about the eyes*"; "*million-footed, superb-faced* Manhattan"; "the wind with girlish laughter"; the "gentle, soft-born, *measureless*, light"; "the gorgeous, *indolent*, sinking sun, burning, *expanding* the air"; "the *most excellent* sun, so calm and haughty"; "the *huge* and thoughtful night." And in at least three places he shows more sustained, if not higher power. The effect of the news from Sumter upon New York is thus described:—

> "The Lady of this teeming and
>   turbulent city,
> Sleepless, amid her ships, her
>   houses, her incalculable wealth,
> With her million children around
>   her—suddenly
> At dead of night, at news from the
>   South,
> Incensed, struck with clenched hand
>   the pavement."

"Old Ireland" is personified as

> "Crouching over a grave, an ancient,
>   sorrowful mother,
> Once a queen, now lean and
>   tattered, seated on the ground,
> Her old white hair drooping
>   dishevelled round her shoulders;
> At her feet fallen an unused royal
>   harp."

But Mr. Whitman's faculty is, perhaps, most fully shown in the poem entitled, "When Lilacs Last in the Door-Yard Bloomed"; in which the contrast of the beauty and life of the opening spring with the scenes presented and the thoughts awakened by the funeral of Abraham Lincoln is drawn with unexpected power. The poem is, as a whole, remarkable, but we must content ourselves with a brief quotation.

[fifteen-line extract from "When Lilacs Last in the Dooryard Bloom'd"]

LEAVES OF GRASS (1867)

LEAVES

OF

GRASS.

New-York.

1867.

J[ohn] B[urroughs].
"Literary Review."
Boston *Commonwealth*,
10 November 1866,
pp. 1–2.

Perhaps a steady and unshaken faith in one's self—what we call self-reliance—has as much to do with a man's success in what he undertakes as any other single quality. This faith Walt Whitman certainly has in an amazing degree; perhaps no man ever wrote with so much assurance and so regardless of the opinions of the mass of his contemporaries. In his recent little volume, called *Drum Taps*, occur these lines:—

> 'I am more resolute because all have denied me than I could ever have been had all accepted me; I heed not, and have never heeded, either experience, cautions, majorities, nor ridicule.'

The following from *Leaves of Grass* is to the same purport:—

> Not the pilot has charged himself to bring his ship into port, though beaten back, and many times baffled;
> Not the path-finder, penetrating inland, weary and long,
> By deserts parched, snows chilled, rivers wet, perseveres till he reaches his destination,
> More than I have charged myself, heeded or unheeded, to compose a free march for these States,
> To be exhilarating music to them years, centuries hence.

He has worked away like a man building something, the plan or character of which none foresaw, but which he had deliberately settled upon; and amid the jeers and ridicule of the crowd has gone on adding stroke after stroke, part after part, as serenely and good-naturedly as if the rest of mankind were clapping their hands in applause.

As his work approaches, or perhaps has arrived at, completion in this new edition, it turns out that the thing he has been building so long is a man—a new democratic man, whom he believes to be typical of the future American, and of whom he perpetually uses himself as the illustration.

The 'Inscription,' which is one of the new features of this edition, says as much:—

> Small is the theme of the following chant, yet the greatest—namely, ONE'S SELF—that wonderous thing, a simple, separate person. That, for the use of the New World, I sing.
> Man's physiology complete, from top to toe, I sing. Not physiognomy alone, nor brain alone, is worthy for the muse; I say the form complete is worthier far. The female equally with the male, I sing.
> Nor cease at the theme of One's Self. I speak the word of the modern, the word EN-MASSE.
>
> My days I sing, and lands—with interstice I knew of hapless war.
> O friend, whoe'er you are, at last arriving hither to commence, I feel through every leaf the pressure of your hand, which I return. And thus upon our journey link'd together let us go.

This passage, 'To a Historian,' also contains a valuable hint toward understanding the purpose of the author:—

You who have celebrated bygones!
Who have explored the outward, the
   surfaces of the races—the life that
   has exhibited itself;
Who have treated of man as the
   creature of politics, aggregates,
   rulers and priests;
I, habitué of the Alleghanies, treating
   man as he is in himself, in his own
   rights,
Pressing the pulse of the life that has
   seldom exhibited itself, (the great
   pride of man in himself;)
Chanter of personality, outlining
   what is yet to be, I project the
   history of the future.

The arrangement of the pieces, as they
stand in the new volume, favors this view.
The first poem, 'Walt Whitman,' which is
a compend of the book, has for its central purpose, perhaps, to show how a
man is made; what elements and experiences contribute to him, and how wide
the field from which he may draw nutriment. It is a search after power—a ransacking of heaven and earth for something
to try himself on—to measure himself
against. He would soar into heaven, he
would dive into hell, to find himself—to
be published of his own personality.

Following this poem comes a collection of pieces called 'Children of Adam,'
in which the author celebrates amativeness and the principle of sex. It is these
poems which have given so much offense.
They have most likely been very much
misunderstood. The poet attempts to do
justice to every part of a strong, healthy,
unconventional man. In these pieces he
shows us his hero mostly as a breeding
animal—for the moment giving free
swing to his animal nature. When we reflect that this animal nature is the basis
of all else—is the very ground under our
feet—we can pardon this attitude of the
poet toward it, particularly as he has done

an equal proportionate justice to the
moral and aesthetic qualities, and has not
unduly exalted any part.

The poems called 'Calamus,' which follow, celebrate a riper and more mature
feeling, namely, manly affection and the
need of comrades. 'Salut au monde,' or,
Health to the World! shows the geniality
and good wishes of America toward all
other nations, till, in the pieces which follow, the high intellectual powers are fully
recognized and unfolded:—

I have said many times that materials
   and the soul are great, and that all
   depends on physique;
Now I reverse what I said, and affirm
   that all depends on the æsthetic, or
   intellectual,
And that criticism is great—and that
   refinement is greatest of all;
And I affirm now that the mind
   governs—and that all depends on
   the mind.

The 'Song of the Broad Axe' and 'To
Working-Men' comprise most of those
poems which, in other editions, were arranged under the head of 'Chants Democratic.' The Sun-down poem, which Thoreau admired so much, comes near the
close of the volume. This poem represents the soul in an attitude of worship or
adoration. Having examined the world
and the men and women in it, having
tasted and tried all things, it finds all perfect, and that there are and can be no
conceivable failures:—

Splendor of ended day, floating and
   filling me!
Hour prophetic—hour resuming the
   past!
Inflating my throat—you, divine
   average!
You, earth and life, till the last ray
   gleams, I sing.

Open mouth of my soul, uttering
　　gladness,
Eyes of my soul, seeing perfection,
Natural life of me, faithfully praising
　　things;
Corroborating forever the triumph of
　　things.

The 'Song of the Open Road' shows
the man about at maturity. It is a magnificent poem. The newer collection
called *Drum Taps*, which this volume
now includes, and which is the poet's
latest work, comes near the close of the
volume, as it ought. These poems, taken
in connection with the author's services
in the army-hospitals during the war,
form a sort of coloring or atmosphere
through which his entire work is to be
read. Their chief feature is their humanity, and they are unspeakably precious in
filling out and completing the idea of the
work. They sanctify and make beautiful,
like a great heroic act, everything in the
author's previous life or previous poems.
　Walt Whitman has at last justified himself. As he has surpassed all others in
rude force and virility, he has surpassed
all others in tenderness and love. All his
'hairy Pelasgic strength,' all his vast abysmal power, have at last blossomed into a
benevolence such as was never before the
inspiration of poems.

Robert Buchanan. "Walt Whitman" [review of *Leaves of Grass* (1867) and *Drum-Taps*]. *Broadway Magazine* 1 (November 1867), 188–95.

The grossest abuse on the part of the
majority, and the wildest panegyric on
the part of a minority, have for many
years been heaped on the shoulders of the
man who rests his claim for judgment on
the book of miscellanies noted below.
Luckily, the man is strong enough, sane
enough, to take both abuse and panegyric with calmness. He believes hugely
in himself, and in the part he is destined
to take in American affairs. He is neither
to be put down by prudes, nor tempted
aside by the serenade of pipes and tim-
brels. A large, dispassionate, daring, and
splendidly-proportioned animal, he remains unmoved, explanatory up to a certain point, but sphinx-like when he is
questioned too closely on morality or religion. Yet when the enthusiastic and
credulous, the half-formed, the inquiring,
youth of a nation begin to be carried
away by a man's teachings, it is time to
inquire what these teachings are; for assuredly they are going to exercise extraordinary influence on life and opinion.
Now, it is clear, on the best authority,
that the writer in question is already exercising on the youth of America an influence similar to that exercised by Socrates
over the youth of Greece, or by Raleigh
over the young chivalry of England. In a
word, he has become a *sacer vates*—his
ministry is admitted by palpable live disciples. What the man is, and what the

ministry implies, it will not take long to explain. Let it be admitted at the outset, however, that we are in concert with those who believe his to be a genuine ministry, large in its spiritual manifestations, and abundant in capability for good.

Sprung from the masses, as he himself tells us, Walt Whitman has for many years lived a vagabond life, labouring, as the humour seized him, and invariably winning his bread by actual and persistent industry. He has been alternately a farmer, a carpenter, a printer. He has been a constant contributor of prose to the Republican journals. He appears, moreover, at intervals, to have wandered over the North American continent, to have worked his way from city to city, and to have consorted liberally with the draff of men on bold and equal conditions. Before the outbreak of the war, he was to be found dwelling in New York, on "fish-shape Paumanok," basking there in the rays of the almost tropical sun, or sallying forth into the streets to mingle with strange companions—from the lodging-house luminary and the omnibus driver, down to the scowling rowdy of the wharf bars. Having written his first book, *Leaves of Grass*, he set it up with his own hands, in a printing-office in Brooklyn. Some of our readers may dimly remember how the work was briefly noticed by contemporary English reviews, in a way to leave the impression that the writer was a wild maniac, with morbid developments in the region of the *os pelvis*. On the outbreak of the great rebellion, he followed in the rear of the great armies, distinguishing himself by unremitting attention to the wounded in the Ambulance Department, until, on receiving a clerkship in the Department of the Interior, he removed to Washington. Here, to the great scandal of American virtue, he continued to vagabondize as before, but without neglecting his official duties. At the street corner, at the drinking-bar, in the slums, in the hospital wards, the tall figure of Walt Whitman was encountered daily by the citizens of the capital. He knew everybody, from the President down to the crossing-sweeper.

"Well," said Abraham Lincoln, watching him as he stalked by, "*he* looks like a *man*."

Latterly, his loafing propensities appear to have grown too strong for American tolerance, and he was ejected from his clerkship, on the pretext that he had written "indecent verses," and was a "free lover." His admirers, indignant to a man at this treatment, have accumulated protest upon protest, enumerating numberless instances of his personal goodness and self-denial, and laying powerful emphasis on certain deeds which, if truly chronicled, evince a width of sympathy and a private influence unparalleled, perhaps, in contemporary history. With all this personal business we have no concern. His admirers move for a new trial on the evidence of his written works, and to that evidence we must proceed.

In about ten thousand lines of unrhymed verse, very Biblical in form, and showing indeed on every page the traces of Biblical influence, Walt Whitman professes to sow the first seeds of an indigenous literature, by putting in music the spiritual and fleshly yearnings of the cosmical man, and, more particularly, indicating the great elements which distinguish American freedom from the fabrics erected by European politicians. Starting from Paumanok, where he was born, he takes mankind in review, and sees everywhere but one wondrous life—the movement of the great masses, seeking incessantly under the sun for guarantees of personal liberty. He respects no particular creed, admits no specific morality prescribed by the civil law, but affirms in round terms the universal equality of

138

men, subject to the action of particular revolutions, and guided *en masse* by the identity of particular leaders. The whole introduction is a reverie on the destiny of nations, with an undertone of forethought on the American future, which is to contain the surest and final triumph of the democratical man. A new race is to arise, dominating previous ones, and grander far, with new contests, new politics, new literatures and religions, new inventions and arts. But how dominating? By the perfect recognition of individual equality, by the recognition of the personal responsibility and spiritual significance of each being, by the abrogation of distinctions such as set barriers in the way of perfect private action—action responsible only to the being of whom it is a consequence, and inevitably controlled, if diabolic, by the combined action of masses.

Briefly, Walt Whitman sees in the American future the grandest realization of centuries of idealism—equable distribution of property, luminous enlargement of the spiritual horizon, perfect exercise of all the functions; no apathy, no prudery, no shame, none of that worst absenteeism wherein the soul deserts its proper and ample physical sphere, and sallies out into the regions of the impossible and the unknown. Very finely, indeed, does the writer set forth the divine functions of the body—the dignity and the righteousness of a habitation existing only on the condition of personal exertion; and faintly, but truly, does he suggest how from that personal exertion issues *spirituality*, fashioning literatures, dreaming religions, and perfecting arts. "I will make," he exclaims, "the poems of materials, for I think they are to be the most spiritual poems; and I will make the poems of my body and of mortality: for I think I shall then supply myself with the poems of my soul and of immortality."

This, we hear the reader exclaim, is rank Materialism; and, using the word in its big sense, Materialism it doubtless is. We shall observe, further on, in what consists the peculiar value of the present manifestation. In the meantime, we must continue our survey of the work.

Having broadly premised, describing the great movements of masses, Walt Whitman proceeds, in a separate "poem" or "book," to select a member of the great democracy, representing typically the privileges, the immunities, the conditions, and the functions of all the rest. He cannot, he believes, choose a better example than himself so he calls this poem "Walt Whitman." He is for the time being, and for poetical purposes, the cosmical Man, an entity, a representative of the great forces.[1] He describes the delight of his own physical being, the pleasure of the senses, the countless sensations through which he communicates with the material universe. All, he says, is sweet—smell, taste, thought, the play of his limbs, the fantasies of his mind; every attribute is welcome, and he is ashamed of none. He is not afraid of death; he is content to change, if it be the nature of things that he should change, but it is certain that he cannot perish. He pictures the pageant of life in the country and in cities; all is a fine panorama, wherein mountains and valleys, nations and religions, *genre*, pictures and gleams of sunlight, babes on the breast and dead men in shrouds, pyramids and brothels, deserts and populated streets, sweep wonderfully by him. To all those things he is bound:—wherever they force him, he is not wholly a free agent; but on one point he is very clear—that, so far as he is concerned, he is the most important thing of all. He has work to do; life is not merely a suck or a sell; nay, the whole business of ages has gone on with one object only—that he, the democrat, Walt Whitman, might

139

have work to do. In these very strange passages, he proclaims the magnitude of the preparations for his private action:—

"Who goes there? hankering, gross, mystical, nude;
How is it I extract strength from the beef I eat?
What is a man, anyhow? What am I? What are you?
All I mark as my own, you shall offset it with your own,
Else it were time lost listening to me.

I do not snivel that snivel the world over,
That months are vacuums, and the ground but wallow and filth;
That life is a suck and a sell, and nothing remains at the end but threadbare crape, and tears.

Whimpering and truckling fold with powders for invalids—conformity goes to the forth-removed;
I wear my hat as I please, indoors or out.

Why should I pray? Why should I venerate and be ceremonious?
Having pried through the strata, analysed to a hair, counsel'd with doctors, and calculated close,
I find no sweeter fat than sticks to my own bones.

In all people I see myself—none more, and not one a barleycorn less;
And the good or bad I say of myself, I say of them.

And I know I am solid and sound;
To me the converging objects of the universe perpetually flow;
All are written to me, and I must get what the writing means.

I know I am deathless;
I know this orbit of mine cannot be swept by the carpenter's compass;

I know I shall not pass like a child's carlacue cut with a burnt stick at night.

I know I am august;
I do not trouble my spirit to vindicate itself, or be understood;
I see that the elementary laws never apologize;
(I reckon I behave no prouder than the level I plant my house by, after all.)

I exist as I am—that is enough;
If no other in the world be aware, I sit content;
And if each and all be aware, I sit content.

One world is aware, and by far the largest to me, and that is myself;
And whether I come to my own to-day, or in ten thousand or ten million years,
I can cheerfully take it now, or with equal cheerfulness I can wait.

My foothold is tenon'd and mortis'd in granite;
I laugh at what you call dissolution;
And I know the amplitude of time.

I am an acme of things accomplish'd, and I am an encloser of things to be.

My feet strike an apex of the apices of the stairs;
On every step bunches of ages, and larger bunches between the steps;
All below duly travel'd, and still I mount and mount.

Rise after rise bow the phantoms behind me;
Afar down I see the huge first Nothing—I know I was even there;
I waited unseen and always, and slept through the lethargic mist,
And took my time, and took no hurt from the fetid carbon.

Long I was hugg'd close—long and
long.

Immense have been the preparations
for me,

Faithful and friendly the arms that
have help'd me.

Cycles ferried my cradle, rowing
and rowing like cheerful boatmen;

For room to me stars kept aside in
their own rings;

They sent influences to look after
what was to hold me.

Before I was born out of my mother,
generations guided me;

My embryo has never been torpid—
nothing could overlay it.

For it the nebula cohered to an orb,

The long slow strata piled to rest it
on,

Vast vegetables gave it sustenance,

Monstrous sauroids transported it in
their mouths, and deposited it
with care

All forces have been steadily
employ'd to complete and delight
me;

Now on this spot I stand with my
robust Soul."

It is impossible in an extract to convey
an idea of the mystic and coarse, yet living, force which pervades the poem called
"Walt Whitman." We have chosen an extract where the utterance is unusually
clear and vivid. But more extraordinary,
in their strong sympathy, are the portions
describing the occupations of men. In a
few vivid touches we have striking pictures; the writer shifts his identity like
Proteus, but breathes the same deep undertone in every shape. He can transfer
himself into any personality, however
base. "I am the man—I suffered—I was
there." He cares for no man's pride. He
holds no man unclean.

And afterwards, in the poem called

"Children of Adam," he proceeds to par-
ticularize the privileges of flesh, and to
assert that in his own personal living body
there is no uncleanness. He sees that the
beasts are not ashamed; why, therefore,
should he be ashamed? Then comes passage after passage of daring animalism;
the functions of the body are unhesitatingly described, and the man asserts
that the basest of them is glorious. All the
stuff which offended American virtue is
to be found here. It is very coarse, but, as
we shall see, very important. It is never,
however, inhuman; indeed, it is strongly
masculine—unsicklied by Lesbian bestialities and Petronian abominations. It simply chronicles acts and functions which,
however unfit for art, are natural, sane,
and perfectly pure. We shall attempt to
show further on that Walt Whitman is
not an artist at all, not a poet, properly
so called; and that this grossness, offensive in itself, is highly significant—an essential part of very imperfect work. The
general question of literary immorality
need not be introduced at all. No one
is likely to read the book who is not in-
telligently chaste, or who is not familiar
with numberless authors offensive to
prudes—Lucretius, Virgil, Dante, Goethe,
Byron, among poets; Tacitus, Rabelais,
Montaigne, Cervantes, Swedenborg, among
prose thinkers.

The remainder of *Leaves of Grass* is
occupied with poems of democracy, and
general monotonous prophecies. There
is nothing more which it would serve
our present purpose to describe in detail,
or to interpret. The typical man continues his cry, encouraging all men,—on the
open road, in the light of day, in the region of dreams. All is right with the world,
he thinks. For religion he advises, "Reverence all things"; for morality, "Be not
ashamed"; for political wisdom among
peoples, "Resist much—obey little." He
has no word for art; it is not in her temple

that he burns incense. His language, as even a short extract has showed, is strong, vehement, instantaneously chosen; always forcible, and sometimes even rhythmical, like the prose of Plato. Thoughts crowd so thick upon him, that he has no time to seek their artistic equivalent; he utters his thought in any way, and his expressions gain accidental beauty from the glamour of his sympathy. As he speaks, we more than once see a man's face at white heat, and a man's hand beating down emphasis at the end of periods. He is inspired, not angry; yet as even inspiration is not infallible, he sometimes talks rank nonsense.

The second part of the volume, *Drum-Taps*, is a series of poetic soliloquies on the war. It is more American and somewhat less mystical than the *Leaves of Grass*; but we have again the old cry of democracy. Here, in proportion to the absence of self-consciousness, and the presence of vivid emotion, we find absolute music, culminating once or twice in poetry. The monody on the death of Lincoln—"when lilacs last in the door-yard bloomed"—contains the three essentials of poetic art—perfect vision, supreme emotion, and true music. This, however, is unusual in Walt Whitman. Intellectual self-consciousness generally coerces emotion, insincerities and follies ensue, and instead of rising into poetry, the lines wail monotonously, and the sound drops into the circle of crabbed prose.

For there is this distinction between Walt Whitman and the poet—that Whitman is content to reiterate his truth over and over again in the same tones, with the same result; while the poet, having found a truth to utter, is coerced by his *artistic* sympathies into seeking fresh literary forms for its expression. "Bawling out the rights of man," wrote Horne Tooke, "is not singing." Artistic sympathies Walt Whitman has none; he is that curiously-crying bird—a prophet with no

taste. He is careless about beautifying his truth: he is heedless of the new forms—personal, dramatic, lyrical—in which another man would clothe it, and in which his disciples will be certain to clothe it for him. He sees vividly, but he is not always so naturally moved as to sing exquisitely. He has the swagger of the prophet, not the sweetness of the musician. Hence all those crude metaphors and false notes which must shock artists, those needless bestialities which repel prudes, that general want of balance and that mental dizziness which astonish most Europeans.

But when this has been said, all blame has been said, if, after all, a man is to incur blame for not being quite another sort of being than nature made him. Walt Whitman has arisen on the States to point the way to new literatures. He is the plain pioneer, pickaxe on shoulder, working and "roughing." The daintier gentlemen will follow, and build where he is delving.

Whitman himself would be the first to denounce those loose young gentlemen who admire him vaguely because he is loud and massive, gross and colossal, not for the sake of the truth he is teaching, and the grandeur of the result that may ensue. There are some men who can admire nothing unless it is "strong"; intellectual dram-drinkers, quite as far from the truth as sentimental tea-drinkers. Let it at once and unhesitatingly be admitted that Whitman's want of art, his grossness, his tall talk, his metaphorical word-piling, are *faults*—prodigious ones; and then let us turn reverently to contemplate these signs which denote his ministry, his command of rude forces, his nationality, his manly earnestness, and, last and greatest, his wondrous sympathy with men as men. In actual living force, in grip and muscle, he has no equal among contemporaries. He emerges from the mass of unwelded materials—in shape much like the Earth-spirit in *Faust*. He is loud and coarse, like most prophets, "sounding," as he himself phrases it, "his barbaric yawp over the roofs of the world." He is the voice of which America stood most in need—a voice at which ladies scream and gigmen titter, but which clearly pertains to a man who means to be heard. He is the clear forerunner of the great American poet, long longed for, often prophesied, but not perhaps to be beheld till the vast American democracy has subsided a little from its last and grandest struggle. Honour in his generation is of course his due, but he does not seem to solicit honour. He is too thoroughly alive to care about being tickled into activity, too excited already to be much moved by finding himself that most badgered of functionaries, the recognized Sir Oracle.

Note

1 Let it be understood, here and elsewhere, that we shall attach our own significance to passages in themselves sufficiently mystical. We may misrepresent this writer; but, apart from the present constructions, he is to us unintelligible.

143

POEMS BY WALT WHITMAN (1868)

POEMS

BY

WALT WHITMAN.

SELECTED AND EDITED

BY

WILLIAM MICHAEL ROSSETTI.

Or si sa il nome, o per tristo o per buono,
E si sa pure al mondo ch'io ci sono.
MICHELANGELO.

LONDON:

JOHN CAMDEN HOTTEN, PICCADILLY.

1868.

"Walt Whitman: Second Notice."
London *Sunday Times*, 29 March 1868, p. 7.

Somewhat more than a year ago (vide *Sunday Times*, March 3rd, 1867) we called the attention of our readers to the works of an American poet—Walt Whitman— at that moment all but unknown in England. While admitting all that was wild, disorderly, and extravagant in these writings, we did justice to the many high qualities they possessed, spoke of them as the most thoroughly national and characteristic poetry to which America had yet given birth, and anticipated for them, when the first feelings of dislike, which the violation of all received models had occasioned were repressed, a large measure of regard among the more cultivated classes of English readers. At the time we wrote, the volume containing Whitman's poems was one of the rarest in England. A few scattered copies could be found, belonging principally to those who had received the work in their capacity of reviewers. We spoke warmly of the desirability of placing it within the reach of a certain tolerably extensive class of readers, and discussed the feasibility of an English reprint. Sooner than we anticipated has such reprint come. It has taken, moreover, the form we expected a first edition of Whitman to bear;—a form not in itself attractive to scholars and students, but such as in the present case was alone to be expected, and such as the exceeding taste of the editor has rendered as little offensive as possible to the haters of expurgated editions. Many motives induce us to recur for a brief while to the works of Whitman, to do which the appearance of the first English edition affords a favourable opportunity. Enough has not yet been said about the man, and the edition itself is a novelty in English literature, deserving on its own account a few words of comment. Not, however, in the few phrases that follow, nor in many more, for which we have not space, should we hope to do justice to that remarkable kosmos, Walt Whitman. He is not a man to be easily dismissed. A few glibly-spoken phrases will not describe him or his work. His faults and excellences are of the kind least commonly encountered, and have phases enough to render just and satisfactory criticism a task of more than usual difficulty. Walt Whitman is undoubtedly a great man. His position as a poet is not likely to be conceded without much dispute. Conservatives in poetry will shrink from utterances which appear to defy all known canons, and possess scarcely one of the gifts hitherto judged indispensable to verse. Unreflective readers will see nothing but a harsh and over-daring Tupper. Those even, whose sympathies are broad, and who shrink from subjecting all poetry to the tape, may pause ere they bestow the title of verse on these strong and often inharmonious outpourings. But no thinking reader will dispute that he is in the presence of a man and a thinker. Whitman is entitled to rank with those men whose works are the scholar's especial delight. His mind is of the same order with that of Rabelais or Montaigne. Rightly to understand him, however, it is necessary to transport oneself in idea from the over-crowded and, in one sense, over-civilised world of Europe, to the great continent whose first seer he is. American life and institutions have impregnated Whitman's soul. American air has saturated his lungs. He knows nothing of old-world notions and conventions; laughs at them when he hears of them, or passes them by as things unworthy of a thought. He is an American, a Manhattanese, a democrat. The world he lives in is untroubled with questions of kingcraft or priestcraft. Human nature, in the manifold developments which in its fight in city or backwood it assumes, he knows and loves. Comradeship is his motto. Men who work and love like he are his brothers. The question of success never enters into his calculations. He sings forgotten or unknown heroes as soon as those whose names are foremost in the scroll of fame. The imperfections of the human nature he contemplates are as well worthy of study as its perfections. Nothing about manhood is vile or unclean. His contempt for the assumptions of philosophy is not greater nor less than his disregard of the dogmatism of authority. He is the most pantheistic of pantheists. The God he worships reveals himself in all places, even where Egyptian or Phœnician would not have sought him. The divine in the human he understands and worships. Nothing with Whitman is unfit for the uses of poetry. Mr. Buchanan is not more ready to descend for the subject of his poetry to street or slum. Wordsworth is not more enraptured of solitude, or in closer communion with nature. His principal theme is, however, manhood; first, as he sees it in the individual that is himself, next as he sees it in the world at large, the American world that is. "Man's physiology complete, from top to toe, I sing. Not physiognomy alone, nor brain alone, is worthy for the muse: I say the form complete is worthier far. The female equally with the male, I sing." His book is, as Mr. Rossetti admirably observes, the poem of personality and democracy. It is strong, passionate, rhapsodical even, and yet pervaded with matter-of-fact plainness of speech. It is extravagant at times both in reality and ideality. One thing, at least, it never is—

unhealthy or morbid. The edition of Whitman's poems which Mr. Rossetti has published does not pretend to completeness. It is but a book of extracts. In its class, however, it is a model. Never before has the public had a volume of extracts in which it might depend with greater confidence upon the taste of him who chose. Our own dislike to selections is not greater than that which Mr. Rossetti proclaims. If, however, there are books of which one should know much while one cannot afford him to know all, we should like always to have Mr. Rossetti to taste and select for us. Mr. Rossetti announces his volume as intended rather to herald the entire work than to render it unnecessary. He has felt it expedient to give the public some knowledge of the first truly national poet America has produced, and has determined not to frighten away the general reader by printing the poems in which the writer flies in the face of prejudices entertained by a large portion of Englishmen. But Mr. Rossetti is no Bowdler. He has given us many poems entire. Others he has entirely omitted. This we at once admit is the only principle upon which work of this kind can be done, and yet find favour with thoughtful readers. Into the question of the value of English prejudice Mr. Rossetti does not enter. His few remarks are explanatory of his motives, neither deprecatory nor justificatory. The greatest works of all times, from the earliest literature of Greek and Hebrew, to the latest of France and England, are offensive to English prudery. He has given to the English world those writings of a great and unknown writer, which it may read without being shocked. If after reading these the public wants more, and cares to risk the chance of being shocked, it can obtain them. That is its own affair. Only in the preface to the first edition of *Leaves of Grass*, which Mr. Rossetti has most judiciously included in his volume, are one or two passages left out, and these he had the author's permission to omit. For it is a fact, creditable alike to editor and publisher, that this work is published with the express sanction of the author, who will receive a royalty on every copy sold, and who has accorded liberty for the sale of the volume in America, wherein at present the earlier editions of Whitman are scarce and expensive. In Mr. Rossetti's preface—a model of grave thoughtful criticism, and free and elegant English—we have a few particulars of Whitman's biography; a description of his personal appearance, and an account of the reception which attended the first publication of his works in America. Some account is also given of his heroic conduct during the late war. The remainder is composed of criticisms upon Whitman's works, and an explanation of the theory of his workmanship. A portrait of the author, very admirably engraven, accompanies the volume, which is unusually elegant and attractive in appearance. In our previous account of Whitman, to which the present notice is intended as an appendix, we quoted as liberally from the published works as our space would permit. We are now, accordingly, exonerated from the necessity of supporting by extracts the opinions we have pronounced. We regret that we cannot quote one passage from the prose preface of which we have spoken. The whole of the preface is wonderfully powerful, sonorous, and trumpet-like, and is in itself sufficient to render, a desirable possession the volume in which it appears. As an exposition of Whitman's views of art it is profoundly interesting. We trust that now that Whitman's works are easily accessible, few Englishmen will care to leave them unread. For ourselves, we confess to sharing the opinion eloquently expressed by his English editor, "His voice will one day be potential or magisterial wherever the English language is spoken—that is to say, in the four corners of the earth; and in his own American hemisphere the uttermost orators of democracy will confess him not more their announcer than their inspirer."

"Walt Whitman's Poems." London *Sun*, 17 April 1868, p. 31490.

Opening this book has been to us a revelation. Reading it has yielded us exquisite pleasure. The remembrance of it sweetens life. Echoes from it haunt us in the thick of our occupations, 'under the shade of melancholy boughs,' in the throng of the streets, at our meals, in the midst of our conversations, anywhere, everywhere, under the likeliest and the unlikeliest circumstances. Before the volume now under notice came into our hands, the name of Walt Whitman was certainly known to us, but that was all. Now that we have read these selections—observe, these *selections*—from his 'Chants Democratic,' from his *Drum Taps*, from his *Leaves of Grass*, from his 'Songs of Parting,' we have learnt to love that name of his, it has become to us a synonym of pleasure, suggestive of thoughts, emotions, aspirations, expressed as in a new language, and, once so expressed, never afterwards to be altogether forgotten. To William Michael Rossetti, as the selecter of these poems, we are not simply, in old-fashioned phrase, beholden, we are not merely in courtlier terms his most obedient, we are his very gratefully, and that, moreover, in heartfelt truthfulness. Already in the columns of the clever but now dead and gone *Chronicle*, under date 6th July,

1867, the editor of this henceforth to us cherished volume of Walt Whitman's Poems had sounded the trumpet of admiration in praise of that particular poet of America. Here, however, he has made good, in every sense, his high, and, as it might have seemed to some, extravagant commendations. Of the justice of the estimate thus enunciated, these poems yield absolute demonstration. Apart from the selection now given to us by Mr Rossetti, we are desirous that it should be understood at once, however, by our readers, that we know nothing whatever of the writings of Walt Whitman. This we would especially premise. And for a sufficient reason. According to a very general rumour even over here in England, according to the showing of even so enthusiastic an appreciator of his genius as Mr Rossetti has (happily for us all) shown himself to be—Walt Whitman has written things that his own most ardent admirers would willingly let die. Yet, of all this, the volume now in our hand, here submitted to our consideration, bears not a particle of evidence. The leering satyrs have been scared away from among the beautiful umbrage. The dregs lurk no longer in the limpid draught placed at our lips. We can quaff without a qualm. There is no canker in the rose-wreath as it is thus brought within our reach—it is all fragrance and dripping with dew. Not a taint is here, in bloom, or foliage, or fruit. The very atmosphere investing these poems is all purity, like the breath of morning. And yet—though we never should have conjectured as much from these poems themselves—the Collective Writings of Walt Whitman must indubitably be tainted, flawed, polluted—and that, too, with a taint, a flaw, a pollution in no conceivable way to be extenuated. Mr Rossetti himself sets forth in regard to the incriminated poems (*all* of which he has carefully omitted in the process of making his selection) not one word, not one hint of extenuation. He says, indeed, that he considers 'that most of them would be much better away.' And, whatever else can be said of the editor of the present volume as a critic of poetic literature, it certainly cannot be said of him that he is a purist. 'Indecencies, improprieties, deforming erudities' there are, he tells us, scattered, it may even be abundantly scattered, here and there, over the Writings of Walt Whitman. Such they are acknowledged to be, in so many words, even by the critic thanks to whose judicious hands those damning blemishes have been discarded. Of their existence at all, we only know, now, by their own evil reputation. They themselves are not here. Nevertheless this selection is in no respect what we should call, in the ordinary acceptation of the words, an Expurgated Edition. There is here no emasculation. The poems that are given are given in their entirety. Mere parts have been nowhere selected. Abbreviations, elisions, excisions, the Editor has shrunk from as from impertinences. He has done his task well and wisely. And yet, task it can hardly be called—true labour of love as it has been (and no wonder) throughout. Although containing within it 'a little less,' we are told 'that [*sic*] half the entire bulk of Whitman's poetry,' this one volume affords a comprehensive view of the writer's genius in its integrity. It is no broken gem that is here placed in our hands for examination, but—'one entire and perfect chrysolite.' Before commenting upon Walt Whitman's poetical productions, however, so far as those are here brought within our survey, a word or two as to the man himself. Abraham Lincoln's exclamation on seeing him was—'Well, *he* looks like a man!' Nor can that exclamation be wondered at when one comes to sum up his characteristics. Lofty in stature, admirably well proportioned, of vigorous strength, of abounding health—forty-nine years of age on the last day of next month—his eyes of a light blue, his complexion florid, his beard fleecy and flowing, but already quite grey—cheerful and masculine in appearance—having a predilection for the society of common people—intensely fond of fine music, and with a great natural taste for works of art—absolutely indifferent 'as to either praise or blame of what he writes'—such, in brief, is Walt Whitman. Born on the 31st of May, 1819, at the farm village of West Hills, Long Island, in the state of New York, somewhere about thirty miles from the great American capital and outport—he is but now in the prime or meridian of his manhood, though already old-looking in spite of his health, of his wholesome out-door life, his temperate habits, and his vigorous constitution. A schoolboy up to thirteen, afterwards a compositor, then a country teacher, then a press writer, then a newspaper editor, then a master printer, then (like his father) a carpenter and builder, then, throughout the Great Civil War, to the Northern Army, what Miss Nightingale was to the British Army at Scutari throughout the War in the Crimea. And, yet all along, and at last wholly and solely, what he is now for the rest of his days—a Poet. Before considering him as such, it is but justice to remark of him in his capacity as a practical philanthropist when attending the poor soldiers all through that tremendous struggle between North and South, between the Federals and the Confederates in America, that 'It is said that by the end of the war he had personally ministered to upwards of 100,000 sick and wounded.' Honour, therefore, to the brave, true heart, if only in remembrance of that one recorded fact in his history—a fact evidencing that Walt Whitman not only 'looks' but *acts* 'like a man.' Turning our glance, however, from the man himself to his productions, to those Poems of his which have been here selected for us from his 'Songs of Parting,' his *Leaves of Grass*, his *Drum Taps*, and so on—one peculiarity is at once especially noticeable in regard to them, and that is their startling, intense, and absolute originality. In their manner, they are unlike any other poems that have ever previously made their appearance. As a rule, they are rhymeless. But, always, always they are rhythmical, and yet rhythmical after a manner peculiarly and exceptionally their own. The lines are of any length—sometimes abbreviated to a little more than a monosyllable—occasionally running out to the extent of half-a-dozen alexandrines. Now standing, as one might say, on one foot, and that a-tip-toe—now running along upon as many feet as those of a centipede. But—with all this whimsicality and *abandon* of manner, with all this wild defiance of the hitherto dominant laws of poetical, and, for that matter even at times of rhetorical, construction—O the charm, the grace, the tenderness, the pathos, the abounding and captivating beauties scattered broadcast, with a lavish hand, with an affluent fancy, with the royal prodigality of genius, over these pages of true poetry! Nor can the daring originality thus manifested by Walt Whitman in the mere manner of his composition be regarded as so wholly unexampled. As has been admirably well asked—

'Was genius awed by Aristotle's rules
    When Shakespeare burst the cobwebs
        of the schools?'

Flinging to the winds of heaven all the precedents of literature, this new poet of the New World, a poet intensely *sui generis*, one racy of the soil from which he has sprung, carves out his own way with a pen as trenchant as an axe, and goes upon that way of his rejoicing. About the only one rhymed passage in the whole of this otherwise quite rhymeless volume of poetry, is the opening of the song in celebration of the broad-axe in the 'Chants Democratic.' And, having but just now—in total forgetfulness at the moment, alike of that especial passage and of that particular song—likened Walt Whitman's pen, in the trenchant sweep of it, to an axe, such as it might be seen gleaming and crashing when wielded in the grip of a backwoodsman of thews and sinews like his own—upon our sudden remembrance immediately afterwards of his own words, the simile appears more than ever most appropriate. For, thus it is that Walt Whitman, in his 'Song of the Broad Axe,' apostrophises that—

'Weapon, shapely, naked, wan;
Head from the mother's bowels
   drawn!
Wooded flesh and metal bone; limb
   only one, and lip only one!
Grey-blue leaf by red-heat grown!
   helve produced from a light seed
   sown!
Resting the grass amid and upon,
To be leaned, and to lean on.'

A pen no less potent, keen, piercing, than such a broad axe, 'to be leaned and to lean on,' 'resting the grass [*Leaves of Grass*] amid and upon'—is, most assuredly, for us the pen of Walt Whitman. Otherwise than in one fragmentary instance like the foregoing, the book is, as we have said, altogether rhymeless. Wonderfully rhythmical throughout, though in lines of the most oddly varying lengths, the poems of Walt Whitman—when the reader has once passed the Rubicon—exercise over that initiated reader's mind a potent and irresistible fascination. The Rubicon must be passed, however, as a preliminary, as the first and all-essential preliminary of initiation. Meaning by that, simply, that

any one coming to the examination of Walt Whitman's poems with a view to their complete appreciation, must begin by, we won't say taking this and that for granted, we won't even say by making such and such allowances, for, so expressing ourselves, we might seem to be slighting the high inherent claims to respect of a great original writer, such as Walt Whitman: instead of that we will say then simply—that the all-essential preliminary we are alluding to is one purely of concession. Concede to Whitman the fashion of his verse—concede to him his terse but never bald realism—concede to him his exotic verbiage, his coinage of words occasionally, with a daring disregard alike of the laws of syntax and of philology—and the spell of the magician is felt at once and for ever! We are within the circle of his poetic incantations! He 'hath his will' thenceforth—as he lists—at his own pleasure over our hearts, our emotions, our imaginations. As exemplars, to begin with, of his magical power in mere word-painting—take almost haphazard a single line or verse picked out here and there from the midst of his descriptions:—

'Evening—me in my room—the
   setting sun,
The setting summer sun shining in
   my open windows, showing the
   swarm of flies, suspended,
   balancing in the air in the centre
   of the room, darting athwart, up
   and down, casting swift shadows
   in specks on the opposite wall,
   where the shine is.'
'The irregular tapping of rain down
   on the leaves, after the storm is
   lulled.'
'Me observing the spiral flight of two
   little yellow butterflies shuffling
   between each other, ascending high
   in the air.'

152

'And the fish suspending themselves
   below there—and the beautiful
   curious liquid.'
'In the distance the flowing glaze, the
   breast of the river, with a wind-
   dapple here and there.'

These word paintings of Whitman's sometimes pass by their very vividness into
whimsicalities, yet are, for all that, wondrous word-paintings nevertheless: as
where he speaks of—

'. . . dabs of music;
Fingers of the organist skipping
   staccato over the keys of the great
   organ.'

His word-painting power goes with him
everywhere. Into the ship-building yard,
for example, where we see with him, as if
we, too, were there—

'The butter-coloured chips flying off
   in great flakes, and slivers.'

It goes with him, and we with it and with
him through even the swinging of a
door—

'The door passing the dissevered
   friend, flushed and in haste.'

Sometimes the secret of it lies even in a
word—

'The dim-lit church and the
   shuddering organ.'

Or, again, as where conjuring up shapes
before him in his reverie, he speaks,
among others, of—

'The shape of the shamed and angry
   stairs, trod by sneaking footsteps.'

Or, yet more even, where brooding over

many exquisite imaginings, he says most
oddly and whimsically—

'They are so beautiful I nudge myself
   to listen.'

Or, again in the same way, when, by one
subtle word, we note the last agonised
kiss of bereaved affection, when—

'The *twitching* lips press lightly on
   the forehead of the dying.'

The merest specks and atoms of beauty,
however, are these little word-pictures
noticeable in casual lines and phrases in
Walt Whitman's poetry. Immeasurably
more noteworthy are the large humanity
and the wide philosophy evidenced and
inculcated by his utterances. His cry is
that of Happiness and of Adoration—

'For I do not see one imperfection in
   the universe.'

Another while he declares—

'That all the things of the universe
   are perfect miracles, each as
   profound as any.'

And another while he ejaculates:—

'The sun and stars that float in the
   open air;
The apple-shaped earth and we upon
   it—surely the drift of them is
   something grand!'

Adding—

'I do not know what it is, except that
   it is grand, and that it is
   happiness.'

Again, he is full of wonderment at the
abounding wonders around him, among
others at—

'The wonder every one sees in every
one else he sees, and the wonders
that fill each minute of time
forever.'

The wonder of wonders to him, however—the glory and consolation of his
life—(the enunciation of which, of the
joy and solace of which to fellow mortals, is among the most dearly-cherished
aspirations of his ambition)—the one
great end worth living for, being, according to Walt Whitman—Death. Thus he
exclaims—

'And I will show that whatever
happens to anybody it may be
turned to beautiful results—and I
will show that nothing can happen
more beautiful than Death.'

It is thus that he speaks in his 'Song at
Sunset' of—'the superb vistas of Death.'
It is thus that in his poem addressed 'To
one Shortly to Die,' he closes it not in
pity but in felicitation—

'I do not commiserate—I congratulate
you.'

It is thus he sings exultantly—

'I shall go with the rest.
We cannot be stopped at a given
point—that is no satisfaction,
To show us a good thing, or a few
good things, for a space of time—
that is no satisfaction;
We must have the indestructible
breed of the best, regardless of
time.
If otherwise, all these things come
but to ashes of dung
If maggots and rats ended us, then
alarum! for we are betrayed!
Then indeed suspicion of death.
Do you suspect death? If I were to

suspect death I should die now:
Do you think I could walk pleasantly
and well suited toward
annihilation?'

Consonant with his rapturous exultation
in the thought of Death, consonant with
his homage for the perfection of the universe, are his absolute confidence in the
reality of the future, and his profound
sense that all that is holiest has never yet
in any way been adequately realised or
appreciated:—

'I say the whole earth, and all the
stars in the sky, are for religion's
sake.
I say no man has ever yet been half
devout enough,
None has ever yet adored or
worshipped half enough;
None has begun to think how divine
he himself is, and how certain the
future is.'

Hence he sings, hence he is a Poet, hence
he undertakes in these poems of his to
write the 'evangel-poem of comrades and
love.' Akin to his overflowing delight in
the thought of the Now and the Hereafter, are the largeness and the depth,
the exquisite self-abnegation and the all-
embracing comprehensiveness of his humanity. To the very dregs and scum and
squalor of the evil streets of a bad city he
cries out—by a subtle violation of grammar, as it seems to us, i.e., in the verb we
have italicised in the subjoined quotation,
appealing to them as though he spoke
with them from their own level—

'Because you are greasy and pimpled,
or that you *was* drunk, or a thief,
Or diseased, or rheumatic, or a
prostitute, or are so now,
Or from frivolity or impotence, or
that you are no scholar, and never
saw your name in print,

154

Do you give in that you are any less immortal?'

At the City Dead House in his *Leaves of Grass*, we see him standing—gazing—yearning, in tenderest pity and commiseration over—what? over 'an outcast form,' indeed, over the body of a poor dead prostitute—

'The divine woman, her body—I see her body—I look on it alone,
That house, once full of passion and beauty—all else I notice not;
No stillness so cold, nor running water from faucet, nor odours morbific impress me;
But the house alone—that wondrous house—that delicate fair house—that ruin!
That immortal house, more than all the rows of dwellings ever built,
Or white domed Capitol itself, with majestic figures surmounted—or all the old high-spired cathedrals,
That little house alone more than them all—poor desperate house!
Fair, fearful work! tenement of a Soul! itself a Soul!
Unclaimed, avoided house! take one breath from my tremulous lips;
Take one tear, dropped aside as I go, for thought of you,
Dead house of love! house of madness and sin, crumbled! crushed!
House of life—ere while talking and laughing—but, oh, poor house! dead even then;
Months, years, an echoing, garnished house—but dead dead, dead.'

So wide, so profound, so insatiable are the yearnings of this great heart for sympathy, that on turning to his poem on 'Envy' what do we find to be the cause of his Envy? Not a perusal of the records of heroism, not the thought of Mighty Generals or Men in Power, but—when he reads of the brotherhood of lovers—

'How through life, through dangers, odium, unchanging, long and long,
Through youth, and through middle and through old age, how unfaltering, how affectionate, and faithful they were,
Then I am pensive—I hastily put down the book, and walk away, filled with the bitterest envy.'

In illustration of the same thought, or rather of the same tender, yearning for sympathy, read his commemoration of 'Parting Friends,'—

'Two simple men I saw to-day on the pier, in the midst of the crowd parting the parting of dear friends;
The one to remain hung on the other's neck and passionately kissed him,
Whilst the one to depart tightly pressed the one to remain in his arms.'

Or, still more, the Poet's apostrophe 'To a Stranger':—

'Passing stranger! you do not know how longingly I look upon you.'

Most of all this yearning for sympathy shines forth when it is recognised 'Among the Multitude'; when, in other words, the Poet foresees it, thus—

'Among the men and women, the multitude
I perceive one picking me out by secret and divine signs,
Acknowledging none else—not parent, wife, husband, brother, child, any nearer than I am:

Some are baffled—But that one is
  not—that one knows me.
Ah! lover and perfect equal!
I meant that you should discover me
  so, by my faint indirections;
And I, when I meet you, mean to
  discover you by the like in you.'

So, too, he sees them afar off in foreign
lands, those breasts with whom his own
could sympathise could they be brought
into communion:—

'O I know we should be brethren and
  lovers—
I know I should be happy with
  them.'

It were idle, however, attempting to afford the reader any adequate notion of
these poems as a symmetrical whole,
through mere fragmentary or incidental
quotations like those to which a reviewer
is necessarily restricted. It would be worse
than the proffering of the specimen-brick
by the house-vendor in Hierocles—it
would be the production of a handful of
splinters chipped off the Apollo Belvi-
dere, or of a stray finger torn from the
Venus de Medici. Whitman's Poems—as
is the case with every true work of art—
must be viewed each in its entirety before
there can be any hope whatever of
their accurate appreciation. So regarded,
they cannot fail by any possibility, as
we conceive, to win the admiration to
which they are so signally entitled. After
this fashion alone—that is to say at
once, searchingly and comprehensively—
ought at any time to be examined, that
noble apostrophe, beginning at page 310,
To Death, that profound and heart-
penetrating epitome of Human Life, com-
mencing at page 356, that no less effective and affecting poem upon Night and
Death which opens at page 266, but
above all the magnificent Nocturn upon

the Death of President Lincoln beginning
at page 301, and, what is to our mind
even finer than that, the exquisitely pathetic and pre-eminently beautiful celebration
by Walt Whitman of the first revelation to
himself of his own powers and future
path in life as a poet, when, as a little
barefooted child, he stood upon the sea-
shore one evening and far on into the
night, listening to the lamentations of the
song-bird bereaved of its mate, himself
drowned in tears as he listened—standing, there, entranced in the moonlight
drinking in the music of that delicate and
tender death-chant! Never before was the
song of a bird so put into human language—never before was the rapturous
anguish of the poetic summons so articulated. It is Béranger's *Ma Vocation* repeated:
when—speaking of himself as a mere infant—the old Chansonnier sings to us—

'Une plainte touchante,
  De ma bouche sortit;
  Le bon Dieu me dit: Chante,
  Chante, pauvre petit.'

And now that Whitman has sung (and is
still, for that matter, happily singing in
the midst of us) in obedience to the holy
mandate by which every true poet is at
the outset made aware of his vocation, he
has as profound a sense of the reality of
that summons, and of the consequent
permanence or security of his reputation
as a Poet, as ever Horace had when
proudly forecasting his own poetic immortality. Assuming to himself at once
his right position in English Literature,
he has even, as it happens, like almost all
the more remarkable poets in our language, selected, unconsciously it may be,
but unmistakably his own especial em-
blem! Henceforth, as it seems to us, *his*
inalienably and no other's! A floral em-
blem to be worn by him from this time
forth as conspicuously as the sprig of

bloom fastened of old on the helmet of the first Plantaganet. In this, as we have just now intimated, it is with him, as it has been before him with his compeer and his congeners, the majority of the great poets in our language. Has not Moore, for example, in this way taken to himself for ever as his the shamrock—and Scott the purpling heather—and Campbell the red velvet strings of love-lies-bleeding? Has not Keats his sprig of basil—and Blair his branch of funereal yew—and Chatterton his trail of lamenting willow? But that Burns, again, according [to] his own showing, was endowed by his Muse (the Muse of Scotland) with the glistening bough of the holly, he might perchance have contested with Dan Chaucer the latter's now undisputed right to the possession as his of the darling blossom of the daisy. As indubitably, moreover, as the daisy belongs to Chaucer and the holly to Burns—so has Shelley assumed to himself the sensitive plant, and Wordsworth the little celandine and the daffodils, and Cowper the rose and the water lily, and Leigh Hunt the flowering branch of May, and Tennyson the gorgeous blossom of the passion flower, if only by right of the 'splendid tear' shed upon it at the garden porch in 'Maud,' and Milton 'the yellow cowslip and the pale primrose,' and Shakespeare, for that matter, almost every bloom of the parterre or of the wilderness. And, as it has been with those, so it is now and henceforth with this true American Poet Walt Whitman, who has made the lilac—the fragrant, blueish-pink blossoms of the lilac—his own completely. Turning the leaves of these poems, the reader may say before the book is closed as the Poet himself says or rather sings with a sort of rapture—

'Yet the lilac with mastering odour holds me.'

For it blossoms, and breathes forth its haunting perfume, and verdantly unfolds its delicate heart-shaped leaves, again and again, all through these pages—more especially in the great Nocturn on the Death of President Lincoln. And so, with the fragrance of the lilacs in our nostrils, and with the song of the lamenting bird in our ears, and with the thought in our hearts of the manly poet himself going his sickening rounds in the ghastly hospitals, all through the great American War, accompanied, as he went down the wards, by his attendant, bearing sponge, and pail, and lint, and ointment, for the cleansing and the binding up of many loathsome wounds, we close this beautiful volume with a renewal of our grateful acknowledgments to Mr. Rossetti, and with a benison to Walt Whitman.

"Poems by Walt Whitman." *Lloyd's Weekly London Newspaper*, 19 April 1868, p. 8.

Englishmen know nothing of Walt (Walter) Whitman, except the occasional brilliant scraps which English papers copy from their American contemporaries. Englishmen know nothing—excepting the very few cultivated Englishmen who have crossed the Atlantic, met the author, and learned to admire him and his books. Mr. William Michael Rossetti has been for some time what may be called a disciple of Whitman. If he did not absolutely discover him, he was at least one of the very first who heard of the discovery. Here is the result: a volume, a selection of Mr. Whitman's poems, containing probably one-half of what he has written, and that half *not necessarily the best*. And here it must be said, that having read the volume with great interest—for Rumour had been busy—and with deep gratification, for the present we must suffer description to assume the place of criticism, since one reading is quite insufficient, and time is required in order that the strangeness of the beauty may be absorbed and assimilated, before any proper estimate of it could be formed. It is strange, at the outset, to find that the other half of the author's writings is so disfigured by violation of morality and decency, as to be rather too much for the English reader; and, stranger still, to hear Mr. Rossetti praying for a complete edition. As far as can be made out, Mr. Whitman considers everything noble, because of divine origin, and everything a fair subject for words. Therefore he goes on about matters fleshly, spiritual, and mixed—always calling spades spades, in a fashion not to be tolerated by ordinary nerves. It will be observed that the volume is called "Poems," and it is certain that not one man in a thousand would so describe them. And yet we can say that there is not one page which is not thoroughly poetic. The simple thing is, not that there is no rhyme—which is, of course, unessential; but that there is no rhythm, no measure, no attempt at complying with any of the universally known demands of *versification*, and which we are still simple enough to consider one of the absolute demands of poetry. A skin of kid is not a kid glove. This is a dilemma which the ordinary English reader will find difficult to get over; but he must read Mr. Rossetti's prefatory sketch, which is in every way an excellent piece of writing from an accomplished man, and which seems to err only on the side of absolute infatuation. Mr. Rossetti insists that it must be taken as an altogether new poetry: as something as distinctively American as Niagara and the Rocky Mountains, and having no more in common with English poetry than Niagara has with the dripping well at Hastings, or the Rocky Mountains with Primrose-hill! A specimen or two of these strange productions shall be given; but it is proper to say that they are amongst the most musical we can find, and the easiest to understand. The author is always mystical—always democratic—always speaking in ghastly praise of death. But he roams over every or any kind of subject, and seems always to be in "communion with nature." He chatters with the birds, and is sometimes as incomprehensible. And he hurls large sayings at the mountains, who echo back peal after peal, and all of which enthusiasts are humbly entreated to suppose that the author understands! Here is an exquisitely musical little piece, the commencement of President Lincoln's Funeral Hymn:—

When lilacs last in the door-yard
  bloomed,
And the great star early drooped in
  the western sky in the night,
I mourned.... and yet shall mourn
  with ever-returning spring.
O ever-returning spring! trinity sure
  to me you bring;
Lilac blooming perennial, and
  drooping star in the west,
And thought of him I love.

O powerful, western, fallen star!
O shades of night! O moody, tearful
  night!
O great star disappeared! O the black
  murk that hides the star!
O cruel hands that hold me
  powerless! O helpless soul of me!
O harsh surrounding cloud that will
  not free my soul!

In the door-yard, fronting an old
  farm-house, near the whitewashed
  palings,

Stands the lilac bush, tall-growing,
with heart-shaped leaves of rich
green,
With many a pointed blossom, rising
delicate, with the perfume strong I
love,
With every leaf a miracle; and from
this bush in the door-yard,
With delicate-coloured blossoms, and
heart-shaped leaves of rich green,
A sprig, with its flower, I break.

In the swamp, in secluded recesses,
A shy and hidden bird is warbling a
song.
Solitary, the thrush,
The hermit, withdrawn to himself,
avoiding the settlements,
Sings by himself a song.
Song of the bleeding throat!
Death's outlet song of life—for well,
dear brother, I know,
If thou wast not gifted to sing, thou
would surely die.

Page after page of this curiously poetical "Funeral Hymn" might be reprinted
here, for the reader's pleasure; but our
object is to provoke, not to appease, the
taste. Here is another short piece which is
perfect—that is, complete. In it may be
seen with what brilliant novelty the poet
can handle the grimmest possible of all
earthly and spiritual subjects:—

TO ONE SHORTLY TO DIE.

From all the rest I single out you,
having a message for you;
You are to die—Let others tell you
what they please, I cannot
prevaricate,
I am exact and merciless; but I love
you—there is no escape for you.

Softly I lay my right hand upon
you—you just feel it;
I do not argue—I bend my head
close, and half-envelop it,

I sit quietly by—I remain faithful,
I am more than nurse, more than
parent or neighbour,
I absolve you from all except
yourself, spiritual, bodily—that is
eternal—
The corpse you will leave will be but
excrementitious.
The sun bursts through in unlooked
for directions!
Strong thoughts fill you, and
confidence—you smile!
You forget you are sick, as I forget
you are sick.
You do not see the medicines—you
do not mind the weeping friends—I
am with you.
I exclude others from you—there is
nothing to be commiserated,
I do not commiserate—I congratulate
you.

Let people quarrel as they please about
what is or is not poetry; but Mr. Walt
Whitman is beyond all question a poet.

Athenæum 2113
(25 April 1868), 585–6.

The selections here given from the poems of Walt Whitman form, we are told,
nearly half of his entire works. Mr.
Rossetti's objects in the present compila-
tion have been, first, to exclude every
poem that could fairly be deemed offensive; and, secondly, to include whatever, being free from just or unjust censure on the ground of decorum, is at the
same time highest as poetry and most
characteristic of the writer. The editor
has wisely, and with a proper reverence
for one in whose genius he believes,
refrained from culling what are called

"beauties" from such poems as might be thought objectionable. He has hacked and spoilt no piece by depriving it of the unity and continuity which make it vital; and thus, though we have not here the whole of Whitman, what we have is genuinely his own. It follows from the process adopted that we are not now called upon to weigh the accusations which have been brought against the writer in America for his license of expression in morals (morals being, of course, to be understood in a special and restricted sense), but simply to examine his credentials as a poet.

In a Preface which, on the whole, is written with his usual discernment and happiness of exposition, Mr. Rossetti observes of Whitman, "He may be termed formless by those who, not without much reason to show for themselves, are wedded to the established forms and ratified refinements of poetic art; but it seems reasonable to enlarge the canon till it includes so great and startling a genius, rather than to draw it close and exclude him." We see, however, no reason why the usual definition of an art should be changed for the sake of embracing in its limits one who might otherwise stand without them. The question now at issue, is not whether Mr. Whitman is a great thinker, but whether he is a great poet. Now, by common consent the vital constituents of poetry are emotion and imagination. By imagination we mean the power of conceiving ideas and of representing them by adequate symbols to the senses.

Judged by this admitted test, what shall we say of Walt Whitman? That some entire poems in this collection, and many scattered passages in other poems, bear the test triumphantly, few, if qualified to judge, will doubt. On the other hand, we have here many pages (probably the greater number) of which it would be difficult to maintain that they are poetry in any sense of that word which has yet been accepted. Thus, in the address 'To Working Men,' who can say that, however exalted by the prevailing idea of the piece, any item in the following catalogue, with the one exception marked in italics, is in itself poetical?—

House-building, measuring, sawing
    the boards;
Blacksmithing, glass-blowing, nail-
    making, coopering, tin-roofing,
    shingle-dressing,
Ship-joining, dock-building, fish-
    curing, ferrying, flagging of side-
    walks by flaggers,
The pump, the pile-driver, the great
    derrick, the coal-kiln and brick-
    kiln,
Coal-mines, and all that is down
    there,—the lamps in the darkness,
    echoes, songs, what meditations,
    what *vast native thoughts looking
    through smutched faces,*
Iron-works, forge-fires in the
    mountains, or by the riverbanks—
    men around feeling the melt with
    huge crowbars—lumps of ore, the
    due combining of ore, limestone,
    coal—the blast-furnace and the
    puddling-furnace, the loup-lump at
    the bottom of the melt at last—the
    rolling-mill, the stumpy bars of pig-
    iron, the strong, clean-shaped T-rail
    for railroads;
Oil-works, silk-works, white-lead-
    works, the sugar-house, steam-
    saws, the great mills and factories.

Even in the composition called 'A Poet,' which, besides its high strain of thought, is very interesting as a revelation of Whitman's individuality, there is far more of theory than of imagination. When he writes of the poet—

160

Him all wait for—him all yield up
  to—his word is decisive and final,
Him they accept, in him lave, in him
  perceive themselves, as amid light,
Him they immerse, and he immerses
  them.
Beautiful women, the haughtiest
  nations, laws, the landscape,
  people, animals,
The profound earth and its attributes,
  and the unquiet ocean (so tell I my
  morning's romanza),
All enjoyments and properties, and
  money, and whatever money will buy,
The best farms—others toiling and
  planting, and he unavoidably
  reaps,
The noblest and costliest cities—
  others grading and building, and
  he domiciles there,
Nothing for anyone, but what is for
  him—near and far are for him,—
  the ships in the offing,
The perpetual shows and marches on
  land, are for him, if they are for
  anybody—

the reader may or may not find in the
lines truth of doctrine, but he assuredly
will not find beauty of expression. Turning, on the contrary, to the pieces named
respectively 'Assimilations,' 'Burial,' 'The
Waters,' 'A Ship,' 'President Lincoln's Funeral Hymn,' and 'A Word out of the Sea,'
he will scarcely deny that they possess
striking truth and beauty of description,
and, still better, that subtle and informing
power which unobtrusively converts all
outward things into symbols, just as the
soul makes for itself a symbol of the
body which it pervades and rules. This
unconscious power of symbolization—
quite distinct from, and even opposed to,
the mechanical ingenuity of allegory—
is nowhere more delightfully evinced by
Whitman than in 'A Word out of the
Sea,' to our thinking *the* poem of the

book. A boy discovers a bird's-nest in
some briars that skirt the sea-shore. Day
after day he watches the movements of
the male bird and his mate, listens to the
singing and the chirping by which they
express their happiness. At length,

  May-be killed unknown to her mate,
  One forenoon the she-bird crouched
    not on the nest,
  Nor returned that afternoon, nor the
    next,
  Nor ever returned again.

The boy continues to note the solitary
bird flitting restlessly from spot to spot
on the shore, and at times pouring forth
a mournful song, the desolation, the longing and the brief beguiling hope of which
the listener translates into human speech.
To the boy's ear the bird sings as follows:—

  Soothe! soothe! soothe!
  Close on its wave soothes the wave
    behind,
  And again another behind, embracing
    and lapping, every one close,—
  But my love soothes not me, not me.
  Low hangs the moon—it rose late;
  O it is lagging—O I think it is heavy
    with love, with love.
  O madly the sea pushes, pushes upon
    the land,
  With love—with love.
  O night! do I not see my love
    fluttering out there among the
    breakers?
  What is that little black thing I see
    there in the white?
  Loud! loud! loud!
  Loud I call to you, my love!
  High and clear I shoot my voice over
    the waves;
  Surely you must know who is here, is
    here;
  You must know who I am, my love.

161

Low-hanging moon!
What is that dusky spot in your
    brown yellow?
O it is the shape, the shape of my
    mate!
O moon, do not keep her from me
    any longer!
Land! land! O land!
Whichever way I turn, O I think you
    could give me my mate back again,
    if you only would;
For I am almost sure I see her dimly
    whichever way I look.
O rising stars!
Perhaps the one I want so much will
    rise, will rise with some of you.
O throat! O trembling throat!
Sound clearer through the
    atmosphere!
Pierce the woods, the earth;
Somewhere, listening to catch you,
    must be the one I want.

Shake out, carols!
Solitary here—the night's carols!
Carols of lonesome love! Death's
    carols!
Carols under that lagging, yellow,
    waning moon!
O, under that moon, where she
    droops almost down into the sea!
O reckless, despairing carols!
But soft! sink low;
Soft! let me just murmur;
And do you wait a moment, you
    husky-nosed sea;
For somewhere I believe I heard my
    mate responding to me,
So faint—I must be still, be still to
    listen;
But not altogether still, for then she
    might not come immediately to me.
Hither, my love!
Here I am! Here!
With this just sustained note I
    announce myself to you;
This gentle call is for you, my love,
    for you!

Do not be decoyed elsewhere!
O I am very sick and sorrowful!
O brown halo in the sky, near the
    moon, drooping upon the sea!
O troubled reflection in the sea!
O throat! O throbbing heart!
O all!—and I singing uselessly,
    uselessly all the night!
Yet I murmur, murmur on!
O murmurs—you yourselves make
    me continue to sing, I know not
    why.
O past! O life! O songs of joy!
In the air—in the woods—over fields;
Loved! loved! loved! loved! loved!
But my love no more, no more with
    me!
We two together no more!

The plaint of the bird arouses in the
boy, too, the sense of something missed
and yearned for. A joy has vanished from
the soul as its mate from the bird. Shall
the ideal of youth that has taken wing return to earth no more? Shall the yearning
for it ever be satisfied, and by what?—

Answering, the Sea,
Delaying not, hurrying not,
Whispered me through the night and
    very plainly before daybreak,
Lisped to me the low and delicious
    word death.

Of the sublimated passion and sweetness of the above, of the minuteness with
which the most delicate transitions of
feeling are caught, and of the grand yet
melancholy suggestiveness which sets the
whole picture, as it were, in a frame of
sad sunset glory, we can hardly speak in
terms of praise too high. That Whitman
can write noble poetry, this one example
conclusively testifies.

Of the writer, generally, it may be
said, that he is universal in his sympathies, (with the sole exception that he
cannot recognize the possibility of good-

ness in any man who happens to be born an aristocrat,)—that (with this exception) he believes in the capacity for virtue, latent or developed, of all his fellows—believes that the best man is but the full and perfected expression of the worth and power hidden in the worst,—believes that in point of art it is right to express in speech all that is true in fact, and to regard all processes and things, natural or mechanical, that have once been associated with man as sanctified thereby. The "*homo sum*" and the deductions drawn from it, have never found a more zealous advocate.

It is difficult to describe a mind so varied and yet so peculiar in a few phrases. Yet we will venture to designate Mr. Whitman as a wide, sincere, passionate thinker,—presenting in himself a new combination of separate views, which are not particularly new in themselves. This is not said to his disadvantage, for truisms, after all, lie at the root of the world's progress. The expansiveness of his mind includes imagination, no doubt, but rather as a constituent than as a characteristic. He resembles those vast tracts of country in which is found the utmost diversity of surface, and in which long intervals of homely or even barren scenery precede and succeed glorious manifestations of Nature. He is so large and generic in his mode of thinking that he often scatters beauty in the seed rather than reveals it in the flowers; at other times, nothing can surpass the truthful minuteness with which he paints the most delicate *nuances* of feeling. He is a fine poet, though it would be a great error to say that all is poetry to which he has given the name.

For a brief and excellent summary of Whitman's life and writings, we refer the reader to Mr. Rossetti's Preface—a composition disfigured only by a somewhat puerile display of contempt for his fellow critics. His allegations against them may or may not be just; but their errors, if real, would have been more gracefully improved by that superior example which Mr. Rossetti so consciously affords, than by his unnecessary invectives.

"Walt Whitman's Poems." *Saturday Review* 25 (2 May 1868), 589–90.

Some years ago, when a few copies of a volume called *Leaves of Grass* found their way into this country from America, the general verdict of those who had an opportunity of examining the book was that much of it was indescribably filthy, most of it mere incoherent rhapsody, none of it what could be termed poetry in any sense of the word, and that, unless at the hands of some enterprising Holywell Street publisher, it had no chance of the honour of an English reprint. In part this opinion is already proved to have been a mistaken one, for a West-end publisher has taken compassion on the stranger, and now presents it to the British public in a comely form. It may be as well to state at the outset, that the volume published by Mr. Hotten is not precisely a reprint of the original *Leaves of Grass*. It contains much new matter written since the appearance of that work, and does *not* contain any of the pieces marked by that peculiar freedom of speech which is generally associated in men's minds with the name of Walt Whitman. For the sake of all parties, the prurient as well as the prudish, lest the one should be unnecessarily alarmed or the other led into an unremunerative venture, it is only fair to say that there is nothing in the present edition to disqualify it for decent society, not to say qualify it for a place in the *Bibliothèque bleue*. It has cost Mr. Rossetti severe pangs, so he informs us, to part with so much as, from considerations of prudence, he has been obliged to exclude. "This peculiarly nervous age," this "mealy-mouthed British nineteenth century," with its present absurd notions about decency, morality, and propriety, could not be expected to receive "the indecencies scattered through Whitman's writings" in that æsthetic spirit in which they should be accepted; and, as he was unwilling to mutilate, "the consequence is that the reader loses *in toto* several important poems, and some extremely fine ones—notably one of quite exceptional value and excellence, entitled *Walt Whitman*." In one respect we are willing to admit the loss sustained in this last instance. The "poem" here referred to is the one which contains the key to Walt Whitman's philosophy and poetic theory. It is in it that he describes himself and his qualifications for the office of poet of the future, grounding his claim upon the fact of his being "hankering, gross, mystical, nude, one of the roughs, a kosmos, disorderly, fleshy, sensual, no more modest than immodest"; and proposing to produce poetry of corresponding qualities, a promise which we must say he most conscientiously fulfils. Its excellence may be open to question, but about its value to the reader who wishes to understand Walt Whitman there can be no doubt whatever.

The present edition is to be considered as an experiment. By excluding everything offensive, the editor hopes to induce people to reconsider the case of Walt Whitman, and reverse the verdict which has been already pronounced. This, we need scarcely observe, is rather more than they can be fairly asked to do, while the evidence which supports the gravest of the charges brought against him is suppressed. But this is not all that Mr. Rossetti expects. The present selection is so to brace and fortify the British mind that in a short time, he trusts, it will be able to relish what now in its weakness it rejects. A complete edition of Walt Whitman, with all the dirt left in, he looks forward to as "the right and crowning result" of his labours. This is but the schoolboy's pudding, which, if we only finish it off, is to be succeeded by a full meal of the uncommonly strong meat he has in reserve for us. A fellow-countryman of the poet's, who had unsuccessfully besieged the virtue of a married lady, is said to have consoled himself with the reflection that, at any rate, he had "lowered her moral tone some." Though he himself had not gained his point, his labours, he thought, had diminished the difficulties in the way of the next comer. Something of this sort appears to be the modest mission of the present volume. We must confess we should very much prefer to see Mr. Rossetti employing himself on some task more worthy of his abilities. He has on many occasions done good service as a critic to literature and art, but we cannot look upon his present enterprise as one in any way beneficial to either. He desires to have Walt Whitman recognised, not merely as a great poet, but as the founder of a new school of poetic literature which is to be greater and more powerful than any the world has yet seen. He is not, it is true, entirely alone in this attempt. There have been already certain indications of a Walt Whitman movement in one or two other quarters. More than a year ago there was a paper in the *Fortnightly Review*, which, however, was not so much a criticism of his poetry as of his person, the writer having had, as well as we recollect, the privilege of reviewing him as he bathed—an important advantage, certainly, in the case of a poet whose principal theme is his own body. Then Mr. Robert Buchanan took him up in the *Broadway* magazine, and, saying nearly all that has ever been said against Walt Whitman—that he is no poet and no artist, that he is gross, monotonous, loud, obscure, prone to coarse animalism and to talking rank nonsense—nevertheless arrived at pretty much the same conclusion as Mr. Rossetti, at least as to the powerful influence he is to exercise over the literature of the future. Something of this sort we might, indeed, have expected. There are people whose reading of the Horatian saying about popular opinion is "*nunquam* vulgus rectum videt," and who always set themselves to find virtues in everything that is generally condemned. Besides, it would be idle to deny that Walt Whitman has many attractions for minds of a certain class. He is loud, swaggering, and self-assertive, and so gets credit for strength with those who worship nothing that is not strong. He is utterly lawless, and in consequence passes for being a great original genius. His produce is unlike anything else that has ever appeared in literature, and that is enough for those who are always on the look-out for novelty. He is rich in all those qualities of haziness, incoherence, and obscurity which seem to be the first that some readers nowadays look for in poetry. But, above all, he runs amuck with conventionalities and decencies of every sort, which naturally endears him to those silly people who take a childish delight in seeing the respectabilities of the world pulled by the nose, and what they consider its stupid prejudices shocked. We need scarcely say we do not suspect a man of Mr. Rossetti's taste and judgment of this kind of enthusiasm. If we were to hazard a theory, we should be inclined to attribute his advocacy of Walt Whitman's poetical claims to an impatience of the feebleness, emptiness, and sentimentality so abundant in modern poetry. The feeling is one with which we do not quarrel; we only object to the form in which it finds expression. A plague of tinkling cymbals is not to be met by a counter-treatment of sounding brass.

An admirer of Walt Whitman has one immense advantage. There is no standard by which his idol can be measured, no known test which can be applied to prove his quality. There is, therefore, a wide field for that dogmatic assertion which is the favourite argument of the transcendental critic. You must not object that his poetry has no melody, music, or form. It is something above and beyond all requirements of that kind. You are not to raise the objection that in a great deal of what he writes there is no meaning at all, and in a great deal more the meaning, when got at, is utterly commonplace. Poetry like Walt Whitman's is not to be judged of by any one who is influenced by narrow considerations of meaning. You are not to take exception to his language, that it is a vile jargon of his own coining. A poet of this order naturally rises above the trammels of precedent in the matter of language. As to the absence of imagination, invention, fancy, art, and sundry other things more or less looked for in poetry, to complain of this in the present instance only shows that you are incapable of understanding the subject. This sort of argument always tells powerfully with the timid, with those people who are haunted by a nervous dread of being set down as dull and commonplace if they allow common sense to influence their judgment; and besides, it has the merit of being unanswerable, except by contradiction. When a man shows you something with all the outward and visible signs of a wheelbarrow, and tells you it is an Act of Parliament, it is very hard to know what to say to him; and it is just as hard to know what to say when you are offered something like the following and told it is poetry, and poetry of a very high order. As the admirers of Walt Whitman always protest against his being judged of fragmentarily, we take the shortest poem we can find, instead of giving the queerest extract:—

VISAGES.

Of the visages of things—And of
    piercing through to the accepted
    hells beneath.
Of ugliness—To me there is just as
    much in it as there is in beauty—
    And now the ugliness of human
    beings is acceptable to me.
Of detected persons—To me, detected
    persons are not, in any respect,
    worse than undetected persons—
    and are not in any respect worse
    than I am myself.
Of criminals—To me, any judge, or
    any juror, is equally criminal—and
    any reputable person is also—and
    the President is also.

Now it may be that this is not balderdash, though we must confess to a strong suspicion that it is; but if it is poetry, all we can say is, we must find some other word for Shakespeare. Walt Whitman himself is much more candid on this point than his advocates. He certainly declares himself to be a poet, but at the same time he describes the offspring of his muse as a "barbaric yawp." We have no very definite idea as to the precise nature of a yawp, but, whatever it may be, it can scarcely be poetry.

We must do Mr. Rossetti the justice of admitting that he does not entirely rely on dogmatism in pleading the cause of his *protégé*. He does assign some few reasons why Walt Whitman should be accepted as "the poet of the epoch." In a paper which appeared in a weekly journal, he puts the claim on the rather curi-

ous ground of his being "an initiator in the scheme and structure of his writings, and an individual of audacious personal ascendant." But in the preface to the present volume he comes more plainly to the point. The reader, he says, is not to ask himself, or return any answer to the questions, whether or not Walt Whitman is like other poets, or whether or not the particular application of rules of art which is found to hold good in the works of other poets, and to constitute a part of their excellence, can be traced also in his work. "Let the questions rather be—Is he powerful? Is he American? Is he new? Is he rousing? Does he feel, and make me feel?" To each of these questions we should be disposed to answer simply "No," were it not that an unqualified negative is scarcely polite. We can see no reason for considering Walt Whitman powerful. Strong he may be, but it is only in the sense in which an onion is strong. His noise, bluster, and arrogance are no more indications of true strength than the swagger of the professional athlete at a country fair, who struts up and down the stage in salmon-coloured tights, and passes for a Hercules with the crowd from the way in which he feels his muscles in public. That he is American in one sense we must admit. He is something which no other country could have produced. He is American as certain forms of rowdyism and vulgarity, excrescences on American institutions, are American. But that he is American in the sense of being representative of American taste, intellect, or cultivation, we should be very sorry indeed to believe. New he certainly is, but it is only in his audacity, and in the abnormal structure of his poetry; there is not a new thought in his writings from beginning to end. As to the other questions, the answer must depend very much on individual temperament. Whether or not he himself feels we cannot tell, but, so far from being rousing or making his reader feel, we should say that with ninety-nine out of a hundred average readers Walt Whitman, taken in any quantity, would be found to be about as soporific a poet as ever produced a yawn. But even if all these questions could be answered in the affirmative—even if we were to concede that Walt Whitman is powerful and new and American and rousing, and throw into the bargain what his friends invariably lay great stress upon, his magnificent physique and his irreproachable character in private life—still all this, we submit, does not make him out to be a poet. To call a man a poet merely because he holds forth in rhapsodical style about one man being as good as another, everything being all right, every one having a right "to do as he dam pleases"—if we may venture to quote the concise language of Transatlantic liberty—and other dogmas of the same sort, is to confuse the functions of the poet and the stump orator; and generally, when Walt Whitman has any meaning at all, it amounts to no more than this. Very often he has no meaning whatever. In his fury he breaks out into a mere perspiration of words, and strings substantives together for pages on a stretch, the result being a something which is as much like poetry as an auctioneer's catalogue. To be sure there is scattered through his pages a vast amount of that vagueness which to some tastes has the true poetic charm. No doubt there are people who consider this sort of thing very fine:—

OF THE TERRIBLE DOUBT OF
APPEARANCES.

The skies of day and night—colours,
densities, forms—May-be these are
(as doubtless they are) only
apparitions, and the real something
has yet to be known;

May-be seeming to me what they are
(as doubtless they indeed but seem)
as from my present point of view—
And might prove (as of course they
would) naught of what they
appear, or naught anyhow, from
entirely changed points of view.

But if it is very fine, then so is Miss Codger's outburst on being introduced to Elijah Pogram:—

But why we call them so, or why
impressed they are, or if impressed
they are at all, or if at all we are, or
if there really is, oh gasping one! a
Pogram or a Hominy, or any active
principle, to which we give those titles, is a topic, spirit-searching, light-
abandoned, much too vast to enter on.

But of course the special charm of Walt Whitman is that he is so—what his admirers call—unconventional; that is, that he says things which other people do not say, and in language which other people do not generally use. His unconventionality, however, is of a very cheap sort. It is nothing more than the unconventionality of the man who considers clothes conventional, and goes about without them. It is true that for the present we are spared the bolder strokes of his genius in this respect, but, as has been already mentioned, it is only for the present; and besides, Walt Whitman's grossness is not accidental, but constitutional. It arises partly from an insensibility to the difference between that which is naturally offensive and that which is not, partly from his peculiar theory of poetry. As it is a fundamental principle of his to recognise no law of any kind, and to submit to no restrictions of artistic propriety, it follows that with him all subjects are equally fit for poetic treatment. As Mr. Rossetti puts it, "he knows of no reason why what is universally seen and known, necessary and right, should not also be allowed and proclaimed in speech," and it is just this ignorance of his which, independently of other reasons, makes any attempt to set him up as a poetic model mischievous to the interests of literary art. It is not a question of squeamishness or hyper-sensitiveness. There is no prudery in objecting to nastiness, nor is there any originality, honesty, manliness, or courage in obtruding what even instinct teaches us to avoid. We cannot say, however, that we anticipate any serious injury to English or American literature from the influence or popularity of Walt Whitman's poetry, so long at least as people are courageous enough to use their common sense, and do not allow themselves to be led away by transcendental "highfalutin" into pretending an admiration which they do not feel.

"Walt Whitman."
Chambers's Journal of Popular Literature, Science, and Art 45 (4 July 1868), 420–5.

Faint praise may harm the prose-writer, but there is nothing which predisposes us against a poet so much as extravagant praise; if we are not very young, and have little enthusiasm to spare about anything, we especially resent it. The unreasonable laudation (now so common) makes us as unreasonably despise its object. 'As it is impossible to conceive a world without a Shakespeare, so we cannot picture it to ourselves without this new sweet singer, Jones.' Bother Jones! We that have known Keats and Shelley, and Byron, and Wordsworth and Coleridge, to be told that there has been no such poet as Jones!

Not a little ludicrous eulogy of this sort has been poured of late upon the American poet whose name stands at the head of this paper, but he is really noteworthy nevertheless. He is the first characteristic poetical writer that the United States have produced. Longfellow is but Tennyson and water; and as for the other Transatlantic bards, they have produced solitary poems of great merit, but none which might not have been written by an Englishman of genius, who had paid great attention to the panoramas of the Mississippi or of the Prairies which have been unfolded from time to time in Leicester Square. Whitman's very faults are national. The brag, and bluster, and self-assertion of the man are American only; the fulsome 'cracking-up' of his own nation is such as would not be ventured upon by a British bard; the frequent bathos—the use of newspaper terms and of terms which have no existence out of New York, and in which you almost hear the American nasal twang, are all characteristic. He is Yankee to the backbone; Yankee, also, it must however be added, in his outspoken independence of thought, in his audacious originality, in his perfect freedom from conventional twaddle, and in his contempt for accidental rank of all sorts. He has named half his volume 'Chants Democratic,' and though they are not chants, nor anything like it, they are certainly democratic. He does not write verse at all, which is fortunate, for he would certainly not be particular about his rhymes; nor does he even write blank verse; but he has invented a certain rolling changeful metre of his own, with, as his English editor truly remarks, 'a very powerful and majestic rhythmical sense throughout.' He sometimes furnishes long strings of detached items—very like the list of goods furnished by shops to their customers; but they are 'not devoid of a certain primitive effectiveness' by any means.

The doctrine of *nihil humanum*, &c. was never pushed to such extreme limits as by Walt Whitman. If a man could gain the suffrages of the human race by flattering them with the sense of their tremendous importance, this poet would be king of the world.

> Small is the theme of the following
> chant, yet the greatest—namely,
> ONE'S-SELF; that wondrous thing, a
> simple separate person. That, for
> the use of the New World, I sing.
> Man's physiology complete, from top
> to toe, I sing. Not physiognomy
> alone, nor brain alone, is worthy
> for the Muse: I say the form
> complete is worthier far. The
> female equally with the male I sing.
> Nor cease at the theme of One's-self.
> I speak the word of the modern,
> the word *En Masse*.

Such is Mr Whitman's programme. If he did not speak 'the word of the modern' quite so often, or, at least, not borrow it from the penny-a-liner, it would be better for his fame. Also, through singing 'Man's physiology complete,' he has caused Mr Rossetti to be at the trouble of preparing the present 'Bowdlerised,' or excised edition of his works, to suit the squeamish tastes of the Old Country. So please, ladies, be particular to ask for the above-mentioned edition. There is nothing in that which you may not read, or the book would not be noticed in these columns.

Whitman's poetry reminds us, as we have said, of no other poet, but in his prose we seem to recognise some kinship to Emerson's. Here is a fine passage from the preface to his *Leaves of Grass* (the titles of his poems are unattractive, being almost always affected or unmeaning), insisting upon the importance of human act, word, thought, and the indestructibility of their results.

'All that a person does or thinks is of consequence. Not a move can a man or woman make that affects him or her in a day or a month, or any part of the direct lifetime, or the hour of death, but the same affects him or her onward afterward through the indirect lifetime. The indirect is always as great and real as the direct. The spirit receives from the body just as much as it gives to the body. Not one name of word or deed—not of the putrid veins of gluttons or rum-drinkers—not peculation, or cunning, or betrayal, or murder—no serpentine poison of those that seduce women—not the foolish yielding of women—not of the attainment of gain by discreditable means—not any nastiness of appetite—not any harshness of officers to men, or judges to prisoners, or fathers to sons, or sons to fathers, or of husbands to wives, or bosses to their boys—not of greedy looks or malignant wishes—nor any of the wiles practised by people upon themselves—ever is or ever can be stamped on the programme, but it is duly realised and returned, and that returned in further performances, and they returned again. Nor can the push of charity or personal force ever be anything else than the profoundest reason, whether it bring arguments to hand or no. No specification is necessary—to add, or subtract, or divide is in vain. Little or big, learned or unlearned, white or black, legal or illegal, sick or well, from the first inspiration down the windpipe to the last expiration out of it, all that a male or female does that is vigorous, and benevolent, and clean, is so much sure profit to him or her in the unshakable order of the universe, and through the whole scope of it for ever. If the savage or felon is wise, it is well—if the greatest poet or savant is wise, it is simply the same—if the

President or chief-justice is wise, it is the same—if the young mechanic or farmer is wise, it is no more or less. The interest will come round—all will come round. All the best actions of war and peace—all help given to relatives and strangers, and the poor, and old, and sorrowful, and young children, and widows, and the sick, and to all shunned persons—all furtherance of fugitives and of the escape of slaves—all the self-denial that stood steady and aloof on wrecks, and saw others take the seats of the boats—all offering of substance or life for the good old cause, or for a friend's sake or opinion's sake—all pains of enthusiasts scoffed at by their neighbours—all the vast sweet love and precious suffering of mothers—all honest men baffled in strifes recorded or unrecorded—all the grandeur and good of the few ancient nations whose fragments of annals we inherit—and all the good of the hundreds of far mightier and more ancient nations unknown to us by name or date or location—all that was ever manfully begun, whether it succeeded or not—all that has at any time been well suggested out of the divine heart of man, or by the divinity of his mouth, or by the shaping of his great hands—and all that is well thought or done this day on any part of the surface of the globe, or on any of the wandering stars or fixed stars by those there as we are here—or that is henceforth to be well thought or done by you, whoever you are, or by any one—these singly and wholly inured at their time, and inure now, and will inure always, to the identities from which they sprung or shall spring.' A fine lay-sermon, surely.

From common humanity our author rises to the American Citizen, with a portrait of whom he furnishes us, which will not easily be recognised by those who have only been accustomed to see English photographs of the individual in question. Other states, he says, indicate themselves by their deputies, but the United States always most in its common people. 'Their manners, speech, dress, friendships—the freshness and candour of their physiognomy—the picturesque looseness of their carriage—their deathless attachment to freedom—their aversion to anything indecorous, or soft, or mean—the practical acknowledgment of the citizens of one state by the citizens of all other states—the fierceness of their roused resentment—their curiosity and welcome of novelty—their self-esteem and wonderful sympathy—their susceptibility to a slight—the air they have of persons who never knew how it felt to stand in the presence of superiors—the fluency of their speech—their delight in music, the sure symptom of manly tenderness and native elegance of soul—their good temper and open-handedness—the terrible significance of their elections, the President's taking off his hat to them, not they to him—these, too, are unrhymed poetry. It awaits the gigantic and generous treatment worthy of it.'

In the meantime, however, Walt Whitman will try his hand.

Starting from fish-shape Paumanok,[1]
  where I was born,
Well-begotten, and raised by a perfect
  mother;
After roaming many lands—lover of
  populous pavements;
Dweller in Mannahatta,[2] city of ships,
  my city—or on southern savannas;
Or a soldier camped, or carrying my
  knapsack and gun—or a miner in
  California;
Or rude in my home in Dakotah's
  woods, my diet meat, my drink
  from the spring;
Or withdrawn to muse and meditate
  in some deep recess,
Far from the clank of crowds,

170

intervals passing, rapt and happy;
Aware of the fresh free giver, the
flowing Missouri—aware of mighty
Niagara;
Aware of the buffalo herds, grazing
the plains—the hirsute and strong-
breasted bull;
Of earths, rocks, fifth-month flowers,
experienced—stars, rain, snow, my
amaze;
Having studied the mocking-bird's
tones, and the mountain hawk's,
And heard at dusk the unrivalled one,
the hermit thrush, from the
swamp-cedars,
Solitary, singing in the West, I strike
up for a New World.

He even dates from the United States era;
in 1856, he writes:

In the Year 80 of the States,
My tongue, every atom of my blood,
formed from this soil, this air,
Born here of parents born here, from
parents the same, and their parents
the same,
I, now thirty-six years old, in perfect
health begin,
Hoping to cease not till death.

Creeds and schools in abeyance
(Retiring back a while, sufficed at
what they are, but never forgotten),
I harbour, for good or bad—I permit
to speak, at every hazard—
Nature now without check, with
original energy.

Yet he is so good as to say that former
experience and instruction have not been
altogether thrown away; he is grateful,
only let it be distinctly understood, that
he is under no slavish sense of obligation;
that the gratitude must be reciprocal.

I conned old times;
I sat studying at the feet of the great
masters:

Now, if eligible, O that the great
masters might return and study me!

If eligible? One would think he pictured
himself as an investment. You must not
be put off your liking, reader, by these
blots. 'Whitman is a poet who bears and
needs to be read as a whole, and then the
volume and torrent of his power carry
the disfigurements along with it and
away.' He is really a fine fellow.

Dead poets, philosophs, priests,
Martyrs, artists, inventors,
governments long since,
Language-shapers on other shores,
Nations once powerful, now reduced,
withdrawn, or desolate,
I dare not proceed till I respectfully
credit what you have left, wafted
hither:
I have perused it—own it is
admirable (moving a while among
it);
Think nothing can ever be greater—
nothing can ever deserve more than
it deserves;
Regarding it all intently a long while,
then dismissing it,
I stand in my place, with my own
day, here.

It is as the poet of his own day, of his
own nation (as also of Humanity, though
in a less degree), that Whitman is to be
considered. Half a century ago, he would
have been wholly unintelligible; and half
a century hence, it is possible that he will
be forgotten; but he will leave much seed
behind him, and perhaps found a school
whose pupils will be greater than their
master. His messages to the Poor and
Fallen (who will most certainly never receive them, by the by) are full of tenderness and fraternal love, but never of pity:
why should they be pitied, who are as
high as the highest, and as good as the

best? Nay, even crime does not cut them off from their equality with him, or him from his sympathy with them.

> If you become degraded, criminal, ill, then I become so for your sake;
> If you remember your foolish and outlawed deeds, do you think I cannot remember my own foolish and outlawed deeds?
> If you carouse at the table, I carouse at the opposite side of the table;
> If you meet some stranger in the streets, and love him or her—why, I often meet strangers in the street, and love them.
>
> Why, what have you thought of yourself?
> Is it you then that thought yourself less?
> Is it you that thought the President greater than you?
> Or the rich better off than you? or the educated wiser than you?
>
> Because you are greasy or pimpled, or that you was once drunk, or a thief,
> Or diseased, or rheumatic, or a prostitute, or are so now;
> Or from frivolity or impotence, or that you are no scholar, and never saw your name in print,
> Do you give in that you are any less immortal?

Whitman does not pretend to read 'the riddle of the painful earth;' but he takes leave to admire, after his fashion, the great Cosmos;

> The sun and stars that float in the open air;
> The apple-shaped earth, and we upon it—surely the drift of them is something grand!
> I do not know what it is, except that it is grand, and that it is happiness,

And that the enclosing purport of us here is not a speculation, or bon-mot, or reconnaissance,
And that it is not something which by luck may turn out well for us, and without luck must be a failure for us,
And not something which may yet be retracted in a certain contingency.

Yet it is Man, and not external Nature, which has his worship:

> When the psalm sings instead of the singer;
> When the script preaches instead of the preacher;
> When the pulpit descends and goes, instead of the carver that carved the supporting desk;
> When I can touch the body of books, by night or by day, and when they touch my body back again;
> When a university course convinces, like a slumbering woman and child convince;
> When the minted gold in the vault smiles like the night-watchman's daughter;
> When warrantee deeds loafe in chairs opposite, and are my friendly companions;
> I intend to reach them my hand, and make as much of them as I do of men and women like you.
>
> The sum of all known reverence I add up in you, whoever you are;
> The President is there in the White House for you—it is not you who are here for him.
> · · · · · · · · · · · ·
> List close, my scholars dear!
> All doctrines, all politics and civilisation, exsurge from you;
> All sculpture and monuments, and anything inscribed anywhere, are tallied in you;

The gist of histories and statistics, as
    far back as the records reach, is in
    you this hour, and myths and tales
    the same;
If you were not breathing and
    walking here, where would they all
    be?
The most renowned poems would be
    ashes, orations and plays would be
    vacuums.

Whitman is practical beyond all poets
before him; and, indeed, in one sense (but
not in the anti-theological one), material.
It delights him to contemplate the visible
instruments of labour, and he sings, in
minutest detail, the works which they accomplish. The axe leaps, and the solid
forest, says he, gives blind utterances, and
the manifold shapes arise in his mind's
eye, which are hewn out of the wood.

The coffin-shape for the dead to lie
    within in his shroud;
The shape got out in posts, in the
    bedstead posts, in the posts of the
    bride's bed;
The shape of the little trough, the
    shape of the rockers beneath, the
    shape of the babe's cradle;
The shape of the floor-planks, the
    floor-planks for dancers' feet;
The shape of the planks of the family
    home, the home of the friendly
    parents and children,
The shape of the root of the home of
    the happy young man and woman,
    the roof over the well-married
    young man and woman,
The roof over the supper joyously
    cooked by the chaste wife, and
    joyously eaten by the chaste
    husband, content after his day's
    work.
The shapes arise!
The shape of the prisoner's place in
    the court-room, and of him or her

seated in the place;
The shape of the liquor-bar leaned
    against by the young rum-drinker
    and the old rum-drinker;
The shape of the shamed and angry
    stairs, trod by sneaking footsteps;
·   ·   ·   ·   ·   ·   ·   ·

The shape of the gambling-board
    with its devilish winnings and
    losings;
The shape of the step-ladder for the
    convicted and sentenced murderer,
    the murderer with haggard face
    and pinioned arms.
·   ·   ·   ·   ·   ·   ·   ·   ·

Shapes of doors giving many exits
    and entrances;
The door passing the dissevered
    friend, flushed and in haste;
The door that admits good news and
    bad news;
The door whence the son left home,
    confident and puffed up;
The door he entered again from a
    long and scandalous absence,
    diseased, broken down, without
    innocence, without means.

These picturings may be somewhat weird
and fanciful, but they are expressed with
power, and the conception of them is certainly original and striking. They are, however, too prolonged, and remind one of
what somebody writes of the minuteness
of Crabbe's verse—that he was like a bro-
ker appraising furniture.

Under the unsatisfactory title of 'Assimilations,' Whitman describes the influence of association upon the human mind,
and, incidentally, depicts most graphi-
cally the surroundings and circumstances
of the somewhat unenviable home in
which he himself was reared.

The mother at home, quietly placing
    the dishes on the supper-table;
The mother with mild words—clean
    her cap and gown, a wholesome

odour falling off her person and clothes as she walks by;
The father, strong, self-sufficient, manly, mean, angered, unjust;
The blow, the quick loud word, the tight bargain, the crafty lure,
The family usages, the language, the company, the furniture—the yearning and swelling heart,
Affection that will not be gainsayed—the sense of what is real—the thought if after all it should prove unreal,
The doubts of day-time and the doubts of night-time—the curious whether and how,
Whether that which appears so is so, or is it all flashes and specks?
Men and women crowding fast in the streets—if they are not flashes and specks, what are they?
The streets themselves, and the façades of houses, and goods in the windows,
Vehicles, teams, the heavy-planked wharfs—the huge crossing at the ferries,
The village on the highland, seen from afar at sunset—the river between,
Shadows, aureola and mist, light falling on roofs and gables of white or brown, three miles off,
The schooner near by, sleepily dropping down the tide—the little boat slack-towed astern,
The hurrying tumbling waves quick-broken crests slapping,
The strata of coloured clouds, the long bar of maroon-tint, away solitary by itself—the spread of purity it lies motionless in,
The horizon's edge, the flying sea-crow, the fragrance of salt-marsh and shore-mud:
These became part of that child who went forth every day, and who now goes, and will always go forth every day.

In Mr Rossetti's Preface, we learn in plain prose what Walt Whitman's life has been. Walt, it appears, is merely a characteristic appellation; he was named Walter, like his father before him, who was first a farmer, afterwards a carpenter and builder (hence, doubtless, that eulogy on the axe), and an adherent to the religious principles of 'the great Quaker iconoclast, Elias Hicks,' of whom, if our readers have never heard, they are no worse off than we are. 'Walt—born in 1819—was schooled at Brooklyn, a suburb of New York, and began life at the age of thirteen, working as a printer, later on, as a country teacher, and then as a miscellaneous press-writer in New York.' He changed his pursuits, after the national fashion: became newspaper editor, and then builder, like his father; from 1837 to 1848, was, we fear, a rowdy, since his American biographer informs us that, during that period, 'he sounded all experiences of life, with all their passions, pleasures, and abandonments;' but in 1862, on the breaking out of the Civil War, he undertook the (gratuitous) service of nursing the wounded. He was a Northerner, of course, but the Southern sick were tended by him with equal care; 'the strongest testimony is borne to his self-devotion and kindliness;' and in a Washington hospital, when attending upon a case of gangrene, he absorbed the poison into his system, and was disabled for six months. In 1865, he obtained a clerkship in the Department of the Interior; but this was taken from him when he published his audacious *Leaves of Grass*. 'He soon after, however, obtained another modest, but creditable post in the office of the Attorney-general. He still visits the hospitals on Sundays, and often on other days as well.'

174

The poet is 'much above the average size, and noticeably well-proportioned. . . . . He has light-blue eyes, a florid complexion, a fleecy beard, now gray, and a quite peculiar sort of magnetism about him in relation to those with whom he comes in contact. . . . . He has always been carried by predilection towards the society of the common people; but is not the less for that open to refined and artistic impressions.' As 'an accessible human individual,' he is thus described by a writer in the *Fortnightly Review*: 'Having occasion to visit New York soon after the appearance of Walt Whitman's book, I was urged by some friends to search him out. . . . . The day was excessively hot, the thermometer at nearly 100°, and the sun blazed down as only on sandy Long Island can the sun blaze. . . . . I saw stretched upon his back, and gazing up straight at the terrible sun, the man I was seeking. With his gray clothing, his blue-gray shirt, his iron-gray hair, his swart sunburned face and bare neck, he lay upon the brown-and-white grass—for the sun had burned away its greenness—and was so like the earth upon which he rested that he seemed almost enough a part of it for one to pass by without recognition. I approached him, gave my name and reason for searching him out, and asked him if he did not find the sun rather hot. "Not at all too hot," was his reply; and he confided to me that this was one of his favourite places and attitudes for composing "poems." He then walked with me to his home, and took me along its narrow ways to his room. A small room of about fifteen feet square, with a single window looking out on the barren solitudes of the island; a small cot; a washstand, with a little looking-glass hung over it from a tack in the wall; a pine-table, with pen, ink, and paper on it; an old line-engraving, representing Bacchus, hung on the wall—and opposite, a similar one of Silenus: these constituted the visible environments of Walt Whitman. There was not, apparently, a single book in the room. . . . . The books he seemed to know and love best were the Bible, Homer, and Shakespeare: these he owned, and probably had in his pockets while we were talking. He had two studies where he read: one was the top of an omnibus; and the other a small mass of sand, then entirely uninhabited, far out in the ocean, called Coney Island. . . . . The only distinguished contemporary he had ever met was the Rev. Henry Ward Beecher, of Brooklyn, who had visited him. . . . . He confessed to having no talent for industry, and that his forte was "loafing and writing poems:" he was poor, but had discovered that he could, on the whole, live magnificently on bread and water. . . . . On no occasion did he laugh, nor indeed did I ever see him smile.'

If he does not laugh, he is humorous enough in his poems, although, it may be, without being aware of it. Under the head of 'Wonders'—and if he has the bump of Wonder, I am afraid he has not that of Veneration—he thus discourses:

> The great laws take and effuse
>   without argument;
> I am of the same style, for I am their
>   friend,
> I love them quits and quits—I do not
>   halt and make salaams.
>
> I lie abstracted, and hear beautiful
>   tales of things, and the reasons of
>   things;
> *They are so beautiful, I nudge myself*
>   *to listen.*
> I cannot say to any person what I
>   hear—I cannot say it to myself—it
>   is very wonderful.

The notion of nudging one's self to listen is capital, but suggests that there may be a tinge of *Irish*-American in Mr Walt

175

Whitman's otherwise *pur sang* (as he would term it). Here is something which, while reminding one in its form of Mr Martin Tupper, would, if the idea should be attributed to him, give that respectable gentleman a fit:

> Of detected persons—To me, detected persons are not in any respect worse than undetected persons— and are not in any respect worse than I am myself.
>
> Of criminals—To me, any judge, or any juror, is equally criminal—and any reputable person also—and the President is also.

We cannot more fitly conclude our notice of this really remarkable man than by quoting his most characteristic poem. It is from the *Leaves of Grass*, and is called 'Burial.' It expresses very strikingly in his strange rhythm the thought that has struck most of us who have any egotism. How strange that the world should have wagged on for ages before we came into it, and how still stranger (and more audacious) that it will still continue to wag on, when we have ceased to wag.

> To think of it!
> To think of time—of all that retrospection!
> To think of to-day, and the ages continued henceforward!
> . . . .
> To think that the sun rose in the east! that men and women were flexible, real, alive! that everything was alive!
> To think that you and I did not see, feel, think, nor bear our part!
> To think that we are now here, and bear our part!
>
> Not a day passes—not a minute or second, without an accouchement!
> Not a day passes—not a minute or second, without a corpse!

> The dull nights go over, and the dull days also;
> The soreness of lying so much in bed goes over;
> The physician, after long putting off, gives the silent and terrible look for an answer;
> The children come hurried and weeping, and the brothers and sisters are sent for;
> Medicines stand unused on the shelf (the camphor-smell has long pervaded the rooms);
> The faithful hand of the living does not desert the hand of the dying;
> The twitching lips press lightly on the forehead of the dying;
> The breath ceases, and the pulse of the heart ceases;
> The corpse stretches on the bed, and the living look upon it;
> It is palpable as the living are palpable.
>
> The living look upon the corpse with their eyesight,
> But without eyesight lingers a different living, and looks curiously on the corpse.
>
> To think that the rivers will flow, and the snow fall, and the fruits ripen, and act upon others as upon us now—yet not act upon us!
> To think of all these wonders of city and country, and others taking great interest in them—and we taking no interest in them!
>
> To think how eager we are in building our houses!
> To think others shall be just as eager, and we quite indifferent!

The poet considers the universalness of this thing called Death:

> Slow-moving and black lines creep over the whole earth—they never

cease—they are the burial-lines;
He that was President was buried,
and he that is now President shall
surely be buried.

But the particular illustration which Walt
Whitman characteristically selects of Burial is by no means that of the President,
but of an old Broadway stage-driver. It is
so graphic, that it might be a sketch by
Dickens, and yet it has a weird sort of
rhythm about it that separates it from
prose of any sort:

Cold dash of waves at the ferry-
wharf—posh and ice in the river,
half-frozen mud in the streets, a
gray discouraged sky overhead, the
short last day-light of Twelfth-
month;
A hearse and stages—other vehicles
give place—the funeral of an old
Broadway stage-driver, the cortège
mostly drivers.

Steady the trot to the cemetery, duly
rattles the death-bell, the gate is
passed, the new-dug grave is halted
at, the living alight, the hearse
uncloses,
The coffin is passed out, lowered and
settled, the whip is laid on the
coffin, the earth is swiftly shovelled
in,
The mound above is flatted with the
spades—silence;
A minute, no one moves or speaks—
it is done;
He is decently put away—is there
anything more?

He was a good fellow, free-mouthed,
quick-tempered, not bad-looking,
able to take his own part, witty,

sensitive to a slight, ready with life
or death for a friend, fond of
women, gambled, ate hearty, drank
hearty, had known what it was to
be flush, grew low-spirited toward
the last, sickened, was helped by a
contribution, died, aged forty-one
years—and that was his funeral.

Thumb extended, finger uplifted,
apron, cape, gloves, strap, wet-
weather clothes, whip carefully
chosen, boss, spotter, starter,
hostler, somebody loafing on you,
you loafing on somebody, headway,
man before and man behind, good
day's work, bad day's work, pet
stock, mean stock, first out, last
out, turning-in at night:
To think that these are so much and
so nigh to other drivers—and he
there takes no interest in them!

Notes

1   'Paumanok is the native name of Long Island, state of New York. It presents a fish-
like shape on the map.'
2   'Mannahatta, or Manhattan, is (as many
readers will know) New York.'

Checklist of Additional Reviews

"Walt Whitman," *London Review* 16
(21 March 1868), 288–9.
London *Morning Star*, 6 April 1868,
[page numbers unknown].
Examiner 3142 (18 April 1868), 245–6.

LEAVES OF GRASS (1871), PASSAGE TO INDIA (1871),
DEMOCRATIC VISTAS (1871)

PASSAGE

to

INDIA.

Washington, D. C.
1871.

New-York: J. S. REDFIELD, Publisher, 140 Fulton St., (up stairs.)

Edward Dowden.
Westminster Review 96 (July 1871), 33–68.

That school of criticism which has attempted in recent years to connect the history of literature and art with the larger history of society and the general movement of civilizations, creeds, forms of national life and feeling, and which may be called emphatically the critical school of the present century, or the naturalist as contradistinguished from the dogmatic school, has not yet essayed the application of its method and principles to the literature and art of America. For a moment one wonderingly inquires after the cause of this seeming neglect. The New World, with its new presentations to the senses, its new ideas and passions, its new social tendencies and habits, must surely, one thinks, have given birth to literary and artistic forms corresponding to itself in strange novelty, unlike in a remarkable degree those sprung from our Old-world, and old-world hearts. A moral soil and a moral climate so different from those of Europe must surely have produced a fauna and flora other than the European, a fauna and flora which the writers of literary natural history cannot but be curious to classify, and the peculiarities of which they must endeavour to account for by the special conditions of existence and of the development of species in the new country. It is as much to be expected that poems and pictures requiring new names should be found there as that new living things of any other kind, the hickory and the hemlock, the mocking bird and the katydid, should be found. So one reasons for a moment, and wonders. The fact is, that while the physical conditions, fostering certain forms of life, and repressing others, operated without let or hindrance, and disclosed themselves in their proper results with the simplicity and sureness of nature, the permanent moral powers were met by others of transitory or local, but, for the time, superior authority, which put a hedge around the literature and art of America, enclosing a little paradise of European culture, refinement, and aristocratic delicatesse from the howling wilderness of Yankee democracy, and insulating it from the vital touch and breath of the land, the winds of free, untrodden places, the splendour and vastness of rivers and seas, the strength and tumult of the people. Until of late indigenous growths of the New World showed in American literature like exotics, shy or insolent. We were aware of this, and expected in an American poet some one who would sing for us gently, in a minor key, the pleasant airs we knew. Longfellow's was a sweet and characteristic note, but, except in a heightened enjoyment of the antique—a ruined Rhine castle, a goblet from which dead knights had drunk, a suit of armour, or anything frankly mediæval—except in this, Longfellow is one of ourselves—an European. *Evangeline* is an European idyl of American life, Hermann and Dorothea having emigrated to Acadie. *Hiawatha* might have been dreamed in Kensington by a London man of letters who possessed a graceful idealizing turn of imagination, and who had studied with clear-minded and gracious sympathy the better side of Indian character and manners. Longfellow could amiably quiz, from a point of view of superior and contented refinement, his countrymen who went about blatant and blustering for a national art and literature which should correspond with the large proportions and freedom of the Republic. "We want," cries Mr. Hathaway in *Kavanagh*, "a national drama, in which scope enough shall be given to our gigantic ideas, and to the unparalleled activity and progress of our people.... We want a national literature, altogether shaggy and unshorn, that shall shake the earth, like a herd of buffaloes, thundering over the prairies!" And Mr. Churchill explains that what is best in literature is not national but universal, and is the fruit of refinement and culture. Longfellow's fellow-countryman, Irving, might have walked arm-in-arm with Addison, and Addison would have run no risk of being discomposed by a trans-Atlantic twang in his companion's accent. Irving, if he betrays his origin at all, betrays it somewhat in the same way as Longfellow, by his tender, satisfied repose in the venerable, chiefly the venerable in English society and manners, by his quiet delight in the implicit tradition of English civility, the scarcely-felt yet everywhere influential presence of a beautiful and grave Past, and the company of unseen beneficent associations. In Bryant, Europe is more in the background; prairie and immemorial forest occupy the broad spaces of his canvas, but he feels pleasure in these mainly because he is not native to their influences. The mountains are not his sponsors; there are not the unconsciousnesses between him and them which indicate kinship, nor the silences which prove entire communion. Moreover, the life of American men and women is almost absolutely unrepresented in the poetry of Bryant. The idealized red man is made use of as picturesque, an interesting and romantic person; but the Yankee is prosaic as his ledger. The American people had evidently not become an object of imaginative interest to itself in the mind of Bryant.

That the historical school of criticism should not have occupied itself with American literature is then hardly to be wondered at. A chapter upon that literature until recently must have been not a criticism but a prophecy. It was this very fact, the absence of a national literature, which the historical school was called on to explain. And to explain it evident and sufficient causes were producible, and were produced. The strictly Puritan origin of the Americans, the effort imposed upon them of subduing the physical forces of the country, and of yoking them to the service of man, the occupation of the entire community with an absorbing industry, the proximity of Europe, which made it possible for America to neglect the pursuit of the sciences, literature, and the fine arts without relapsing into barbarism—these causes were enumerated by De Tocqueville as having concurred to fix the minds of the Americans upon purely practical objects. "I consider the people of the United States as that portion of the English people which is commissioned to explore the wilds of the New World; whilst the rest of the nation enjoying more leisure, and less harassed by the drudgery of life, may devote its energies to thought, and enlarge in all directions the empire of the mind." Besides which, before a nation can become poetical to itself, consciously or unconsciously, it must possess a distinctive character, and the growth of national as of individual character is a process of long duration in every case, of longer duration than ordinary when a larger than ordinary variety of the elements of character wait to be assimilated and brought into harmony.

In Emerson a genuine product of the soil was perhaps for the first time apparent to us. We tasted in him the flavour of strange sap, and knew the ripening of another sun and other winds. He spoke of what is old and universal, but he spoke in the fashion of a modern man, and of his own nation. His Greek head pivoted restlessly on true Yankee shoulders, and when he talked Plato he did so in a dialectical variety of Attic peculiar to Boston.[1] Lowell, at times altogether feudal and European, has also at times a trans-Atlantic air, in the earnest but somewhat vague spiritualism of his earlier poems, his enthusiasm about certain dear and dim general ideas, and more happily in a conception of the democratic type of manhood which appears in some of the poems of later years, especially in that very noble "Ode recited at the Harvard Commemoration, July 21, 1865." But taken as a whole, the works of Lowell do not mirror the life, the thoughts, and passions of the nation. They are works, as it were, of an English poet who has become a naturalized citizen of the United States, who admires the institutions, and has faith in the ideas of America, but who cannot throw off his allegiance to the old country, and its authorities.

At last steps forward a man unlike any of his predecessors, and announces himself, and is announced with a flourish of critical trumpets, as Bard of America, and Bard of democracy. What cannot be questioned after an hour's acquaintance with Walt Whitman and his *Leaves of Grass* is that in him we meet a man not shaped out of old-world clay, not cast in any old-world mould, and hard to name by any old-world name. In his self-assertion there is a manner of powerful nonchalantness which is not assumed; he does not peep timidly from behind his works to glean our suffrages, but seems to say, "Take me or leave me, here I am a solid and not an inconsiderable fact of the universe." He disturbs our classifications. He attracts us; he repels us; he excites our curiosity, wonder, admiration, love; or, our extreme repugnance. He does anything except leave us indifferent. However we feel towards him we cannot despise him. He is "a summons and a challenge." He must be understood and so accepted, or must be got rid of. Passed

by he cannot be. To English readers Whitman is already known through Mr. Conway's personal reminiscences, published in the *Fortnightly Review*, through the judicious criticism of Mr. Rossetti prefixed to his volume of selections, and through other reviews, favourable and unfavourable. His critics have, for the most part, confined their attention to the personality of the man; they have studied him, for the most part, as a phenomenon isolated from the surrounding society, the environment, the *milieu*, which has made such a phenomenon possible. In a general way it has been said that Whitman is the representative in art of American democracy, but the meaning of this has not been investigated in detail. It is purposed here to consider some of the characteristics of democratic art, and to inquire in what manner they manifest themselves in Whitman's work.

A word of explanation is necessary. The representative man of a nation is not always the nation's favourite. Hebrew spiritualism, the deepest instincts, the highest reaches of the moral attainment of the Jewish race, appear in the cryings and communings of its prophets; yet the prophets sometimes cried in the wilderness, and the people went after strange gods. American democracy is as yet but half-formed. The framework of its institutions exists, but the will, the conscience, the mature desires of the democratic society are still in process of formation. If Whitman's writings are spoken of as the poetry of American democracy, it is not implied that his are the volumes most inquired after in the libraries of New York or Boston. What one means is that these are the poems which naturally arise when a man of imaginative genius stands face to face with a great democratic world, as yet but half-fashioned, such as society is in the United States of the present day. Successive editions of his

183

works prove that Whitman has many readers. But whether he had them now, or waited for them in years to come, it would remain true that he is the first representative democrat in art of the American Continent. At the same time he is before all else a living man, and must not be compelled to appear as mere official representative of anything. He will not be comprehended in a formula. No *view* of him can image the substance, the life and movement of his manhood, which contracts and dilates, and is all over sensitive and vital. Such views are, however, valuable in the study of literature, as hypotheses are in the natural sciences, at least for the collocation of facts. They have a tendency to render criticism rigid and doctrinaire; the critic must therefore ever be ready to escape from his own theory of a man, and come in contact with the man himself. Every one doubtless moves in some regular orbit, and all aberrations are only apparent, but what the precise orbit is we must be slow to pronounce. Meanwhile we may legitimately conjecture, as Kepler conjectured, if only we remain ready as Kepler was to vary our conjectures as the exigencies of the observed phenomena require.

A glance at the art of an aristocratic period will inform us in the way of contrast of much that we may expect to find under a democracy. And before all else we are impressed by the great regard which the artists of an aristocratic period pay to form. The dignity of letters maintains itself, like the dignity of the court, by a regulated propriety of manners. Ideas and feelings cannot be received unless they wear the courtly costume. Precise canons applicable to the drama, the ode, the epic, to painting, sculpture, architecture, music, are agreed upon, and are strictly enforced. They acquire traditional authority, the precedents of a great period of art (such, for example, as that of Louis XIV.)

being final and absolute with succeeding generations. "Style is deemed of almost as much importance as thought. . . . The tone of mind is always dignified, seldom very animated, and writers care more to perfect what they produce than to multiply their productions."[2] The peril to which an aristocratic literature is hereby exposed is of a singular kind; matter or substance may cease to exist, while an empty and elaborately studied form, a variegated surface with nothing below it, may remain. This condition of things was actually realized at different times in the literatures of Italy, of Spain, of France, and of England, when such a variegated surface of literature served for disport and display of the wits of courtiers, of ingenious authors, of noble and gentle persons male and female, and when reflection and imagination had ceased to have any relation with letters.

Again, the literature of an aristocracy is distinguished by its striving after selectness, by its exclusive spirit, and the number of things it proscribes. This is especially the case with the courtly art which has a great monarchy for its centre of inspiration. There is an ever-present terror of vulgarity. Certain words are ineligible in poetry; they are mean or undignified, and the things denoted by them must be described in an elegant periphrasis. Directness and vividness are sacrificed to propriety. The acquired associations of words are felt to be as important, and claim as much attention as their immediate significance, their spiritual power and personal character. In language as in life there is, so to speak, an aristocracy and a commonalty; words with a heritage of dignity, words which have been ennobled, and a rabble of words which are excluded from positions of honour and of trust. But this striving after selectness in forms of speech is the least important manifestation of the exclusive spirit of aristocratic art. Far the greater number of men and women, classes of society, conditions of life, modes of thought and feeling, are not even conceived as in any way susceptible of representation in art which aspires to be grave and beautiful. The common people do not show themselves *en masse* except as they may follow in a patient herd, or oppose in impotent and insolent revolt the leadership of their lords. Individually they are never objects of equal interest with persons of elevated worldly station. Even Shakespeare could hardly find in humble life other virtues than a humorous honesty and an affectionate fidelity. Robin Hood, the popular hero, could not be quite heroic were he not of noble extraction, and reputed Earl of Huntingdon. In the decline of an aristocratic period, dramatic studies of individual character and the life of the peasant or artisan may be made *from a superior point of view*. The literature of benevolence and piety stooping down to view the sad bodies and souls of men tends in this direction. And there are poems and novels, and paintings and sculptures, which flatter the feeling of mild benevolence. Pictures like those of Faed, in which some aged cottager, some strong delver of the earth, or searcher of the sea, some hardworked father of children, says appealingly, "By virtue of this love I exhibit towards my offspring, by virtue of the correct sense I have of the condescension of my betters, by virtue of this bit of pathos—indubitably human—in my eye, confess now *am* I not a man and a brother?"—pictures like these are produced, and may be purchased by amiable persons of the upper classes who would honour the admirable qualities which exist in humble life. But when the aristocratic period is in its strength, and especially in courtly art and literature, these condescending studies, not without a certain affection and sincerity in them, are

unknown. It is as if the world were made up of none but the gently born and bred. At most rustic life is glanced at for the sake of the suggestions of pretty waywardness it may supply to the fancy of great people tired of greatness. To play at pastoral may be for a while the fashion, if the shepherds and shepherdesses are permitted to choose graceful classical names, if the crooks are dainty, and the duties of the penfold not severe, if Phillis may set off a neat ankle with the latest shoe, and Corydon may complain of the cruel fair in the bitterness of roundel or sonnet. The middle classes, however, the *bourgeoisie*, figure considerably in one department of poetry—in the comic drama. Molière indeed, living under a stricter rule of courtliness, suffered disgrace in consequence of the introduction of so low-bred a person as the excellent M. Jourdain. But to the noble mind of our own Caroline period how rich a material of humour, inexhaustibly diverting, if somewhat monotonous in theme, was afforded by the relations of the high-born and the moneyed classes. The *bourgeois* aping the courtier, the lord making a fool of the merchant, while he makes love to the merchant's wife and daughter—what unextinguishable laughter have variations upon these elementary themes compelled from the occupants of the boxes in our Restoration theatres! There is an innocence quite touching in their openness to impressions from the same comic effects repeated again and again. Harlequin still at the close of the pantomime belabouring Pantaloon is not more sure of his success with the wide-eyed on-lookers in the front row than was the gallant engaged in seducing the draper's or hosier's pretty wife with gold supplied by her husband, in the playhouses favoured by our mirthful monarch and his companions.

All that is noblest in an aristocratic age embodies itself not in its comedy, but its serious art, and in the persons of heroic men and women. Very high and admirable types of character are realized in the creation of epic and dramatic poetry. All the virtues which a position of hereditary greatness, dignity, and peril calls forth—energy of character, vigour of will, disregard of life, of limb, and of property in comparison with honour, the virtues of generosity, loyalty, courtesy, magnificence—these are glorified and illustrated in man; and in woman all the virtues of dependence, all the graces insensibly acquired upon the surface of an externally beautiful world, and at times the rarer qualities called forth by occasional exigencies of her position, which demand virtues of the masculine kind. It is characteristic and right that our chief chivalric epic, the *Faerie Queene*, should set before itself as the general end of all the book "to fashion a gentleman or noble person in virtuous and gentle discipline." The feudal world with Artegall and Calidore, with Britomart and Una, was not wanting in lofty conceptions of human character, male and female.

Other characteristics of the art of an aristocratic period may be briefly noted. It is not deeply interested in the future, it gazes forward with no eyes of desire. Why should it? when nothing seems better than that things should remain as they are, or at most that things should be ameliorated, not that a new world should be created. The aristocratic society exists by inheritance, and it hopes from to-morrow chiefly a conserving of the good gifts handed down by yesterday and to-day. Its feeling of the continuity of history is in danger of becoming formal and materialistic; it does not always perceive that the abandonment of old things and the acceptance of new may be a necessary piece of continuity in government, in social life, in art, in religion. At the present the artist of the period of aristocracy

looks not very often, and then askance upon certain approved parts of the Present. But he loves to celebrate the glories of the Past. He displays a preference accordingly for antique subjects, chosen out of the history of his own land, or the histories of deceased nations. Shelley with his eyes fixed upon the golden age to come may stand as representative of the democratic tendencies in art; Scott, celebrating the glories of feudalism, its heroism and its refinements, will remain our great aristocratic artist of the period subsequent to the first French Revolution. The relation of the art to the religion of an age of aristocracy is peculiarly simple. The religious dogma which constitutes the foundation and formative principle of the existing society must have been fully established, and of supreme power, before the aristocratic form of social and political life can have acquired vigour and stability; the intellectual and moral habits favoured by the aristocratic polity—loyalty, obedience, veneration for authority, pride in the past, a willingness to accept things as they come to us from our fathers, a distrust of new things, all favour a permanence of belief. The art, therefore, will upon the whole (peculiar circumstances may of course produce remarkable exceptions) be little disturbed by the critical or sceptical spirit, and, untroubled by doubts, that art will either concern itself not at all with religion, or, accepting the religious dogma without dispute, will render it into artistic form in sublime allegory and symbol, and as it is found embodied in the venerable history of the Church. We may finally note from De Tocqueville the shrinking in an aristocratic society from whatever, even in pleasure, is too startling, violent, or acute, and the especial approval of choice gratifications, of refined and delicate enjoyments.

Now in all these particulars the art of a democratic age exhibits characteristics precisely opposite to those of the art of an aristocracy. Form and style modelled on traditional examples are little valued. No canons of composition are agreed upon or observed without formal agreement. No critical dictator enacts laws which are accepted without dispute, and acquire additional authority during many years. Each new generation, with its new heave of life, its multitudinous energies, ideas, passions, is a law to itself. Except public opinion, there is no authority on earth above the authority of a man's own soul, and public opinion being strongly in favour of individualism, a writer is tempted to depreciate unduly the worth of order, propriety, regularity of the academic kind; he is encouraged to make new literary experiments as others make new experiments in religion; he is permitted to be true to his own instincts, whether they are beautiful instincts or the reverse. The appeal which a work of art makes is to the nation, not to a class, and diversities of style are consequently admissible. Every style can be tolerated except the vapid, everything can be accepted but that which fails to stimulate the intellect or the passions.

Turning to Whitman, we perceive at once that his work corresponds with this state of things. If he had written in England in the period of Queen Anne, if he had written in France in the period of the *grand monarque*, he must have either acknowledged the supremacy of authority in literature and submitted to it, or on the other hand revolted against it. As it is, he is remote from authority, and neither submits nor revolts. Whether we call what he has written verse or prose, we have no hesitation in saying that it is no copy, that it is something uncontrolled by any model or canon, something which takes whatever shape it possesses directly from the soul of its maker. With the Bible, Homer, and Shakespeare familiar to him, Whitman writes in the presence of great models, and some influences from each have doubtless entered into his nature; but that they should possess authority over him any more than that he should possess authority over them, does not occur to him as possible. The relation of democracy to the Past comes out very notably here. Entirely assured of its own right to the Present, it is prepared to acknowledge fully the right of past generations to the Past. It is not hostile to that Past, rather claims kinship with it, but also claims equality, as a full-grown son with a father:—

> "I conn'd old times;
>   I sat studying at the feet of the great
>   masters:
>   Now, if eligible, O that the great
>   masters might return and study
>   me!
>   In the name of These States, shall I
>   scorn the antique?
>   Why These are the children of the
>   antique, to justify it.
>   Dead poets, philosophs, priests,
>   Martyrs, artists, inventors,
>   governments long since,
>   Language-shapers on other shores,
>   Nations once powerful, now
>   reduced, withdrawn or desolate,
>   I dare not proceed till I respectfully
>   credit what you have left, wafted
>   hither:
>   I have perused it, own it is
>   admirable (moving awhile among
>   it);
>   Think nothing can ever be greater,—
>   nothing can ever deserve more
>   than it deserves;
>   Regarding it all intently a long
>   while,—then dismissing it,
>   I stand in my place, with my own
>   day, here."

It is the same thought which finds expression in the following enumeration of the benefactors of the soul of man in

Whitman's prose essay *Democratic Vistas*; after which enumeration, they are dismissed, and a summons is sent forth for the appearance of their modern successors:—

"For us along the great highways of time, those monuments stand—those forms of majesty and beauty. For us those beacons burn through all the nights. Unknown Egyptians, graving hieroglyphs; Hindus with hymn and apothegm and endless epic; Hebrew prophet, with spirituality, as in flashes of lightning, conscience, like red-hot iron, plaintive songs and screams of vengeance for tyrannies and enslavement; Christ, with bent head, brooding love and peace, like a dove; Greek, creating eternal shapes of physical and esthetic proportion; Roman, lord of satire, the sword, and the codex;—of the figures some far-off and veiled, others nearer and visible; Dante, stalking with lean form, nothing but fibre, not a grain of superfluous flesh; Angelo, and the great painters, architects, musicians; rich Shakespeare, luxuriant as the sun, artist and singer of Feudalism in its sunset, with all the gorgeous colours, owner thereof, and using them at will; and so to such as German Kant and Hegel, where they, though near us, leaping over the ages, sit again impassive, imperturbable, like the Egyptian gods. Of these, and the like of these, is it too much, indeed, to return to our favourite figure, and view them as orbs and systems of orbs, moving in free paths in the spaces of that other heaven, the kosmic intellect, the Soul?

"Ye powerful and resplendent ones! ye were in your atmospheres, grown not for America, but rather for her foes, the Feudal and the old—while our genius is Democratic and modern. Yet could ye, indeed, but breathe your breath of life into our New World's nostrils—not to enslave us, as now, but for our needs, to breed a spirit like your own—perhaps (dare we to say it?) to dominate, even destroy, what you yourselves have left! On your plane, and no less, but even higher and wider, will I mete and measure for our wants to-day and here. I demand races of orbic bards, with unconditional, uncompromising sway. Come forth, sweet democratic despots of the west!"

As in all else, so with regard to the form of what he writes, Walt Whitman can find no authority superior to himself, or rather to the rights of the subject which engages him. There is, as Mr. Rossetti has observed, "a very powerful and majestic rhythmical sense," throughout his writings, prose and verse (if we consent to apply the term *verse* to any of them), and this rhythmical sense, as with every great poet, is original and inborn. His works, it may be, exhibit no perfect crystal of artistic form, but each is a menstruum saturated with form in solution. He fears to lose the instinctive in any process of elaboration, the vital in anything which looks like mechanism. He does not write with a full consciousness of the processes of creation, nor does any true poet. Certain combinations of sound are preconceived, and his imagination excited by them works towards them by a kind of reflex action, automatically. His *ars poetica* is embodied in the precept that the poet should hold himself passive in presence of the material universe, in presence of society, in presence of his own soul, and become the blind but yet unerringly guided force through which these seek artistic expression. No afterthought, no intrusion of reasoning, no calculating of effects, no stepping back to view his work is tolerated. The artist must create his art with as little hesitation, as little questioning of processes, and as much sureness of result as the beaver builds his house. Very nobly Whitman has spoken on this subject, and let those who, because they do not know him, suppose him insensible to any attractions in art except those of the extravagant, the incoherent, and the lawless, read what follows from the preface to *Leaves of Grass*:—

"The art of art, the glory of expression, and the sunshine of the light of letters is simplicity. Nothing is better than simplicity—nothing can make up for excess, or for the lack of definiteness. To carry on the heave of impulse, and pierce intellectual depths, and give all subjects their articulations, are powers neither common nor very uncommon. But to speak in literature with the perfect rectitude and insouciance of the movements of animals, and the unimpeachableness of the sentiment of trees in the woods, and grass by the roadside, is the flawless triumph of art. If you have looked on him who has achieved it, you have looked on one of the masters of the artists of all nations and times. You shall not contemplate the flight of the grey-gull over the bay, or the mettlesome action of the blood-horse, or the tall leaning of sunflowers on their stalk, or the appearance of the sun journeying through heaven, or the appearance of the moon afterward, with any more satisfaction than you shall contemplate him. The greatest poet has less a marked style, and is more the channel of thoughts and things without increase or diminution, and is the free channel of himself. He swears to his art. . . . . What I tell I tell for precisely what it is. Let who may exalt, or startle, or fascinate, or soothe, I will have purposes as health, or heat, or snow has, and be as regardless of observation."

Seeing much of deep truth in this, it must be added that, when the poet broods over his half-formed creation, and fashions it with divine ingenuity, and gives it shapeliness and completion of detail, and the lustre of finished workmanship, he does not forsake his instincts, but is obedient to them; he does not remove from nature into a laboratory of art, but is the close companion of nature. The vital spontaneous movement of the faculties, far from ceasing, still goes on like "the flight of the grey-gull over the bay," while the poet seeks after order, proportion, comeliness, melody—in a word beauty; or rather, as Whitman himself is fond of saying, does not seek but is sought—the perfect form preconceived but unattained, drawing the artist toward itself with an invincible attraction. An artist who does not yield to the desire for perfect order and beauty of form, instead of coming closer to nature is really forsaking nature, and doing violence to a genuine artistic instinct. Walt Whitman, however, knows this in all probability well enough, and does not need to be taught the mysteries of his craft. We will not say that his poems, as regards their form, do not, after all, come right, or that for the matter which he handles his manner of treatment may not be the best possible. One feels, as it has been well said, that although no counting of syllables will reveal the mechanism of the music, the music is there, and that "one would not for something change ears with those who cannot hear it." Whitman himself anticipates a new theory of literary composition for imaginative works, and especially for highest poetry, and desires the recognition of new forces in language, and the creation of a new manner of speech which cares less for what it actually realizes in definite form than "for impetus and effects, and for what it plants and invigorates to grow."

189

Nevertheless, when we read not the lyrical portions of Whitman's poetry, but what may be called his poetical statements of thoughts and things, a suspicion arises that if the form be suitable here to the matter, it must be because the matter belongs rather to the chaos than the kosmos of the new-created world of art.

The principle of equality upon which the democratic form of society is founded, obviously opposes itself to the exclusive spirit of the aristocratical polity. The essential thing which gives one the freedom of the world is not to be born a man of this or that rank, or class, or caste, but simply to be born a man. The literature of an aristocratic period is distinguished by its aim at selectness, and the number of things it proscribes; we should expect the literature of a democracy to be remarkable for its comprehensiveness, its acceptance of the persons of all men, its multiform sympathies. The difference between the President and the Broadway mason or hodman is inconsiderable—an accident of office; what is common to both is the inexpressibly important thing, their inalienable humanity. Rich and poor, high and low, powerful and feeble, healthy and diseased, deformed and beautiful, old and young, man and woman, have this in common, and by possession of this are in the one essential thing equal, and brethren one of another. Even between the virtuous man and the vicious the difference is less than the agreement; they differ by a quality, but agree by the substance of their manhood. The *man* in all men, however it may be obscured by cruel shocks and wrenches of life which distort, by long unnatural uses which deform, by ignorance, by the well-meaning stupidity of others, or by one's own stupidity, by foul living, or by clean, hard, worldly living, is surely somewhere discoverable. How can any human creature be rejected, any scorned, any mocked?

Such satire and such comedy as appear in aristocratic society are discouraged by the genius of democracy. The spirit of exclusiveness will, it is true, never fail to find material for its support, and baser prizes may replace the calm, conservative, but unaggressive pride of hereditary dignity. Nevertheless it remains no less true that the spectacle of a great democracy present to the imagination, and the temper of the democracy accepted by the understanding heart, favour only such prides as are founded on nature—that is, on the possession, acquired or inherited, of personal qualities, personal powers, and virtues, and attainments.

If this be a true account of some characteristics of the art which rises when a man of imaginative genius stands face to face with a great democracy, Walt Whitman in these particulars is what he claims to be, a representative democrat in art. No human being is rejected by him, no one slighted, nor would he judge any, except as "the light falling around a helpless thing" judges. No one in his poems comes appealing "Am I not interesting, am I not deserving, am I not a man and a brother?" We have had, he thinks, "ducking and deprecating about enough." The poet studies no one from a superior point of view. He delights in men, and neither approaches deferentially those who are above him, nor condescendingly gazes upon those who are beneath. He is the comrade of every man, high and low. His admiration of a strong, healthy, and beautiful body, or a strong, healthy, and beautiful soul, is great when he sees it in a statesman or a savant; it is precisely as great when he sees it in the ploughman or the smith. Every variety of race and nation, every condition in society, every degree of culture, every season of human life, is accepted by Whitman as admirable and best, each in its own place. Working men of every name—all who engage in fieldwork, all who toil upon the sea, the city artisan, the woodsman and the trapper, fill him with pleasure by their presence; and that they are interesting to him not in a general way of theory or doctrine (a piece of the abstract democratic creed), but in the way of close, vital human sympathy appears from the power he possesses of bringing before us with strange precision, vividness, and nearness in a few decisive strokes the essential characteristics of their respective modes of living. If the strong, full-grown working man wants a lover and comrade, he will think Walt Whitman especially made for him. If the young man wants one, he will think him especially the poet of young men. Yet a rarer and finer spell than that of the lusty vitality of youth, or the trained activity of manhood, is exercised over the poet by the beautiful repose or unsubdued energy of old age. He is "the caresser of life, wherever moving." He does not search antiquity for heroic men and beautiful women; his own abundant vitality makes all the life which surrounds him a source of completest joy; "what is commonest, cheapest, nearest, easiest, is Me. . . . not asking the sky to come down to my good-will; scattering it freely for ever." Let a few passages illustrate Whitman's joyous sympathy with men:—

> "I have perceiv'd that to be with
>   those I like is enough,
>   To stop in company with the rest at
>   evening is enough,
>   To be surrounded by beautiful,
>   curious, breathing, laughing flesh
>   is enough,
>   To pass among them, or touch any
>   one, or rest my arm ever so
>   lightly round his or her neck for a
>   moment—what is this, then?
> I do not ask any more delight. I
>   swim in it, as in a sea."

> "The big doors of the country barn
>   stand open and ready;
> The dried grass of the harvest-time
>   loads the slow-drawn wagon;
> The clear light plays on the brown
>   grey and green intertinged;
> The armfuls are pack'd to the
>   sagging mow.
> I am there, I help, I came stretch'd
>   atop of the load;
> I felt its soft jolts, one leg reclined
>   on the other;
> I jump from the cross-beams, and
>   seize the clover and timothy,
> And roll head over heels, and tangle
>   my hair full of wisps."

> "The negro holds firmly the reins of
>   his four horses, the block swags
>   underneath on its tied-over chain;
> The negro that drives the dray of
>   the stone-yard, steady and tall he
>   stands, pois'd on one leg on the
>   string-piece;
> His blue shirt exposes his ample
>   neck and breast, and loosens over
>   his hip-band;
> His glance is tall and commanding,
>   he tosses the slouch of his hat
>   away from his forehead;
> The sun falls on his crispy hair and
>   moustache, falls on the black of
>   his polished and perfect limbs.
> I behold the picturesque giant, and
>   love him."

The following loses much by being removed from its place at the end of the poem of "Faces," which it closes with calm melodious chords:—

> "The old face of the mother of many
>   children!
> Whist! I am fully content.
> Lull'd and late is the smoke of the
>   First-day morning,
> It hangs low over the rows of trees
>   by the fences,

191

It hangs thin by the sassafras, the
wild-cherry, and the cat-brier
under them.
I saw the rich ladies in full dress at
the soirée,
I heard what the singers were
singing so long,
Heard who sprang in crimson youth
from the white froth and the
water-blue.
Behold a woman!
She looks out from her quaker-cap—
her face is clearer and more
beautiful than the sky.
She sits in an arm-chair, under the
shaded porch of the farmhouse,
The sun just shines on her old white
head.
Her ample gown is of cream-hued
linen;
Her grandsons raised the flax, and
her granddaughters spun it with
the distaff and the wheel.
The melodious character of the
earth,
The finish beyond which philosophy
cannot go, and does not wish to
go,
The justified mother of men."

But it is not those alone who are beautiful and healthy and good who claim the
poet's love. To all "the others are down
on" Whitman's hand is outstretched to
help, and through him come to us the
voices—petitions or demands—of the diseased and despairing, of slaves, of prostitutes, of thieves, of deformed persons, of
drunkards. Every man is a divine miracle
to him, and he sees a *redeemer*, whom
Christ will not be ashamed to acknowledge a comrade, in every one who per-
forms an act of loving self-sacrifice:—

"Three scythes at harvest whizzing in
a row, from three lusty angels
with shirts bagged out at their
waists;

The snag-tooth'd hostler with red
hair redeeming sins past and to
come,
Selling all he possesses, travelling on
foot to fee lawyers for his brother,
and sit by him while he is tried
for forgery."

Is there no limit to the poet's acceptance of the persons of men? There is one
test of his tolerance more severe than can
be offered by the vicious or the deformed.
Can he tolerate the man of science? Yes,
though he were to find him peeping and
botanizing upon his mother's grave. Science and democracy appear before Whitman as twin powers which bend over the
modern world hand in hand, great and
beneficent. Democracy seems to him that
form of society which alone is scientifi-
cally justifiable; founded upon a recognition of the facts of nature, and a resolute
denial of social fables, superstitions, and
uninvestigated tradition. Moreover he
looks to science for important elements
which shall contribute to a new conception of nature and of man, and of their
mutual relations, to be itself the ideal basis of a new poetry and art—"after the
chemist, geologist, ethnologist, finally shall
come the Poet worthy that name; the
true Son of God shall come singing his
songs." Lastly, Whitman has a peculiar
reason of his own for loving science; he is
a mystic, and such a mystic as finds positive science not unacceptable. Whitman's
mysticism is not of the Swedenborgian
type. He beholds no visions of visible
things in heaven or hell unseen to other
men. He rather sees with extraordinary
precision the realities of our earth, but
he sees them, in his mystical mood, as
symbols of the impalpable and spiritual.
They are hieroglyphs most clear-cut, most
brilliantly and definitely coloured to his
eyes, but still expressive of something unseen. His own personality as far as he can

give it expression or is conscious of it—that identity of himself, which is the hardest of all facts, and the only entrance to all facts, is yet no more than the image projected by another ego, the real *Me*, which stands "untouched, untold, altogether unreached:"—

> "Withdrawn far, mocking me with
>   mock-congratulatory signs and
>   bows,
> With peals of ironical laughter at
>   every word I have written,
>
> .   .   .   .
>
> Now I perceive I have not
>   understood anything—not a single
>   object; and that no man ever can.
> I perceive Nature, here in sight of
>   the sea, is taking advantage of
>   me, to dart upon me, and sting
>   me,
> Because I have dared to open my
>   mouth to sing at all."

To such mysticism science cannot succeed in opposing itself: it can but provide the mystic with a new leaf of the sacred writing in which spiritual truths are recorded. Note the pregnant parenthesis in the following:

> "Gentlemen! [men of science] to you
>   the first honours always.
> Your facts are useful and real, and
>   yet they are not my dwelling;
> (I but enter by them into an area of
>   my dwelling.)"

If Whitman seems suspicious of any class of men, disposed to be antagonistic to any, it is to those whose lives are spent among books, who are not in contact with external nature, and the stir and movement of human activity, but who receive things already prepared, or, as Whitman expresses it, "distilled." He knows that the distillations are delightful, and

would intoxicate himself also, but he will not let them. Rather he chooses to "lean and loafe at his ease, observing a spear of summer grass," to drink the open air (that is, everything natural and unelaborated); he is "enamoured of growing outdoors." At the same time his most ardent aspiration is after a new literature, accordant with scientific conceptions, and the feelings which correspond with democracy. And to the literature of the old world and of feudalism he willingly does justice. "American students may well derive from all former lands, ... from witty and warlike France, and markedly, and in many ways, and at many different periods, from the enterprise and soul of the great Spanish race, bearing ourselves always courteous, always deferential, indebted beyond measure to the mother-world, to all its nations dead, as to all its nations living—the offspring, this America of ours, the daughter not by any means of the British Isles exclusively, but of the Continent, and of all continents." True culture and learning Whitman venerates; but he suspects men of refinement and polite letters and dainty information, the will-o'-the-wisps of Goethe's "Mährchen," who "lose themselves in countless masses of adjustments," who end by becoming little better than "supercilious infidels," whose culture, as Carlyle long since observed, is of a "sceptical-destructive" kind.

Men of every class then are interesting to Whitman. But no individual is pre-eminently interesting to him. His sketches of individual men and women, though wonderfully vivid and precise, are none of them longer than a page; each single figure passes rapidly out of sight, and a stream of other figures of men and women succeeds. Even in "Lincoln's Burial Hymn" he has only a word to say of "the large sweet soul that has gone;" the chords of his nocturn, with their implicated threefold sweetness, odour and sound and light, having passed into his strain, really speak not of Lincoln but of death. George Peabody is celebrated briefly, because through him, a "stintless, lavish giver, tallying the gifts of earth," a multitude of human beings have been blessed, and the true service of riches illustrated. No single person is the subject of Whitman's song, or can be; the individual suggests a group, and the group a multitude, each unit of which is as interesting as every other unit, and possesses equal claims to recognition. Hence the recurring tendency of his poems to become catalogues of persons and things. Selection seems forbidden to him; if he names one race of mankind the names of all other races press into his page; if he mentions one trade or occupation, all other trades and occupations follow. A long procession of living forms passes before him; each several form, keenly inspected for a moment, is then dismissed. Men and women are seen *en masse*, and the mass is viewed not from a distance, but close at hand, where it is felt to be a concourse of individuals. Whitman will not have the people appear in his poems by representatives or delegates; the people itself, in its undiminished totality, marches through his poems, making its greatness and variety felt. Writing down the headings of a Trades' Directory is not poetry; but this is what Whitman never does. His catalogues are for the poet always, if not always for the reader, *visions*—they are delighted—not perhaps delightful—enumerations; when his desire for the perception of greatness and variety is satisfied, not when a really complete catalogue is made out, Whitman's enumeration ends; we may murmur, but Whitman has been happy; what has failed to interest our imaginations has deeply interested his; and even for us the impression of multitude, of variety, of equality is produced,

as perhaps it could be in no other way. Whether Whitman's habit of cataloguing be justified by what has been said, or is in any way justifiable, such at least is its true interpretation and significance.

One can perceive at a glance that these characteristics of Whitman's work proceed directly from the democratic tendencies of the world of thought and feeling in which he moves. It is curious to find De Tocqueville, before there existed properly any native American literature, describing in the spirit of philosophical prophecy what we find realized in Whitman's *Leaves of Grass*:—

"He who inhabits a democratic country sees around him, on every hand, men differing but little from each other; he cannot turn his mind to any one portion of mankind without expanding and dilating his thought till it embraces the whole world.... The poets of democratic ages can never take any man in particular as the subject of a piece, for an object of slender importance, which is distinctly seen on all sides, will never lend itself to an ideal conception..... As all the citizens who compose a democratic community are nearly equal and alike, the poet cannot dwell upon any one of them; but the nation itself invites the exercise of his powers. The general similitude of individuals which renders any one of them, taken separately, an improper subject of poetry, allows poets to include them all in the same imagery, and to take a general survey of the people itself. Democratic nations have a clearer perception than any other of their own aspect; and an aspect so imposing is admirably fitted to the delineation of the ideal."

The democratic poet celebrates no individual hero, nor does he celebrate himself. "I celebrate myself," sings Whitman, and the longest poem in *Leaves of Grass* is named by his own name; but the self-celebration throughout is celebration of himself as a man and an American; it is what he possesses in common with all others that he feels to be glorious and worthy of song, not that which differentiates him from others; manhood, and in particular American manhood, is the real subject of the poem "Walt Whitman;" and although Whitman has a most poignant feeling of personality, which indeed is a note of all he has written, it is to be remembered that in nearly every instance in which he speaks of himself the reference is as much impersonal as personal. In what is common he finds what is most precious. The true hero of the democratic poet is the nation of which he is a member, or the whole race of man to which the nation belongs. The mettlesome, proud, turbulent, brave, self-asserting young Achilles, lover of women and lover of comrades of Whitman's epic, can be no other than the American people; his Ulysses, the prudent, the 'cute, the battler with the forces of nature, the traveller in sea-like prairie, desolate swamp, and dense forest is brother Jonathan. But if the American nation is his hero, let it be observed that it is the American nation as the supposed leader of the human race, as the supposed possessor in ideas, in type of character, and in tendency if not in actual achievement, of all that is most powerful and promising for the progress of mankind.

To the future Whitman looks to justify his confidence in America and in democracy. The aspect of the present he finds both sad and encouraging. The framework of society exists; the material civilization is rich and fairly organized. Without any transcendentalism or political mysticism about the principle of universal suffrage, not glossing over its "appall-ing dangers," and for his own part content that until its time were come self-government should wait, and the condition of authoritative tutelage continue, he yet approves the principle as "the only safe and preservative one for coming times," and sees in America its guardian. He dwells with inexhaustible delight upon certain elements in the yet unformed personal character of the average American man and woman. And his experience, and the experience of the nation during the civil war—proving the faithfulness, obedience, docility, courage, fortitude, religious nature, tenderness, sweet affection of countless numbers of the unnamed, unknown rank and file of North and South—practically justifies democracy in Whitman's eyes "beyond the proudest claims and wildest hopes of its enthusiasts." But at the same time no one perceives more clearly, or observes with greater anxiety and alarm, the sore diseases of American society; and leaving us to reconcile his apparently contradictory statements, he does not hesitate to declare that the New World democracy, "however great a success in uplifting the masses out of their sloughs, in materialistic development, products, and in a certain highly deceptive superficial popular intellectuality, is so far an almost complete failure in its social aspects, in any superb general personal character, and in really grand religious, moral, literary, and æsthetic results." A vast and more and more thoroughly appointed body Whitman finds in the American world, and little or no soul. His senses are flattered, his imagination roused and delighted by the vast movement of life which surrounds him, its outward glory and gladness, but when he inquires, What is behind all this? the answer is of the saddest and most shameful kind. The following passage is in every way, in substance and in manner, highly characteristic of Whitman; but the reader must remember that in spite of all that he discerns of evil in democratic America, Whitman remains an American proud of his nationality, and a believer who does not waver in his democratic faith:—

"After an absence, I am now (September, 1870) again in New York City and Brooklyn, on a few weeks' vacation. The splendour, picturesqueness, and oceanic amplitude and rush of these great cities, the unsurpassed situation, rivers and bay, sparkling sea-tides, costly and lofty new buildings, the façades of marble and iron, of original grandeur and elegance of design, with the masses of gay colour, the preponderance of white and blue, the flags flying, the endless ships, the tumultuous streets, Broadway, the heavy, low, musical roar, hardly ever intermitted even at night; the jobbers' houses, the rich shops, the wharves, the great Central Park, and the Brooklyn Park of Hills (as I wander among them this beautiful fall weather, musing, watching, absorbing)—the assemblages of the citizens in their groups, conversations, trade, evening amusements, or along the by-quarters—these, I say, and the like of these, completely satisfy my senses of power, fulness, motion, &c., and give me, through such senses and appetites, and through my æsthetic conscience, a continued exaltation and absolute fulfilment. Always, and more and more, as I cross the East and North rivers, the ferries, or with the pilots in their pilothouses, or pass an hour in Wall Street, or the gold exchange, I realize (if we must admit such partialisms) that not Nature alone is great in her fields of freedom, and the open air, in her storms, the shows of night and day, the mountains, forests, seas—but in the artificial, the work of man too is equally great—in this profusion of teeming humanity, in these ingenuities, streets, goods, houses, ships—these seething, hurrying, feverish crowds of men, their complicated business genius (not least among the geniuses), and all this mighty, many-threaded wealth and industry concentrated here.

"But sternly discarding, shutting our eyes to the glow and grandeur of the general effect; coming down to what is of the only real importance, Personalities, and examining minutely, we question, we ask, Are there, indeed, *Men* here worthy the name? Are there athletes? Are there perfect women, to match the generous material luxuriance? Is there a pervading atmosphere of beautiful manners? Are there crops of fine youths and majestic old persons? Are there arts worthy Freedom, and a rich people? Is there a great moral and religious civilization—the only justification of a great material one?

"Confess that rather to severe eyes, using the moral microscope upon humanity, a sort of dry and flat Sahara appears, these cities, crowded with petty grotesques, malformations, phantoms, playing meaningless antics. Confess that everywhere in shop, street, church, theatre, bar-room, official chair, are pervading flippancy and vulgarity, low cunning, infidelity—everywhere the youth puny, impudent, foppish, prematurely ripe—everywhere an abnormal libidinousness, unhealthy forms, male, female, painted, padded, dyed, chignoned, muddy complexions, bad blood, the capacity for good motherhood deceasing or deceased, shallow notions of beauty, with a range of manners, or rather lack of manners (considering the advantages enjoyed) probably the meanest to be seen in the world."

Such a picture of the outcome of American democracy is ugly enough to satisfy the author of "Shooting Niagara—and after?" but such a picture only represents the worst side of the life of great cities. Whitman can behold these things, not without grief, not without shame, but without despair. He does not unfairly contrast the early years of confusion and crudity of a vast industrial and democratic era with the last and perfected results of an era of feudalism and aristocracy. He finds much to make him sad; but more to make him hopeful. He takes account of the evil anxiously, accurately; and can still rejoice. Upon the whole his spirit is exulting and prompt in cheerful action; not self-involved, dissatisfied, and fed by indignation. Contrast with the passage given above Whitman's preface to *Leaves of Grass* prefixed to Mr. Rossetti's volume of Selections, with its joyous confidence and pride in American persons and things, or that very noble poem "A Carol of Harvest, for 1867," in which the armies of blue-clad conquering men are seen streaming North, and melt away and disappear, while in the same hour the heroes reappear, toiling in the fields, harvesting the products, glad and secure under the beaming sun, and under the great face of Her, the Mother, the Republic, without whom not a scythe might swing in security, "not a maize-stalk dangle its silken tassels in peace." If all enthusiasm about political principles be of the nature of *Schwärmerei*, Whitman's feeling towards the Republic deserves that name; but he would have the principles of democracy sternly tested by results,—results not only present but prospective and logically inevitable, and he has faith in them not because they seem to him to favour freedom any more than because they seem to favour law and self-control, and security, and order. He, as much as Mr. Carlyle, admires "disciplined men," and believes

that with every disciplined man "the arena of *Anti*-Anarchy, of God-appointed *Order* in this world" is widened; but he does not regard military service as the type of highest discipline, nor the drill-sergeant as highest conceivable official person in the land.

The principle of political and social equality once clearly conceived and taken to heart as true, works outward through one's body of thought and feeling in various directions. If in the polity of the nation every citizen be entitled by virtue of the fact of his humanity to make himself heard, to manifest his will, and in his place to be respected, then in the polity of the individual man, made up of the faculties of soul and body, every natural instinct, every passion, every appetite, every organ, every power, may claim its share in the government of the man. If a human being is to be honoured as such, then every part of a human being is to be honoured. In asserting one's rights as a man, one asserts the rights of everything which goes to make up manhood. It is the democratic temper to accept realities unless it is compelled to reject them; to disregard artificial distinctions, and refer all things to natural standards, consequently to honour things because they are natural and exist. Thus we find our way to the centre of what has been called the "materialism" of Whitman— his vindication of the body as it might be more correctly termed. Materialist, in any proper sense of the word, he is not; on the contrary, as Mr. Rossetti has stated, "he is a most strenuous asserter of the soul," but "with the soul, of the body, as its infallible associate and vehicle in the present frame of things." And as every faculty of the soul seems admirable and sacred to him, so does every organ and function and natural act of the body. But Whitman is a poet; it is not his manner to preach doctrines in an abstract form, by means of a general statement; and the doctrine, which seems to him of vital importance, that a healthy, perfect body—male or female—is altogether worthy of honour, admiration, and desire, is accordingly preached with fulness and plainness of detail. The head of his offending with many who read, and who refuse to read him, lies of course here. That lurking piece of asceticism, not yet cast out of most of us, which hints that there is something peculiarly shameful in the desire of the sexes for one another, of the man for the woman, and of the woman for the man, will certainly find matter enough of offence in one short section of *Leaves of Grass*, that entitled "Children of Adam." And one admission must be made to Whitman's disadvantage. If there be any class of subjects which it is more truly natural, more truly human *not* to speak of than to speak of (such speech producing self-consciousness, whereas part of our nature, it may be maintained, is healthy only while it lives and moves in holy blindness and unconsciousness of self), if there be any sphere of silence, then Whitman has been guilty of invading that sphere of silence. But he has done this by conviction that it is best to do so, and in a spirit as remote from base curiosity as from insolent licence. He deliberately appropriates a portion of his writings to the subject of the feelings of sex, as he appropriates another, "Calamus," to that of the love of man for man, "adhesiveness," as contrasted with "amativeness," in the nomenclature of Whitman, comradeship apart from all feelings of sex. That article of the poet's creed, which declares that man is very good, that there is nothing about him which is naturally vile or dishonourable, prepares him for absolute familiarity, glad, unabashed familiarity with every part and every act of the body. The ascetic teaching of many Mediæval writers is un-

favourable to morality by its essential character: Whitman's may become unfavourable by accident. "As to thy body, thou art viler than muck. Thou wast gotten of so vile matter, and so great filth, that it is shame for to speak, and abomination for to think. Thou shalt be delivered to toads and adders for to eat." "If thou say that thou lovest thy father and thy mother because thou art of their blood and of flesh gotten, so are the worms that come from them day by day. If thou love brethren or sisters or other kindred, because they are of the same flesh of father and mother and of the same blood, by the same reason should thou love a piece of their flesh, if it be shorn away." "All other sins [but wedlock] are nothing but sins, but this is a sin, and besides denaturalizes thee, and dishonours thy body. It soileth thy soul, and maketh it guilty before God, and moreover defileth thy flesh."[3] These were the views of pious persons of the thirteenth century. Here the body and the soul are kept in remote severance, each one the enemy of the other. Such spirituality, condemned alike by the facts of science and by the healthy natural human instincts, is seen by Whitman to be, even in its modern modifications, profoundly immoral. The lethargy of the soul induces it willingly to take up under some form or another with a theory which directs it heavenwards on the swift wings of devotional aspiration, rather than heavenwards for joy, but also earthwards for laborious duty, to animate, to quicken, to glorify all that apart from it is dull and gross. Both directions of the soul are declared necessary to our complete life by Whitman—the one in solitude, the other in society.

"Only in the perfect uncontamination and solitariness of individuality may the spirituality of religion positively come forth at all. Only here, and on such terms, the meditation, the devout ecstasy, the soaring flight. Only here, communion with the mysteries, the eternal problems, whence? whither? Alone, and identity, and the mood,—and the soul emerges, and all statements, churches, sermons, melt away like vapours. Alone, and silent thought, and awe, and aspiration,—and then the interior consciousness, like a hitherto unseen inscription, in magic ink, beams out its wondrous lines, to the sense. Bibles may convey, and priests expound, but it is exclusively for the noiseless operation of one's isolated self, to enter the pure ether of veneration, reach the divine levels, and commune with the unutterable."

Then the soul can return to the body, and to the world, and possess them, and infuse its own life into them:—

"I sing the Body electric;
  The armies of those I love engirth
    me, and I engirth them;
  They will not let me off till I go
    with them, respond to them,
  And discorrupt them, and charge
    them full with the charge of the
    soul."

Having acknowledged that Whitman at times forgets that the "instinct of silence," as it has been well said, "is a beautiful, imperishable part of nature," and consequently that Whitman in a few passages falls below humanity, falls even below the modesty of brutes, everything has been acknowledged, and it ought not to be forgotten that no one asserts more strenuously than does Whitman the beauty, not indeed of asceticism, but of holiness or healthiness, and the shameful ugliness of unclean thought, desire, and deed. If he does not assert holiness as a duty, it is because he asserts it so strongly

as a joy and a desire, and because he loves to see all duties transfigured into the glowing forms of joys and of desires. The healthy repose and continence, and the healthy eagerness and gratification of appetite, are equally sources of satisfaction to him. If in some of his lyrical passages there seems entire self-abandonment to passion, it is because he believes there are, to borrow his own phrase, "native moments," in which the desires receive permission from the supreme authority, conscience, to satisfy themselves completely:

"From the master—the pilot I yield
    the vessel to;
  The general commanding me,
    commanding all—from him
    permission taking."

Whitman's most naked physical descriptions and enumerations are those of a robust, vigorous, clean man, enamoured of living, unashamed of body as he is unashamed of soul, absolutely free from pruriency of imagination, absolutely inexperienced in the artificial excitements and enhancements of jaded lusts. "I feel deeply persuaded," writes one of Whitman's critics who has received the impression of his mind most completely and faithfully,[4] "that a perfectly fearless, candid, ennobling treatment of the life of the body (so inextricably intertwined with, so potent in its influence on the life of the soul), will prove of inestimable value to all earnest and aspiring natures, impatient of the folly of the long prevalent belief that it is because of the greatness of the spirit that it has learned to despise the body, and to ignore its influences; knowing well that it is, on the contrary, just because the spirit is not great enough, not healthy and vigorous enough, to transfuse itself into the life of the body, elevating that and making it holy with its own triumphant intensity; knowing too how the body avenges this by dragging the soul down to the level assigned itself. Whereas the spirit must lovingly embrace the body, as the roots of a tree embrace the ground, drawing thence rich nourishment, warmth, impulse. Or rather the body is itself the root of the soul—that whereby it grows and feeds. The great tide of healthful life that carries all before it must surge through the whole man, not beat to and fro in one corner of his brain. 'O the life of my senses and flesh, transcending my senses and flesh.' For the sake of all that is highest, a truthful recognition of this life, and especially of that of it which underlies the fundamental ties of humanity—the love of husband and wife, fatherhood, motherhood—is needed."

The body then is not given authority over the soul by Whitman. Precisely as in the life of the nation a great material civilization seems admirable to him and worthy of honour, yet of little value in comparison with or apart from a great spiritual civilization, a noble national character, so in the life of the individual all that is external, material, sensuous, is estimated by the worth of what it can give to the soul. No Hebrew ever maintained the rights of the spiritual more absolutely. But towards certain parts of our nature, although in the poet's creed their rights are dogmatically laid down, he is practically unjust. The tendencies of his own nature lead him in his preaching to sink unduly certain articles of his creed. The logical faculty, in particular, is almost an offence to Whitman. The processes of reasoning appear to him to have elaboration for their characteristic, and nothing elaborated or manufactured seems of equal reality with what is natural and has grown. Truth he feels to be, as Wordsworth has said, "a motion or a shape instinct with vital functions;" and were

Whitman to seek for formal proof of such truth, he, like Wordsworth, would lose all feeling of conviction, and yield up moral questions in despair. "A slumbering woman and child convince as an university course can never convince:"

"Logic and sermons never convince,
    The damp of the night drives deeper
        into my soul."

Whitman becomes lyrical in presence of the imagination attempting for itself an interpretation of the problems of the world; he becomes lyrical in presence of gratified senses and desires; but he remains indifferent in presence of the understanding searching after conclusions. There is something like intolerance or want of comprehensiveness here; one's heart, touched by the injustice, rises to take the part of this patient, serviceable, despised understanding.

Whitman, as we have seen, accepts the persons of all men, but for a certain make of manhood he manifests a marked preference. The reader can guess pretty correctly from what has gone before what manner of man best satisfies the desires of the poet, and makes him happiest by his presence; and what is the poet's ideal of human character. The man possessed of the largest mass of manhood, manhood of the most natural quality, unelaborated, undistilled, freely displaying itself, is he towards whom Whitman is instinctively attracted. The heroes honoured by the art of an aristocracy are ideal, not naturalistic. Their characters are laboriously formed after a noble model, tempered as steel is tempered, welded together and wrought into permanent shape as their armour is. The qualities which differentiate them from most men are insisted upon. They are as little a growth of nature (in the vulgar sense of the word *nature*) as is a statue. Corneille's stoical heroes, for example, are the work of a great *art* applied to human character. Our true nature can indeed only be brought to light by such art processes, but there is an art which works with nature, and another art which endeavours to supersede it. Only through culture, only through the strenuous effort to conceive things at their best, not as they are, but as they may and ought to be, only through the persistent effort to constrain them to their ideal (that is their most real) shapes, can human character and human society and the works of man become truly natural. Such art does not supersede nature, but is rather nature obtaining its most perfect expression through the consciousness of man. So declares Polixenes in *A Winter's Tale*:—

> "Nature is made better by no mean,
> But nature makes that mean; so, over that art,
> Which, you say, adds to nature, is an art
> That nature makes. You see, sweet maid, we marry
> A gentler scion to the wildest stock;
> And make conceive a bark of baser kind
> By bud of nobler race: This is an art
> Which does mend nature—change it rather: but
> The art itself is nature."

Whitman has not failed to perceive this truth, but he fears that it may be abused. Meddling with nature is a dangerous process. Any idea or model, after which we attempt to shape our humanity, must proceed from some *view* of human nature, and our *views* are too often formal and contracted, manufactures turned out of the workshop of the intellect, of which the ultimate product cannot but be a formal and contracted character. But human nature itself is large and incalculable; and, if allowed to grow unconstrained and unperverted, it will exhibit the superb vitality and the unimpeachable rectitude of the perfect animal or blossoming tree. Using *natural*, then, in the vulgar sense, there are some men more than others a part of nature; men not modelled after an idea remote from the instincts of manhood; vigorous children of the earth, of wholesome activity, passionate, gay, defiant, proud, curious, free, hospitable, courageous, friendly, wilful. In such men Whitman sees the stuff of all that is most precious in humanity. "Powerful uneducated persons" are the comrades he loves to consort with:—

> "I am enamour'd of growing outdoors;
> Of men that live among cattle, or taste of the ocean, or woods;
> Of the builders and steerers of ships, and the wielders of axes and mauls, and the drivers of horses;
> I can eat and sleep with them week in and week out."

These are certainly not the persons who engage the imagination in the literature of an aristocracy.

It must not, however, be supposed that Whitman sets himself against culture. He would, on the contrary, studiously promote culture, but a culture which has another ideal of character than that growth of feudal aristocracies, and which, accepting the old perennial elements of noblest manhood, combines them "into groups, unities appropriate to the modern, the democratic, the West." No conception of manhood can be appropriate unless it be of a kind which is suitable not to the uses of a single class or caste, but to those of the high average of men. The qualities of character which are judged of most value by the democratic standard

201

are not extraordinary, rare, exceptional qualities; the typical personality, which the culture sets before itself as its ideal, is one attainable by the average man. The most precious is ever in the common. Such a culture, Whitman holds, will be that of "the manly and courageous instincts, and loving perceptions, and of self-respect." Central in the character of the ideal man is the simple, unsophisticated Conscience, the primary moral element. "If I were asked to specify in what quarter lie the grounds of darkest dread, respecting the America of our hopes, I should have to point to this particular. . . . . Our triumphant, modern Civilizee, with his all-schooling, and his wondrous appliances, will still show himself but an amputation while this deficiency remains." If Whitman appears to be antagonistic to culture, as we commonly understand or misunderstand the term, to refinement, intellectual acquisition, multiform and delicate sympathies, the critical spirit, it is "not for absolute reasons, but current ones." In our times, he believes, refinement and delicatesse "threaten to eat us up like a cancer. . . . . To prune, gather, trim, conform, and ever cram and stuff, is the pressure of our days. . . . . Never, in the Old World, was thoroughly upholstered Exterior Appearance and show, mental and other, built entirely on the idea of caste, and on the sufficiency of mere outside acquisition—never were glibness, verbal intellect more the test, the emulation—more loftily elevated as head and sample,—than they are on the surface of our Republican States this day." In antagonism to the conception of culture which bears such fruit as this, Whitman desires one which, true child of America, shall bring joy to its mother, "recruiting myriads of men, able, natural, perceptive, tolerant, devout, real men, alive and full." In like manner Whitman's portraits of models of womanly Personality—the young American woman who works for herself and others, who dashes out more and more into real hardy life, who holds her own with unvarying coolness and decorum, who will compare, any day, with superior carpenters, farmers, "and even boatmen and drivers," not losing all the while the charm, the indescribable perfume of genuine womanhood, or that resplendent person down on Long Island, known as the Peacemaker, well toward eighty years old, of happy and sunny temperament, a sight to draw near and look upon with her large figure, her profuse snow-white hair, dark eyes, clear complexion, sweet breath, and peculiar personal magnetism—these portraits, he admits, are frightfully out of line from the imported Feudal models—"the stock feminine characters of the current novelists, or of the foreign court poems (Ophelias, Enids, Princesses, or Ladies of one thing or another), which fill the envying dreams of so many poor girls, and are accepted by our young men, too, as supreme ideals of female excellence to be sought after. But I present mine just for a change."

In the period of chivalry there existed a beautiful relation between man and man, of which no trace remains in existence as an institution—that of knight and squire. The protecting, encouraging, downward glance of the elder, experienced, and superior man was answered by the admiring and aspiring, upward gaze of the younger and inferior. The relation was founded upon inequality; from the inequality of the parties its essential beauty was derived. Is there any possible relation of no less beauty, corresponding to the new condition of things, and founded upon equality? Yes, there is manly comradeship. Here we catch one of the clearest and most often reiterated notes of Whitman's song. The feelings of equality, individualism, pride, self-maintenance, he would not repress; they are to be as great as the soul is great; but they are to be balanced by the feelings of fraternity, sympathy, self-surrender, comradeship. European Radicals have for the most part been divided into two schools, with the respective watchwords of *Equality* and *Fraternity*. Whitman expresses the sentiments of both schools, while his position as poet rather than theorist or politician, saves him from self-devotion to any such socialistic or communistic schemes, as the premature interpretation of the feeling of fraternity into political institutions has given birth to in untimely abortion. One division of *Leaves of Grass*, that entitled "Calamus" (Calamus being the grass with largest and hardiest spears and with fresh pungent *bouquet*), is appropriated to the theme of comradeship. And to us it seems impossible to read the poems comprised under this head without finding our interest in the poet Walt Whitman fast changing into hearty love of the man, these poems, through their tender reserves and concealments and betrayals, revealing his heart in its weakness and its strength more than any others. The chord of feeling which he strikes may be old—as old as David and Jonathan—but a fulness and peculiarity of tone are brought out, the like of which have not been heard before. For this love of man for man, as Whitman dreams of it, or rather confidently expects it, is to be no rare, no exceptional emotion, making its possessors illustrious by its singular preciousness, but it is to be widespread, common, unnoticeable.

"I hear it was charged against me
    that I sought to destroy
    institutions;
But really I am neither for nor
    against institutions:
(What indeed have I in common
    with them?

Or what with the destruction of
    them?)
Only I will establish in the
    Mannahatta, and in every city of
These States, inland and seaboard,
And in the fields and woods, and
    above every keel, little or large,
    that dents the water,
Without edifices, or rules, or
    trustees, or any argument,
The institution of the dear love of
    comrades."

In this growth of America, comradeship, which Whitman looks upon as a sure growth from seed already lying in the soil, he believes the most substantial hope and safety of the States will be found. In it he sees a power capable of counterbalancing the materialism, the selfishness, the vulgarity of American democracy—a power capable of spiritualizing the lives of American men. Many, Whitman is aware, will regard this assurance of his as a dream; but such loving comradeship seems to him implied in the very existence of a democracy, "without which it will be incomplete, in vain, and incapable of perpetuating itself." In the following poem the tenderness and ardour of this love of man for man finds expression, but not its glad activity, its joyous fronting the stress and tumultuous agitation of life:—

"When I heard at the close of the day
    how my name had been receiv'd
    with plaudits in the capitol, still it
    was not a happy night for me that
    follow'd;
And else, when I carous'd, or when
    my plans were accomplished, still
    I was not happy;
But the day when I rose at dawn
    from the bed of perfect health,
    refresh'd, singing, inhaling the
    ripe breath of autumn,

When I saw the full moon in the
     west grow pale and disappear in
     the morning light,
When I wander'd alone over the
     beach, and undressing, bathed,
     laughing with the cool waters,
     and saw the sun rise,
And when I thought how my dear
     friend, my lover, was on his way
     coming, O then I was happy;
O then each breath tasted sweeter—
     and all that day my food
     nourish'd me more—and the
     beautiful day pass'd well,
And the next came with equal joy—
     and with the next at evening,
     came my friend;
And that night, while all was still, I
     heard the waters roll slowly
     continually up the shores,
I heard the hissing rustle of the
     liquid and sands, as directed to
     me, whispering, to congratulate
     me,
For the one I love most lay sleeping
     by me under the same cover in
     the cool night,
In the stillness, in the autumn
     moonbeams, his face was inclined
     toward me,
And his arm lay lightly around my
     breast—and that night I was
     happy."

Various workings in the poems of Whitman of the influence of the principle of
equality as realized in the society which
surrounds him have now been traced. No
portion of the poet's body of thought and
emotion escapes its pervading power, and
in a direct and indirect manner it has
contributed to determine the character
of his feeling with respect to external
nature. In the way of crude mysticism
Whitman takes pleasure in asserting the
equality of all natural objects, and forces,
and processes, each being as mysterious

and wonderful, each as admirable and
beautiful as every other; and as the multitude of men and women, so, on occasions, does the multitude of animals, and
trees, and flowers press into his poems
with the same absence of selection, the
same assertion of equal rights, the same
unsearchableness, and sanctity, and beauty, apparent or concealed in all. By another working of the same democratic
influence (each man finding in the world
what he cares to find) Whitman discovers
everywhere in nature the same qualities,
or types of the same qualities which he
admires most in men. For his imagination
the powers of the earth do not incarnate
themselves in the forms of god and demi-
god, faun and satyr, oread, dryad, and
nymph of river and sea—meet associates,
allies or antagonists of the heroes of an
age, when the chiefs and shepherds of the
people were themselves almost demigods. But the great Mother—the Earth—
is one in character with her children of
the democracy, who, at last, as the poet
holds, have learned to live and work in
her great style. She is tolerant, includes
diversity, refuses nothing, shuts no one
out; she is powerful, full of vitality, generous, proud, perfect in natural rectitude,
does not discuss her duty to God, never
apologizes, does not argue, is incomprehensible, silent, coarse, productive, chari-
table, rich in the organs and instincts of
sex, and at the same time continent and
chaste. The grass Whitman loves as much
as did Chaucer himself; but his love has a
certain spiritual significance which Chaucer's had not. It is not the "soft, swete,
smale grass," embroidered with flowers,
a fitting carpet for the feet of glad knights
and sportive ladies, for which he cares.
In the grass he beholds the democracy
of the fields, earthborn, with close and
copious companionship of blades, each
blade like every other, and equal to every
other, spreading in all directions with lusty

life, blown upon by the open air, "coarse, sunlit, fresh, nutritious." The peculiar title of his most important volume, *Leaves of Grass*, as Mr. Rossetti has finely observed, "seems to express with some aptness the simplicity, universality, and spontaneity of the poems to which it is applied."

The character of Whitman's feeling with respect to external nature bears witness to the joyous bodily health of the man. His communication with the earth, and sea, and skies, is carried on through senses that are never torpid, and never overwrought beyond the measure of health. He presses close to nature, and will not be satisfied with shy glances or a distant greeting. He enjoys the strong sensations of a vigorous nervous system, and the rest and recuperation which follow. His self-projections into external objects are never morbid; when he employs the "pathetic fallacy" the world shares in his joyousness; he does not hear in the voices of the waters or of the winds echoes of a miserable egotism, the moan of wounded vanity, or the crying of insatiable lust. He is sane and vigorous. But his relation with nature is not one in which the senses and perceptive faculty have a predominant share. He passes through the visible and sensible things, and pursues an invisible somewhat—

"A motion and a spirit that impels
   All thinking things, all objects of all
      thought,
   And rolls through all things;"

and of this he can never quite possess himself. "There is [in his poems] a singular interchange of actuality and of ideal substratum and suggestion. While he sees men with even abnormal exactness as men, he sees them also 'as trees walking,' and admits us to perceive that the whole show is in a measure spectral and unsubstantial, and the mask of a larger and profounder reality beneath it, of which it is giving perpetual intimations and auguries."[5]

In the direction of religion and philosophy there is in the democratic state of society a strong tendency, as De Tocqueville has shown, towards a pantheistic form of belief, and a strong tendency towards the spirit of optimism. The equality existing between citizens, and the habit of mind which refuses to observe the ancient artificial social distinctions, give the general intellect a turn for reducing things to unity, a passion for comprehending under one formula many objects, and reducing to one cause many and various consequences.[6] Where castes or classes of society exist, one caste or class seems to object singularly little to the perdition of the inferior breeds of the human race— "this people who knoweth not the law are cursed." The Hindú could contemplate the fate of a Mlechha, the Jew, that of a Gentile, the Mahommedan, that of a Giaour, without overwhelming concern. But when the vision of a common life of the whole human race has filled the imagination, when a real feeling of solidarity is established between all the members of the great human community, the mind seems to shrink in horror from the suspicion that the final purposes of God or nature, with respect to man, can be other than beneficent. Society, in the democratic condition, is not fixed and desirous of conservation, but perpetually moving, and men's desires (apart from the results of scientific observation) induce them to hope, to conjecture, to believe that this movement is progressive. Biology and natural history with their doctrine of development and evolution, the science of origins with its surveys of the earliest history of our race seems to confirm the conviction, so flattering to men's desires, that nature and man harmoniously work under laws which tend towards a great and fortunate result. The events of the past are interpreted in the light of this conviction. Faith in the future becomes passionate, exists in the atmosphere, and obtaining nutriment from every wind, appears to sustain itself apart from all evidence—that miracle which belongs to every popular faith. The past progress of the race, the great future of the race to match the greatness of its past, the broad dealings of Providence or of natural law with mankind—when the thoughts of these, and feelings corresponding to such thoughts, have occupied the mind and heart, there appears something not only horrible, but something artificial, inconsequent, non-natural, in the notion of endless and fruitless penal suffering. And it is a noteworthy fact—the more remarkable when we bear in mind the Puritanical basis of American religion—that in the many new forms of religion which America has put forth as a tree puts forth leaves, in the many attempts towards the realization of a new conception of our relation to God and to one another, an almost constant element is the belief in the final happiness of all men.

The religious faith of Whitman, as far as it has definite form, reminds one of that taught in the Pedagogic Institution of Wilhelm Meister's *Wanderjahre*, in which from the Three Reverences inculcated, reverence for what is above us, reverence for what is around us, reverence for what is beneath us, springs the highest reverence, reverence for oneself. And with Whitman as with the Pedagogic company perfect reverence casts out fear. But he is not anxious to give his creed a precise form; he is so little interested in the exclusion of heretics that he does not require very accurate symbols and definitions.

"And I say to mankind, Be not
     curious about God,

For I, who am curious about each,
     am not curious about God,
(No array of terms can say how
     much I am at peace about God,
     and about death)."

Finding the present great and beautiful, contented with the past, but not driven into the past to seek for ideals of human character, and a lost golden age, Whitman has entire confidence in what the future will bring forth. He knows not what the purposes of life are for us, but he knows that they are good. Nowhere in nature can he find announcements of despair, or fixity of evil condition. He is sure that in the end all will be well with the whole family of men, and with every individual of it. The deformed person, the mean man, the infant who died at birth, the "sacred idiot," will certainly be brought up with the advancing company of men from whose ranks they have dropped:—

"The Lord advances, and yet
     advances;
Always the shadow in front—always
     the reach'd hand, bringing up the
     laggards."

At times this optimism leads Whitman to the entire denial of evil; "he contemplates evil as, in some sense, not existing, or, if existing, then as being of as much importance as anything else;" in some transcendental way, he believes, the opposition of God and Satan cannot really exist. Practically, however, he is not led astray by any such transcendental reducing of all things to the Divine. Any tendency of a mystical kind to ignore the distinction between good and evil, is checked by his strong democratic sense of the supreme importance of personal qualities, and the inevitable perception of the superiority of virtuous over vicious personal qualities. By one who feels profoundly that the differences between men are determined, not by rank, or birth, or hereditary name or title, but simply by the different powers belonging to the bodies and souls of men, there is small danger of the meaning of *bad* and *good* being forgotten. And Whitman never really forgets this. The formation of a noble national character, to be itself the source of all literature, art, statesmanship, is that which above all else he desires. In that character the element of religion must, according to Whitman's ideal, occupy an important place, only inferior to that assigned to moral soundness, to conscience. "We want, for These States, for the general character, a cheerful, religious fervour, imbued with the ever-present modifications of the human emotions, friendship, benevolence, with a fair field for scientific inquiry [to check fanaticism], the right of individual judgment, and always the cooling influences of material Nature." These are not the words of one who moves the landmarks of right and wrong, and obscures their boundaries. For Whitman the worth of any man is simply the worth of his body and soul; each gift of nature, product of industry, and creation of art, is valuable in his eyes exactly in proportion to what it can afford for the benefit of body and soul. Only what belongs to these, and becomes a part of them, properly belongs to us—the rest is mere "material." This mode of estimating values is very revolutionary, but to us it seems essentially just and moral. The rich man is not he who has accumulated unappropriated matter around him, but he who possesses much of what "adheres, and goes forward, and is not dropped by death."

Personality, character, is that which death cannot affect. Here again Whitman's democratic feeling for personality over-masters his democratic tendency towards pantheism. He clings to his iden-tity and his consciousness of it, and will not be tempted to surrender that consciousness in imagination by the attractions of any form of *nirvana*. Death, which is a name to him full of delicious tenderness and mystery not without some element of sensuousness curiously blended with it— ("O the beautiful touch of Death, soothing and benumbing a few moments, for reasons"), is but a solemn and immortal birth:—

"Dark Mother, always gliding near, with soft feet,
Have none chanted for thee a chant of fullest welcome?
Then I chant it for thee—I glorify thee above all;
I bring thee a song that when thou must indeed come, come unfalteringly."

From such indications as these, and others that have gone before, the reader must gather, as best he can, the nature of Whitman's religious faith. But the chief thing to bear in mind is that Whitman cares far less to establish propositions than to arouse energy and supply a stimulus. His pupil must part from him as soon as possible, and go upon his own way.

"I tramp a perpetual journey—(come listen all!)
My signs are a rain-proof coat, good shoes, and a staff cut from the woods;
No friend of mine takes his ease in my chair;
I have no chair, no church, no philosophy;
I lead no man to a dinner-table, library, or exchange;
But each man and each woman of you I lead upon a knoll,
My left hand hooking you round the waist,

My right hand pointing to
    landscapes of continents, and a
    plain public road."

That plain public road each man must travel for himself.

Here we must end. We have not argued the question which many persons are most desirous to put about Walt Whitman—"Is he a poet at all?" It is not easy to argue such a question in a profitable way. One thing only need here be said,— no adequate impression of Whitman's poetical power can be obtained from this article. A single side of his mind and of his work has been studied, but we have written with an abiding remembrance of the truth expressed by Vauvenargues:— "Lorsque nous croyons tenir la vérité par un endroit, elle nous échappe par mille autres."[7]

Notes

1 "A Greek head on right Yankee shoulders."———Lowell.
2 *Democracy in America*, vol. iii. p. 115, ed. 1840.
3 Quotations from the "Mirror of S. Edmund" and "Hali Meidenhead," published by the Early English Text Society.
4 "A Woman's Estimate of Walt Whitman." From late letters by an English Lady to

W. M. Rossetti. *The Radical*, May, 1870.
5 W. M. Rossetti. Prefatory notice to *Poems by Walt Whitman*.
6 See *La Démocratie en Amérique*, tome 3, chaps. vii. viii.
7 Since this article was begun another original voice has been heard from America. It would have been interesting to have compared, or rather contrasted (for they are far more unlike than like), the poems of Joaquin Miller with those of Whitman. Miller represents a barbaric age, and barbaric virtues, with an ancient civilization, that of Spain and Mexico, in the background. The Californian digger, the filibuster chief, the woman of the Indian tribes, are represented in the "Songs of the Sierras" as never before in American poetry. But in New York their author saw nothing except "a great place for cheap books, and a big den of small thieves." Whitman seeing this, sees also much beside this. In reading Miller's poems we are haunted by two lines of Whitman, in which his affinities with the South find expression:—

"O magnet South! O glistening, perfumed South! my South!
O quick mettle, rich blood, impulse and love! good and evil! O all dear to me!"

What Whitman names hero in abstractions, Miller represents embodied in the characters of individual men and women.

208

TWO RIVULETS (1876)

For the Eternal Ocean bound,
These ripples, passing surges, streams of Death and Life.

TWO

RIVULETS

Including DEMOCRATIC VISTAS, CENTENNIAL
SONGS, *and* PASSAGE TO INDIA.

AUTHOR'S EDITION.
CAMDEN, NEW JERSEY.
1876.

Edmund W. Gosse.
"Walt Whitman's New Book."
Academy 9
(24 June 1876), 602–3.

The new volume by Walt Whitman will not be found to contain any very important illustrations of his theory of poetic composition, or any very original ethical statements, but it throws a good deal of light upon his personal character, and embraces much individual and incidental matter which is of very high interest. In the first place, we fancy that it will be difficult for any sincere critic, desirous of judging without prejudice on either side, to read the "Memoranda during the War" without acknowledging that the author is personally brave and self-sacrificing, and the preface to the whole without admitting that his aims are pure and his belief in his own mission genuine. It has become difficult to speak of Whitman without passion. His opponents expend upon him every term of obloquy, private and public, which their repertory contains; his more extreme admirers claim for him all the respect reserved, long after their deaths, for the founders of successful religions. Between the class that calls Whitman an immoral charlatan bent on the corruption of youth, and the class that accounts him an inspired prophet, sent, among other iconoclastic missions, to abolish the practice of verse, there lies a great gulf. One would like to ask if it be not permitted that one should hold, provisionally, an intermediate position, and consider him a pure man of excellent intentions, to whom certain primitive truths with regard to human life have presented themselves with great vividness, and who

has chosen to present them to us in semi-rhythmic, rhetorical language, which rises occasionally, in fervent moments, to a kind of inarticulate poetry, and falls at others into something very inchoate and formless. A wise admirer might even say that the book called *Leaves of Grass* was intended to give a section, as it were, of the ordinary daily life of a normal man, and therefore properly falls, as every life does, occasionally into shapeless passages of mere commonplace or worse, Poetry proper being always occupied with the rapid and ecstatic moments of life, whether in sorrow or pleasure. The folly of refusing to admit any beauty in Whitman's work seems obvious in the face of a dozen such passages as the famous "Burial Hymn," or the picturesque parts of the rhapsody called "Walt Whitman;" the danger of acknowledging him with too little reserve is best realised if one conceives the dread possibility of the arising of a school of imitators of his tuneless recitative.

The book before us contains all the small miscellaneous writings of Whitman now collected for the first time. In verse (or recitative) we have the "Passage to India," which appeared in 1872 [*sic*], and "As a Strong Bird on Pinions Free," dating from the same year. The prose book called *Democratic Vistas* was printed in 1871, and all, therefore, which we have to consider here is the opening cluster of rhythmical pieces called "Two Rivulets," the "Centennial Songs," and the prose "Memoranda during the War," all which are now published for the first time. Of the brief but varied contents of the first of these, the most remarkable is a dramatic soliloquy put into the mouth of the dying Columbus, who, sick to death with grief and disappointment, but indomitable still, paces the shores of Jamaica and utters his piteous and majestic lament:—

211

"I am too full of woe!
  Haply I may not live another day;
  I cannot rest, O God, I cannot eat
  Or drink or sleep, till I put forth
      myself,
  My prayer, once more to Thee,
  Breathe, bathe myself once more in
      Thee, commune
  With Thee, report myself once more
      with Thee."

The division into lines is our own, the sequence of no words being altered, and it will be seen how naturally the slow march falls into scarcely irregular blank verse. This piece, which might take a place among the death-songs of "A Passage to India" may be contrasted with "The Ox-Tamer," a very fine study of life in the West, where

  "In a far-away northern county, in
      the placid, pastoral region,
  Lives my farmer-friend, the theme of
      my recitative, a famous Tamer of
      Oxen."

This is a worthy pendent to the description of the bridal of the Trapper, and the similar passages of marvellous picturesque directness to be found in *Leaves of Grass*. An address "To a Locomotive in Winter" is certainly the most vivid and imaginative view of an apparently hopeless subject yet achieved. "From that Sea of Time" presents a remarkably beautiful idea of the poet holding to his ear, one after another, the limpid and voiceless shells blown up on the shore of history, and hopelessly striving to gain from their murmurs some tidings of the sea of Time from whence they come, a thought kindred to the famous fancies of Wordsworth and of Landor. There is not much else in the section which possesses special merit, and there is one piece, called "Eidolons," which contains almost every vicious habit of style which Whitman has ever adopted, and which is quite enough, alone, to make the general objection to his writings plausible.

Of the four "Centennial Songs," one, "The Song of the Redwood Tree," has something primitive or Vedic in the strength of imagination which links in it in one great chorus the vast forces of nature, rain and snow and the wild winds, colossal trees, and huge mountains, and the serene skies above them all. This heroic chant is full of an arrogance appropriate to the occasion, and is far above any perfunctory trickle of complimentary song. The other three rhapsodies are hardly poetic, though vigorous and sympathetic. In the determination "to sing a song no poet yet has chanted," Whitman forces into his page an enumeration, of necessity fragmentary and whimsical, of the mechanical inventions and natural products of America. The result is decidedly grotesque. There is a very advanced Swedish poet of our day who has introduced "petroleum" into his verse, but that was in singing of the French Commune, and even he, and certainly every other bardic person, small or great, would shrink from inditing such a line as:—

  "Steam-power, the great express-lines,
      gas, petroleum."

The catalogue of the limbs of the human body, which has been so much laughed at in *Leaves of Grass*, was better than this. To Whitman the world and all it contains is so ceaselessly exciting and delightful that he is willing to let any objects whatever pass before his imagination in a kind of ceaseless phantasmagoria. This, however, is not enough for a poet; he has a constructive and elective work to do. Shelley has described the poet's enjoyment in the mere lazy observation of the current facts of nature, but he has not neglected to observe that this is not in itself poetry, any more than food or even chyle is in itself blood, for he has been careful to add:—

"Out of these create he can
Forms more real than living man."

It would be too much to assert that no poet will ever arise great enough to create nurselings of immortality out of the observation of such matters as express-lines, gas or petroleum, but certainly to recapitulate with emphasis the names of these things is not to produce poetry.

Space is not left us to characterise fully the "Memoranda during the War." They are notes, fragments, ejaculations of the most unaffected kind, and do more than any other writing to endear Whitman to us. There is something inexpressibly tender and manly in the tone of these notes; and something exceedingly stirring in the description of the alternate excitement and depression of the war-time: the pleasure in the presence around him of so many brave and handsome men, all fired with the same patriotic exaltation; the sadness of watching the deaths of so many of these in the prime of life. In the true spirit of his own passionate "Calamus," he wandered from tent to tent, ministering to the dying, comforting the wounded, bearing everywhere about with him that fragment of fragrant reed, that fascination of personal character, which he values so highly, and which he exercises over many who know him only through his books. From a literary point of view, his prose style may be justly criticised as heavy and disjointed, but the intrinsic interest of the story easily carries the reader above it. In some cases, as in the marvellously powerful description of the scene in the theatre when President Lincoln was shot, he is swept away into real eloquence, as in his recitatives into real poetry, by the fervour of his imagina-

tion. The ethical purpose of the book—and it is needless to say that it has one—manifestly is to exemplify in a very tragical passage of real life the possibility of carrying out that principle of sane and self-sacrificing love of comrades for one another which Whitman has so often celebrated in his most elevated and mystical utterances. It is the old story of Achilles and Patroclus transferred from windy Troy to the banks of the Potomac. It is conceivable that when all Whitman's theories about verse and democracy and religion have been rejected or have become effete, this one influence may be still at work, a permanent bequest of widened emotion to all future generations.

[J. H. McCarthy].
"Songs Oversea."
Examiner 3586
(21 October 1876),
1191–3.

It is now many years since the peace and placidity of the Republic of Letters, beginning to be shaken a little here at home by new songs of new singers, was first disturbed by the announcement of the advent of a great new poet on the other side of the Atlantic, a poet who, according to the expressions of the little band—small indeed but rapidly waxing—was to answer to the desire of one of Longfellow's prose-characters, and be the Bard of America with a song appropriate to the vastness of the subject. The poet's name was Walt Whitman, and by this magic name his faithful followers conjured until they got people to read these poems they loved so much. Then, indeed, the storm broke on the heads of the devoted adherents. The form of his song was not that to which so many centuries of European civilisation had been accustomed, therefore it was wholly unmusical, discordant, monstrous, horrible, and shapeless. But this was not all. Behind chaos came hell. The giant who broke light-hearted through the meshes of sonnet and sextain and rondel, who would have laughed with hearty Titanic laughter had he but known of them, at the quaint conceits and recipes of good Master George Puttenham for proportion poeticall, in staffe and in measure, and who recked not of lozenge or Tricquet, Pillaster, spire, sphere, or ovall, was discovered daring to speak of the body to a goodly and God-fearing generation, and for this Homeric simplicity was held as one of the company of the Arbiter or the Aretine. But, if many opposed him, many were of his party, and the most opposite and opposed schools of poetry agreed on this one point—admiration of the new master. But whether praised or blamed, Walt Whitman, with Carlyle's Danton, walked his own wild road whither it led him. But it has led him from the *Pays de l'amour*, and from passion of any sort, as it has led one of our own sweet chief poets, who once sang love and was cried at for singing, into the fierce arena of political struggle. In the *Two Rivulets* will be found no stream, no little runlet, that has passed through the Eden-garden of the children of Adam, nor are the waters ruffled by any wind-blown echo of Calamus, nor does the amorous animal—man—roll on and trample down the grass-leaves. Walt Whitman's new volume consists of *Two Rivulets*,

For the eternal ocean bound
These ripples, passing surges, streams
    of death and life,

twin channels of poetry and prose; the already familiar "Democratic Vistas," "Centennial Songs," "As a Strong Bird on Pinions free," "Memoranda during War," and "Passage to India." There is no need to revive here, even in slightest measure, any part of the old quarrel as to the exact designation suitable for such of the works of Walt Whitman as their author considers to be fitly baptised as poems. The power of the singer may be seen still vigorous in the poems "Eidolons" and "To a Locomotive in Winter;" the latter wonderful in its investiture of the mechanical monster with the parament of poetry and poetic thought, perhaps not wholly to be understood or appreciated except by those who have been in America; who have with it, in the "driving snow" of "a winter day declining," been

Launched o'er the prairies wide—
    across the lakes
To the free skies, unpent and glad
    and strong.

Here, too, in the "After the Sea-ship," as in "The Song of All Seas," which concludes the series of Centennial Songs, is found evidence of the writer's strong love and feeling for the sea and for its children, the rivers and lakes, which are found at their mightiest on the American continent. And this strong love for the sea he feels for all Nature. Truly Mr. Symonds says of him in 'The Greek Poets,' "Hopeful and fearless, accepting the world as he finds it, recognising the value of each human impulse, shirking no obligation, self-regulated by a law of perfect health, he, in the midst of a chaotic age, emerges clear and distinct, at one with nature, and therefore Greek." It was this admiration, this passionate worship of Nature, which led to much denunciation of the worshipper; it is this which still inspires and informs his work. But the present volume is distinctly a political, a historical, or, perhaps more correctly still, a prophetic book, and it deals with and treats of the mighty future of America.

214

Walt Whitman has been often, and with justice, compared to the painter—poet—prophet William Blake; like him he has not, it may be, obtained the recognition due to him; in this at least he suffers more than Blake, that he is better known in the land of the stranger than at home. Americans question his right to be the typical singer of America. Yet Walt Whitman has merits that no American prose-writer or poet ever yet had, with virtues and strength sufficient for claiming laureateship of the great American nation. Nothing in its way could be more splendidly dramatic and grandly descriptive than the account of the assassination of President Lincoln, one of the greatest and noblest of the central figures of modern political evolution. Space will not permit of its complete quotation from the Memoranda of the War, "these soiled and creas'd little *livraisons*, each composed of a sheet or two of paper, folded small to carry in the pocket, and fasten'd with a pin ... blotched here and there with more than one blood stain," which are amongst the most precious of Whitman's possessions—amongst the most precious of his gifts.

After relating how it was announced that Lincoln would be at the theatre on the night of April 14, 1865, and describing the contrast of the fearful tragedy about to be performed with the nature of the performance—*Our American Cousin*—at which Lincoln, who enjoyed theatrical performances, was present, he proceeds:—

Through the general hum following the stage pause, with the change of positions, etc., came the muffled sound of a pistol shot which not one hundredth part of the audience heard at the time—and yet a moment's hush—somehow, surely a vague startled thrill—and then, through the ornamented, draperied, starr'd and striped spaceway of the President's box, a sudden figure, a man, raises himself with hands and feet, stands a moment on the railing, leaps below to the stage (a distance of perhaps fourteen or fifteen feet), falls out of position, catching his boot-heel in the copious drapery (the American flag), falls on one knee, quickly recovers himself, rises as if nothing had happen'd (he really sprains his ankle, but unfelt then), and so the figure, Booth, the murderer, dress'd in plain black broadcloth, bareheaded, with a full head of glossy raven hair, and his eyes like some mad animal flashing with light and resolution, yet with a certain strange calmness, holds aloft in one hand a large knife—walks along not much back from the footlights, turns fully towards the audience his face of statuesque beauty, lit by those basilisk eyes, flashing with desperation, perhaps insanity—launches out in a firm and steady voice the words, *Sic semper tyrannis*—and then walks with neither slow nor very rapid pace diagonally across to the back of the stage, and disappears ... (Had not all this terrible scene—making the mimic ones preposterous—had it not all been rehears'd in blank, by Booth, beforehand?)

A moment's hush, incredulous—a scream—the cry of *murder*. Mrs. Lincoln leaning out of the box, with ashy cheeks and lips, with involuntary cry, pointing to the retreating figure, *He has killed the President* ... And still a moment's strange, incredulous suspense—and then the deluge!—then that mixture of horror, noises, uncertainty—the sound, somewhere back, of a horse's hoofs clattering with speed—the people burst through chairs and railings, and break them up—that noise adds to the queerness of the scene—there is inextricable confusion and terror—women faint— quite feeble persons fall and are trampled on—many cries of agony are heard—the broad stage suddenly fills to suffocation with a dense and motley crowd, like some horrible carnival—the audience rush generally upon it, at least the strong men do—the actors and actresses are all there in their play costumes and painted faces, with mortal fright showing through the rouge; some trembling, some in tears—the screams and calls, confused talk—redoubled, trebled—two or three manage to pass up water from the stage to the President's box—others try to clamber up, etc., etc., etc.

In the midst of all this, the soldiers of the President's Guard, with others, suddenly drawn to the scene, burst in (some two hundred altogether)—they storm the house, through all the tiers, especially the upper ones, inflamed with fury, literally charging the audience with fixed bayonets, muskets and pistols, shouting "*Clear out! clear out! you sons of———*." Such the wild scene, or a suggestion of it rather, inside the play-house that night.

. . . .

And in the midst of that night-pandemonium of senseless hate, infuriated soldiers, the audience and the crowd—the stage and all its actors and actresses, its paint-pots, spangles, and gas lights—the life-blood from those veins, the best and sweetest of the land, drips slowly down, and death's ooze already begins its little bubbles on the lips. . . . Such, hurriedly sketched, were the accompaniments of the death of President Lincoln. So suddenly, and in murder and horrors unsurpassed, he was taken from us. But his death was painless.

Such descriptive power as this would of right entitle Walt Whitman to place and name among the sons of men; and it is this, and such as this, which make the faults that must undoubtedly be admitted—among others, and perhaps most flagrant, the idle and unnecessary dislike of the poet to "old romance," to "novels, plots, and plays of foreign courts," and worst of all to "love-verses sugar'd in rhyme"—seem comparatively unimportant. Could he apply this power to the whole as to this one chapter, Walt Whitman might abandon all other titles for that of America's first historian.

W. Hale White. "The Genius of Walt Whitman." *The Secular Review,* 20 March 1880, pp. 180–2.

It is rather remarkable that Walt Whitman's last book, the *Two Rivulets*, should have received so little recognition in this country. There has been no English edition, and so far as the present writer knows, nothing has been said about it in any of the Reviews. Yet this book contains, perhaps, the best defence of Democracy which has been offered of late years, some of the truest poetry, and not a few arrowy sayings, which, if they have not pierced the core of the great problems which have eternally troubled humanity, have at any rate penetrated them profoundly.

The *Two Rivulets* consists of prose and verse. The prose is made up of an essay called "Democratic Vistas," and of memoranda written during the great Civil War of the States. The author was a volunteer in the hospitals, and he tells us his experiences in the wards and in the camps. The verse, with one or two exceptions, is unmetrical and unrhymed, in the same style as the *Leaves of Grass*. No man more clearly than Whitman has seen the seamy side of Republicanism, as it is presented in the United States. At times his faith in the people has apparently been altogether shattered, and passages might be cited which, taken by themselves, would lead us to believe that he is without hope. He sees "the chaotic confusion of labour in the Southern States, the growing and alarming spectacle of countless squads of vagabond children, the hideousness and squalor of certain quarters of the cities; the advent of late years, with increasing frequency, of these pompous, nauseous, outside shows of vulgar wealth," and what he calls his "darkest dread," the decay of the "simple, unsophisticated conscience, the primary moral element." "Our triumphant modern civilisee," he proclaims, "with his all-schooling and his wondrous appliances, will still show himself but an amputation while this deficiency remains."

"The underlying principles of the States are not honestly believed in (for all this hectic glow and these melodramatic screamings), nor is humanity itself believed in. What penetrating eye does not everywhere see through the mask? The spectacle is appalling. We live in an atmosphere of hypocrisy throughout. The men believe not in the women, nor the women in the men. A scornful superciliousness rules in literature. The aim of all the *littérateurs* is to find something to make fun of. A lot of churches, sects, &c., the most dismal phantasms I know, usurp the name of religion. Conversation is a mass of badinage. From deceit in the spirit, the mother of all false deeds, the

offspring is already incalculable. An acute and candid person in the Revenue department at Washington, who is led by the course of his employment to regularly visit the cities, north, south, and west, to investigate frauds, has talked much with me (1869, 1870) about his discoveries. The depravity of the business classes of our country is not less than has been supposed, but infinitely greater. The whole of the official services of America, national, State, and municipal, in all their branches and departments, except the Judiciary, are steeped, saturated, in corruption, bribery, falsehood, maladministrations; and the Judiciary is tainted. The great cities reek with respectable as much as non-respectable robbery and scoundrelism. In fashionable life, flippancy, tepid amours, weak infidelism, small aims, or no aims at all, only to kill time . . . I say that our New World Democracy, however great a success in uplifting the masses out of their sloughs, in materialistic-development products, and in a certain highly deceptive, superficial, popular intellectuality, is so far an almost complete failure in its social aspects, in any superb, general-personal character, and in really grand, religious, moral, literary and æsthetic results."

Nevertheless, on the whole, his doubts are over-mastered, and, as against any other form of government, he decides for self-government. He believes "the ulterior object of political and all other government (having, of course, provided for the police, the safety of life, property, and for the basic statute and common law, and their administration, always first in order) to be among the rest, not merely to rule and to repress disorder, but to develop, to open up to cultivation, to encourage the possibilities of all beneficent and manly outcroppage, and of that aspiration for independence and the pride and self-respect latent in all characters (or if there be exceptions, we cannot, fixing our eyes on them alone, make theirs the rule for all). I say the mission of government henceforth, in civilised lands, is not repression alone, and not authority alone, not even of law, nor by that favourite standard of the eminent writer (Carlyle), the rule of the best men, the born heroes and captains of the race (as if such ever, or one time out of a hundred, get into the big places, elective or dynastic!), but higher than the highest arbitrary rule, to train communities through all their grades, beginning with individuals and ending there again, to rule themselves."

"What Christ appeared for in the moral-spiritual field for humankind—namely, that in respect to the absolute soul there is, in the possession of such by each single individual, something so transcendent, or incapable of gradations (like life), that, to that extent, it places all beings on a common level, utterly regardless of the distinctions of intellect, virtue, or station, or any height or lowliness whatever, is tallied in like manner, in this other field, by Democracy's rule, that men, the nation, as a common aggregate of living identities, affording in each a separate and complete subject for freedom, worldly thrift, and happiness, and for a fair chance for growth, and for protection in citizenship, &c. must to the political extent of the suffrage or vote, if no further, be placed, in each and in the whole, on one broad, primary, universal, common platform." Walt Whitman's creed in this matter has been largely shaped by the war. He found the average American in the United States' armies, under pressure of want, disease, danger, and at one time in presence of failure, to be nobler than a mere glance at the outside of political life would have reported him to be. He records with joy that once, when he stood by the bedside of a Pennsylvania soldier,

who lay conscious of approaching death, yet perfectly calm "and with noble spiritual manner," an old surgeon observed that "he had not seen yet the first case of man or boy that met the approach of dissolution with cowardly qualms or terror." He insists on the grandeur of the great uprising of the people for the sake of an idea, and the equally grand spectacle of the peaceful disbanding of the gigantic armies, and their absorption, without a word, into the ranks of the citizens. Lastly, he is convinced that, whatever follies Democracy may commit, owing mainly to its indifference, there resides in it a power of enthusiastic self-assertion on all great occasions when appeal is fairly made to it.

This is but a poor and brief account of Whitman's argument. The subject is one too large for discussion in a couple of columns; but those who care for it, if they turn to the "Democratic Vistas," will assuredly find that Whitman's plea is not school logic nor mere vapouring, but that it is *from himself*, and that every line has life in it.

After reading Whitman's poetry, we are apt to condemn nine-tenths of modern poetry as nothing but jingle. Some of his verses, like "After the Sea Ship," for example, are merely expressive of nature— that is to say, a natural phenomenon, commonplace enough, is selected, described, and set in a frame. But we recognise a peculiar charm—the charm of the picture, the secret of all art, and we say to ourselves, the man who takes anything which lies around us unnoticed, and holds it up to us as something worthy of admiration; who signalises its special beauty; who gives it voice; who acts as the tongue of the dumb world to us, is one of our greatest benefactors. Whitman never leaves the Present for the Past, in order to find his romance. He is utterly free from that miserable modern sentimentality which discerns nothing in our own time worth seeing, but must take all its subjects from a century, or ten centuries, or twenty centuries ago; a sentimentality morally pernicious, because, under its influence, life passes away like a dream, all the messages of the Present lying entirely disregarded. To Whitman the nineteenth century is emphatically the century for him; and he is not afraid even to write an ode to a locomotive. The poetry of the present epoch is infected with a scepticism worse than anything ever condemned by council or synod. It parades before us a weak despair, an insistence on the irreconcileable in nature, the parting of friends never to meet again, the obliteration of the landscape by the advancing ugliness of cities, the insolubility of the riddles of life, death, and the infinite. The trick, for trick it is, is easy enough. Every man with the least capacity for anything beyond the pleasures of the senses is full enough of such stuff as this; but he ought to consider himself bound not to speak it. Unless he can help his fellow creatures to courage and to faith, let him hold his tongue. Whitman refuses to be cowed even by death.

"O what shall I hang on the chamber walls?
And what shall the pictures be that I hang on the walls,
To adorn the burial house of him I love?
Pictures of growing spring, and farms, and homes,
With the fourth-month eve at sundown, and the grey smoke lurid and bright,
With floods of the yellow gold, and the gorgeous, indolent, sinking sun burning, expanding the air;
With the fresh sweet herbage under foot, and the pale, green leaves of the trees prolific,

In the distance the flowing glaze, the breast of the river, with a wind-dapple here and there;
With ranging hills on the banks, with many a line against the sky, and shadows;
And the city at hand, with dwellings so dense, and stacks of chimneys,
And all the scenes of life, and the workshops, and the workmen homeward returning."

He believes that thought will be its own cure; that if we are afflicted by doubt, we must not hesitate—least of all must we stop short and hide ourselves in a fiction; but that we must go forward.

"O my brave soul!
O farther, farther sail!
O daring joy, but safe! Are they not all the seas of God?
O farther, farther, farther sail!"

The reader of the *Two Rivulets* will notice, what was so obvious in the *Leaves of Grass*, a determination to make men satisfied with their own lives. Whitman does not teach that life is to be reckoned by a few consummate moments, to which we are to look back, or for which we are to wait. He sings the sweetness of common occupations. He knows that in mere life itself there is something, there is much that is good, and that we must find our happiness in the common day's work, relationships, and visitations, unless we wish our existence to be excavated, a mere hollow reminiscence or anticipation.

Finally, he holds that it is possible for man, even in his last extremity, to preserve his serenity, and still to hope. It is almost murder to mutilate his exquisite "Prayer of Columbus" by not quoting it entire; but nevertheless, the closing verses must be given by way of illustrating the sublimity of his faith:—

219

"One effort more—my altar this
  bleak sand;
That thou, O God, my life hast
  lighted,
With ray of light, steady, ineffable,
  vouchsafed of thee
(Light rare, untellable—lighting the
  very light!
Beyond all signs, descriptions,
  languages)!
For that, O God—be it my latest
  word, here on my knees,
Old, poor, and paralysed—I thank
  thee.

"My terminus near,
The clouds already closing in upon
  me,
The voyage balk'd, the course
  disputed, lost,
I yield my ships to thee,
Steersman unseen! henceforth the
  helms are thine;
Take thou command—what to my
  petty skill thy navigation?

"My hands, my limbs, grow
  nerveless;
My brain feels rack'd, bewilder'd;
Let the old timbers part, I will not
  part;
I will cling fast to thee, O God,
  though the waves buffet me—
Thee, thee, at least, I know.

"Is it the prophet's thought I speak,
  or am I raving?
What do I know of life? What of
  myself?
I know not even my own work, past
  or present;
Dim, ever shifting guesses of it
  spread before me,
Of nearer, better worlds; their
  mighty parturition
Mocking, perplexing me.

"And these things I see suddenly—
  what mean they?
As if some miracle, some hand

divine unseal'd my eyes:
Shadowy, vast shapes smile through
  the air and sky;
And on the distant waves sail
  countless ships;
And anthems in new tongues I hear
  saluting me."

In this "Prayer of Columbus" Whitman has reached the highest point of self-negation—a point which it seems sometimes impossible to attain. It is almost beyond us to be able to say: "I am perfectly content if only the evolution goes on which my existence has helped. Whatever may happen to me—whether I live or die; whether our immortality be a truth or a figment—I am altogether resigned and happy." It is clear that this must be the goal of our ethics; and, until we have overcome even to that end, we shall be the victims of unceasing despairs. Till then we build on illusions, which for a moment seem to possess reality, and presently vanish, mocking our hopes.

If a motto were to be chosen for the *Two Rivulets*, and for Walt Whitman generally, it should be that noble sentence from the preface to "The Hesperus" of Jean Paul:—

The stones and rocks, which two veiled shapes, necessity and sin, like Deucalion and Pyrrha, throw behind them at the good, shall become new men.

And on the western gate of this century stands written:

'Here is the road to Virtue and
  Wisdom.'

Just as on the western gate of Cherson stood the sublime inscription—

'Here leads the way to Byzantium.
Infinite Providence, thou wilt make
  the day dawn.'

LEAVES OF GRASS (1881–2)

LEAVES

of

GRASS

BOSTON
JAMES R. OSGOOD AND COMPANY
1881-2

"Whitman's *Leaves of Grass.*"
Critic [New York] 1 (5 November 1881), 302–3.

Practically, but not actually, this is the first time that Mr. Whitman has issued his poems through a publishing house instead of at his private cost. The two volumes called *Leaves of Grass* and the *Two Rivulets*, which he had printed and himself sold at Camden, N. J., are now issued in one, under the former title, without special accretions of new work, but not without a good deal of re-arrangement in the sequence of the poems. Pieces that were evidently written later, and intended to be eventually put under *Leaves of Grass* now find their place; some that apparently did well enough where they were have been shifted to other departments. On the whole, however, the changes have been in the direction of greater clearness as regards their relation to the sub-titles. It is not apparent, however, that the new book is greatly superior to the old in typography, although undeniably the fault of the privately printed volumes, a variation in types used, is no longer met with. The margins are narrower, and the look of the page more commonplace. The famous poem called 'Walt Whitman' is now the 'Song of Myself.' It still maintains:

I too am not a bit tamed, I too am
    untranslatable;
I sound my barbaric yawp over the
    roofs of the world.

It still has the portrait of Whitman when younger, standing in a loose flannel shirt and slouched hat, with one hand on his hip, the other in his pocket. 'Eidolons' has been taken from the second volume and placed, for good reasons that the reader may not be ready to understand, among the first pieces gathered under the sub-title 'Inscriptions.' It ends with the 'Songs of Parting,' under which the last is 'So Long,' a title that a foreigner and perhaps many an American might easily consider quite as untranslatable as Mr. Whitman proclaims himself to be. The motive for the publication seems to be to take advantage of that wider popularity which is coming somewhat late in life to him whom his admirers like to call 'the good gray poet.'

One great anomaly of Whitman's case has been that while he is an aggressive champion of democracy and of the working-man, in a broad sense of the term working-man, his admirers have been almost exclusively of a class the farthest possibly removed from that which labors for daily bread by manual work. Whitman has always been truly caviare to the multitude. It was only those that knew much of poetry and loved it greatly who penetrated the singular shell of his verses and rejoiced in the rich, pulpy kernel. Even with connoisseurs, Whitman has been somewhat of an acquired taste, and it has always been amusing to note the readiness with which persons who would not or could not read him, raised a cry of affectation against those who did. This phenomenon is too well known in other departments of taste to need further remark; but it may be added that Mr. Whitman has both gained by it and lost. He has gained a vigorousness of support on the part of his admirers that probably more than outbalances the acrid attacks of those who consider his work synonymous with all that is vicious in poetical technique, and wicked from the point of morals. As to the latter, it must be confessed that, according to present standards of social relations, the doctrines taught by Whitman might readily be construed, by the overhasty or unscrupulous, into excuses for foul living: for such persons do not look below the surface, nor can they grasp the whole idea of Whitman's treatment of love. However fervid his expressions may be, and however scornful he is of the miserable hypocrisies that fetter but also protect the evilly disposed, it is plain that the idea he has at heart is that universal love which leaves no room for wickedness because it leaves no room for doing or saying unkind, uncharitable, unjust things to his fellow-man. With an exuberance of thought that would supply the mental outfit of ten ordinary poets, and with a rush of words that is by no means reckless, but intensely and grandly labored, Whitman hurls his view of the world at the heads of his readers with a vigor and boldness that takes away one's breath. This century is getting noted among centuries for singular departures in art and literature. Among them all, there is none bolder or more original than that of Whitman. Perhaps Poe in his own line might be cited as an equal. It is strange, and yet it is not strange, that he should have waited so long for recognition, and that by many thousands of people of no little culture his claims to being a poet at all are either frankly scouted or else held in abeyance. Literature here has remarkably held aloof from the vital thoughts and hopes of the country. It seems as if the very crudity of the struggle here drove people into a petty dilettante atmosphere of prettiness in art and literature as an escape from the dust and cinders of daily life. Hence our national love for 'slicked up' pictures, for instance, by which it is often claimed in Europe that promising geniuses in painting, there, have been ruined for higher work. Hence our patronage of poets that have all the polish of a cymbal, but all a cymbal's dry note and hollowness. Hence, at one time, our admiration for orators that were ornate to the verge of inanity. Into this hot-house air of literature Walt Whitman bounded, with the vigor and suppleness of a clown at a funeral. Dire were the grimaces of the mourners in high places, and dire are their grimaces still. There were plenty of criticisms to make, even after one had finished crying Oh! at the frank sensuality, the unbelievable nakedness of Walt. Everything that decent folk covered up, Walt exhibited, and boasted of exhibiting! He was proud of his nakedness and sensuality. He cried, Look here, you pampered rogues of literature, what are you squirming about, when you know, and everybody knows, that things are just like this, always have been, always will be? But it must be remembered that this was what he wrote, and that he did with a plan, and by order from his genius. It has never been heard of him that he was disgusting in talk or vile in private life, while it has been known that poets celebrated for the lofty tone of their morality, for the strictness of their Christianity, the purity of their cabinet hymns, can condescend in private life to wallow in all that is base. That is the other great anomaly of Whitman. He rhapsodizes of things seldom seen in print with the enthusiasm of a surgeon enamoured of the wonderful mechanism of the body. But he does not soil his conversation with lewdness. If evil is in him, it is in his book.

Whitman's strength and Whitman's weakness lie in his lack of taste. As a mere external sign, look at his privately printed volumes. For a printer and typesetter, reporter and editor, they do not show taste in the selection and arrangement of the type. A cardinal sin in the eyes of most critics is the use of French, Spanish, and American-Spanish words which are scattered here and there, as if Whitman had picked them up, sometimes slightly incorrectly, from wandering minstrels, Cubans, or fugitives from one of Walker's raids. He shows crudely the American way of incorporating into the language a handy or a high-sounding word without elaborate examination of its original meaning, just as we absorb the different nationalities that crowd over from Europe. His thought and his mode of expression is immense, often flat, very often monotonous, like our great sprawling cities with their endless scattering of suburbs. Yet when one gets the 'hang' of it, there is a colossal grandeur in conception and execution that must finally convince whoever will be patient enough to look for it. His rhythm, so much burlesqued, is all of a part with the man and his ideas. It is apparently confused; really most carefully schemed; certainly to a high degree original. It has what to the present writer is the finest thing in the music of Wagner—a great booming movement or undertone, like the noise of heavy surf. His crowded adjectives are like the mediæval writers of Irish, those extraordinary poets who sang the old Irish heroes and their own contemporaries, the chiefs of their clans. No Irishman of to-day has written a nobler lament for Ireland, or a more hopeful, or a more truthful, than has Walt Whitman. Yet it is not said that he has Irish blood. Nor is there to be found in our literature another original piece of prose so valuable to future historians as his notes on the war. Nor is there a poet of the war-time extant who has so struck the note of that day of conflict as Whitman has in 'Drum Taps.' He makes the flesh creep. His verses are like the march of the long lines of volunteers, and then again like the bugles of distant cavalry. But these are parts of him. As he stands complete in *Leaves of Grass,* in spite of all the things that regard for the decencies of drawing-rooms and families may wish away, he certainly represents, as no other writer in the world, the struggling, blundering, sound-hearted, somewhat coarse, but still magnificent vanguard of Western civilization that is encamped in the United States of America. He avoids the cultured few. He wants to represent, and does in his own strange way represent, the lower middle stratum of humanity. But, so far, it is not evident that his chosen constituency cares for, or has even recognized him. Wide readers are beginning to guess his proportions.

"Walt Whitman's Poems." *Literary World* 12 (19 November 1881), 411–12.

This is the collected and revised poetry of Walt Whitman, who, some will have it, is by preeminence of art and nature our representative American poet. It will be noticed that at last he has found a publisher other than himself. What this nation may become it might not be wise to prophesy; but we may at the start humbly entertain the hope, at least, that at this present writing our nationality, in root and fiber, is something else than what Mr. Whitman sings. His book is one of courage, most downright in its dogmatics, and says its say apparently without the slightest consideration for the fact that much it says must cross and shock the deepest ethical instincts of a great multitude—we should certainly hope the vast majority of those American men and women who by any misfortune are led to read him. For these poems are of that breed that they force the honest critic into a corner where he must either speak plain words, or step down and out from his judgment-seat. This is a book which makes not only war upon nearly all traditional theories of true poetry, but in many places a very brutal assault upon our fixed ideas of human decency and purity. For instance, it has long been held that poetry is not merely the prose of any philosophy, history, geography, anthropology, or, we might add, anatomy or sexual physiology; but must have some sort of inherent rhythm and melody—the heartbeats and spiritual pulsations of the poet. This, for want of a better term, we call the *form* of poetry. Tennyson, for example, is a master of poetic form. The poems under review, as to form, run to a chaos of monotonies. It is not the chaotic diversity of the wild woods, or the sea waves, or the autumn leaves, or the sand grains in a gravel-pit, in all which there is the articulated beauty and inbred virtue of nature obedient to the Great Craftsman. The chaos of Mr. Whitman's verse, to compare great with small, reminds us of the gray clay bluffs of Truro Beach. Would it were as clean! In form he reminds us of Martin Farquhar Tupper.

There is vastly more to be said as to his substance. First of all, and gladly, this: that he has, in his nigh four hundred pages, spurts and flashes of some things which say: "This could and should have been a noble creature." He has a quick, sharp sight for the surfaces of natural scenery, as when he speaks of the "heart-shaped" leaf of the lilac; but somehow he seems incapable of grasping the inner spiritual lessons of field and flood, or a spiritual analogy. The best instance of the opposite we have found on a careful search is this:

I believe a leaf of grass is no less than the journey work of the stars (p. 53).

His grasp of the detail of an event, but not of its ethical quality, is shown in his description of a sea-fight [pp. 62–63]. Somehow he never shows us the soul of anything. We may ask even, "Does he believe there is any such thing as a soul?" American he is, of the ruder and more barbaric type, a prairie cow boy in a buffalo robe, with a voice of the east wind, shouting prophecies and incantations about what he thinks he sees and knows. But from civilized speech or melody he seems strangely remote. Egotism, if a virtue, is certainly an unfragrant one, and Walt Whitman's egotism, grotesque as it is, is perhaps less grotesque than gigantic. He describes himself well enough in the lines,

I am not a bit tamed, I too am untranslatable—
I sound my barbaric yawp over the roofs of the world.

Mr. Whitman's religion is no doubt to him a serious matter, and it is a somewhat serious matter to discover what in the world it is. He often discourses eloquently of God, as when (p. 76) he says:

I find letters from God dropt in the street and every one is signed by God's name,
And I leave them where they are for I know that wheresoever I go
Others will punctually come forever and ever.

Yet the prevalent tone of his verses is curiously Asiatic, as though he were an incarnation of Brahma, and a pantheist. He says (p. 31):

Clear and sweet is my soul, and clear and sweet is all that is not my soul.

(A cess-pool, for instance).

In fact, he declares himself to be all that the universe is, even to being at the same moment each of two exactly opposite things, as though a man at any given instant were and were not. Indeed, it is this rapt but noisy mysticism which makes it rather hard to finger Mr. Whitman and touch his quality. Not that true poetry does not allow mysticism, or that mystics are not often poets. Indeed, high poetry is often a blessed hint, and only a hint, of a vaster world within the veil of the unreachable and the non-measurable. Uhland's ballad, "The Two Locks of Hair," for instance, hints at the draped and veiled world of sorrow, whose mysteries are only revealed to the mourners after here. Mr. Whitman's mysticism is a fog-bank that cloaks all, even the possible hint itself. Add to this his all-pervading oracularity of speech, and he is certainly a man hard to be "understanded" of common folk. And yet there are gleams in his book, not only of great things, but of possibly magnificent ones. His tribute to Abraham Lincoln (p. 262), beginning "O Captain! my Captain!" is a weird and rare performance. "The Singer in the Prison" (p. 292) beginning

O sight of pity, shame and dole
O fearful thought—a convict soul,

is full of tenderness and pathos.

The ethical quality of Mr. Whitman's poems remains to be examined. Here, in all honesty, it is hard to know what to say or what to leave unsaid. Gray hairs have their rights, and ought to be a shield against taunt and bitterness; but woman's purity and human society have their rights also, and there are little children growing up into the arena of the world's toil and trial who have their rights as well. We go now upon the assumption that there are certain elements of decency which pervade all human society, heathen and otherwise, and that the world is not too old to blush. We say that there are passages in this book that never ought to

have been written, much less published; passages which sound like a lecture on the obstetrics of lust and (may we say it with all deference to our well-bred readers) the apotheosis of the Phallus. It is hard to overstate this matter. When a man with such physical imagery of shame summons the very wind (p. 49) to be assistant in a poetical concubinage as realistic as a French invisible card, and the salt sea also (p. 46), it is certainly time for us common mortals who have still some respect for the seventh commandment to stay in doors from the elements, or, if at sea, to make all speed for the shore. The offense in this wise is not all-pervading, but it is very acute and deep.

His apologists will say of him that he is only another Adam in the Garden, naked and not ashamed. We say of him, and of all who have assisted in the making of his book, that they are guilty of an act of indecent exposure.

For the rest, what Mr. Whitman might have been in poetry we have tried to fairly state. We can only add that if in these *Leaves of Grass* he has shown himself to be a poet, then the great and shining ones whom the English-speaking race have been wont to honor with this high title, are not.

E[dward] P. M[itchell]. "Walt Whitman and the Poetry of the Future." New York *Sun*, 19 November 1881, p. 2.

The publication of the *Leaves of Grass* by a reputable bookmaking house, as a business enterprise, and without expurgation, marks very distinctly an epoch in

Walt Whitman's career. It was inevitable that the force of his genius should carry, sooner or later, the inner citadel of respectable literature; but the event has been delayed for a quarter of a century. During that time he has been his own printer and bookseller. Containing passages which under a strict construction of certain statutes of the United States could not be permitted to pass through the mails, the privately printed volumes have found a constantly increasing number of purchasers and readers. The accessions have not been from the ranks of the depraved and prurient. Walt Whitman's audience has grown, not by reason of, but in spite of, his frank disregard of some of the proprieties of utterance. Of this side of the matter it is enough to say that if the new edition is a triumph for the poet, it has been achieved without any concession on his part. He has modified nothing. He has cancelled no objectionable line or offensive phrase. He has confessed no sin against good taste or decency. In pushing his way into his present company he has not for an instant hauled in his elbows.

In another respect the appearance of the new edition of *Leaves of Grass* is an interesting event. For the first time, the poet can be judged by his poetic scheme in its entirety. The additional verses are not so important in themselves as in the relation of parts to a completed whole. Walt Whitman's admirers have always insisted that criticism before the final development of the plan was premature. The poet has compared his work to one of those ambitious old architectural edifices, built part by part at long intervals, and showing the designer's idea only when the last stone was in place. The gaps have now all been filled. The revision of the several poems, and their rearrangement with reference to the sub-titles and to each other, leave them, we are told, as they were designed to be.

While Walt Whitman has kept steadily on his way, unshaken in belief in his mission and uncompromising as to his methods, he has provoked a difference of public opinion more marked, perhaps, than in the case of any author now alive. His aggressiveness seems to leave no middle ground. He is either a genius of colossal proportions or an immense windbag; either to be hailed and worshipped or to be punctured. A considerable part of his contemporaries hold him to be beneath criticism; a small circle of ardent admirers exalt him above it. The poet himself, it is to be feared, is prone to encourage the latter view. Every page that he has written discloses an egotism that reaches the verge of sublimity. He is impatient even of discriminating eulogy. He is said to hold as no better than a vender of scurrilities a friend of his, himself a poet, who not long ago published a magazine article in which the laudation of *Leaves of Grass* was measured instead of being unreserved. With Walt it is: Take me or leave me; but if you take me, take me as the Consummate Man. In estimating a singer and seer this indomitable self-confidence is a quality that ought not to be overlooked. To refuse to admit it as corroborative proof of genius would be to reject one of the lessons of biography. Walt's vigorous personality and the purity and naïve simplicity of his private life have drawn about him a circle of devoted friends. They cannot understand why his genius should be denied or overlooked any more than they can see how the existence of the sun can be denied or overlooked when it is shining in a clear sky at noonday. They are exasperated because the great public is so slow to accept the poet at their valuation and his own. On the other hand, those to whom Whitman is a noisy madman, or a disturber of the poetic peace, or a bawler of platitudes, are reluctant to give the poet's adherents credit for any better motive than the affectation of eccentricity. The "good gray poet" business disgusts them. They are puzzled by the admiration with which Whitman's achievements are regarded by Emerson and Tennyson and other bards who are as unlike the Bard of Paumanok as so many gentlemen in evening dress are unlike a gentleman in a diving suit. And all the while the belief is growing in cultivated minds that in Walt Whitman we have one of the most remarkable and original individualities in literature.

Let us look first at his method. It is from the superficial and non-essential characteristics of *Leaves of Grass* that the popular conception of the poet is derived. The oddities, the whim-whams, the grotesque contrasts lie on the surface, lending themselves readily to burlesque, and affording plenty of material for ridicule.

Whitman's versification proceeds in the loosest possible fashion, discarding rhyme altogether, except in rare instances. A vague effect of rhythm is preserved, the cæsura recurring at irregular and often widely unequal intervals. It is an informal but roughly harmonious flow of words, sustaining the same relation to finished verse as the recitative to the aria. It is regarded by many as a startling innovation, but is really nothing more than a return to the earliest and most nearly spontaneous form of poetic expression. For purpose of comparison, as regards external form only, we place a passage from "The Return of the Heroes" side by side with passages from the Sixty-fifth and One Hundred, and Fourth Psalms in the English version:

Loud O my throat, and clear O soul!
The season of thanks and the voice of full yielding,
The chant of joy and power for boundless fertility.

All tilled and untilled lands expand before me,

I see the true arenas of my race, or first or last,
Man's innocent and strong arenas.

I see the heroes of other toils,
I see well wielded in their hands the better weapons.

I see where the Mother of All.
With full-spanning eye gazes forth, dwells long.
And counts the varied gathering of the products.

Busy the far, the sunlit panorama,
Prairie, orchard, and yellow grain of the North,
Cotton and rice of the South, and Louisiana cane,
Open unseeded follows, rich fields of clover and timothy,
Kine and horses feeding, and droves of sheep and swine,
And many a stately river flowing and many a jocund brook,
And healthy uplands with herby-perfumed breezes,
And the good, green grass, that delicate miracle the ever-recurring grass.

Praise walketh for thee, O God, in Zion;
O thou that hearest prayer, unto thee shall all flesh come.
Thou crownest the year with thy goodness.

Thy paths drop fatness, they drop upon the pastures of the wilderness;
And the little hills rejoice on every side.

The pastures are clothed with flocks.
The valleys also are covered over with corn.

Bless the Lord, O my soul!
O Lord, my God, thou art very great;
Thou art clothed with honor and majesty.

He watereth the hills from his
chambers;
The earth is satisfied with the fruit of
thy works.
He sendeth the springs into the
valleys;
By them shall the fowls of the
heavens have their habitation.
They give drink to every beast of the
field; the wild asses quench their
thirst.
He causeth the grass to grow for the
cattle, and the herb for the service
of man.

Again, we present the "Address to the Sun," of Ossian-Macpherson, in passages alternate with those of Walt Whitman's invocation of the same orb. In neither case is assistance given to the rhythm by artificial division of the verses. The interest of the comparison will be found to extend beyond the matter of form:

OSSIAN.

O thou that rollest above, round as the shield of my fathers. Whence are thy beams, O Sun! thy everlasting light? Thou comest forth in thy awful beauty; the stars hide themselves in the sky; the moon, cold and pale, sinks in the western way; but thou thyself movest alone.

WALT WHITMAN.

Thou orb aloft full-dazzling, thou hot October noon! Flooding with sheeny light the gray beach sand, the sibilant near sea with vistas far, and foam, and tawny streaks and shades and spreading blue; O sun of noon refulgent! my special word to thee.

OSSIAN.

Who can be a companion of thy course! The oaks of the mountains fall; the mountains themselves decay with years:

the ocean shrinks and grows again; the moon itself is lost in heaven; but thou art forever the same, rejoicing in the brightness of thy course.

WALT WHITMAN.

Hear me illustrious! Thy lover me, for always have I loved thee, even as basking babe, then happy boy alone by some wood-edge, thy touching-distant beams enough, or man matured, or young or old, as now to thee I launch my invocation.

OSSIAN.

When the world is dark with tempests, when thunder rolls and lightning flies, thou lookest in thy beauty from the clouds, and laughest at the storm. But to Ossian thou lookest in vain, for he beholds thy beams no more: whether thy yellow hair flows on the eastern clouds, or thou tremblest at the gates of the west.

WALT WHITMAN.

Thou that with fructifying heat and light, o'er myriad farms, o'er land and waters North and South, o'er Mississippi's endless course, o'er Texas' grassy plains, Kanada's woods, o'er all the globe that turns its face to thee shining in space; thou that impartially infoldest all, not only continents, seas: thou that to grapes and weeds and little wild flowers givest so liberally, shed, shed thyself on mine and me, with but a fleeting ray out of the million million. Strike through these chants.

OSSIAN.

But thou art, perhaps, like me, for a season: thy years will have an end. Thou shalt sleep in thy clouds, careless of the voice of the morning. Exalt, then, O Sun, in the strength of thy youth! Age is dark and unlovely: it is like the glimmering light of the moon when it shines through broken clouds, and the mist is on the hills; the blast of the North is on the plain, the traveller shrinks in the midst of his journey.

WALT WHITMAN.

Nor only launch thy subtle dazzle and thy strength for these; prepare the later afternoon of me myself—prepare my lengthening shadows, prepare my starry nights.

This reversion to a primitive mode of poetic expression is particularly interesting, occurring as it does at a time when a certain school of English-speaking poets are paying so much heed to the merely mechanical and musical qualities of verse. Whitman wastes no strength in the elaboration of metres, of rhyme, of assonance, of refrain. He does not stop to think of melody. There is no doubt that his method is that of the least friction—the least amount of idea rubbed off in the process of conformation. Nor is there any doubt that it is the method best suited to his genius; it seems to be the natural language of his genius. His sturdy egotism, his sympathy with living Nature and with Man in action, are poured forth in a torrent of words unhampered by the laws of prosody. Fancy the untamable, untranslatable Walt pottering over rondeaux, or elaborating canzonets, or measuring off fourteen lines to the idea! In the three or four poems which have rhyme and the stanza, the rhymes are of the crudest and the stanzas are fetters:

O Captain! my Captain! our fearful
  trip is done.
The ship has weathered every rack,
  the prize we sought is won;
The port is near, the bells I hear, the
  people all exulting,
While follow eyes the steady keel, the

vessel grim and daring;
But O heart! heart! heart!
O, the bleeding drops of red,
Where on the deck my Captain lies,
  Fallen cold and dead.

A strange thing about Whitman's rugged recitative is that it never becomes monotonous. Within apparently narrow limits of possible variation, he manages to secure a wonderful variety. His longest cumulative passages, his catalogues of natural objects, catalogues of occupations, geographical and physiological lists, are something more than catalogues and lists. The art may be unconscious, but the result shows him a perfect master of the poetic accent. Walt Whitman would have made the catalogue of ships in the "*Iliad*" a poem in itself. Where his voice sounds in the minor key the music is often so dainty that we fail to notice the absence of the conventional lyric forms. Some lines in "Sea Drift" sound like a snatch of one of Shakespeare's songs:

> *Two together!*
> *Winds blow south, or winds blow*
>   *north,*
> *Day come white, or white come*
>   *black,*
> *Home, or rivers and mountains*
>   *from home,*
> *Singing all time, minding no time,*
> *While we two keep together.*
> *Low hangs the moon, it rose late,*
> *It is lagging—O I think it is heavy*
>   *with love, with love———*

We have been speaking of some of the surface characteristics of Walt Whitman's poetry. If all poets were in the habit of using this recitative rhythm as a vehicle for their thoughts, what qualities would still distinguish him from the rest?

It seems to us that Walt Whitman is the truest representative of the reactionary movement against romanticism—the

231

movement in which Emile Zola is a noisy and mercenary incidental. What he has undertaken to do is to exhibit with absolute unreserve the mind of a modern man in its relations to nature and to modern society. See me, says Walt, the average man of the nineteenth century, just as I am, with all the conventions and lies and shame stripped off, leaving my intellectual and emotional processes absolutely naked to view. See me as I am, bodily, too, if you care for the spectacle—every rag stripped off. And thus unclad, morally and physically, he proceeds to execute all the gymnastic antics that suggest themselves to the imagination of the child of nature when he is freed from the restraint of clothing and set out in the sunlight.

It is not from any lack of conscientious intention that the poet fails in part of his purpose, and instead of achieving a portrait of the real Walt gives us an approximate Walt, a partly real, partly ideal Walt. No man that ever lived has succeeded in making a complete exposure of himself. In the most intimate confidences there are still nooks and corners over which vanity does and always will insist on drawing the veil. Still, Whitman goes at his work lustily, and with many advantages. The individuality which he exhibits is interesting. His courage is dauntless. His sympathy with the external world is genuine; his heart beats in true accord with the heart of nature. He is a born poet, with imagination of a high order—the imagination which creates new material instead of moulding old stuff into new forms. As compared with Tennyson, for instance, who justly admires him, he is an architect who has conceived a plan and built an edifice, not merely an artist engaged in beautifying with exquisite skill the walls of a structure centuries old. Walt Whitman has found poetry in the so-called commonplace objects of Nineteenth century life. He views at night the "far-sprinkled systems," but he views them through a Nineteenth century scuttle, constructed by a carpenter of today. The scuttle is as poetic an orifice as the oriel or the mullioned window of the bartizan tower; but, being an essentially modern conception, it does not enjoy the prestige which they have in conventional verse. Whitman exults in showing side by side the sublime or the beautiful that has always been acknowledged as such, and the sublime or the beautiful unacknowledged and unrecognized by everybody but himself. He goes forth at night and sings:

I am he that walks with the tender
  and growing night,
I call to the earth and sea half-held
  by night.
Press close, bare-bosomed night; press
  close magnetic, nourishing night!
Night of south winds—night of the
  large few stars!
Still nodding night—mad naked
  summer night!

Smile O voluptuous cool breath'd
  earth!
Earth of the slumbering and liquid
  trees!
Earth of departed sunset—earth of
  the mountains misty-topt!
Earth or the vitreous pour of the full
  moon just tinged with blue!
Earth of shine and dark mottling the
  tide of the river!
Earth of the limpid gray of clouds
  brighter and clearer for my sake!
Far swooping elbow'd earth—rich
  apple blossom'd earth!
Smile, for your lover comes.

Prodigal, you have given me love—
  therefore I to you give love!
O unspeakable passionate love.

And with equal joy he contemplates the gigantic black driver of a dray:

The negro holds firmly the reins of
his four horses, the block swags
underneath it on its tied-over
chain,
The negro that drives the long dray
of the stone yard, steady and tall
he stands pois'd on one leg on the
stringpiece.
His blue shirt exposes his ample neck
and breast and loosens over his hip
band,
His glance is calm and commanding,
he tosses the slouch of his hat
away from his forehead.
The sun falls on his crispy hair and
mustache, falls on the black of his
polished and perfect limbs.

His idea of supreme beauty is man,
at his best, in contact with nature—
the naked body of the swimmer battling
with the waves, the locomotive driving
through the snowdrift, the woodsman
swinging his broadaxe, the lusty farmer
swinging his scythe, outdoor life, the ship
at sea, muscle and pluck forever! No poet
has ever echoed more accurately the
whirr and roar of the restless, every-day
life of the world, the infinitely complex
movement of human activity, the rush of
the planet through space, the resultant
sound of all mingled sounds. This booms
like the distant voice of the ocean in
some of Goethe's lines, but Goethe never
came nearer the laboratory of the universe than Whitman in "Eidólons":

> Ever the dim beginning,
> Ever the growth, the rounding of the
>   circle,
> Ever the summit and the merge at
>   last (to surely start again),
>   Eidólons! Eidólons!
> Ever the mutable,
> Ever materials changing, crumbling,
>   re-cohering,
> Ever the ateliers, the factories divine,
>   Issuing Eidólons!

The misfortune is that Walt Whitman,
not content with his discovery of the value
of the spirit of the Nineteenth century
and the Modern Man as poetic material,
seeks to elevate it into a democratic philosophy, or new religion of humanity.
That he regards himself as the prophet of
new ideas which loom awfully, but somewhat vaguely, behind the framework of
his verses, is shown by abundant evidence. It would perhaps puzzle him to
write out in cold prose the cardinal
points of his social and religious philosophy, or, having done so, to demonstrate
that they contain anything more than the
ancient commonplaces. The abstract idea
of universal brotherhood, of which the
kiss between man and man is his not
agreeable poetic type, the equality of man
with man and of man with God, some
taking truisms afforded by an imperfect
acquaintance with the literature of metaphysical thought, a constant insistence on
the doctrines of stirpiculture, a firm conviction in the majesty of the People—is
not this the sum of the new creed of
which he declares himself over and over
again the embodiment, and which leads
him to the final audacity of a comparison
of his own mission with that of Christ?

"Walt Whitman's Claim to Be Considered a Great Poet." Chicago *Tribune*, 26 November 1881, p. 9.

Walt Whitman has issued a new and complete edition of his poems, with the same
title as that given to his first volume, published in 1855, and reissued at Camden,
N. J., some twenty years later. In his volume

all the objectionable passages which were the cause of so much complaint at the time of their first appearance are given entire without a word changed or omitted. It was said of Mr. Mallock by an English reviewer, that in his last novel he had introduced "the beastly into literature." Considering some of the unexpurgated lines in this volume, Mr. Whitman is entitled to the honorable position of the apostle of the beastly in poetry. Nothing that Swinburne—a kindred unclean spirit, of greater intellectual power, however—ever wrote compares with the foulness of some of the "good gray poet's" verse. The lines might be appropriate over the portals of a bawdy house, but not in a volume of poetry from a respectable publishing firm, intended for general circulation.

Mr. Whitman has been so long silent that the leading facts in his career are generally forgotten. He is now in his 63d year, having been born in 1819 at West Hills, on Long Island. His father was an Englishman and his mother from Holland. During his life he has worked as printer, carpenter, school-teacher, army-nurse, and clerk in the office of the Attorney-General. He has traveled quite extensively, and has suffered of late years from partial paralysis. For a proper appreciation of his poetry a peculiarly cultured taste is required. Claiming to be a writer for and of the people, those to whom Whitman appeals have shown the least sympathy with him and the greatest ignorance of the inspirations of his muse. Possibly we do not comprehend Whitman. Certainly we fail to enjoy what he is pleased to call his poetry. To any of Carlyle's heavily-capitalized pages the same title might be applied with equal force. The difficulty is to understand why it would not be equally effective and striking if entitled "prose." Take as an instance the poem entitled "Our Old Feuillage":

Always our old feuillage!
Always Florida's green peninsula—
always the priceless delta of
Louisiana—always the cotton-fields
of Alabama and Texas,
Always California's golden hills, and
hollows, and the silver mountains
of New Mexico—always
soft-breath'd Cuba,
Always the vast slope drain'd by the
Southern Sea, inseparable with the
slopes drain'd by the Eastern and
Western Seas,
The eighteen thousand miles of
sea-coast and bay-coast on the
main, the thirty thousand miles of
river navigation,
The seven millions of distinct families
and the same number of
dwellings—always these, and
more, branching forth into
numberless branches,
Always the free range and diversity—
always the continent of Democracy;
Always the prairies, pastures, forests,
vast cities, travelers, Kanada the
snows:
Always these compact lands tied at
the hips with the belt stringing the
huge oval lakes—

Thus, in the same strain, this so-called poetry runs on for four pages without a single period! It is true that Walt Whitman has been praised by such high authorities in literature as Emerson, Tennyson, and Ruskin. Their eulogies, however, were rather on the thoughts and sentiments of the author than praise of his versification. His power is rugged and his controlling impulse, apart from his egotism, is to say whatever occurs to him at the moment, whether relevant or irrelevant. He lacks both rhyme and rhythm. His is imaginative, but not metrical, composition; the fruit of an excited imagination, but without measured form. If we call him a great poet, and judge him by his writings, where shall we assign our Longfellow or Whittier, tried on the same kind of evidence? Macaulay has as broad and liberal a definition of *ars poetica* as anyone. "By poetry," he says, "we mean the art of employing words in such a manner as to produce an illusion on the imagination; the art of doing by means of words what the painter does by means of colors." Now, if we take one or two of Walt Whitman's best efforts, how does he fulfill these requirements? Here is a little bit called "Aboard at a Ship's Helm":

Aboard at a ship's helm,
A young steersman steering with care.

Through fog on a seacoast dolefully
ringing,
An ocean-bell—O a warning bell
rocked by the waves.

O you give a good notice indeed, you
bell by the sea-reefs ringing,
Ringing, ringing, to warn the ship
from its wreck-place.

For as on the alert O steersman, you
mind the loud admonition.
The bows turn, the freighted ship
tacking speeds away under her gray
sails,
The beautiful and noble ship with all
her precious wealth speeds away
gayly and safe.

But O the ship, the immortal ship! O
ship aboard the ship!
Ship of the body, ship of the soul,
voyaging, voyaging, voyaging.

Or take a few lines from another poem:

Sauntering the pavement or riding the
country by road, lo, such faces!
Faces of friendship, precision,
caution, suavity, ideality,
The spiritual prescient face, the
always welcome common
benevolent face,

The face of the singing of music, the
grand faces of natural lawyers and
judges broad at the back-top,
The faces of hunters and fishers,
bulged at the brows, the shaved
blanched faces of orthodox
citizens,
The pure, extravagant, yearning,
questioning artist's face,
The ugly face of some beautiful soul,
the handsome detested or despised
face.

This now is too lamentable a face for
a man.
Some abject louse asking leave to be,
cringing for it,
Some milk-nosed maggot blessing
what lets it wrig to its hole.

The face is a haze more chill than the
Arctic sea,
Its sleepy and wabbling icebergs
crunch as they go.

Milton defines poetry as "thoughts that voluntary move harmonious numbers"; and Chatfield says, "Poetry is the music of thought, conveyed to us in the music of language." Joubert happily puts it, "Nothing which does not transport is poetry. The lyre is a winged instrument." Let us see, then how a few lines from Whitman's "Song of Myself" come up to the requirements of these authorities:

I celebrate myself, and sing myself,
and what I assume you shall
assume,
For every atom belonging to me as
good belongs to you.

I loafe and invite my soul,
I lean and loafe at my ease observing
a spear of summer grass.

My tongue, every atom of my blood,
form'd from this soil, this air.
Born here of parents born here from
parents the same, and their parents
the same,

I, now thirty-seven years old in
   perfect health begin,
Hoping to cease not till death.

Creeds and schools in abeyance,
Retiring back awhile sufficed at what
   they are, but never forgotten,
I harbor for good or bad, I permit to
   speak at every hazard,
Nature without check with original
   energy.

Take some of the shorter poems. Here
is an ode to "Beautiful Women":

Women sit or move to and fro, some
   old, some young,
The young are beautiful—but the old
   are more beautiful than the young.

Here is another, entitled "Thought":

Of obedience, faith, adhesiveness;
As I stand aloof and look there is to
   me something profoundly affecting
   in large masses of men following
   the lead of those who do not
   believe in men.

Ruskin considers that "It is a shallow
criticism that would define poetry as confined to literary productions in rhyme
and metre. The written poem is only poetry *talking*, and the statue, the picture,
and the musical composition are poetry
acting. Milton and Goethe, at their desks,
were not more truly poets than Phidias
with his chisel, Raphael at his easel, or
deaf Beethoven bending over his piano,
inventing and producing strains which he
himself could never hope to hear"—and
this great critic, Ruskin, say Whitman's
admirers, has praised our hero! So be it!
Phidias and Raphael and Beethoven were
judged in accordance with the merits of
what they produced. Their "*acted* poetry"
stood the test of the most acute analysis
and was given prominent rank because it

was perfection. In the same manner "*talking*
poetry," by whoever written, must satisfy
the eye, the ear, the mind, the heart, all
the higher mental faculties in order to be
classed as true, genuine inspired poetry.
Does this short poem meet these demands:

A GLIMPSE

A Glimpse, through an interstice
   caught,
Of a crowd of workmen and drivers
   in a barroom around the stove late
   of a winter night, and I unremark'd
   seated in a corner,
Or a youth who loves me and whom
   I love, silently approaching and
   seating himself near, that he may
   hold me by the hand,
A long while amid the noises of
   coming and going, of drinking and
   oath and smutty jest,
There we two, content, happy in
   being together, speaking little,
   perhaps not a word.

See how easily Whitman's verse becomes prose, and what would be the
spontaneous criticism on any author who
should write such prose:

Thou orb aloft full-dazzling, thou hot
October noon! Flooding with sheeny
light the gray beach sand, the sibilant
near sea with vistas far, and foam, and
tawny streaks and shades and spreading blue; O sun of noon refulgent! My
special word to thee. Hear me illustrious! Thy lover me, for always have I
loved thee, even as basking babe, then
happy boy alone by some woodedge,
thy touching-distant beams enough, or
man matured, or young or old, as
now to thee I launch my invocation.
Thou that with fructifying beat and
light, o'er myriad farms, o'er land and
waters North and South, o'er Mississippi's endless course, o'er Texas' gras-

sy plains, Kanada's woods, o'er all the globe that turns its face to thee shining in space; thou that impartially infoldest all, not only continents, seas; thou that to grapes and weeds and little wild flowers givest so liberally, shed, shed thyself on mine and me, but with a fleeting ray out of the million millions. Strike through these chants. Nor only launch thy subtle dazzle and thy strength for these; prepare the later afternoon of me myself—prepare my lengthening shadows, prepare my starry nights.

There is no thought of melody, of the mechanical requirements of verse. It is simply a combination of words like unto the bits of glass in the child's kaleidoscope. Is it the language of a real genius or the voice of a ponderous fool? Whitman himself partially answers the question in a song from which we have already quoted. He is:

Walt Whitman, a kosmos, of
   Manhattan the son,
Turbulent, fleshy, sensual, eating,
   drinking, and breeding.
No sentimentalist, no stander above
   men and women, or apart from
   them.
No more modest than immodest.
I dote on myself, there is that lot of
   me and all so luscious.

This is the pen picture of himself by the man claiming to be the apostle of a new art, instead of being really the apostle of a great art in its most degraded form.

There is no necessity for further quotation. We can admire the native, rugged strength of Whitman's unhampered genius. His active, brilliant imagination and his far-reaching enthusiasm seeking expression in language—in words that shall fire the heart and excite the mind—are char-acteristics of an extraordinary nature. So too his command of language and, apparently inexhaustible vocabulary is remarkable in a man with such antecedents and personal history. But these qualities do not make him a great poet. And to rank him as such is, to our thinking, to establish an entirely new standard from that which we have been wont to apply to the great masters of song. If they are true poets, then is Whitman a false one; if he is a poetic genius, then were the most honored names of literature but poetasters and "pitiful rhymers."

"Leaves of Grass." Liberty [Boston] 1 (26 November 1881), 3.

Liberty has received from the publishers, and joyfully welcomes Leaves of Grass, the collective title of Walt Whitman's poems. It is a convenient, compact, and tastefully "got up" volume of 382 pages, and contains a number of hitherto unpublished poems, besides those of the earlier editions. Leaves of Grass have lost nothing of their original native simplicity, freshness, and vigor from being more carefully arranged and placed in a more artistic, though it may be a more conventional vase. The book will be more readily purchased and read, at any rate; and that is the main point. The titles of some of the poems have been changed, and the table of contents newly arranged and made much more convenient for reference to special passages.

We have not discovered that the book has lost anything of its characteristic outspoken independence, nor that any concession has been made to Mrs. Grundy. It still retains all its naked truthfulness and purity, like its prototype in marble, the Greek Slave.

Walt Whitman is preeminently, above all and before all, the poet of innovation, the poet of change, the poet of growth, the poet of evolution. There is not a drop of stagnant blood in his veins. Every fibre of him quivers with life, energy, and fire. His spirit is at the same time the spirit of content and discontent. He is satisfied with whatever is and as it is—for *to-day*, but not for *to-morrow*, nor that for *any future tomorrow*.

> Urge and urge and urge,
> Always the procreant urge of the
>   world.

That seems to him to be the key-note of the universe.

A study, "By Blue Ontario's Shore," affords a good idea of what he himself considers his mission, and shows how thoroughly one in purpose that mission is with *Liberty*'s. He shall speak for himself from that poem.

[seventy-nine–line extract]

"Notes of New Books." Philadelphia *Times*, 3 December 1881, p. 6.

Walt Whitman, complete at last, thanks to the patience and pluck of James R. Osgood & Co., the Boston publishers, speaks to the world by his new book, just issued in such shape and under such auspices as will win the world's wider attention. The book is running over with the writer's own personality and the two must be treated as one. Walt and his work are older, whiter, more mature; not wiser, but quieter; the mad turbulence hushed a little and some pruning done; yet the same sight, undimmed, immortal; *Leaves of Grass*, still green and vital as ever, but now growing close about many a solid rock of fame; the man and his work, among the oddest, if not the most beautiful, things of the present century.

> I, the Titan, the hard-mouthed
>   mechanic, spending my life in the
>   hurling of words.

In an age of short hair, and cropped beards, and close-fitting contained "pants," and neck wear, a man that persists in letting his hair and beard grow long, wears loose clothing, low-necked shirts and no collar or hatter at all, out-Byrons Byron, and if he can do all this, as Whitman does, and still maintain his self-respect, and not get hooted at on every street corner, that is, keep on his own way without fastening upon himself the obloquy of a quack and charlatan, it argues pretty strongly that there is unusual stuff in the animal somewhere. And the man who can name three hundred little songs and songlets, and somehow permeate each name with instinctive life that laughs at commonplace and each name an original fixed streak of genius in its way, not only not dull, but vividly descriptive, suggestive, is something out of the ordinary ranks of hacks in all lines. As to the poems, Emerson long ago said they were poetry; Tennyson, Swinburne, not to speak of vapid critics at home or abroad, affirm that Walt has written poetry. What is there left to be said? Much every day were there room to say it. Short and clear let the words be. It would be easy to pick a thousand lines from Whitman's three hundred and eighty-two pages that fairly breathe and bristle with power, that sparkle and flash with beauty, that are as unique in modern poetry as the brightest aurora that has filled the north skies for a generation and as rare as the few gem-like days of June. Now and then there are eclipses; sunlight and stars all gone out of the man and his word; but nature swings back to him, lo to it, and there is light again when the orbit is bound and nature attuned. It is life, seen and recorded. Never mind the egotism. That must come in somehow in all work. To jot it down more definitely, Whitman has eyes, looks into things, not at them. No long or steady gaze, no masterful comprehension of the great laws of the facts, but the facts he sees; furthermore, has the ability to report the fact as he sees it, as it is; yet further, to saturate all facts so seen and recorded with the momentary intense splendor of his own being. Name the being? The grade of it? Well, not Homeric; that was warlike, heroic, grand. Read the lines of Whitman's face and of his poetry: nothing of the Homeric or heroic is there. Not Shakespearean; that is art incarnate. Whitman is not an artist; not Virgilic or Dantic—that is culture and morality and sentiment and piety of a kind. Whitman has none of these. Not Emersonian or Tennysonian—that is scholarly—Whitman is the farthest removed from all that. What then? We answer, that what these all were to the distinctive spirit of their generations, though in utter contrast with them, Whitman is to the characteristic spirit of this generation—gigantic, rude, loud, prosy, mechanic, conceited. Whirling, unsettled, abounding in vitality, extent and power. In this light read Whitman's book, and lines fine, in their way, as any in Homer or Shakespeare shall flash on your soul, if you have a soul, and pleasure rich and rare as the lover finds in love, the poet in nature, and the banker in his margins shall press and pierce you almost to pain.

[T. W. Higginson]. "Recent Poetry." *Nation* 33 (15 December 1881), 476–7.

We have read anew, from a sense of duty, the original and unexpurgated *Leaves of Grass*, by Walt Whitman, as now reprinted, with some milder additions. It cannot be said of them, as Sir Charles Pomander, in "Christie Johnstone," says of his broken statues, that "time has impaired their indelicacy." This somewhat nauseating quality remains in full force, and we see no good in their publication except to abate the outcries of the Liberal League against Mr. Anthony Comstock and his laws respecting obscene publications. So long as *Leaves of Grass* may be sent through the mails, the country is safe from over-prudery, at least. Mr. Whitman is often ranked with the "fleshly school," and his circle of English admirers is almost identical with the coterie whose apostles are Swinburne and Wilde. But the erotic poems of these authors are to those of Whitman as rose-water to vitriol. The English poets have at their worst some thin veneering of personal emotion; with Whitman there seems no gleam of anything personal, much less of that simple, generous impulse which makes almost every young man throw some halo of ideal charm about the object of his adoration. Whitman's love, if such it can be called, is the sheer animal longing of sex for sex—the impulse of the savage, who knocks down the first woman he sees, and drags her to his cave. On the whole, the condition of the savage seems the more wholesome, for he simply gratifies his brute lust and writes no resounding lines about it.

Leaving this disagreeable aspect of the matter, we are impressed anew, on reading these poems, by a certain quality of hollowness, which is nowhere more felt than in the strains called "Drum-Taps." It would be scarcely worth while to bring these strains to any personal test, perhaps, did not Mr. Whitman's admirers so constantly intrude his personality upon us; but we cannot quite forget what Emerson says, that "it makes a great difference to a sentence whether there be a man behind it or no." When Mr. Whitman speaks with utter contempt of the "civilian" (p. 252), and claps the soldier on the back as "camerado" (p. 251), we cannot help thinking of Thackeray's burly and peaceful Jos. Sedley at Brussels, just before the battle of Waterloo, striding and swaggering between two military officers, and looking far more warlike than either. One can be aroused to some enthusiasm over the pallid shop-boy or the bookish undergraduate who knew no better than to shoulder his musket and march to the front in the war for the Union; but it is difficult to awaken any such emotion for a stalwart poet, who—with the finest physique in America, as his friends asserted, and claiming an unbounded influence over the "roughs" of New York— preferred to pass by the recruiting-office and take service in the hospital with the non-combatants.

When we come to purely intellectual traits, it is a curious fact that Mr. Whitman, by the production of one fine poem, has overthrown his whole poetic theory. Dozens of pages of his rhythmic prose are not worth "My Captain," which among all his compositions comes the nearest to accepting the restraints of ordinary rhyme. His success in this shows that he too may yet be compelled to recognize form as an element in poetic power. The discovery may have come too late, but unless he can regard its lessons he is likely to leave scarcely a complete work that will be remembered; only here and there a phrase, an epithet, a fine note—as when the midnight tolling for General Garfield is called "The sobbing of the bells." These are the passages which his especial admirers style "Homeric," but which we should rather call Ossianic. The shadowy Gaelic bard rejected the restraints of verse, like Whitman, and reiterated his peculiar images with wearisome diffuseness and minuteness. To be sure, he was not an egotist, and he kept within the limits of decency; but he gave fine glimpses and pictures, while there was always a certain large, free atmosphere about all his works. They were translated into all languages; he was ranked with Homer and Virgil; Goethe and Napoleon Bonaparte were his warm admirers—and the collections of English poetry do not now include a line of his composing. If Whitman, after the same length of time, proves more fortunate, it will be because he wrote "My Captain."

[Francis F. Browne]. "Briefs on New Books." *Dial* [Chicago] 2 (January 1882), 218–19.

After a quarter of a century's probation in the obscurity of author's editions and desultory proofsheets, Walt Whitman's *Leaves of Grass* have at last been taken in hand by a reputable publisher. To Mr. Whitman, this success, after so long a period of suppression and literary outlawry, is no doubt particularly grateful; and in the enjoyment of his triumph he may not unnaturally reject all hints afforded by its long postponement as to the value of his literary wares. Though the period during which he has been known as a writer has been one of great activity and enterprise in the publishing trade, and one in which publishers have keenly sought for what was new and fresh in literature, none of them have been willing to risk either money or reputation on him in an unedited state, and his refusal to abridge or modify his work is understood to have been imperative. He is doubtless glad now that it was so, and will be very likely to find his personal independence and self-sufficiency reinforced by the event: though we could not easily call to mind a case in which reinforcements of this sort are less needed. The self-poise of one whose motto is "I blab myself" is not to be suspected lightly. Not wishing to repress sympathy rightly due to perseverance in the face of obstacles, we would yet suggest that congratulations in the present case may not imprudently be restricted as regards both promptness and effusiveness. A literary revolt, like a political one, must not be lauded too hastily. Having found a publisher, it remains to be seen if Mr. Whitman shall find a public. Before declaring him to be the new messiah of poetry, it may be well to take time at least to note the magnitude of the task to which he has set himself—which, practically, is not to found a new poetic school, but to work a poetic revolution. We do not purpose to undertake now any extended analysis of Mr. Whitman's characteristics. The most obvious and distinguishing of them—that which relates to poetic form—is, in our judgment, one which it is a waste of time to consider seriously. If his method of writing poetry be correct or even admissible, we might as well drop distinctions between poetry and prose, at least so far as expression is concerned,—a merchant's inventory or lawyer's brief being as good poetry as a ballad or sonnet, and the average political "leader" being as truly po-

etical (we will not say imaginative) as Shelley's Ode to the West Wind. The untutored citizen who avowed his inability to see anything in Whitman's poetry beyond "a lot of ——— cataloging" is an entirely competent witness in the case; and we would be quite willing to rest it upon his evidence, without recourse to the concurrent testimony of all poets who ever wrote—from the Hebrew melodists and the "impudent Highlander" Macpherson to the Sweet Singer of Michigan. Mr. Whitman, indeed, appears not to be content with the abrogation of all conventional notions of poetry and artificial contrivances for constructing and testing it. Not only are rhymes avoided by him and even measures shunned—spondees, dactyls, trochees, iambics, anapests, odes, ballads, and sonnets, kicked into chaos together, as frippery suited only to poets who lull their readers with "piano tunes,"—but he overrides and crushes out with remorseless effort even those innocently recurring cadences and natural rhythms which are so often the involuntary accompaniment of the expression of impassioned thought. He thus succeeds not only in avoiding all semblance of piano tunes or any other musical thing, but in producing singularly harsh and disagreeable prose. Whatever may be Mr. Whitman's powers of imagination and description, his lack of a sense of poetic fitness, his failure to understand the business of a poet, is certainly astounding. His disqualifications in these respects are scarcely less phenomenal than those of a painter who should be insensible to shades of color, or of a draughtsman without perception of form. As the particular apostle and expounder of Nature, there is something inexplicable in his obtuseness to the existence of rhythm and cadence as elements in both Nature and the human soul. In view of his savage contempt for anything musical in poetry, it will be a fine stroke of the irony of fate if he shall be destined to be remembered only by the few pieces which are marked by the "piano-tune" quality that he derides—the true and tender lyric of "My Captain" and the fine poem on "Ethiopia Saluting the Colors." These pieces, with the magnificent threnody on Lincoln—"When Lilacs Last in the Dooryard Bloomed"—and a few others in which there is an approach to metrical form, with fine lines and passages scattered here and there, are likely to be preserved in memory when his more characteristic pieces—those which are without form and void—shall exist only as curiosities of literature or are performing for their author the very proper function of sounding his "barbaric yawp over the roofs of the world." Of the more purely intellectual quality of these writings we have but little to say. It is not to our taste, even in prose, to dissociate the thing said from the manner of saying it; and such separation is quite impossible in poetry. We are aware how strongly Mr. Whitman is praised for his virility and freedom; but his virility, as applied to the purposes of poetry, seems to us not unlike what the virility of a buffalo bull might be as applied to carriage purposes, and his freedom such as might more properly be expected of an irresponsible and rampant savage. His democracy, so loudly proclaimed and oft reiterated, is of a sentimental and dramatic kind which addresses everyone with stagecries of "*Camerado*," salutes as equal the "Caffre, Patagonian, Hottentot, Feejeeman, Greenlander, Lapp, Austral Negro, naked, red, sooty, with protrusive lip," and causes surprise only at his moderation in not including in his good-fellowship apes and baboons also. The grossness of Mr. Whitman's poetry is also a matter on which we do not care to dwell. In fact, some of his pieces are so very gross that it is almost indelicate to call attention to

them even for purposes of condemnation. Grossness in literature is bad enough when introduced incidentally and apologetically; but when it is paraded without veil or foil, and not only toleration for it but admiration for its author's candor is demanded, it is difficult to avoid a feeling of injury and resentment. We have no wish to make this matter in any way a question of personal moral quality. We are inclined to the opinion that if Mr. Whitman had been possessed of but a little humor, his poetry would have been less immoral; and we prefer to think that it is but a part of his general lack of the sense of poetic fitness and propriety that he fails to distinguish between what is erotic in poetry and what is simply bestial. The pieces of this class are not numerous in his volume, but it would be both difficult and undesirable to express their rankness of quality. The real gems which he offers us are furnished with a most unclean and offensive setting—in disregard of the fact that selection and decoration are precisely the business of the poet. It is doubtful if there was ever before a writer, much less a poet, who showed such utter lack of taste in the selection of material. Under the plea—repeated so often as almost to discredit its sincerity, that he despises affectations and hypocrisies, and wishes to be as open and as free as Nature is, he invites us to clinical studies of men's lusts and to æsthetic considerations of carrion. The really good and beautiful things in his pages are blotched and fouled by their associations. The literary delicacies which he offers are garnished with garbage; he requires his readers to extract scattering grains of nourishment after the fashion of barnyard fowls. Perhaps his most serious error is in estimating the strength of the common poetic stomach by his own. Nature's impulses are usually unmistakable; and it is a triumph of that original

242

Adam in man which Mr. Whitman celebrates that most unvitiated stomachs reject with involuntary but decided symptoms of disapproval the mixture of wine and bilge-water, nectar and guano, which he has compounded and for which Messrs. Osgood & Co. have consented (let us hope not without some furtive qualms and indignation of the nostrils) to become the cup-bearers.

"New Publications." Detroit *Free Press*, 7 January 1882, p. 3.

That Walt Whitman is genuine and thoroughly believes in himself is beyond question. It does not therefore follow that he is a poet, though we have noticed that those who insist most strenuously upon his claim to be so considered, base the claim mainly on his genuineness and self-confidence, waiving for the moment all discussion as to the beastliness of certain of his verses—there really is no other word which fitly characterizes them—his poems, so-called, very rarely furnish any excuse for their appearance in the poetic form. There is no rhyme or pretense of any, nor is there any attempt at meter. With one or two exceptions they might just as well be written like other prose.

Of course this does not settle the question. There is a great deal of poetry in the English language without either rhyme or meter. But it is recognized as such in spite of the prosaic form; while Walt Whitman's ebullitions, if put in that form, would not be. Printed as prose they would strike the reader as grandiloquent, sonorous, rhetorical, sometimes as imaginative, almost always as egotistical, but very rarely as poetical. Take, for example, such a verse

as the following, strike out the misplaced capitals and the spaces, in short, print it as prose is printed, and see how much of the "divine afflatus" can be detected in it:

Sauntering the pavement or riding the country by road, lo, such faces!
Faces of friendship, precision, caution, suavity, ideality,
The spiritual prescient face, the always welcome common benevolent face.
The face of the singing of music, the grand faces of natural lawyers and judges, broad at the back-top.
The faces of hunters and fishers, bulged at the brows, the shaved, blanched faces of orthodox citizens.
The pure, extravagant, yearning, questioning artist's face.
The ugly face of some beautiful soul, the handsome, detested or despised face.
This now is too lamentable a face for a man.
Some abject louse asking leave to be, cringing for it,
Some milk-nosed maggot blessing what lets it wrig to its hole.

As for the beastly portion of the volume, "The Children of Adam," it is an outrage upon the decencies of literature. It is open, undisguised sensualism of the grossest sort; and its publication is a grave mistake. We have no special fear that it will corrupt the rising generation, for its indecency is so potent that intelligent parents and guardians will look out for it. But when such a work, with the imprint of a highly respected publishing house, has free circulation and transmission through the mails, an argument almost unanswerable is furnished for the professional perverters of youth whose vile trash, heretofore excluded from the mails, is really less indecorous in form—whatever it may be in spirit—than some portions of *Leaves of Grass*.

"The Poetry of the Future."
New York *Examiner*,
19 January 1882, p. 1.

Here we have it, the real Simon-pure article, and no doubt about it. At least we are so assured by the author and by his admirers. Let us see wherein the poetry of the future differs from the poetry of the past and the present, and whether it can make good its title to be considered the poetry of the future.

Walt Whitman is a great poet—in his own estimation, and in that of critics who make up in noise what they lack in numbers. This volume is intended to demonstrate to the world that his claim is well-founded; for, like other great men who have an original message to deliver to the world, he has been misunderstood. He should not complain, however, but remember that obloquy is the ordinary lot of genius. This volume, we repeat, is intended to be his vindication. We have read it carefully and curiously—curiously, because though we had heard much of Whitman before, we confess to dense ignorance of all but a hundred lines or so of his writings—and we do not hesitate to say that it is a volume admirably calculated to convince those who were previously of his opinion. That it will convince others we—but this is to pass judgment before the cause is argued.

We should not be true to our own convictions if we neglected to protest, on the very threshold of the subject, against the coarse filthiness of the book. The author is by turns blasphemous and obscene, for the mere sake of showing that he dare do anything and say anything that he chooses. We are not sure that the book is not amenable to the laws against sending obscene literature through the mails; and were the Society for the Suppression of Vice to test the matter, any ordinary jury would give a verdict in its favor. The plea that the book is "literature" does not excuse such unmitigated and indefensible nastiness as disfigures some of its pages. Byron and Swinburne and Oscar Wilde are as modest as a young maiden by comparison. To write such a book and send it forth to the world with a complacent smirk required great courage—or brazen effrontery—on the part of its author; and it is strange that he should have obtained the imprint for it of so respectable a publishing house.
[. . .]
Walt Whitman's artistic creed is easily understood. He states it on the very first page of this volume:

> *I too haughty Shade also sing war,*
> *and a longer and greater one than*
> *any,*
> *Waged in my book with varying*
> *fortune, with flight, advance and*
> *retreat, victory deferr'd and*
> *wavering,*
> *(Yet methinks certain, or as good as*
> *certain, at the last), the field the*
> *world,*
> *For life and death, for the Body and*
> *for the eternal Soul.*

That is it, war on the social customs and opinions of the age, on its morals, its religion—on everything. Again he says:

> I am not the poet of goodness only, I
> do not decline to be the poet of
> wickedness also.

Decline? He jumps at the chance, and wallows in vice and crime at every opportunity. The poet's friends tell us that his life has been correct, that only in his verse is he a libertine; so much the worse for him, he cannot even plead in extenuation of his offence that he had become so accustomed to evil that it is second nature to him. Deliberate baseness is always worse than the baseness that is the outcome of a depraved and bestial nature.

No one will dispute Byron's place in the temple of fame, however severely he may condemn the poet's character and the impress it has left on his work. Walt Whitman may be a poet in spite of his immorality. He asks us to accept him as a poet, as a great poet, with a bold egotism which must be either the height of sublimity or the height of folly. Is he a poet?

That depends, of course, on what one means by poetry. If by poetry we mean verse composed according to regular rhythmical laws, with or without rhyme, Walt Whitman is not a poet. Regular he never is; rhythmical he is at times, but in a wild and irregular way; and of rhyme he is very sparing, for the most part avoiding it altogether. If there are in this volume six consecutive lines to be found anywhere that will "scan" perfectly according to any one known metre, it may safely be assumed that they exist wholly by accident, not by the poet's design. He simply happened to express himself in that way. But we do not believe that six such lines are to be found; we have looked diligently, and have not discovered them. To return: if poetry be admitted to be, as to its essence, independent of mere form; if irregular, capricious and rugged rhythmical forms be conceded fittingly to embody poetical thought and constitute a different thing from merely poetical prose; then it will be hard to deny that Walt Whitman is, at infrequent intervals, a true poet.

That he is a great poet is a preposterous claim, that is not worth the trouble of serious refutation.

Let us illustrate. Are the following passages poetry or are they not?

The Lord reigneth; let the earth
    rejoice;
Let the multitude of isles be glad.
Clouds and darkness are round about
    him;
Righteousness and judgment are the
    habitation of his throne.
A fire goeth before him,
And burneth up his enemies round
    about.
His lightnings enlightened the world:
The earth saw and trembled;
The hills melted like wax at the
    presence of the Lord,
At the presence of the Lord of the
    whole earth.
The heavens declare his
    righteousness,
And all the people see his glory.

Departed then over the wavy sea
The floater, foamy-necked, most like
    to a bird,
Till about an hour of the second day
The twisted prow had sailed,
That the voyagers saw land, ocean
    shores shine,
Mountains steep, spacious sea-nesses.
Then was the sea-sailer
At the end of its watery way.

The first passage is from Psalm 97; the second a faithful translation from *Beowulf*, one of the oldest and most valuable relics of Anglo-Saxon literature. The Psalms are commonly called poetry, yet they have neither rhyme nor regular rhythm; *Beowulf* is called poetry, yet it has nothing to distinguish it from prose but a sort of alliteration. If it be admitted that the above are poetry—of a genuine, though perhaps not of the most perfect, sort—Walt Whitman's claim to be a poet is, perhaps, borne out, but his claim to be an *original* poet is made ridiculous. At the best he has done ill what David did well over three thousand years ago. But admitting that the Psalms are poetry, can we deny the same title to these lines?

Smile O voluptuous cool breath'd
earth!
Earth of the slumbering and liquid
trees!
Earth of the departed sunset—earth
of the mountains misty-topt!
Earth of the vitreous pour of the full
moon just tinged with blue!
Earth of shine and dark mottling the
tide of the river!
Earth of the limpid gray of clouds
brighter and clearer for my sake!
Far-swooping elbow'd earth—rich
apple-blossom'd earth!
Smile, for your lover comes.

Whether the thought in the above was really worth the trouble of expressing may be a question, but that it is poetically expressed can there be doubt? And where in all English literature should we look for two more exquisite pictures than these, from a poem on Lincoln's death, "When lilacs last in the dooryard bloomed"?

In the dooryard fronting an old
farmhouse near the white-wash'd
palings,
Stands the lilac-bush tall-growing
with heart-shaped leaves of rich
green,
With many a pointed blossom rising
delicate, with the perfume strong
I love,
With every leaf a miracle—and from
this bush in the dooryard,
With delicate–color'd blossoms and
heart-shaped leaves of rich green,
A sprig with its flower I break.

. . . .
Pictures of growing spring and farms
and homes.
With the Fourth-month eve at
sundown, and the gray smoke lucid
and bright.
With floods of the yellow gold of
the gorgeous, indolent, sinking
sun, burning, expanding the air,
With the fresh sweet herbage under
foot, and the pale green leaves
of the trees prolific,
In the distance the flowing glaze,
the breast of the river, with a
wind dapple here and there,
With ranging hills on the banks, with
many a line against the sky, and
shadows,
And the city at hand with dwellings
so dense, and stacks of chimneys,
And all the scenes of life and the
workshops, and the workmen
homeward returning.

Tennyson never wrote a more dainty love-song than this from "Sea-drift:"

Two together!
Winds blow south, or winds blow
north,
Day come white, or white come
black,
Home, or rivers and mountains from
home.
Singing all time, minding no time,
While we two keep together.

Occasionally he is capable of setting a sublime truth in words that are as beautifully fitted for the purpose as the jeweller's fine gold is to receive and hold the diamond; as when he says of the grass:

Or I guess it is the handkerchief of
the Lord.
A scented gift and remembrancer
designedly dropt,

246

Bearing the owner's name someway
  in the corners, that we may see and
  remark, and say *Whose?*

Or where he says in the same poem, "I
believe a leaf of grass is no less than the
journey-work of the stars."

On the other hand, while one is wading
through the unnumbered lines of dreary
trash in this volume, how often is he
tempted to declare that Walt Whitman
has not the poet's gift in the slightest
measure—that he is only an ignorant
American youth whose culture has been
gained wholly from the street-corner and
the daily newspaper, who has been smit-
ten with a desire for notoriety, and has
shrewdly determined that to be odd and
singular is the shortest cut to that end. In
what respect do his writhings and contor-
tions, his twistings and turnings of our
good old English tongue, differ from the
affected attitudes and "intense" dialect of
the "consummately utter" æsthete who
gives us so much sport today? After all,
does the ability to write a few fine lines
constitute one a poet? Does one kernel of
wheat in a bushel of chaff warrant us in
giving the name "grain" to the whole?
Evidently not, but evidently also, the
single kernel of wheat *is* wheat in spite of
the vast preponderance of chaff. May the
question not be answered somewhat like
this: Walt Whitman is a poet, after a
fashion, but he has written very little poetry. If he is not of those who "die with
all their music in them," as Dr. Holmes
sings, he yet may have succeeded in uttering but a small part of the music that is
in him. For noise, be it remembered, is
not music.

One further characteristic needs to be
touched on in forming a complete and
final judgment of the value of Whitman's
work. He shows an aptness now and
then for coining those

Jewels five-words-long
That on the stretched forefinger of all
  Time
Sparkle forever.

What could be better, for example, than
his description of the sound of the carpenter's plane, as it "whistles its wild ascending lisp"? Anybody who has ever heard
the sound will appreciate the striking fitness of the phrase. "Far-sprinkled systems" is a most happy epithet for the
clear sky of a winter's night; and nothing could better picture in words the
thronged thoroughfares of New York than
this line:

When million-footed Manhattan
  unpent descends to her pavements.

What poet has apostrophized Death
more happily than this: "Dark mother
always gliding near with soft feet"? And
in all the poetry written about the death
of President Garfield, has there been a
single phrase so peculiarly happy as "the
sobbing of the bells ... those heartbeats
of a Nation in the night"? But if one shall
say of these things, One swallow does
not make a summer, nor do a few happy
turns of phrase make a poet—for our
part we could only assent.

But, it may be asked, does Walt Whitman never submit to the trammels of poetry, as poetry is ordinarily conceived?
Never fully, yet once he comes very near
to doing so—in a poem on the death of
Lincoln—and this is the result:

O Captain! my Captain! our fearful
  trip is done,
The ship has weather'd every rock,
  the prize we sought is won,
The port is near, the bells I hear, the
  people all exulting,
While follow eyes the steady keel,
  the vessel grim and daring;
But O heart! heart! heart!

O the bleeding drops of red,
　Where on the deck my
　　Captain lies
　Fallen cold and dead.

O Captain! my Captain! rise up and
　hear the bells;
Rise up—for you the flag is hung—
　for you the bugle trills,
For you bouquets and ribbon'd
　wreaths—for you the shores
　a-crowding,
For you they call, the swaying mass,
　their eager faces turning;
　Here Captain! dear father!
　　This arm beneath your head!
　　　It is some dream that on the
　　　deck
　　　　You've fallen cold and
　　　　dead.

My Captain does not answer, his
　lips are pale and still,
My father does not feel my arm, he
　has no pulse nor will,
The ship is anchor'd safe and sound,
　its voyage closed and done,
From fearful trip the victor ship
　comes in with object won;
　Exult O shores, and ring O bells!
　　But I with mournful tread,
　　　Walk the deck my Captain
　　　lies,
　　　　Fallen cold and dead.

The most prejudiced will not deny
that that is poetry, but Walt Whitman is
not half so proud of it himself as he is of
some of his "barbaric yawps." Nevertheless, he will be known fifty years hence—
if he is known then at all, which we more
than half-doubt—only as the author of
"My Captain," on the whole, probably,
the most stirring lyric that the civil war
produced. Contrast with such a poem
lines like these:

Southward there, I screaming, with
　wings slow flapping, with the

myriads of gulls wintering along
　the coasts of Florida,
Otherways, there atwixt the banks of
　the Arkansaw, the Rio Grande, the
　Nueces, the Brazos, the Tombigbee,
　the Red River, the Saskatchawan or
　the Osage, I with the spring waters
　laughing and skipping and running.

[. . .]

Not every writer can drop so quickly
and so naturally as he from the level of
pure poetry to what is not even prose,
but mere drivel.

Walt Whitman is the peculiar product of
a peculiar condition of things. He is the
"Bowery Bhoy" in literature, a rowdy with
the *cacoethes scribendi* (in plain English,
the itch for writing). He could not have
been bred anywhere but in a certain part
of New York city a generation ago—in
any other place or at another time he
could no more have been developed than
Plymouth Rocks can be hatched out of
cobble-stones. And American letters were
in a peculiar transition state when he made
his first appearance in print, which fact
alone made his career possible. A few devoted admirers have diligently puffed him,
and the more judicious critics have ridiculed him into a sort of fame. It is a common saying among publishers that next
to very warm praise of a book downright
abuse on the part of the critics will best
promote its sale. But a popularity thus
created is always short-lived; people buy
the book for a few weeks just to see
whether the critics have told the truth
about it, and finding that they have, toss
it aside never to look at it again.

Walt Whitman has certain artistic virtues, it is true; he can paint a pretty pen-
picture of nature as it presents itself to
the eye, but he has no word for us of
"the still, sad music of humanity" heard
throughout nature. How can he tell us

what he has never seen—what he has no eyes to see? He has a certain rough power, an aboriginal gift, so to speak, of poetic language, but he is uncouth and barbaric. He has fire, but it destroys oftener than it warms. Though he affects to be as broad as the universe, he is narrow—he has but one note to his pipe, and that a cracked one. Pathos is an element of his power, but it must be allowed that bathos is much more frequent in his writings. As Landor said of Byron, "there are things in him as strong as poison and original as sin." He is, after all, too many-sided to be characterized in a single phrase—many-sided in good qualities as well as in evil: At one time he is a dithyrambic Emerson calmly philosophizing on the spiritual truths of the universe; at another he is a prose Swinburne run mad. He is a wicked Tupper; he is an obscene Ossian; he is a poetical Zola; he is—Walt Whitman.

Catholic World 34 (February 1882), 719–20.

The animus underlying the songs of Walt Whitman entitled *Enfans d'Adam* is characteristic of nearly all he has written, and if these had been given their true heading they would have been entitled *Enfans de la Bête*. Why not? The animal in Walt was free from all conscious restraint, young and lusty, and why should he not sing of its liberties and joys, such as they are? Had not his master proclaimed the precept, "Act out thyself"? and, having the courage of his convictions, with youthful vigor on his side, the disciple was resolved, in spite of obtrusive advice, to act out fearlessly, at least as far as language and type serve, what was in him.

Walt Whitman is a more recent and more genuine outcome of transcendentalism. Less tutored, and for that reason—education being what it is—less perverted, he is more a creature of his instincts, and, as it happens, not of the higher sort; and taking his stand on these, he utters himself in accents which at times make the more cultivated transcendentalists hold their breath. Walt is the "enfant terrible" of transcendentalism. His birth was hailed by the corypheus of this sect with a burst of parental joy; subsequently, on close inspection, he appeared to entertain suspicions of his legitimacy, but now, with maturer examination, his doubts have vanished and he recognizes his lineage.

The difference between the master and the disciple is this: Mr. Emerson revolted against the false restraints of Calvinism, and, in the righteous indignation of his repressed nature, expressed himself passionately and not seldom unguardedly; while Walt Whitman, unconscious of the impious and paralyzing repression of Puritanism, not having the inherited restraints of seven or eight Puritan ministers wrapt in his skin, takes his master's utterances to the letter and acts them out with all the force of the characteristics of his personality, and in great glee "sounds his barbaric yawp over the roofs of the world."

Is it a matter for congratulation that the sage of Concord, so-called by his disciples, has not sufficiently recovered from the early strain which was put upon him, seriously to listen in his advanced age to wise misgivings and lawfully-begotten fears?

But man is a rational animal, and not like the beasts, which have no sense; and all effort on his part to play the irrational beast would be ridiculous, were it not a degradation exacting so great a depravation of his nature. But this attempt is never made with impunity, for man's rational nature sooner or later will surely take revenge on him who makes, whether maliciously or otherwise, the experiment. No, it is not a thing for laughter, but a serious matter, when a man is led to believe that he can with impunity violate any one essential law of his rational being. It is a more serious matter when the leaders of public opinion encourage in a community a belief of this kind, or aid in the spreading of literature infected with such opinions. It is a most serious matter, considering their effect on the coming generation; for the harvest of the poisonous seeds sown in the tender minds of this, will be reaped in the next. And until men gather grapes from thorns and figs from thistles every intelligent, every religious, every moral man, every sincere lover of his race, will set his face fixedly against the teachers and upholders of opinions so degrading to man and so pernicious in their tendency.

Let us have songs of the "Enfans d'Adam"—not of the old Adam, but the new! Let us have songs of that blissful communion which existed between God and man in the Garden of Eden—communion lost, alas! by the first Adam, but graciously restored by the second Adam. Songs that spring from this source rise upward and imparadise men's hearts! These are the songs men's souls crave, the age hopes for and is ready to receive.

[Lafcadio Hearn]. "*Leaves of Grass*!" New Orleans *Times-Democrat*, 30 July 1882, p. 4.

There are minds which, seeking beauty in all things, tint with their own iridescence of fancy whatever they gaze upon and claim the discovery of beauty where ordinary intelligences can perceive only ugliness, and the nakedness of ugliness! Such a mind seems to be that of the very eminent critic and scholar who not long since contributed an extraordinary eulogium to one of the leading magazines upon Walt Whitman's *Leaves of Grass*. After having read the essay, we sought in vain for those immortal beauties which he discovered in that eccentric, tiresome, flatulent, raw volume of rhapsodies by Walt Whitman, suppressed in Massachusetts. Mr. Whitman has found another publisher in Philadelphia, and a copy bearing the imprint of Rees, Welsh & Co., lies upon our table—entire, priapic, undraped.

The eminent critic himself, already alluded to, could not, with all his artistic ingenuity, discover any gems of fine thought in the scoriac deposit of that lava-flow of lust, that orgiastic outpouring of coarseness entitled "Children of Adam." He certainly did himself the justice to condemn this portion of the work, more or less mildly, to the great annoyance of its creator. Even granting that Walt Whitman has immense genius, lofty sentiment, artistic strength—which we cannot—the "Children of Adam" would condemn him beyond redemption. Piron was a genius, indeed; but his name will ever be associated with that infamous Ode which befouls his place in literature.

Yet we would not pretend to judge this portion of Mr. Whitman's work from the standpoint of religious or purely social ethics. In art even that which is highly condemnable by such standards finds indulgence; and perfection of form excuses nudity. There is a holiness about the marble nakedness of an antique goddess that compels respect;—there is a holiness in the passion loveliness creates. The Soul of the Universe is love, permeating, divinizing—finding its loftiest expression in dreams marble-frozen and gem-chiselled—in songs of poets—in the wizard work of musicians—in all the longing of humanity for the Ideal and Impossible. But the duty of art is to elevate our conceptions, to inspire the desire for what is nobler and better than what we have known—to create ideals for future generations to realize—even as Greek mothers brought forth children comely and graceful as the statues of the sculptors. The Naturalists are not artists. They describe only that which is; they are mere dissectors when they are not mere photographers. They acknowledge their work disgusts; and by disgusting people with what is, they hope to inspire them with a thirst for what is not! They are the Nihilists of literature.

Well, Mr. Whitman is an American Naturalist, quite as reckless as Zola or Maupassant, but withal infinitely less talented, less skillful. The chief difference between the American Naturalist and his ultra-Atlantic brethren, is that he does not profess to revolt his readers for a good purpose—although he does revolt them to no purpose that we can discover. In fact, he imagines that he charms! He describes what is as he conceives it; and seems to imagine himself a great revelator of nature's secrets. There are things which should not be described unless idealized, and therefore only by the high-priests of art. Mr. Whitman imagines himself to be

such; and breaks through all canons of good taste, all rules of decency, all conventionalities that the boldest art respects. The result is more or less disgusting;—it is like a navvy trying to model nudities out of mud!

Pages 86 and 87—("I Sing the Body Electric")—are evidence of this indecency of taste. We do not refer to lasciviousness so much as to coarseness—not to immorality, so much as vulgarity. Swinburne's muse is in some respects more immoral than Mr. Whitman's, but her nudity is of the grand antique sort and her dancing graceful. Her unclad splendor may be judged admiringly, apart from her reputation. But Mr. Whitman's muse is at once indecent and ugly, lascivious and gawky, lubricous and coarse.

What nobler theme for art than a perfect human body?—the noblest monuments of the world's literatures all contain niches for unclad types of beauty—from the earliest Indian epics to the latest masterpieces of modern verse! But what does Mr. Whitman offer us on these two hideous pages? A series of scenes alternately suggesting a dissecting room and a butcher's shop! He talks about "naked *meat*!" What is meat? It is dead flesh!

Cannibalism?

And "jaw-hinges," "roof of the mouth," "knee-pans," "leg-fibre," "thin red jellies," "lung-sponges," "bowels," "sweat," "scapula," "elbow-sockets," "the bones and the marrow within the bones"—and many other things which none but Mr. Whitman would mention at all!

But he tells us these things are the soul! Would it not be more decent to say that he does not believe in individual souls? Is it philosophy even to declare that the "sweat" and the "bowels" and "the toe-joints" are not only parts of the soul, but the soul itself!

In the downright lubricity of certain

lines, we can only say that Mr. Whitman has fully equalled, if not exceeded the extant writers of antiquity, and has used phraseology only to be expected in those surreptitiously circulated works the publication whereof is accounted a crime by the law of all civilized nations.

He may claim to deal only with legitimate passion; but his treatment of it is illegitimate to the degree of outrage. He has one advantage over his critics, however;—they cannot quote him!

Elsewhere, there is some philosophy in the book; there are pages of force and rough beauty; there is originality, depth, strong feeling. The book is not the creation of a literary quack. It is the work of an honest man—rude in his conceptions, reckless in his expressions, erroneous occasionally in his deductions, eccentric, erratic, inartistic, enthusiastic, dogmatic likewise. What he writes he believes to be good and beautiful. Some agree with him. We do not. We hold much of his book to be infamous according to the universal code of ethics; and contrary to all just standards of taste; largely shapeless, nebulous—with here and there an appearance of bright and solid nuclei. *Leaves of Grass* may be preserved awhile by curiosity, like ferns in a mantel-vase;— but they will crumble away, withered by public contempt or indifference, just as soon as curiosity has been satiated.

[T. Francis Gordon]. "Walt Whitman's Complete Volume: The Realism of Walt Whitman." *American* 2 (12 August 1882), 282.

[The publication of Walt Whitman's complete and unexpurgated volume, relinquished by his Boston publishers on account of the objections of the Attorney-General of Massachusetts to certain of its contents, has been undertaken by a Philadelphia publisher. We present, in this connection, some views concerning Whitman's poetry generally, and add some further remarks concerning the propriety of issuing the volume in its present shape.— ED. THE AMERICAN.]

"If we look at the matter widely, there is really no such thing as good or bad subjects in poetry, but good or bad poets. Anything, everything, is a fit subject. Art has no business with leading-strings or handcuffs or gags. It says to you, 'Go;' and turns you loose into the great garden of poetry where there is no forbidden fruit." This is Victor Hugo's protest against the disapprobation of those French critics whose conventional imaginations were very much disturbed by the astonishing leaps through time and space that were made by this untrammelled and disorderly genius. It is this same "*quidquid agunt homines*," unrestrained freedom of choice, that Walt Whitman has so urgently insisted upon, when the well-regulated public has remonstrated at what he calls liberty, and society license. If we "look at the matter widely," as Hugo recommends, we shall be inclined to agree with the French poet that art should not be handcuffed, and admit as the final test only that the result shall be good poetry; but then this final test must be firmly insisted upon. If a poet has produced really fine poetry, no matter what his material may have been, he has justified himself, at least from the standpoint of his art. But in order to apply this test substantially, we must consider what really good art is; and we find it to be the noble expression of noble ideas; and if it fail in either of these directions it ceases to be the best art. If the ideas are no longer worthy, while the form remains perfect, we have an art that rapidly deteriorates and becomes trivial, and bears within it the germ of decay. If, on the other hand, the ideas are noble and the form indifferent, we have an imperfect, incomplete art, that if it be in a healthy state must soon develop into fuller and finer expression. There is, therefore, not the danger that those concerned with the merely moral side of the question might suppose, in setting art free and cutting her leading strings, as long as the real function of art is recognized. There are plenty of restrictions left, in the severe restraint on hand and eye and speech that true art imposes on her honest servants. What matters it how poor, how mean, how simple the material, if the touch of the artist can turn it to gold, if the imagination can glorify it? There is a certain superb license that brings its own apology with it, when a man of genius is carried over the bounds of convention by the rush of passion, or the glory of beauty, or the heat of a fervid imagination, and is grand at the same time that he is gross, as Shakespeare was sometimes, or Rubens. But if he is only gross without being grand, then there is no quarter for him anywhere, and he is rejected both by morals and art. Realism, for its own sake, has no place in art, least of all in poetry; for poetry, by its very form, separates itself from prose as an imaginative manner of expressing the ideal side of nature and of man's emotions, passions and actions. In prose even brutal realism sometimes justifies itself, when there is need to make reality seem as terribly real as possible and to present facts impressively; but we see to what degradation poetry can be reduced by conscientiously applied realism, even in the hands of a poet of imagination and the most refined sensibilities, a poet who had produced the finest imaginative poetry, in Wordsworth's "Simon Lee." And we see to what infinitely lower degradation realism can bring a man without refined sensibilities and a cultivated imagination in Whitman's "Children of Adam."

It is only another proof of the enormous egotism of the man, that he should claim to have made a new departure in insisting on the physical basis of passion, as there is scarcely a poet from Anacreon to Swinburne who has failed to do it ample justice. All that he has done is to tear off, with a rude hand, the thin veil of ideality that "shadowed its form though not concealed," and drag it bare before the public, shorn of the finer, higher, purer emotions that sentiment has so intimately associated with it, and stripped of all imaginative charm. This he assuredly has done. It is true that Whitman is a son of the people, and has naturally missed the refining influences of early associations; but then one is forced to remember another son of the people, Robert Burns, and one involuntarily thinks of his

"O, my Love's like a red, red rose,
  That's newly sprung in June:
O my Love's like a melodie
  That's sweetly played in tune,"

when one comes to lines like these,—verses they can scarcely be called:

"Sometimes with one I love I fill
    myself with rage for fear I effuse
    unreturned love.
But now I think there is no such
    thing as unreturned love; the pay
    is certain one way or another.
(I loved a certain person ardently
    and my love was unreturned,
Yet out of my love have I written
    these songs.)"

Or put this beside it, so full of spontane-
ousness and the emotion of the hour.

"O, wha can prudence think upon,
    And sic a lassie by him?
O, wha can prudence think upon,
    And sae in love as I am?"

But it is not only to noble or graceful
ideas, but to worthy expression of them
as well, that poetry owes its power and
charm; and it is in this sense of form that
Walt Whitman is so essentially lacking. A
poet must be an artist, as well as a man
of imagination, and however much of an
outlaw or rebel he may be in spirit, must
submit himself to the laws of his art.
Methods he must have though they be of
his own choosing, and the man of genius
always recognizes the necessity of such
restraints. A poet who absolutely ignores
the charm of verse, has missed the secret
of his art. An English poet who neglects
the language of poetry, which is something set apart from the common terms
of daily speech, and by preference employs the most hackneyed, prosaic literal
expressions of everyday life, has no sense
of the sacredness of poetry. When one
thinks of what real poetry is, one has
hardly patience with a man who could
offer the public lines like these, and call
them poetry:

"I tucked my trowser-ends into my
    boots, and went and had a good
    time."

"Do I contradict myself?
Very well then I contradict myself.
(I am large, I contain multitudes.)"
"I reckon I am their boss, and they
    make me a pet besides."
"I assert that all fast days were what
    they must have been,
And that they could no-how have
    been better than what they were,
And that to-day is what it must be,
    and that America is,
And that to-day and America could
    no-how be better than what they
    are."

Could indifference of ideas and contempt of form be carried further than this?
In Whitman's case, it is especially unfortunate that he should have failed to
conceive of poetry as an art, for every
now and then one comes across a burst
of something that might have been poetry, and fine poetry too, if it had been
shaped by an artist. There is this from the
"Song of Myself":

"I am he that walks with the tender
    and growing night.
I call to the earth and the sea half
    held by the night,
Press close, bare-bosomed night—
    press close, magnetic, nourishing
    night!
Night of the south-winds—night of
    the large few stars!
Still, nodding night—mad, naked
    summer night."

There are passages of this quality scattered through the volume in "Drum Taps,"
"Sea Drift," "From Noon to Starry Night,"
but they shine like oases among weary
pages that are an inextricable tangle
of incoherent emotions, epithets, invectives, detached thoughts, inconsequent reflections, un-analyzable, divigations, that
spread in straggling unmetrical lines. The

author of *Leaves of Grass* entirely lacks, or has never cultivated any sustained power of construction, and the fact that he has been taken so seriously in Europe is partly due to his astonishing egotism, his defiant tone and fierce assertion of his own individuality, and partly to the undiscriminating manner that prevails in certain English literary circles to find something that shall be unmistakably typical of the new civilization of the crude Western world, something that might pass for the poetry of the self-made man.

It is not from an ethical standpoint, not from narrow, conservative prejudice, that Walt Whitman's insistent realism is inevitably condemned, but from the vital principles of his art, which it offends beyond reconciliation. He is judged by a canon that he himself would hardly refuse to accept: "In poetry, there is no such thing as good or bad subjects, but good or bad poets."

"Late Publications."
Boston *Commonwealth*,
2 September 1882, p. 1.

The new edition of *Leaves of Grass*, by Walt Whitman, is a compact volume of four hundred pages, handsomely printed, and with all of the author's permanent verse included. There ever will be a divided opinion, probably, as to Whitman's claim to rank as a poet. Certain is it that he discards all the canonical rules pertaining to composition, and gives just the expression, regardless of "feet," that answers his thought's need. Much of his work, therefore, seems but the record of ideas in the baldest of prose. Here and there is a sentiment embodied which touches the highest poetic afflatus. Yet with a feeling

throughout that conventional "poetry" has all been derided, we find many passages that bear reading again and again, and their strength grows upon one as familiarity is achieved. The author seems to us to be laboring with great thoughts, which he must indite at once to rescue from oblivion, with purpose later to set their excellence in flowing rhyme. They are rough diamonds of poetic thought awaiting the inspired lapidary's skill. The "fleshly" pieces, of which so much has been said, and which endangered the circulation of the book hereabouts, are to our mind but beatific adorations of the great gift of maternity, and to the purist can be as welcome as the nude statue. With the limitations of our civilization, however, there are but few purists, and the intent of the author can easily be misunderstood by very excellent people, and wholly perverted by the depraved. They are not necessary to any representation of the force or originality of the writer, and as they offend large sections of the community, and furnish prurient curiosity with food for lascivious thought, they had better, as Mr. Emerson originally suggested, be curtailed, if not wholly omitted. It is absurd, however, to rank the work as an obscene or reprehensible one in the broad and literal sense.

"New Books."
Philadelphia *Press*,
11 September 1882, p. 7.

"The good gray poet," stands by his colors and indicates his principles. Having been driven from the modern Athens he now appears undimmed and, it is to be hoped, victorious in the neighbor city of his home. The controversy about the

255

morality of his poems need not here be continued. It is a question to which the old motto of the Garter can be well applied—*Honi soit qui mal y pense*. The lewd imagination which would gloat over Whitman's virile lines would find rot to feed on in the best of books. Here, let it be said, however, that *Leaves of Grass*, as it stands, is not a book for girls or children. It pictures freely or frankly, without winking at, the evils in the world—the evils which every man and woman knows exist, and has to face every day. A great part of Whitman's poems is perfectly sound and safe reading for even the tenderest of girlhood. It seems as if it would be worth while to publish for a more indiscriminate public an edition of *Leaves of Grass* with the sixty or hundred dubious lines omitted. It might injure the perspective of the work from an ideal point of view, but the gain to the young to be able to read the best of Whitman would certainly amply pay for the sacrifice. The Philadelphia issue of *Leaves of Grass* is identical in make-up to the Osgood edition.

G. C. Macaulay.
"Walt Whitman."
Nineteenth Century
[London] 12
(December 1882),
903–18.

In publishing, some fifteen years ago, a volume of selections from the works of Whitman, Mr. Rossetti considered that he was preparing the ground for the ultimate publication in England of a complete edition of the poems of that remarkable, if rather eccentric, writer. That event has now at length taken place (though not, it seems, without unforeseen difficulty of some kind, marked by a long interval between the advertisement and the appearance of the volume, and by a change of publishers apparently at the last moment), and London can at length supply us from its own resources with copies of *Leaves of Grass*, under which title the author apparently now wishes to include all his poetical works up to the present time. We are presented at the same time with another work of the same author, the preface to the first edition of *Leaves of Grass* (published 1855 in a thin quarto, type set up by the author himself), which is now not easily to be met with. This preface was not reprinted in subsequent editions, but was prefixed with some omissions by Mr. Rossetti to his volume of selections. For what has been given us we must be thankful, though we may mildly complain that Whitman's other prose works, consisting of two books—one a magnificent political prophecy, and the other a personal narrative of deep interest—are apparently to be withheld from the English reader, though long ago advertised as published or to be published in company with the preface afore-mentioned. Even in America, says a personal friend of the author, these books can hardly be said to have been published, though readers occasionally find them out, and certainly in England they are little enough known. The reader at the British Museum may find there a copy of *Democratic Vistas*, but he will search in vain for *Memoranda during the War*.

Meanwhile, however, a real service has been rendered to us by the publication in London of *Leaves of Grass*, and against the printing of the volume there is nothing to be said; it is, in fact, a fine specimen of typography, with few apparent misprints, excellencies which no doubt are fully appreciated by the author, who knows practically what printing is. For those who are acquainted with previous editions of the poems this publication has an interest of its own quite apart from the fact that it is the first complete English edition. There are poems contained in it which have either never appeared before, or only in a separate form not readily to be obtained in this country, as for instance, the "Song of the Exposition," "After all not to create only," with its funeral chant for feudalism, which has passed now to its charnel vault—

Coffin'd with crown and armour on,
Blazoned with Shakspere's purple
   page
And dirged by Tennyson's sweet sad
   rhyme.

There are also throughout the poems changes of title, omissions, and corrections, such as the author continually makes in his works, for, rough as they seem and often are, the roughness is not caused by want of revision, and finally, the poems are rearranged, sometimes under new heads altogether, such as "Autumn Rivulets," while "Passage to India" remains only as the title of a single poem, which in 1872 [sic] gave its name to a whole volume. But to mention these in detail, and to estimate the effect of them taken together, would be impossible without assuming in the reader a previous knowledge which in most cases he would not possess. We must confine ourselves at present to more general considerations.

Whitman has been the object of a good deal of enthusiastic and rather undiscriminating admiration, and also of a certain amount of furious and equally undiscriminating abuse. Neither is deserved, but he lays himself open, it must be said, almost equally to both. It is time, however, that an attempt were made to

arrive at a sober estimate of his real value; and to the formation of such an estimate those should contribute who, having carefully considered the writings of the man, feel his influence strongly indeed, as all such will, but are not overpowered by it, and see his great merits plainly without being thereby prevented from seeing plainly also his great excess and defects. A few of such critics have already essayed the task, but it will hardly be said that there is no room for more.

It is said, and, so far as I know, said truly, that this prophet is not honoured in his own country. This does not mean that his books have not been bought and read: indeed, the number of copies sold of the first editions of *Leaves of Grass* is to me rather a subject of surprise. Astonishment at the audacity of the venture must have had some share in raising the public interest, for the book unquestionably sold well. Nor does it mean that the merit of the author was quite unrecognised: on the contrary, by some who were most competent to judge, he was estimated at a very high value. "The most extraordinary piece of wit and wisdom that America has yet contributed" was Emerson's verdict on the book, and Thoreau thought he saw something almost more than human in the personality of the man. But the mass of his countrymen were not and are not strong enough to accept him; they have perhaps too little confidence in their own literary originality to appreciate duly one from among themselves who breaks through all the conventional usages of literature; they have too much squeamish delicacy to admit to their society one who is so brutally outspoken and unrefined. It is necessary perhaps that this writer, for we need not be zealous to claim for him the title of poet, should be first accepted in the Old World before he can be recognised by the New, which at

257

present can see nothing in literature but by reflected light. Strange irony of fate, if such should be the destiny of one who cast off the conventional forms in order to free himself and his country from Old World influences! "The proof of a poet shall be sternly deferr'd till his country absorbs him as affectionately as he has absorbed it." This he has said and still believes, waiting in confidence for that proof of his title to be forthcoming. But there are many reasons why he should be slowly if at all admitted to his rights, whether in Old World or in New, and to glance at some of these reasons before we proceed further will not be amiss.

He is perhaps of all writers the most repellent to the reader who glances at him superficially. In the first place he is indecent, and that too not accidentally but on principle. Whatever may be thought of his morality, and that I hold to be essentially sound and healthy, it cannot be denied that in one section of his work, and occasionally throughout the poems and prose, he outrages every ordinary rule of decency. There is nothing impure in this kind of exposure; it has indeed the direct antithesis to prurient suggestion, and the intention of it is unquestionably honest, but from an artistic point of view it is the gravest of faults, it is essentially and irredeemably ugly and repulsive. We are most of us agreed that there is and ought to be a region of reticence, and into this region the writer has rushed himself and drags us unwillingly after him. He stands convicted of ἀπειροκαλία, if of nothing worse. Akin to this first instance of defect in artistic perception is a second—his use, namely, of words which are either not English or essentially vulgar; and to this must be added a not unfrequent neglect of syntax, which, together with looseness in the application of some words, makes him at times vague or unintelligible. Occasionally there occur words or expres-

sions which, though not ordinarily found in literature, have a native force which justifies them; but generally it is the case that for the French word or for the vulgarism savouring either of the gutter on the one hand or of the Yankee penny-a-liner on the other might be substituted a good English word equally expressive. But here also we too probably have before us a fault of wilfulness, for we know that he will not allow the language of English literature to be large enough for the poets of America, but expects accessions to it from Tennessee and California. If, however, he has in his choice of words sought that simplicity which (to quote his own words) is "the art of art, the glory of expression, and the sunshine of the light of letters," he has certainly not seldom failed to attain it, and it was hardly to be attained by pouring out indiscriminately into his pages the words which ran naturally off his pen. The "art of sinking" is illustrated in his juxtaposition of the most incongruous things, and this especially in his well-known catalogues, which, though sometimes picturesque and interesting, are generally only absurd and dull. The fact that they are introduced on principle is not to be admitted as an excuse for their inartistic and formless character, any more than a similar excuse is to be allowed for offenses against decency. From many of these faults a sense of humour would have protected him, and this also might have preserved him from some of that violently feeble exaggeration with which he speaks especially of his own countrymen and their institutions, and from the parade with which he sometimes announces truisms, as if they had been just now for the first time discovered by himself. His defence on the general charge is finely given in a poem now published for the first time, written in Platte Cañon, Colorado.

Spirit that formed this scene,
These tumbled rock-piles grim and
   red,
These reckless heaven-ambitious
   peaks,
These gorges, turbulent-clear streams,
   this naked freshness,
These formless wild arrays . . .
Was't charged against my chants they
   had forgotten art? . . .
But thou that revelest here, spirit that
   formed this scene,
They have remembered thee.

But the grandeur of nature is not always to be attained by heaping together uncouth masses. We complain not so much that the work lacks polish, as that the writer has not been preserved by his own native genius from ugly excrescences.

These artistic defects and his general disregard of form make many of his works repulsive, and do not allow us to accept any one as faultless. But they are mostly such as expurgation could remove, and therefore are not vital. The characteristic which cannot be got rid of, and yet repels, is his intense egotism and self-assertion. His longest, and in some respects most important, work—a poem of twelve or fourteen hundred lines, with which the original *Leaves of Grass* opened—has or had his own name as the title[1] and his own personality as the subject; and this self-assertion of the individual is perhaps the prevailing characteristic of Whitman's work, that which makes it in fact representative in some degree of the spirit of the age; and the egotism, after all, is not so much personal as typical. The poet is a Kosmos, and contains within himself all unity and all diversity. What he claims for himself he thereby claims for others on the same terms. "Underneath all, to me is myself, to you yourself." We feel when the poet proclaims himself "an acme of things ac-

complished," for whose birth all the forces of the universe have been a preparation, he is speaking less for himself individually than for humanity, the humanity of his own day and of future days. The egotism becomes more offensive when it is obviously personal and indicates himself as the Michael Angelo of literature; and that, it must be admitted, is not unseldom, though here too he claims to be speaking less for himself than for the future race of democratic poets. To these charges it may be added that, not withstanding his boasted freedom from the trammels of conventionality, he is in his more ordinary work a mannerist of the most vulgar kind. "Oh! to realise space!" "Have you reckoned a thousand acres much?" "Has any one supposed it lucky to be born? I hasten to inform him or her that it is just as lucky to die." "I have said that the soul is not more than the body, and I have said that the body is not more than the soul." "I swear I think there is nothing but immortality, that the exquisite scheme is for it, and the nebulous float is for it, and the cohering is for it!" If these are not all exact quotations, every one will recognise them as genuine types. No style lends itself more readily to parody and burlesque. But when he is at his best the mannerism is in a great measure shaken off.

The disregard of metrical uniformity is another fact which is observed by the most superficial reader, and probably repels him, but with far less reason than the points above mentioned. It is not indeed correct to say that "there is no trace of rhyme or metre" in these poems. There is at least one poem which affords an instance of perfectly regular metre and rhyme throughout, and in another the regularity in these respects is all but complete; while in some others, such as "Pioneers" and the "Dirge for two Veterans," though there is no rhyme nor an absolute uniformity in the length of lines, there is a stanzaic uniformity, which satisfies, or almost satisfies, the conventional expectations. As for the rest, some is quite formless; but for the most part there is a strongly marked and characteristic rhythm, not strictly metrical, though with metrical tendencies, nor properly to be called the rhythm of prose. It has rather the monotony of a chant than the varied tones of the best rhythmical prose, though it must be said that it not only resembles but is identical with the early prose rhythm of the same author.[2] Every reader of the preface before us will perceive this; and we are relieved from the possibility of doubt by the fact that passages from this preface have been introduced word for word, or with insignificant changes, into subsequently published poems, being divided stichometrically into lines by the natural pauses of the sentence. The words which he himself uttered in this preface on the subject of the rhythmical uniformity are among the best which have been spoken on that subject yet, and no apology is needed for quoting them.

"The poetic quality is not marshalled in rhyme or uniformity. . . . but is the life of these and much else, and is in the soul. The profit of rhyme is that it drops seeds of a sweeter and more luxuriant rhyme, and of uniformity that it conveys itself into its own roots in the ground out of sight. The rhyme and uniformity of perfect poems show the free growth of metrical laws, and bud from them as unerringly and loosely as lilacs and roses on a bush, and take shapes as compact as the shapes of chestnuts, and oranges, and melons, and pears, and shed the perfume impalpable to form. The fluency and ornaments of the finest poems, or music, or orations, or recitations are not independent but dependent. . . . Who troubles himself about his ornaments or fluency is lost."

It has been said already that though Whitman's lines are not ordinarily metrical, yet they have metrical tendencies, and this will readily be perceived by any one who reads them aloud. The prevailing rhythm is dactylic. Every reader of Whitman will recognise as characteristic the following examples, chosen purely to illustrate the movement:—

Vigil strange I kept on the field one
  night;
When you, my son and my comrade,
  dropt at my side that day,
One look I but gave, which your dear
  eyes return'd with a look I shall
  never forget;
One touch of your hand to mine, O
  boy, reach'd up as you lay on the
  ground,
Then onward I sped in the battle. . . .

Or again—

It is well—against such I say not a
  word, I am their poet also;
But behold such swiftly subside,
  burnt up for Religion's Sake;
For not all matter is fuel to heat,
  impalpable flame, the essential life
  of the earth,
Any more than such are to Religion.

Not unseldom we find regular or slightly irregular hexameters, sometimes several in succession, and occasionally also pentameters, e.g.—

Do you know, O speech, how the
  buds beneath you are folded?

Or,

Borne through the smoke of the
  battles and pierced with missiles I
  saw them,
And carried hither and yon through
  the smoke, and torn and bloody.

260

Or again (an elegiac couplet)—

Chants going forth from the centre,
from Kansas, and thence
equidistant
Shooting in pulses of fire, ceaseless,
to vivify all.

But these are accidents. Let me call the reader's attention to one form of this rhythm which is doubtless the result of design, the occasional lengthening of line in passionate lyrical outbursts, which produces sometimes a remarkable effect of intensity in that it "crowds and hurries and precipitates" the notes in the eagerness as it were of the verse to find a cadence.

Whichever way I turn, O I think you
could give me my mate back again,
if you only would.

From these dactylics we pass to the inspiriting trochaics of "Pioneers," and finally, as the poet grows graver in the more deeply spiritual songs of the soul and of death, which are among his last productions, with the rapid flow of the earlier rhythm mingles the graver tone of the iambic, as in the remarkable poem called "Passage to India."

Passage indeed, O soul, to primal
thought,
Not lands and seas alone, thy own
clear freshness,
The young maturity of brood and
bloom,
To realms of budding bibles.

Or again, in the still more recent "Song of the Redwood Tree"—

Nor yield we mournfully, majestic
brothers,
We who have grandly filled our time;
With nature's calm content, with tacit
huge delight,

We welcome what we wrought for
through the past,
And leave the field for them.

But enough of the outward form; it is time that we examine more closely the value of the contents.

If we were asked for justification of the high estimate of this poet, which has been implied, if not expressed, in what has been hitherto said, the answer would be perhaps first, that he has a power of passionate expression, of strong and simple utterance of the deepest tones of grief, which is almost or altogether without its counterpart in the world. Not often has he exerted his power, but often enough to let us understand that he possesses it, and to stamp him as a poet inferior to few, if any, of our time in strength of native genius, however he may fall behind many in artistic perception. Two poems of death, indicated often by himself as the highest theme, though not faultless, for none of his work is so, are enough in themselves to rest his claim upon. The first is "Out of the Cradle Endlessly Rocking;" and the other that funeral hymn for President Lincoln which begins, "When Lilacs Last in the Dooryard Bloomed." Nothing illustrates more strongly than these two poems the intense sympathy of the writer with nature, animate and inanimate, and the deep emotional significance which it has for him. Both are saturated with influences of sky, sea, or forest. The first is of the ocean, whose husky moaning is a fit accompaniment to the song of desolate loneliness; the second is of the forest, whose pine-fragrance is as the perfume of the sweet soul that is gone. In both the most passionate outpourings come forth in the notes of birds— the mocking-bird, the most magnificent of songsters, and the hermit thrush, the grey-brown minstrel of the cedar swamp,

261

lyrical mourners whose chant is fused and translated into words by the ecstatic listener. Shelley's skylark pours forth harmonious madness of joy, Keats' nightingale seems to be intoxicated with passionate yearning; but never before has a bird poured forth to a poet a song so capable of stirring the depths of emotion in the heart, so heart-breaking indeed in its intensity of grief, as that of the lone singer "on the prong of a moss-scalloped stake, down almost among the slapping waves." The burden of the first division of the chant is "Two together."

> Shine! shine! shine!
> Pour down your warmth, great sun!
> While we bask, we two together.
> Two together!
> Winds blow south, or winds blow
>   north,
> Day come white or night come black,
> Home, or rivers and mountains from
>   home,
> Singing all time, minding no time,
> While we two keep together.

Such is the joyous and careless song of the two feathered guests on the seashore of Paumanok, when the snows had melted and the lilac scent was in the air, while every day the boy, curious but never disturbing them, peered cautiously at the he-bird flitting to and fro, and the she-bird "crouch'd on her nest, silent with bright eyes," till of a sudden, "may-be killed unknown to her mate," she disappeared, nor returned that day nor the next, nor ever appeared again. And thenceforward all the summer, day and night over the surging of the fierce mother the sea, the boy hears at intervals the solitary one who is left.

> Blow! blow! blow!
> Blow up, sea winds, along
>   Paumanok's shore.

I wait and I wait till you blow my
    mate to me.

Often the child, gliding down to the beach, had stood with bare feet, the wind wafting his hair, with "the white arms out in the breakers tirelessly tossing," to listen and translate the notes of the demon or bird.

> Soothe! soothe! soothe!
> Close on its wave soothes the wave
>   behind,
> And again another behind, embracing
>   and lapping, every one close,
> But my love soothes not me not me.
> Low hangs the moon, it rose late,
> It is lagging—O I think it is heavy
>   with love, with love.
> O madly the sea pushes upon the
>   land,
> With love, with love.
> O night! do I not see my love
>   fluttering out among the breakers?
> What is that little black thing I see
>   there in the white?
> Loud! loud! loud!
> Loud I call to you, my love!
> High and clear I shoot my voice over
>   the waves.
> Surely you must know who is here, is
>   here,
> You must know who I am, my love.
> Low-hanging moon!
> What is that dusky spot in your
>   brown yellow?
> O it is the shape, the shape of my
>   mate!
> O moon, do not keep her from me
>   any longer.
> Land! land, O land!
> Whichever way I turn, O I think you
>   could give me my mate back again,
>   if you only would,
> For I am almost sure I see her dimly
>   whichever way I look.
> . . . .

But soft! sink low!
Soft! let me just murmur.
And do you wait a moment, you
    husky-noised sea,
For somewhere I believe I heard my
    mate responding to me,
So faint, I must be still, be still to
    listen,
But not altogether still, for then she
    might not come immediately to me.
Hither, my love!
Here I am! here!
With this just-sustained note I
    announce myself to you,
This gentle call is for you, my love,
    for you.
Do not be decoyed elsewhere,
That is the whistle of the wind, it is
    not my voice;
That is the fluttering, the fluttering of
    the spray;
Those are the shadows of the leaves.
O darkness! oh in vain!
O I am very sick and sorrowful.
· · · · · · · · · ·
O past! O happy life! O songs of joy!
In the air, in the woods, over fields,
Loved! loved! loved! loved! loved!
But my mate no more, no more with
    me!
We two together no more.

It stirs the boy's heart, and he feels that
it is toward him and not really toward its
mate that the bird sings, and a thousand
echoes have started to life in his soul.

O give me the clew! (it lurks in the
    night here somewhere),
O if I am to have so much, let me
    have more!
Whereto answering, the sea,
Delaying not, hurrying not,
Whispered me through the night, and
    very plainly before daybreak,
Lisped to me the low and delicious
    word death,

And again death, death, death, death,
Hissing melodious neither like the
    bird nor like my arous'd child's
    heart,
But edging near as privately for me
    rustling at my feet,
Creeping thence steadily up to my
    ears and laving me softly all over,
Death, death, death, death, death.

This is the only solution of the cries of
unsatisfied love, and here lies the highest
problem which awaits the poet always
with its unconquerable, almost unassail-
able, mysteriousness. This word it is which
he gives as the key to the thousand re-
sponsive songs awakened in him from
that hour, the word, which the sea whispered, "like some old crone rocking the
cradle, swathed in sweet garments, bending aside."[3] "Whispers of Heavenly Death"
is the title of one section of these poems,
and it is the "Carol of Death" which forms
the centre of the second of the two poems
to which attention has now been called.
Splendidly imaginative is this "nocturne,"
with its three ever-recurring chords, "lilac, and star, and bird." Of more intricate
construction than the other and less directly passionate, because expressive of
a more reflecting sorrow, it is yet a composition which few can read or hear unmoved.

Ever-returning Spring, trinity sure to
    me you will bring,
Lilac blooming perennial and
    drooping star in the west,
And thought of him I love.

The star is disappearing in the black
murk of clouds, while cruel hands hold
him powerless; but his senses are steeped
in the perfume of the lilac and the song
from secluded recesses, "death's outlet
song of life," of the singer among the
cedars, while "over the breast of the

spring," through lanes and through streets of cities,

> Passing the yellowspear'd wheat,
> every grain from its shroud in the
> dark brown field uprisen,
> Passing the apple-tree blows of white
> and pink in the orchards,
> Carrying a corpse to where it shall
> rest in the grave,
> Night and day journeys a coffin.

To the coffin that slowly passes, with the great cloud darkening the land, with the people's mourning and "the tolling tolling bells' perpetual clang," he brings a sprig with its flower broken from the lilac bush, with its delicate blossoms and heart-shaped leaves. Nor for this coffin alone, but for all he would bring blossoms and branches and chant a song "for you, O sane and sacred Death." This, after all, was what the great star must have meant a month since—

> As I saw you had something to tell as
> you bent to me night after night,
> As you drooped from the sky low
> down as if to my side, while the
> other stars all look'd on,
> As we wander'd together the solemn
> night (for something, I know not
> what, kept me from sleep).

But he is drawn by the song of the bird, though for a moment he lingers, detained by the star, his departing comrade, and by the mastering odour of the lilac. Sea winds blown from east and west, from the Atlantic and from the Pacific, shall be the perfume for the grave of the man he loves. Pictures of growing spring "with floods of the yellow gold of the gorgeous indolent sinking sun," of all the scenes of life in country or city of this varied and ample land, these shall adorn his burial house. But over all these falls the dark cloud,

And I knew death, its thought, and the sacred knowledge of death.
Then with the knowledge of death as walking one side of me,
And the thought of death close-walking the other side of me,
And I in the middle as with companions, and as holding the hands of companions,
I fled forth to the hiding receiving night, that talks not,
Down to the shores of the water, the path by the swamp in the dimness,
To the solemn shadowy cedars and ghostly pines so still.

The bird sang the "Carol of Death."

> Prais'd be the fathomless universe,
> For life and joy, and for objects and
> knowledge curious,
> And for love, sweet love—but praise!
> praise! praise!
> For the sure-enwinding arms of cool-
> enfolding death.

The hearer stands rapt by the charm and holding as if by the hand his mystic companions, while the sight that was bound in his eyes "unclosed, as to long panoramas of visions." He sees the vision of armies, of battle flags borne through the smoke, of the corpses of all the slain soldiers of the war, and he sees that they were not as had been thought.

> They themselves were fully at rest,
> they suffered not;
> The living remained and suffer'd.

Passing from the visions and from the song, he unlooses the hold of his comrades' hands, and leaves the cedars and the lilac with heart-shaped leaves; yet each and all he keeps.

> The song, the wondrous chant of the
> grey-brown bird,

And the tallying chant, the echo
 arous'd in my soul,
With the lustrous and drooping star,
 with the countenance full of woe,
With the holders holding my hand
 nearing the call of the bird,
Comrades mine, and I in the midst,
 and their memory ever I keep, for
 the dead I loved so well,
For the sweetest, wisest soul of all my
 days and lands—and this for his
 dear sake,
Lilac and star and bird twined with
 the chant of my soul,
There in the fragrant pines and the
 cedars dusk and dim.

The passage from this region of pure imagination and passion to the other works
of the same writer compels us to deal
with his religious and political philosophy. In religion, if he is to be labelled
with a name, it must be perhaps "Pantheist;" he is an exponent of "Cosmic Emotion." "I hear and behold God in every
object, yet understand not God in the
least." It is the contemplation of "the
fathomless universe," and all its movements and rests, its organic and inorganic
existences, which stirs the religious emotion in his soul. Men are inclined to cry,
"What is this separate nature so unnatural? What is this earth to our affections?
(unloving earth without a throb to answer
ours, cold earth, the place of graves)." To
answer this question is the function of
the poet, to soothe "the sad incessant refrain, Wherefore, unsatisfied soul? and
Whither, O mocking Life?" His answer is
"Bathe in the Spirit of the Universe, intoxicate thyself with God."

Thoughts, silent thoughts, of Time,
 and Space, and Death, like waters
 flowing,
Bear me indeed as through the
 regions infinite,

Whose air I breathe, whose ripples
 hear, lave me all over,
Bathe me, O God, in thee, mounting
 to thee,
I and my soul to range in range of
 thee.
O Thou transcendent,
Nameless, the fibre and the breath,
Light of the light, shedding forth
 universes. . . .
Thou pulse, thou motive of the stars,
 suns, systems,
That, circling, move in order, safe,
 harmonious,
Athwart the shapeless vastnesses of
 space,
How should I think, how breathe a
 single breath, how speak, if out of
 myself
I could not launch to those superior
 universes?

God, as he includes all, includes personality, and from God will come somehow
a satisfaction of the longing of the soul.
What conclusions, if any, are to be drawn
from the alteration in the new edition of
the poem called "Gods," I leave it to the
curious to consider; but in it clearly, as
elsewhere, we find anticipation of the

Lover divine, and perfect comrade,
Waiting content, invisible yet, but
 certain,

of whom, whether he be ideal or real, we
cannot pronounce.

About immortality he doubts, yet
strongly believes. In moments of cool reflection he feels that the question of "identity beyond the grave" is the great un-
solved problem. Yet his poetical optimism
continually leads him to assert immortality, and that not merely the merging of
our life in the vital forces of the universe,
though that is sometimes his meaning,
but actual personal identity of the human

soul after death. We have, on the one hand, among his first utterances—

I bequeath myself to the dirt, to grow from the grass I love;

and, on the other hand, we have later the picture of the chamber of death, where

The living look upon the corpse with their eyesight,
But without eyesight lingers a different living and looks curiously on the corpse;

and again the cry—

If maggots and rats ended us, then alarum! for we are betrayed,
Then indeed suspicion of death.

On the whole he seems to become more definite as he proceeds, in his anticipation of "identity after the grave." As for defined creeds, it is not they which give the life;

Leaves are not more shed from the trees, or trees from the earth, than they are shed out of you.
God and the soul are not to be argued about;
Logic and sermons never convince;
The damp of the night strikes deeper into my soul.

But religion is the thing above all, and he rarely fails to point the way to spiritual meanings.

His morality is almost comprised in the one word "health," health of body and health of soul, the healthy and sane man to be the ultimate standard. These are Greek ethics, and the maxim on which they seem to be based—

Whatever tastes sweet to the most perfect person, that is finally right—

is thoroughly Aristotelian. A "sane sensu-

ality," as it is called by one of his friends, is a necessary part of the ideal man. The body is sacred as well as the soul, and to assert its sacredness is the purpose of his sometimes outrageous physiological details, which can hardly have the desired effect, but are clearly not meant, nor indeed adapted, to minister to vicious tastes; they may disgust, but they can hardly corrupt. There is indeed something in this tearing away of veils which, however justly it may offend true modesty, is to unhealthiness and pruriency as sunlight and the open air; they shrink from the exposure, and shiver at the healthy freshness; it is not an atmosphere in which they can long survive: mystery is the region in which they thrive, and here all mystery is rudely laid bare. This man's nature is itself as healthy as the sea, which endangers not us with all the fevers deposited in it.

His judgment of actions is rather aesthetic than strictly moral, and he admires the unconscious blossoming out of good and kindly deeds more than all the moral struggles which proceed from religious introspection. He envies the careless rectitude of the movements of animals who are placid and self-contained, and do not "sweat and whine about their condition." He is sure that good deeds have their happiness in themselves and not in any external or future reward, and that bad deeds have their misery in themselves and not in any external or future punishment.

The song is to the singer, and comes back most to him;
The teaching is to the teacher, and comes back most to him;
The theft is to the thief, and comes back most to him;
The love is to the lover, and comes back most to him;
The gift is to the giver, and comes back most to him, it cannot fail.

266

And again of a future life—

I have dreamed that we are not to be
   changed so much, nor the law of
   us changed;
I have dreamed that heroes and good-
   doers shall be under the present
   and past law,
And that murderers, drunkards, and
   liars shall be under the present and
   past law,
For I have dreamed that the law they
   are under now is enough.

But underlying all, so far as he himself
is concerned, is a sympathy embracing all
human beings, however vile, and all animals and plants, however irresponsive. It
is this which leads him at times to em-
phasise his own sensuality, that he may
make himself the equal of the most depraved, to draw them if it may be in the
bonds of sympathy to himself. It is this
which is the open secret of that magnetic
influence which he is said to exercise over
those whom he casually meets. It was this
which led him to the hospitals rather
than to the field of battle, and makes him
recall in memory now the experiences of
the "Dresser," rather than the great battles and sieges at which he was present.
No study of the poet would be complete
which did not include the section of his
work which deals with the war and after,
which indeed contains some of the most
magnificent and spirit-stirring trumpet-
blasts, as well as some of the most
deeply-moving aspects of suffering and
death ever expressed by a poet. Here was
a great theme, and he treated it nobly;
with all notes of patriotism and devotion
to the flag is beautifully blended sympathy for the vanquished, and deep desire
to relieve the sufferings of the wounded.
On the whole no part of his work is more
interesting than this; it is as if he were the
born poet of emancipation, tender to all

suffering persons, yet with nerve strong
enough to endure without fainting or
shrieking the stroke of necessary surgery.
Magnificent is his war cry, as in the "Song
of the Banner at Daybreak," and his note
of triumph, "The war is completed, the
price is paid, the title settled beyond recall;" yet finer still is the "Vigil on the
Field of Battle," the memories of the hospital tent with its long row of cots, the
vision of the Mother of All gazing desperate on her dead, the reflection on those
"Camps of Green" where friend and foe
without hatred sleep, and need not any
longer provide for outposts, nor word
for the countersign, nor drummer to beat
the morning drum. Other things, too, he
gathered from the experiences of the war:
he gathered from them more than from
all else the steadfastness of his belief in
democracy, in the nobleness and courage
of common men. But to speak of this
would belong rather to a review of the
Democratic Vistas, which is not my task;
the poetical aspects of the theme are
enough. The poet then believes in the
power of sympathy, but he believes also
in individuality "underneath all-individ-
uals." At least half his work is devoted
to the assertion of this, and yet with this
sympathy and "adhesiveness" is to go hand
in hand, and he has as his watchword
still the word of democracy, the word En-
masse. The reconciliation is to be found
in the prose more clearly than in the verse,
but Whitman is not over-anxious for reconciliation; he is large, he contains multitudes, and has room for contradictions.

Do I contradict myself?
Very well then, I contradict myself.

That being so, his optimism is the more
comprehensible; and it is upon a basis of
optimism after all that he builds his whole
religion and philosophy. He has too firm
a grasp of fact to ignore the existence of

evil. If he exclaims at times, "There is no evil," he adds, "or if there is, it is just as important to you as anything else." "I am not the poet of goodness only; I am just as much the poet of evil." But he believes that evil is transient and relative; he holds that the drift of things is towards good; that all is, not at once, but finally for the best. This he says, in plain prose, is the growing conviction of his life and in verse, of the souls of men and women going forward along the roads of the universe,

> They go, they go, I know that they
>   go, but I know not where they go,
> But I know that they go forward
>   toward the best.

This it is which makes him so much at peace about God and about death. "No array of words can describe how much I am at peace about God and about death;" the heroic failures of this world are to him eternal successes. "Battles are lost in the same spirit in which they are won;" therefore, "Vivas to those who have failed!" And above all the cause of liberty will finally succeed.

> Revolt! and still revolt! revolt!
> .   .   .   .
> When liberty goes out of a place, it is
>   not the first to go, nor the second
>   or third to go,
> It waits for all the rest to go, it is the
>   last.
> When there are no more memories of
>   heroes and martyrs,
> And when all life and all the souls of
>   men and women are discharged
>   from any part of the earth,
> Then only shall liberty, or the idea
>   liberty, be discharged from that
>   part of the earth,
> And the infidel come into full
>   possession.

Too much, perhaps, has been said of the religion and morality of the poet, and too little of the literary aspect of his works. But this it is difficult to illustrate sufficiently by quotation, and impossible to set forth without illustration. It seemed to me that suggestions of the drift of the whole were more likely to be useful than attention to particular points. Everyone will remark first the too frequent infelicity of sentiment and phrase, and then the striking directness of utterance, and the stumbling, as if by accident, on the absolutely best words in the absolutely best order, which characterises his finest work. Whether these be truly poems or fine imaginings only we need not be much concerned to inquire. His own claim to be the poet of America is based on other than purely literary grounds.

> Give me the pay I have served for,
> Give me to sing the songs of the great
>   Idea, take all the rest.
> I have loved the earth, sun, animals; I
>   have despised riches; I have given
>   alms to everyone that asked. . . .
> I have dismissed whatever insulted
>   my own soul or defiled my body,
> Claimed nothing to myself which I
>   have not carefully claimed for
>   others on the same terms,
> Sped to the camps, and comrades
>   found and accepted from every
>   state,
> (Upon this breast has many a dying
>   soldier leaned to breathe his last).
> Say, O mother, have I not to your
>   thought been faithful?
> Have I not through life kept you and
>   yours before me?

Notes

1 The title 'Walt Whitman,' which this poem has generally borne in American editions, is now altered to 'Song of Myself.'

2　It should be observed that in the later prose of *Democratic Vistas*, a book which is comparatively free from his characteristic weaknesses, the writer attains to a prose style of much greater excellence. This book, with its Carlylian eloquence and anti-Carlylian optimism, is not more remarkable on account of the robust faith of the writer in the future of American democracy, than on account of his keen perception and vigorous denunciation of its present faults and failings, and is enough by itself to stamp him as a master of the English language and a prose poet of the first order. The English reader who would understand the author's drift and hear the key-note of his philosophy could not do better than begin with this book, but that it is in England almost unobtainable.

3　A line added in this edition.

SPECIMEN DAYS & COLLECT (1882–3)

Specimen Days & collect

By WALT WHITMAN,

Author of " LEAVES OF GRASS."

PHILADELPHIA:

DAVID McKAY,

No. 23 SOUTH NINTH STREET.

1882–'83.

"New Publications."
New York *Tribune*,
14 October 1882, p. 6.

Rees Welsh & Co., Philadelphia, have published a volume of Walt Whitman's prose, under the title, *Specimen Days and Collect*. Externally it bears a close resemblance to *Leaves of Grass*, but the likeness does not run through. The strong animalism of this astonishing author seems to be thoroughly aroused only under the influence of the muse; and though it is plain enough even when he writes in the prose form, it is not then offensive. We are inclined to suspect that a better test of his intrinsic quality will be found in these random and fugitive papers, some of them recording his experiences as a hospital nurse, many gathered from the pages of periodicals, than in the wilder and less genuine strains in which he has been accustomed to shout for the edification of feather-brained disciples. There is little in these confessions, communings with nature, forcible and often original descriptions of common-place objects, which can very well stir the enthusiasm of the howling dervishes of the new criticism; but there is a certain freshness and individuality which are always impressive, and an imaginative quality which sometimes rises very near the level of poetry if it does not reach it. And yet that Whitman has any new message to deliver to the world, that life, literature, philosophy have anything to gain from his thoughts, no perfectly sane person is likely to decide after a reading of his prose. In the "Pieces in Early Youth" reprinted with the miscellania called *Collect*, it is apparent that Whitman once wrote very much like other people.

"Whitman's New Book."
Boston *Sunday Herald*,
15 October 1882, p. 9.

Walt Whitman's new book, with the odd, but thoroughly characteristic and descriptive title, *Specimen Days and Collect*, is a prose companion to *Leaves of Grass*, being a complete collection of the author's prose writings, as the former comprises all his verse. It is a meaty, compact volume, and is more directly comprehensible to the understanding of the multitude than the greater and more famous work. And yet this is as much Whitman as his verse is, and the same characteristics pervade it: grand healthiness of tone, largeness of view, universal reach, and, at the same time, deliberate perception and sensitiveness, and identity with nature, indissoluble and knit through and through with its fabric. Had *Leaves of Grass* never been written this book alone would be enough to establish the author's fame as a great poet. In a personal letter Whitman writes: "It is a great jumble (as man himself is)—is an autobiography after its sort—(sort o' synonymous with Montaigne, and Rousseau's 'Confessions', etc.)—is the gathering up and formulation and putting in identity of the wayside itemizings, memoranda and personal notes of 50 years under modern American conditions—a good deal helter-skelter, but, I am sure, with a certain sort of orbic compaction and oneness as the final result. It dwells long on the secession war, gives glimpses of that event's strange interiors, especially the army hospitals; in fact, makes the resuscitation and putting on record of the emotional aspect of the war of 1861–65 one of its principal features." Indeed, too

273

much stress cannot be laid upon this phase of the book. No history or description of the war that has yet been written probably gives such vivid and graphic pictures of its events—its heroism, its horror, its sadness, the pathetic tenderness of countless of its incidents, and, above all, its grand significance. For this reason it ought to be dear to every soldier. During the years from 1876 to the present date Whitman has been a partial paralytic. Very much of his days (and nights, also, it appears) he has spent in the open air down in the country in the woods and fields, and by a secluded little New Jersey river. His memoranda, on the spot, of these days and nights, fill a goodly portion of the volume. Then comes the *Collect*, embodying "Democratic Vistas," the noble prose preface to *Leaves of Grass* of the edition of 1855, and much other prose, together with a number of youthful efforts in prose and poetry, which, in a note, the author explains he would have preferred to have them quietly dropped in oblivion, but, to avoid the annoyance of their surreptitious issue, he has, with some qualms, tacked them on. The whole volume, in its arrangement, is pregnant with Whitman's personality, and it seems more a part of its author than paper and printers' ink usually do. It also exhibits, as far as possible for any public record, that most wonderful and intricate of processes, the working of a poet's mind, and affords an insight into the mysterious interior depths and rambling galleries and chambers of the cosmic sphere whose large and rugged exterior is clothed with the fresh beauty of leaves of grass.

The contents of the book take a wide range, as may be seen by the following samples: The old Whitman and Van Velsor Cemeteries . . . Paumanok (Long Island, N. Y.) and My Life on It as Child and Young Man . . . Printing Office— Old Brooklyn . . . Lafayette . . . Broadway Sights . . . My Passion for Ferries . . . Omnibus Jaunts and Drivers . . . Plays and Operas . . . Opening of the Secession War . . . Down at the Front . . . The Army Hospitals . . . Cases . . . Preparations for Visits . . . A New York Soldier . . . A Yankee Antique . . . Two Brothers, one South, one North . . . the Grand Review . . . New Themes Entered upon (1876–'80) . . . to the Spring and Brook . . . A July Afternoon by the Pond . . . Locusts and Katydids . . . Full Starr'd Nights . . . Mulleins . . . A Sun-Bath—Nakedness . . . Human and Heroic New York . . . Hours for the Soul . . . Delaware River—Days and Nights . . . Scenes on the Ferry . . . Begin a Long Jaunt West . . . Missouri, Kansas, Colorado . . . The Prairies, and an Undelivered Speech . . . Denver Impressions . . . The Spanish Peaks—Evening on the Plains . . . the Arkansas . . . The Silent General . . . the Women of the West . . . St. Louis . . . Edgar Poe's Significance . . . Loafing in the Woods . . . Jaunting through Canada . . . the Saguenay . . . Capes Eternity and Trinity . . . Carlyle from American Points of View . . . A Week in Boston . . . Collect . . . Democratic Vistas . . . Prefaces to *Leaves of Grass*, 1855, 1872, 1876 . . . Poetry Today in America . . . Death of Abraham Lincoln . . . Stories and Sketches Written in Youth (1834–1842).

In *Specimen Days* there is a vein of playfulness, and a humor—if it may be called so—probably different from anything yet in literature. The following is an example of this quality, and it is also an excellent characterization of the book:

CEDAR-PLUMS LIKE—NAMES

One time I thought of naming this collection "Cedar-Plums Like" (which I still fancy wouldn't have been a bad name, nor inappropriate.) A melange of loafing, looking, hobbying, sitting, traveling—a little thinking thrown in for salt but very little—not only summer but all seasons—not only days but nights—some literary meditations—books, authors examined, Carlyle, Poe, Emerson tried (always under my cedar tree, in the open air, and never in the library)—mostly the scenes everybody sees, but some of my own caprices, meditations, egotism—truly an open air and mainly summer formation—singly or in clusters—wild and free and somewhat acrid—indeed more like cedar plums than you might guess at first glance.

But do you know what they are? (To city man, or some sweet parlor lady, I now talk.) As you go along roads, or barrens, or across country, anywhere through these states, middle, eastern, western or southern, you will see, certain seasons of the year, the thick woody tufts of the cedar mottled with bunches of china-blue berries, about as big as fox grapes. But first a special word for the tree itself; everybody knows that the cedar is a healthy, cheap, democratic wood, streaked red and white—an evergreen—that it is not a cultivated tree—that it keeps away moths—that it grows inland or seaboard, all climates, hot or cold, any sort—in fact, rather prefers sand and bleak side spots content if the plough and fertilizer and the trimming axe will but keep away and let it alone. After a long rain, when everything looks bright, often have I stopt in my wood saunters, south or north, or far west, to take in its dusky green washed clean and sweet, and specked copiously with its fruit of clear, hardy blue. The wood of the cedar is of use—but what profit on earth are those sprigs of acrid plums? A question impossible to answer satisfacto-

rily. True, some of the herb doctors give them for stomache affections, but the remedy is as bad as the disease. Then, in my rambles down in Camden county, I once found an old crazy woman gathering the clusters with zeal and joy. She showed, as I was told afterward, a sort of infatuation for them, and every year placed and kept profuse bunches high and low about her room. They had a strange charm about her uneasy head, and effected docility and peace. (She was harmless, and lived near by with her well-off married daughter.) Whether there is any connection between these bunches and being out of one's wits I cannot say, but I myself entertain a weakness for them. Indeed, I love the cedar, anyhow—its naked ruggedness, its just palpable odor (so different from the perfumer's best), its silence, its equable acceptance of winter's cold and summer's heat, of rain or drought, its shelter to me from those, at times, its associations (well, I never could explain why I love anybody or anything). The service I now specially owe to the cedar is, while I cast around for a name for my proposed collection, hesitating, puzzled—after rejecting a long, long string, I lift my eyes, and lo; the very term I want. At any rate, I go no further—I tire in the search. I take what some invisible kind spirit has put before me. Besides, who shall say there is not affinity enough between (at least the bundle of sticks that produced) many of these pieces or granulations and those blue berries? Their lusciousness growing wild—a certain aroma of nature I would so like to have in my pages—the thing soft whence they come—their content in being let alone—their stolid and deaf repugnance to answering questions (this latter the nearest, dearest trait affinity of all). Then, reader dear, in conclusion, as to the point of the name for the present collection, let us be satisfied to have a name—something to identify and bind it together, to concrete all its vegetable, mineral, personal memoranda, abrupt raids of criticism, crude gossip of philosophy, varied sands and clumps—without bothering ourselves because certain pages do not present themselves to you or me as coming under their own name with entire fitness or amiability. (It is a profound, vexatious, never-explicable matter—this of names. I have been exercised deeply about it my whole life.)

After all of which the name "Cedar-Plums Like" got its nose put out of joint; but I cannot afford to throw away what I pencil'd down the lane there, under the shelter of my old friend, one warm October noon. Besides, it wouldn't be civil to the cedar tree.

The parts that deal with the war have been emphasized as forming one of the most important phases of the work. Here is an incident from the author's war experience which gives a better glance into the secession contest than all the formal military reports and statistics of the period:

A YANKEE ANTIQUE

March 27, 1885. Sergt. Calvin F. Harlowe, company C. 29th Massachusetts, 3d brigade, 1st division, 9th corps—a mark'd sample of heroism and death (some may say bravado, but I say heroism, of grandest, oldest order)—in the late attack by the rebel troops, and temporary capture by them, of Fort Steadman, at night. The fort was surprised at dead of night. Suddenly awaken'd from their sleep, and rushing from their tents, Harlowe, with others, found himself in the hands of the secesh—they demanded his surrender—he answered: "Never while I live." (Of course it was useless. The others surrender'd; the odds were too great.) Again he was ask'd to yield, this time by a rebel captain. Though surrounded, and quite calm, he again refused, call'd sternly to his comrades to fight on, and himself attempted to do so. The rebel captain then shot him—but at the same instant he shot the captain. Both fell together mortally wounded. Harlowe died almost instantly. The rebels were driven out in a very short time. The body was buried next day, but soon taken up and sent home (Plymouth county, Mass.). Harlowe was only 22 years of age—was a tall, slim, dark-hair'd, blue-eyed young man—had come out originally with the 29th; and that is the way he met his death after four years' campaign. He was in the seven days' fight before Richmond, in second Bull Run, Antietam, first Fredericksburg, Vicksburg, Jackson, Wilderness, and the campaigns following—was as good a soldier as ever wore the blue, and every old officer in the regiment will bear that testimony. Though so young, and in a common rank, he had a spirit as resolute and brave as any hero for the books, ancient or modern; it was too great to say "I surrender"—and so he died. [. . .]

There are many scattered dashes of poetic and literary criticism, evidently negligent and impromptu. On one of the concluding pages, for instance, the following:

I tried to read a beautifully printed and scholarly volume on "the Theory of Poetry" received by mail this morning from England—but gave it up at last for a bad job. Here are some capricious pencillings that followed, as I find them in my notes.

In youth and maturity poems are charged with sunshine and varied pomp of the day, but as the soul more and more takes precedence (the sensuous still included), the dusk becomes the poet's atmosphere. I, too, have sought, and ever seek, the brilliant sun, and make my songs according. But, as I grow old, the half-lights of evening are far more to me.

The play of imagination, with the sensuous objects of nature for symbols, and faith—with love and pride as the unseen impetus and moving power of all, make up the curious chess game of a poem.

Common teachers or critics are always asking: "What does it mean?" Symphony of the fine musician, or sunset, or sea waves rolling up the beach—what do they mean? Undoubtedly, in the most subtle elusive sense, they mean something—as love does, and religion does, and the best poem—but who shall fathom and define those meanings? I do not intend this as a warrant for wildness and frantic escapades, but to justify the soul's frequent joy in what cannot be defined to the intellectual part or to calculation:

At its best, poetic lore is like what may be heard of conversation in the dusk, from speakers near or far, of which we get only a few broken mummers. What is not gather'd is far more—perhaps the main thing.

Grandest poetic passages are only to be taken at free remove, as we sometimes look for stars at night, not by gazing directly toward them, but off one side.

(To a poetic student and friend.) I only seek to put you in rapport. Your own brain, heart, evolution, must not

only understand the matter, but largely supply it.

His criticism on "Edgar Poe's Significance" is an example of the best critical powers, and shows a high moral judgment. He says "there is another shape of personality dearer far to the artist sense (which likes the play of strongest lights and shades), where the perfect character, the good, the heroic, although never attained, is never lost sight of, but, through failures, sorrows, temporary downfall, is return'd to again and again, and while often violated is passionately alluded to as long as mind, muscles, voice obey the power we call volition. This sort of personality we see more or less in Burns, Byron, Schiller and George Sand. But we do not see it in Poe.... Almost without the first sign of moral principle or of the concrete or its heroisms, or the simpler affections of the heart, Poe's verses illustrate an intense faculty—for technical and abstract beauty, with the rhyming art to excess, and an incorrigible propensity toward nocturnal themes, a demoniac undertone behind every page, and, by final judgment, probably belong among the electric lights of imaginative literature, brilliant and dazzling, but with no heat." Again, he says: "By its popular poets the calibres of an age, the weak spots of its embankments, its subcurrents (often more significant than the biggest surface ones), are unerringly indicated. The lush and weird that have taken such extraordinary possession of 19th century verse-lovers, what mean they?"

Occasionally throughout the book, and as notable as any parts, are some of Whitman's special letters. Here, for example, is one which tells its own story.

Camden, N. J., U. S. A., Dec. 20, 1881.
To ——— ——— (Dresden, Saxony):

Your letter asking definite endorsement to your translation of my "*Leaves of Grass*" into Russian is just received, and I hasten to answer it. Most warmly and willingly I consent to the translation, and wish a prayerful God speed to the enterprise.

You Russians and we Americans! Our countries so distant, so unlike at first glance—such a difference in social and political conditions, and our respective methods or moral and practical development the last 100 years and yet in certain features, and vastest ones, so resembling each other. The variety of stock elements and tongues, to be resolutely fused in a common identity and union at all hazards—the idea, perennial through the ages—that they both have their historic and divine mission—the fervent element of manly friendship throughout the whole people, surpass'd by no other races—the grand expanse of territorial limits and boundaries—the unform'd and nebulous state of many things, not yet permanently settled, but agreed on all hands to be the preparations of an infinitely greater future—the fact that both peoples have their independent and leading positions to hold, keep, and if necessary, fight for, against the rest of the world—the deathless aspirations at the inmost center of each great community, so vehement, so mysterious, so abysmic—are certainly features you Russians and we Americans possess in common.

As my dearest dream is for an internationality of poems and poets, binding the lands of the earth closer than all treaties and diplomacy; as the purpose beneath the rest in my book is such hearty comradeship, for individuals to begin with, and for all the nations of the earth as a result—how happy I should be to get the healing and emotional contact of the great Russian peoples.

To whom, now and here, (addressing you for Russia and Russians, and empowering you, should you see fit, to print the present letter in your book, as a preface,) I waft affectionate salutation from these shores, in America's name.

W. W.

The following extract from a letter to a German friend gives a picture of the poet's condition at present:

May 31, '82. From today I enter upon my 64th year. The paralysis that first affected me nearly 10 years ago has since remain'd with varying course—seems to have settled quietly down, and will probably continue. I easily tire, am very clumsy, cannot walk far; but my spirits are first-rate. I go around in public almost every day—now and then take long trips, by railroad or boat, hundreds of miles—live largely in the open air—am sunburnt and stout, (weigh 190)—keep up my activity and interest in life, people, progress and the questions of the day. About two-thirds of the time I am quite comfortable. What mentality I ever had remains entirely unaffected; though physically, I am a half-paralytic, and likely to be so, long as I live. But the principal object of my life seems to have been accomplish'd—I have the most devoted and ardent of friends and affectionate relatives—and of enemies I really make no account.

It is understood that Whitman himself considers *Specimen Days* as the exponent and finish of his poetic work, *Leaves of Grass*; that each of the two volumes is indispensable, in his view, to the other, and that both together finally begin and illustrate his literary scheme in the new world. Talking lately, in a half-jocular vein, to a friend, he called them his Adam and Eve, sent out in "this garden, the world."

The book is issued in precisely the same style as *Leaves of Grass*, with the same cloth binding [. . .] and the same price. It contains a faithful likeness of Whitman, in out-door attire, and sitting watching a butterfly that has lit on his finger. Since *Leaves of Grass* was transferred to the Philadelphia house, four editions have been exhausted, and they are now on the fifth.

"All About Walt Whitman." *Literary World* 13 (4 November 1882), 372–3.

We have here Mr. Whitman's collected prose. His prose is better than his poetry. It is clean. It is sane. It is intelligible. It is often readable. Much of it is really interesting, because either of its autobiographical effect, its reminiscential quality, or its frank fresh mirroring of out-of-door life and sensation. The book is virile. In many places it has the smell of damp loam or of new-mown grass. It is honest and justifiable. It contains the prose work of its author's life, and shows him at his best all through. Its title, its title-page in the author's rugged autograph, its make-up, and its literary style are all characteristic; and the heliotype portrait, facing p. 122, is strikingly good. The contents are brief essays or sketches, mostly fragmentary, many of them dated as if they were leaves torn from a diary. The first and

longest group, occupying 200 pages, is denominated *Specimen Days*. Following these, under the heads of *Collect* and "Notes Left Over" come 150 or more pages of nearly similar material. The volume closes with a hundred pages of "Pieces in Early Youth," printed subordinately in fine type. The book is unobjectionable so far as we have noticed, and there is not a little that can be said in its favor.

Many readers will be interested at once in the opening pages for the details they furnish of Mr. Whitman's ancestry and life. He was born on Long Island, May 31, 1819; and grew up on its shores studying sea-fowl, fishes and fishermen, wrecks, and nature generally in her wilder moods. As he writes, he tells us, the whole experience comes back to him:

the soothing rustle of the waves, and the saline smell—boyhood's times, the clam digging, barefoot and with trowsers roll'd up—the hay boat, and the chowder and fishing excursions; or, of later years, little voyages down and out New York bay, in the pilot boats.

From 1824 to 1828 Mr. Whitman's parents lived in Brooklyn. He remembers Lafayette's visit, and going to hear Elias Hicks preach in a ball-room on the Heights. He began life in earnest as an errand boy in a lawyer's office; subscribed to a circulating library; reveled in the Arabian Nights and Scott's novels and poems; and then went to work to learn the trade of a printer. When he was eighteen he was teaching school in Queens and Suffolk Counties, and "boarding round." Then was the time when it was his passion to sail the East River to and fro in the ferry boats, "often up in the pilot-houses;" where he could "get a full sweep, absorbing shows, accompaniments, surroundings." To this succeeded a passion for Broadway and its omnibuses, where he saw Andrew Jackson, Webster, Clay, Seward, Van Buren, Walker the filibuster, Kossuth, Fitz–Greene Halleck, Bryant, the Prince of Wales, Dickens, and a host of other celebrities—among them Cooper and Poe. One of his special reminiscences belonging to this time is this:

> I once saw (it must have been about 1832, of a sharp bright January day) a bent, feeble, but stout-built very old man, bearded, swathed in rich furs, with a great ermine cap on his head, led and assisted, almost carried, down the steps of his high front stoop (a dozen friends and servants, emulous, carefully holding, guiding him) and then lifted and tuck'd in a gorgeous sleigh, envelop'd in other furs, for a ride. . . . I remember the spirited, champing horses, the driver with his whip, and a fellow driver by his side, for extra prudence. . . . It was John Jacob Astor.

In 1848–9 Mr. Whitman was editor of the Brooklyn *Daily Eagle*; then he went South, and worked at journalism a little while in New Orleans; then up into the Northwest and so round to New York again; then took to housebuilding and journalism once more in Brooklyn; and in 1855 began to put his *Leaves of Grass* to press. He was then in his thirty-sixth year.

The next sixty pages of the book are devoted to reminiscences of the Civil War, gathered in the Union hospitals among the sick and wounded soldiers. Mr. Whitman did good service as nurse and attendant in those trying days, and relates scores of pathetic incidents of the familiar type in unconventional terms. There is a powerful picture of the effect at Washington of the first Battle of Bull Run. There are graphic descriptions of field and camp hospitals, of trains and boat-loads of wounded, of individual cases of suffering, heroism, and patience, of visits to "the front," of death scenes, of Mr. Lincoln as he appeared on horseback with his cavalry escort, and, finally, a few concluding paragraphs under the forcible heading "The real war will never get into the books."

Having finished with the War, Mr. Whitman enters upon a range of bucolic themes, and shows himself to us as a sort of muscular Thoreau, fond of out-of-doors, of farm lanes, brooks and springs, bumble-bees, birds, and so on. He invites us to "a July afternoon by the pond." He teaches us "the lesson of a tree." He gives us a handful of "autumn side-bits." He spends "a winter day on the beach." He wanders out in the "full-starr'd nights." He takes a sun-bath, in sheer nakedness, in a secluded dell, once a marl-pit, "now abandon'd, fill'd with bushes, trees, grass, a group of willows, a straggling bank, and a spring of delicious water running right through the middle of it, with two or three little cascades." Look at this sturdy child of Nature playing with his mother:

> Hanging clothes on a rail near by, keeping old broadbrim straw on head, and easy shoes on feet, haven't I had a good time the last two hours! First with the stiff-elastic bristles rasping arms, breast, sides, till they turn'd scarlet—then partially bathing in the clear waters of the running brook—taking everything very leisurely, with many rests and pauses—stepping about barefooted every few minutes now and then in some neighboring black ooze, for unctuous mud-baths to my feet—a brief second and third rinsing in the crystal running waters—rubbing with the fragrant towel—slow negligent promenades on the turf up and down in the sun, varied with oc-

casional rests. . . . Somehow I seem'd to get identity with each and every thing around me, in its condition. Nature was naked, and I was also.

Mingled with rambles and rambling meditations such as these are fragments of wider observations—days on the Delaware, views and experiences in the South and the far West, notes on his visit to Boston a year or two since, and, among distinctively literary topics, paragraphs—they are hardly more than that—on Bryant, Emerson, Carlyle, and Longfellow. These finish the *Specimen Days*.

The *Collect* which follows opens with a long political and sociologic essay on "Democratic Vistas." The several prefaces to *Leaves of Grass*, 1855, 1872, 1876, succeed; then the *North American Review* paper on "Poetry Today in America;" and finally a defense of *Leaves of Grass* from the charge of indecency, and a "lecture" on the death of Lincoln.

As to Mr. Whitman's prose it is obviously quite interchangeable with his poetry. Many pages of this book might be transferred to *Leaves of Grass* by simply a rearrangement of lines. Thus (p. 109):

Cold and sharp last night—
Clear and not much wind—
The full moon shining, and a fine spread of constellations and little and big stars—
Sirius very bright, rising early,
Preceded by many-orb'd Orion, glittering, vast, sworded, and chasing with his dog.

Or again (p. 132):

It was a happy thought to build the Hudson river railroad right along the shore.
The grade is already made by nature;
You are sure of ventilation one side—
And you are in nobody's way.

I see, hear, the locomotives and cars,
Rumbling, roaring, flaming, smoking,
Constantly, away off there, night and day—
Less than a mile distant, and in full view by day.
I like both sight and sound.
Express trains thunder and lighten along;
Of freight trains, most of them very long,
There cannot be less than a hundred a day.

If this is not excellent poetry, measured by the Whitman standard, we are greatly mistaken. But, seriously, in his prose Mr. Whitman shows us a pleasanter side of himself than we have hitherto known.

Edward Dowden. *Academy* 22 (18 November 1882), 357–9.

"Echoes and Escapades," "Drifts and Cumulus," "Notes of a Half-Paralytic"—these and other titles for his bundle of jottings, made during and after the war, were rejected by Whitman; and for a while he hovered about a title which would have suggested a comparison between this cluster of open-air thoughts and observations and the berries of the wild cedar-tree of America.

"A melange of loafing, looking, hobbling, sitting, traveling—a little thinking thrown in for salt, but very little—not only summer but all seasons—not only days but nights—some literary meditations—books, authors examined, Carlyle, Poe, Emerson tried (always under my cedar-tree, in the open air, and never in the library)—mostly the scenes everybody sees, but some of my own caprices, meditations, egotism—truly an open air and mainly summer formation—singly or in clusters—wild and free and somewhat acrid."

The acrid taste is no more than a pleasant sharpness now and again; and in the main these "Notes of a Half-Paralytic" are sweet and sane and nourishing, more, perhaps, than their writer knows or can know. No diary of an invalid is wholesomer reading than this; never a groan or a growl, never a word of complaint; but every bright hour, every breeze of health, every delight in flower and bird and stream and star, and in the kind voice or hand of a friend, remembered and recorded. Always, in this invalid's diary, the pure, fresh air, and the sky overhead; never the blinds drawn down, the table crowded with medicine bottles, and the foot of the spiritual medicine-man upon the threshold:

> "Doubtless in the course of the following, the fact of invalidism will crop out (I call myself a *half-Paralytic* these days, and reverently bless the Lord it is no worse) between some of the lines—but I get my share of fun and healthy hours, and shall try to indicate them. (The trick is, I find, to tone your wants and tastes low down enough, and make much of negatives, and of mere daylight and the skies.)"

From 1876, when Whitman began to get over the worst of the tedious and baffling illness, ascribed by physicians to his exertions in the hospitals during the war, he spent portions of several seasons at a secluded haunt in New Jersey—Timber Creek, its stream (almost a river) entering from the great Delaware twelve miles away, "with primitive solitudes, recluse and woody banks, sweet-feeding springs, and all the charms that birds, grass, wildflowers, rabbits and squirrels, old oaks, walnut-trees, &c., can bring." Down the long farm-lane he would hobble to a lonely pond, where the creek expands and the kingfishers dart and turn; and so, still sauntering on, "to the spring under the willows—musical as soft-clinking glasses—pouring a sizeable stream, thick as my neck, pure and clear, out from its vent, where the bank arches over." And here, enveloped for the month of May in the droning of bumble-bees, listening to the clear quailnotes in June, or the roulades and pensive refrains of the hermit-thrush, Whitman would take his seat on log or stump, and (the journalist's ruling passion strong in age and disablement) would jot down his notes—notes not for the buoyant and healthy alone, but meant just as well for ailing folk:—

> "Who knows (I have it in my fancy, my ambition) but the pages now ensuing may carry ray of sun, or smell of grass or corn, or call of bird, or gleam of stars by night, or snowflakes falling fresh and mystic, to denizen of heated city-house, or tired workman or work-woman?—or may-be in sick room or prison—to serve as cooling breeze, or Nature's aroma, to some fever'd mouth or latent pulse."

Sometimes he would run down by rail to the New Jersey sea-shore; and on those flat and odorous sea-prairies, their sedgy perfume in his nostrils, he would revive the sights and sounds and smells of his Long Island youth, the "stretch of interminable white-brown sand, hard and smooth and broad, with the ocean perpetually, grandly rolling in upon it, with slow-measured sweep, with rustle and hiss and foam, and many a thump as of low bass drums." Or, back again in his Camden home, he would cross and recross the Delaware, helped by the friendly pilots ("Eugene Crosby, with his strong, young arm so often supporting, circling, convoying me over the gaps of the bridge, through impediments, safely aboard"), and would enjoy the stir and play of the delightful "human comedy," or would invite his soul, and absorb the spectacle of the starry heavens.

"*A January Night.*—Fine trips across the wide Delaware to-night. Tide pretty high, and a strong ebb. River, a little after eight, full of ice, mostly broken, but some large cakes making our strong-timber'd steamboat hum and quiver as she strikes them. In the clear moonlight they spread, strange, unearthly, silvery, faintly glistening, as far as I can see. Bumping, trembling, sometimes hissing like a thousand snakes, the tide-procession, as we wend with or through it, affording a grand undertone, in keeping with the scene. Overhead, the splendor indescribable; yet something haughty, almost supercilious, in the night. Never did I realise more latent sentiment, almost *passion*, in those silent interminable stars up there. One can understand, such a night, why, from the days of the Pharaohs or Job, the dome of heaven, sprinkled with planets, has supplied the subtlest, deepest criticism on human pride, glory, ambition."

We have record of visits to New York, and a sail in the bay, with a little lyrical cry at sight of the schooner-yachts going in a good wind—"those daring, careening things of grace and wonder, those white and shaded swift-darting fish-birds (I wonder if sea or shore elsewhere can outvie them), ever with their slanting spars, and fierce, pure, hawk-like beauty

and motion." But the procession of gentility and wealth in Central Park is not altogether to Whitman's liking; and in his criticism of modern society, although at bottom he believes that the American people remains sound, there are pages (to quote Mr. Ruskin's words with respect to Whitman's writings) "deadly true—in the sense of rifles—against our deadliest sins." More than once Whitman voyaged up the Hudson to the honeysuckle-and-rose-embowered cottage of John Burroughs, the delightful writer of *Wake Robin* and *Pepacton*; and in September 1879 he found himself strong enough to begin a long jaunt to the West, seeing Missouri, Kansas, and Colorado, at Denver turning south, and then east again. The sea-like spread of prairies, the wild gorges, the streams of amber and bronze, brawling along their beds with frequent cascades and snow-white foam, the fantastic forms of mountains bathed in transparent browns, faint reds and grays, the free handling and absolute uncrampedness of the landscape, the superb physique of the miners, their character shaped by their victorious tussles with savage nature (but alas, the genteel ladies of the West, copying unsuccessfully their Eastern sisters!)—these, with a few inevitable reserves, were all acceptable to, and accepted by, the author of *Leaves of Grass*. A later journey to Canada, the sight of Niagara, a visit to the hospitable house of his friend Dr. Bucke at London, then up the black waters of the Saguenay a hundred miles, the region more grim, more wildly beautiful, "with a sort of still and pagan *scaredness*," than any he had seen yet, comprised the last of Whitman's wanderings. A Sunday service with the insane at the asylum under the care of Dr. Bucke brought Whitman face to face with some of those "laggards" in the race who have ever been dear to his heart:

"I was furnish'd with an arm-chair near the pulpit, and sat facing the motley, yet perfectly well-behaved and orderly, congregation. The quaint dresses and bonnets of some of the women, several very old and gray, here and there like the heads in old pictures. O the looks that came from those faces! There were two or three I shall probably never forget. Nothing at all markedly repulsive or hideous—strange enough I did not see one such. Our common humanity, mine and yours, everywhere—

'The same old blood—the same red, running blood;' yet behind most, an inferr'd arriere of such storms, such wrecks, such mysteries, fires, love, wrong, greed for wealth, religious problems, crosses—mirror'd from those crazed faces (yet now temporarily so calm, like still waters), all the woes and sad happenings of life and death—now from everyone the devotional element radiating—was it not, indeed, *the peace of God that passeth all understanding*, strange as it may sound?"

Connected with the notes of convalescence in this volume are Whitman's previously published memoranda of the war; and the national frenzy and agony (with underlying sanity and strength) of the one period goes well with the tender calm and restorative happiness of the other. His lecture on Lincoln, a record of his visits to Emerson and Longfellow, a reminiscence and a criticism, severe, yet sympathetic, of Edgar Poe, will interest readers who care to see great or distinguished persons through a poet's eyes. At Emerson's grave he muses:

"A just man, poised on himself, all-loving, all-inclosing, and sane and clear as the sun. Nor does it seem so much Emerson himself we are here to honor—it is conscience, simplicity, culture, humanity's attributes at their best, yet applicable, if need be, to average affairs. . . . How shall I henceforth dwell on the blessed hours when, not long since, I saw that benignant face, the clear eyes, the silently smiling mouth, the form yet upright in its great age—to the very last, with so much spring and cheeriness, and such an absence of decrepitude, that even the term *venerable* hardly seemed fitting?"

The tribute is made of more worth by Whitman's keen perception of the limitations of Emerson's genius. Elsewhere there is eloquent recognition of the work done for American literature by Longfellow, Bryant, Whittier. I miss from this collection of notes an admirable piece of criticism on Burns, published in *Our Land and Time* (January 25, 1875). In Edgar Poe, Whitman finds neither the genius for perfect and noble living and thinking, morally without flaw, happily balanced in activity, nor "that other shape of personality dearer far to the artist-sense (which likes the strongest play of lights and shades) where the perfect character, the good, the heroic, although never attain'd, it never lost sight of, but through failures, sorrows, temporary downfalls, is return'd to again and again" (so with Burns, Byron, George Sand):

"Almost without the first sign of moral principle, or of the concrete and its heroisms, or the simpler affections of the heart, Poe's verses illustrate an intense faculty for technical and abstract beauty, with the rhyming art to excess, an incorrigible propensity towards nocturnal themes, a demoniac undertone behind every page—and, by final judgment, belong among the electric lights of imaginative literature, brilliant and dazzling, but with no heat. . . . In a dream I once had, I saw a vessel on the sea, at midnight, in a storm. It was no great full-rigg'd ship, nor majestic steamer, steering firmly through the gale, but seem'd one of those superb little schooner-yachts I had so often seen lying anchor'd, rocking so jauntily in the waters around New York, or up Long Island Sound—now flying uncontroll'd with torn sails and broken spars through the wild sleet, and winds and waves of the night. On the deck was a slender, slight, beautiful figure, a dim man, apparently enjoying all the terror, the murk, and the dislocation of which he was the centre and the victim. That figure of my lurid dream might stand for Edgar Poe, his spirit, his fortunes, and his poems—themselves all lurid dreams."

Beside "Democratic Vistas," known to all who value Whitman, this volume contains the recent articles by him in the *North American Review* ("Poetry to-day in America" and "A Memorandum at a Venture"), the prefaces to the several editions of his poems, and some pieces written in early youth—short tales and poems—printed now to avoid the annoyance of a surreptitious issue which had been announced.

Among other restoratives of health one could wish that Whitman would some time try a voyage across the Atlantic. With Mr. Tennyson, Mr. Ruskin, Mr. Rossetti, Mr. Symonds, Mr. Swinburne, Mr. W. Bell Scott, Mr. R. Hengist Horne, Mr. Robert Buchanan, Mr. Robert L. Stevenson, the Hon. Roden Noel, and others known and unknown, desirous to give him friendly greeting, he might have among us, in American phrase, "a good time."

"Among Books." *Mace: A Weekly Record of the Glasgow Parliamentary Debating Association* 4 (27 November 1882), 2–3.

In our issue for March 21st 1882, we drew attention to the then recently published English edition of Walt Whitman's volume of Poems, *Leaves of Grass*. The writer of that notice felt bound to hail Whitman as the poet who beyond all others was imbued with, and gave expression to, the Modern Spirit. The chants in the *Leaves of Grass* convey, in a form as beautiful as it is original, the universal wonder and sympathy which fill the mind of a poet who cares not so much to speculate upon the mysterious future as "to loafe" and enjoy the more mysterious present. The problems of existence have a subordinate place in his regard: the fact of existence is the consummate object of his thoughts. Remarkable as are his poems for their originality, their strength, and their beauty, the volume of prose now before us exceeds them in each of these attributes. Not to many poets is given to be great prose writers. Probably Victor Hugo alone of all the writers in this century has achieved supreme excellence in both. We may incur the charge of exaggeration, especially from those whose sympathies in this matter we are not entitled to expect; but we are inclined to trust posterity to endorse the verdict, that Walt Whitman is one of the very greatest writers in prose and poetry which the nineteenth century has produced. The theory that genius is still inspired has new confirmation in his works. Isaiah and Jeremiah, in the "broadsheets" in which they rebuked their Jewish fellow-countrymen for the hollowness of their worship and for their social sins, were not more trenchant than this modern prophet, who denounces the shams of an age more civilized but probably more corrupt than theirs. "Is there," says Whitman, "a great moral and religious civilization—the only justification of a great material one? Confess that to severe eyes, using the moral microscope upon humanity, a sort of dry and flat Sahara appears, these cities, crowded with petty grotesques, malformations, phantoms, playing meaningless antics. Confess that everywhere, in shop, street, church, theatre, bar-room, official chair, are pervading flippancy and vulgarity, low cunning, infidelity."

The first writings of Carlyle and Emerson were despised and rejected; and yet these very writings have had so profound an influence in forming the thought of our period, that it were impossible to imagine, as Whitman remarks, what it would have been without them. The mantle of Carlyle has in a sense fallen upon Whitman. Without Carlyle's historic sense, without his bitter personal irony, he has all Carlyle's contempt for humbug, all his withering scorn of the respectabilities, all his earnestness and enthusiasm for the true democracy. Less a man of books, more a man of men,—less a recluse, more a man of the world,—than either Carlyle or Emerson, he adds new point to their texts, and finds new sermons in them. Learned, Whitman certainly is—a man of vast reading, fulfilled more than most students with what is to be had from books. He is more. His immense pliability of intellect, his subtle power of fixing his gaze with intimate scrutiny, enable him to absorb suggestions from everything. He reads a man—the very spinal marrow of him—not as an anatomist or a psychologist, or a man of business or a tailor, but as they all would do. The separate, special individuality: that seizes Whitman's attention—and he has the man. Thus, he examines the individual, and through him the aggregate. Society, its foibles, its rottenness, is transparent to him, and he does not spare it. While he is one of the most powerful advocates of the rights of the democracy, he never ceases to urge the necessity of its making private and public virtue as much an aim as political power. With the grasp of a true seer, he never sighs for "the old days that are ended," but attempts to urge on a future richer than any past in strong men and women, "in crops of fine youths and majestic old persons." The means he purposes using, and advocating the use of, are not legislative—they are intellectual. "Of all this, and these lamentable conditions," he says, in continuation of [the] passage quoted above, "to breathe into them the breath recuperative of sane and heroic life, I say a new-founded literature, not merely to copy and reflect existing surfaces, or to pander to what is called good taste, not only to amuse, pass away time, celebrate the beautiful, the refined, the past, or exhibit technical, rhythmic, or grammatical dexterity, but a literature underlying life, religious, consistent with science, handling the elements and forces with competent power, teaching and training men—and, perhaps the most precious of its results—achieving the entire redemption of women out of these incredible holds and webs of silliness, millinery and every kind of dyspeptic depletion, and thus ensuring to the States a strong and sweet Female Race—a race of Perfect Mothers—is what is needed."

In "Democratic Vistas" he expounds his political philosophy more consecutively and eloquently than anywhere else:—

The political history of the past may be summed up as having grown out of what underlies the words, order, safety, caste, and especially out of the need of some prompt deciding authority, and of cohesion at all cost. Leaping time, we come to the period within the memory of people now living, when, as from some lair where they had slumbered long, accumulating wrath, sprang up and are yet active (1790, and on even to the present, 1870), those noisy eructations, destructive iconoclasms, a fierce sense of wrongs, amid which moves the power [*sic*], well known in modern history, in the Old World, stain'd with much blood, and marked by savage reactionary clamors and demands. These bear mostly as on one inclosing point of need. For after the rest is said—after the many time-honor'd and really true things for subordination, experience, right of property, &c., have been listen'd to and acquiesced in—after the valuable and well-settled statement of our duties and relations in society is thoroughly conn'd over and exhausted—it remains to bring forward and modify everything else with the idea of that Something a Man is, (last precious consolation of the drudging poor,) standing apart from all else, divine in his own right, and a woman in hers, sole and untouchable by any canons of authority, or any rule derived from precedent, state-safety, the acts of legislatures, or even from what is called religion, modesty, or art. The radiation of this truth is the key of the most significant doings of our immediately preceding three centuries, and has been the political genesis and life of America. Advancing visibly, it still more advances invisibly. Underneath the fluctuations of the expressions of society, as well as the movements of the politics of the leading nations of the world, we see steadily pressing ahead and strengthening itself, even in the midst of immense tendencies toward aggregation, this image of completeness in separatism, of individual personal dignity, of a single person, either male or female, characterized in the main, not from extrinsic acquirements or position, but in the pride of himself or herself alone; and, as an eventual conclusion and summing up (or else the entire scheme of things is aimless, a cheat, a crash), the simple idea that the last, best dependence is to be upon humanity itself, and its own inherent, normal, full-grown qualities, without any superstitious support whatever.

The purpose of democracy—supplanting old belief in the necessary absoluteness of establish'd dynastic ruleship, temporal, ecclesiastical, and scholastic, as furnishing the only security against chaos, crime, and ignorance—is, through many transmigrations, and amid endless ridicules, arguments, and ostensible failures, to illustrate, at all hazards, this doctrine or theory that man, properly trained in sanest, highest freedom, may and must become a law, and series of laws, unto himself, surrounding and providing for, not only his own personal control, but all his relations to other individuals, and to the state; and that, while other theories, as in the past histories of nations have proved wise enough, and indispensable perhaps for their conditions, *this*, as matters now stand in our civilized world, is the only scheme worth working from, as warranting results like those of Nature's laws, reliable, when once establish'd, to carry on themselves.

Literature, strictly considered, has never recognized the People, and whatever may be said does not to-day. Speaking generally, the tendencies of literature, as hitherto pursued, have been to make mostly critical and querulous men. It seems as if, so far, there were some natural repugnance between a literary and professional life, and the rude rank spirit of democracies. There is in later literature, a treatment of benevolence, a charity business, rife enough it is true; but I know nothing more rare, even in this country, than a fit scientific estimate and reverent appreciation of the People—of their measureless wealth of latent power and capacity, their vast, artistic contrasts of lights and shades—with, in America, their entire reliability in emergencies, and a certain breadth of historic grandeur, of peace or war, far surpassing all the vaunted samples of book-heroes, or any *haut ton* coteries, in all the records of the world.

To formulate beyond this present vagueness—to help, live, and put before us the species, or specimen of the species of the democratic ethnology of the future, is a work toward which the genius of our land, with peculiar encouragement, invites her well-wishers. Already certain limnings, more or less grotesque, more or less fading and watery, have appeared. We, too (repressing doubts and qualms), will try our hand. Attempting then, however crudely, a basic model or portrait of personality for general use for the manliness of the States—and doubtless that is most useful which is most simple and comprehensive for all, and toned low enough—we should prepare the canvas well beforehand. Parentage must consider itself in advance.... To our model a clear-blooded, strong-fibered physique is indispensable; the questions of food, drink, air, exercise, assimilation, diges-

tion, can never be intermitted. Out of these we decry a well-begotten selfhood—in youth fresh, ardent, emotional, aspiring, full of adventure; at maturity brave, perceptive, under control, neither too talkative nor too reticent, neither flippant nor somber; of the bodily figure the movements easy, the complexion showing the best blood, somewhat flushed, breast expanded, an erect attitude, a voice whose sound outvies music, eyes of calm and steady gaze, yet capable of flashing, and a general presence that holds its own in the company of the highest, for it is native personality, and that alone, that endows a man to stand before presidents or generals, or in any distinguished collection with *aplomb*, and not culture or any knowledge or intellect whatever.

A large part of the volume is occupied by Whitman's diary during the American War. Some of the sketches were written as letters to friends during the war and afterwards. All of them have the same nervous strength. They are, indeed, as he says, "a batch of convulsively written reminiscences." Why should they not? "They are but parts of the actual distraction, heat, smoke, and excitement of those times. The war itself, with the temper of society preceding it, can indeed be best described by that very word *convulsiveness*." We can only give two of these sketches:—

During those three years in hospital, camp, or field, I made over six hundred visits or tours, and went, as I estimate, counting all, among from eighty thousand to a hundred thousand of the wounded and sick, as sustainer of spirit and body in some degree, in time of need. These visits varied from an hour or two, to all day or night; for with dear or critical cases I generally watch'd all night. Sometimes I took up my quarters in the hospital, and slept or watch'd there several nights in succession. Those three years I consider the greatest privilege and satisfaction, (with all their feverish excitements and physical deprivations and lamentable sights,) and, of course, the most profound lesson of my life.

THE MILLION DEAD, TOO, SUMM'D UP

The dead in this war, there they lie, strewing the fields, and woods, and valleys, and battlefields of the South —Virginia, the Peninsula, Malvern Hill and Fair Oaks, the banks of the Chickahominy, the terraces of Fredericksburgh, Antietam Bridge, the grisly ravines of Manassas, the bloody promenade of the Wilderness; the varieties of the *strayed* dead; Gettysburgh, the West, Southwest; Vicksburgh, Chattanooga, the trenches of Petersburgh; the numberless battles, camps, hospitals everywhere; the crop reap'd by the mighty reapers, and typhoid, dysentery, inflammations, and blackest and loathsomest of all, the dead and living burial-pits, the prison-pens of Andersonville, Salisbury, Belle-Isle, &c. (not Dante's pictured hell, and all its woes, its degradations, filthy torments, excell'd those prisons.) The dead, the dead, the dead,— *our dead*—on South or North, ours all (all, all, all, finally dear to me), or East or West—Atlantic Coast or Mississippi Valley—somewhere they crawl'd to die, alone, in bushes, low gullies, or on the sides of the hills— . . . thousands, aye tens of thousands, of Southerners crumble to-day in Northern earth.

"New Publications: Walt Whitman's Prose." New York *Times*, 18 December 1882, p. 2.

The whole of Walt Whitman's prose writing is included in this closely printed book. So much has been said upon Whitman's place in literature, judgment upon his worth is so various and confused—Prof. Dowden, for instance, associates him with Shakespeare, and a recent commentator of American literature whistles him confidently down the wind to nothingness—that his own expression and elucidation of himself must be regarded with peculiar interest by large numbers of readers. The new book is certainly not wanting in versatility. It contains many of those brief, sketchily written notes on nature which were, it is apparent, jotted down in the open air, amid the freshness of fields and woods and streams; it contains the celebrated "Democratic Vistas," which tell of the politics, progress, and nationality of our Western world; and it includes, above all, those widely discussed prefaces, touching upon American poetry to-day, and especially upon the future of American poetry, as this is viewed by Whitman. At the end of the book there is a series of "notes left over," and there are reprinted some of the author's early work in prose and verse. Persons who are inspired by the cosmic exultation in *Leaves of Grass* should not fail to compare those radical poems with the poet's manner and thought in the verses called "Dough-Face Song," and in a highly moral tale like "Death in a Schoolroom." These early pieces are, it must be seen, not worth reprinting; and Whitman has set them, it is clear, in a somewhat frank spirit of defiance. It has often been stated by his critics that his youthful work was essentially mediocre and imitative, and that he changed his manner in order that he might be accounted an original poet; but Whitman takes the tenable ground, evidently, that he has outgrown his first work and has moved forward progressively. He believes that he can afford to compare *Leaves of Grass* and *Specimen Days* with the labor of his green literary years.

As to Whitman's prose manner—the manner which may be described as his style—that is found to be, throughout this book, a kind of cultivated affectation, not at all forcible because it is unconventional. It is an obscure, involved, harsh manner, frequently ungrammatical and cumbersome: seldom graceful, direct, or simple. It is best when it is most free from the writer's word-torturings. Occasionally Whitman throws off his affectations and composes with straightforward lucidity; the fact that he can do this and does it proves conclusively that he depends for one sort of effect upon literary eccentricity and trickery. It is probable, however, that he has faith to some degree in his own tricks. On the other hand, it may be said of him that he can rise to the dignity of a large subject, as in the preface to the first edition of *Leaves of Grass*. He has, moreover, a certain mastery of picturesque word-painting, which finds an abundant, vigorous outlet in his works on nature. His prose, taken altogether, is not especially distinguishable from his verse—if, indeed, he can be said to have written verse. The constant use which he makes of the hyphen amounts to his fashion of breaking phrases and sentences in "Leaves of Grass."

The picturesqueness and the imaginative feeling, also the spirit of broad human tenderness, which are felt in the notes will, one is apt to think, win the at-

tention of many readers who cannot find their way through the extravagance and garrulity of Whitman's verse; in spite of the fact, too, that his verse has, in a crude state, sound poetic qualities and robustly original conceptions. It is far less what Whitman writes that stirs many observant men than what he sees or suggests. His conceptions of mankind, of present nationality, of the real earth and the world, are vital to the imagination. He is not, it is discovered by thinkers who are abreast of the science of our time, a sentimental idealist. He does not regard longingly the world as it was or as it might be. He is not blind to the thousand and one facts of life to which, seemingly, poets are densely blind. He views broadly, radically, the evolution of man, of nature, and of society. It is his stand-point which is his strong point. His force, his purpose, is new in literature. A poet who searches so deep and high could hardly fail to gain his adherents. It is because Whitman is so little of an artist, because he is a rhapsodist rather than a poet, that he misses his mark with the bulk of readers. Nevertheless, he is more tempered in his prose. The condensation of prose appears to hold him in check. His notes might be read with delight—by one grown accustomed to his spasmodic style—under the open sky. Many of his descriptions charm the fancy. He speaks of "the beautiful, spiritual insects;" of the "rising and falling wind-purr from the tops of the maples and willows;" of "the indolent and spiritual night, inexpressibly rich, tender, suggestive;" of "the monotone and liquid gurgle from the hoarse, sumptuous, copious fall;" of "the flap of a pike leaping out and rippling the water;" of "the guttural twittering" of the kingfishers; of bumble-bees "humming their perpetual rich mellow boom;" and one might quote a long list of still happier phrases. The following note, placed at the end of some war reminiscences, is quite characteristic of Whitman, and exhibits his tendency to dwell on words, no matter how awkwardly he may employ his language: "As I have looked over the proof-sheets of the preceding pages, I have once or twice feared that my diary would prove at best but a batch of convulsively written reminiscences. Well, be it so. They are but parts of the actual distraction, heat, smoke, and excitement of those times. The war itself, with the temper of society preceding it, can indeed be best described by that very word *convulsiveness*." It should be mentioned that Whitman's reminiscences of the civil war are honest, pathetic comments upon serious, at times tragic, episodes. Whitman knows what the war days were; he has felt their horror and mournfulness; and he writes about them with a sincere candor which cannot be confounded with his usual strain for effect. In his prose notes, as in his patriotic chants, his voice is sure and tender. Some of the most imaginative and also realistic of his notes are inspired by night, with all its stars and infinite distances, with its strange and solemn silence, with its universal beauty. He describes, for example, the emotion which is aroused in him by a Winter night: "I don't know anything more thrilling than to be on the wide firm deck of a powerful boat, a clear, cool, extra moonlight night, crushing proudly and resistlessly through this thick, marbly, glistening ice. The whole river is now spread with it—some immense cakes. There is such weirdness about the scene—partly the quality of the light, with its tinge of blue, the lunar twilight—only the large stars holding their own in the radiance of the moon. Temperature sharp, comfortable for motion, dry, full of oxygen. But the sense of power—the steady, scornful, imperious urge of our strong new engine, as she plows her way through the big and little

cakes." In this brief paragraph there may be found that stalwartism of sense and soul which is so enthusiastically admired by the Whitman men, and which is, without doubt, an impressive trait in the poet.

Whitman's notes are not confined to war, reminiscences and descriptions; he gives in a few of them his opinions of certain men and his views upon various subjects. He writes upon the death of Carlyle, upon Carlyle from an American point of view, upon his visit to Boston, upon four American poets—Bryant, Longfellow, Whittier, and Emerson. He rebukes a magazine critic who attacked him for his "attitude of contempt and scorn and intolerance" toward our leading poets. He says: "I can't imagine any better luck befalling these States for a poetical beginning and initiation than has come from Emerson, Longfellow, Bryant, and Whittier." Emerson, he thinks, stands at the head of the four. He is at a loss to give precedence to either of the others. His description of them is flattering, not to put too fine a point upon it: "Each illustrious, each rounded, each distinctive." Emerson, he thinks, is noteworthy for his sweet, vital-tasting melody, rhymed philosophy, and amber-clear poems; Longfellow for rich color, graceful forms, and incidents, a competitor with the singers of Europe on their own ground; Bryant for pulsing the first interior verse-throbs of a mighty world; Whittier for the zeal, the moral energy that founded New-England. One can hardly assert hereafter that Whitman, the least satisfactory and the most original of all our poets, rejects and condemns the body corporate of American poets. It is unfortunate in the circumstances, that he has not presented his views upon more eminent American verse-writers, like Lowell, Stedman, Aldrich, Stoddard, and a few others. It is invariably pleasant to read the opinions, of poets upon poets. In one of his notes concerning Emerson, Whitman refers to the philosopher's condemnation—from a strict standpoint of morality—of that rather notorious and thoroughly objectionable poem, "Children of Adam." According to Emerson and most fine-sighted critics, the immorality of this poem is repulsive. Emerson argued on the subject with Whitman, who was not convinced. When Emerson asked him what he had to say in reply to arguments, Whitman—who is his own reporter here—said: "Only that while I can't answer them at all, I feel more settled than ever to adhere to my own theory and exemplify it." The question is, then, between Whitman and the public taste, and we believe that public taste will decide it sharply. If Whitman's theory of morality, which is, briefly, that everything can be uttered honestly in literature, should be accepted, there would no longer be any mystery in social relation, no charm of modesty in sexual intercourse. It is interesting, however, to read Whitman's opinion upon the question at first hand.

There is some strong, practical writing in "Democratic Vistas," though the majority of persons who take up this book will turn their attention at once to the prefaces, all of them curious contributions to literature and more generally discussed than known. In the preface of 1855, which has aroused the most attentive consideration in England and throughout Europe, Whitman makes several aggressive assumptions. He asserts in the beginning that the Americans, of all the people of the earth, have the fullest poetical nature; that the United States are themselves a great poem. He declares, furthermore, that the American poets—meaning, of course, the poets of the future—are to inclose old and new, since ours is the race of races; they shall excite generosity and affection; they shall be cosmos. The boldest statement in this preface is the following radicalism: "Exact science and its practical movements are no checks on the greatest poet, but always his encouragement and support." In the preface of 1872 Whitman adds eloquently: "The mighty present age! To absorb and express in poetry anything of it—of its world—America—cities and States—the years, the events of our nineteenth century—the rapidity of movement—the violent contrasts, fluctuations of light and shade, of hope and fear—the entire revolution made by science in the poetic method—these great new underlying facts and ideas rushing and spreading everywhere—truly a mighty age." Again, in the preface of 1876, he says: "I count with such absolute certainty on the great future of the United States—different from, though founded on, the past—that I have always invoked that future, and surrounded myself with it, before or while singing my songs." At the end of his article on "Poetry To-day in America," Whitman writes prophetically: "Meanwhile, Democracy waits, the coming of its bards in silence and twilight—but 'tis the twilight of the dawn."

It is clear that Whitman's aspiration is noble and liberal, that his faith is founded in the history of humanity, and that his prophecy is the right prophecy of this "mighty age"—mighty and wonderful though a hundred Ruskins, though a thousand Carlyles had launched their invective against its penetrating power. On the whole, *Specimen Days* is an important contribution to our literature.

"Walt Whitman's New Book."
Critic [New York] 3
(13 January 1883), 3.

There is a word which is a great favorite of Mr. Whitman and will be found in the little motto he has written under his portrait. It is not an English word, nor is it Americanized, according to the standard dictionaries; yet Mr. Whitman has made it good American, so far as in his power lies, and stamped it with more than ordinary significance. Ensemble. What does Walt Whitman mean by that pet word? He brings it in at the oddest moments. It is one of many (such as, for instance, Libertad, clair-obscure, laying-off, barbaric yawp, arrieres, melange, and twenty more) at sight of which, judicious critics educated at universities and suckled on Matthew Arnold and John Ruskin, are seen to be affected by a peculiar spasm of the features that leaves no doubt concerning their views on such additions to the language. Whatever the rights in the case may be, whatever sense there is in tying down the English language to words that have their patents from the old masters, this word is of such importance in examining understandingly the prose and poetry of Whitman, that it alone would be a fitting inscription to his monument. It is a word without legal status, an innovation, a piece of piracy from the French—an awkward word, if the truth must be told. And yet it signifies more than any other the striving which gives the work of Whitman its chief value, its main grandeur. A Democratic Prometheus, Walt Whitman has been battling during most of his literary career against the complacent Jupiter of conventional, popular literature. His chains have been poverty, contempt, shallowness of critics, bad taste on his own side. He has been a failure; even now he is not a success; but every decade of the century will show more clearly that his failure is better than the successes of Longfellow and Tennyson. The selection of the word Ensemble is not the happiest; but he has made it, and it should be respected for the great idea, let us say the grand failure, that lies behind it.

What has impressed Whitman most during his intimate comradeship with Long Island farming folk, New York workmen and roughs, New Jersey 'mudsills,' and the thousands of soldiers belonging to every state of the Union, and both parties to the Civil War, whom he came in personal contact with in the Capital of the country? It is size, quantity, greatness, mass, extent. He sees everything on the biggest scale. A reader of palms who reads his books will assert beforehand that he has broad, long and thick hands, with fingers thick and shorter than those of most people. He sees in everything the big masses, not the little particulars. Hence his love for the gigantic; the tremendous impression crowds, armies, the terrible wastes, the sublime prairies of the West, make on his peculiar individuality. Hence his early discarding of the ordinary forms of versification, and his molding out of the prose of Carlyle, and the prose and poetry of Victor Hugo, a new literary form of expression, which is all that its enthusiastic admirers claim for it, although not always equally successful, and more than any one could have expected, looking merely at Whitman's chances in life. It is only half knowledge that demands absolute originality; for that is something which does not, can not exist. So far as is humanly possible, Whitman is an original poet, representative in literature of a great fact, and, like

293

all such representatives, harder for those to estimate who are near by than those at a distance. For the present, he is a poet for poets and connoisseurs; the people neglect him utterly for men who follow the traditions; woman, the half of humanity which holds to old ideas most tenaciously for good or for evil, rejects him, chiefly because in his gigantic wrestling with the impossible in literature he offends her by writing of things which modesty conceals, but also because woman looks backward instead of forward, and so prevents a too rapid advance over ground not thoroughly discussed and proved. Now what is the task Whitman—half aware of it, half unaware—has grappled with? It is to sing the 'Ensemble,' the whole—everything! He is the painter who, unchastened by failures in the studio, rushes out into the fields and tries to paint a panorama of the whole horizon. Nothing shall be lacking. The microcosm must yield its nudities and sexual impulses, its pangs of agony at being unable to describe the indescribable, its delight in sounds made by human art, its overflow of affection and tenderness toward man, woman and child. The macrocosm must be depicted in the effects on man of its cosmic forces, of the sun and stars, of night and dawn, and effects of fog, haze, atmosphere. The effort made by all this striving must be painful to some sensitive natures; certainly in *Leaves of Grass* and in a hundred passages of this collection under a still queerer name, the struggle beats through in a magnificent, chaotic fashion, which eventually masses itself into something like order, and now discovers to the patient and sympathetic reader that here is the reign of law.

Ensemble is Whitman's strength and his weakness. He fails magnificently, where a better instructed man, or a cautious, would have remained fatally mediocre. It is curious to find in his case, as in many others here, that so far from having no ancestry, Whitman can read back through a line of sturdy, fairly-taught yeomen, to dates which are very often unattainable by Europeans who make such things their greatest boast. He has a good deal of Dutch blood, and his predilection for adaptations of French words may mean that he has some of the old French Protestant blood which did more to form New York in Dutch times than the historians are yet prepared to tell. His fearlessly egotistical account of his derivation and life will be just what readers of *Leaves of Grass* have wanted, for it throws the strongest light on the origin and meaning of that work. Patriotic people, who are not utterly at odds with Whitman, will be glad to find further notes taken during his hospital work at Washington. THE CRITIC might be half filled with passages deserving quotation. The recent Western and Canadian notes show his healthy and big views of things in nature; they are fine, but tantalising in their shortness. What Whitman has to say about Carlyle and Emerson was too recently published (in these pages) to need present notice, and so were 'The Poetry of the Future' and 'A Memorandum at a Venture' (in *The North American*). Many pieces in *Specimen Days* appeared in this paper. The most curious in the 'Collect' are poetical pieces printed long ago in New York papers, before Whitman broke with ordinary verse restrictions, and carved out for himself the elastic system of poetry-prose, in which *Leaves of Grass* appeared. That poem and this volume of essays and notes form in themselves a literary inter-state exhibition or American Institute Fair, such as Whitman has attempted to describe in measures. Every sort of thing is crammed into it, and the manager is the big, good-natured, shrewd and large-souled poet, whose photograph shows him lounging in smoking-jacket and broad felt hat, gazing at his hand, on which a delicate butterfly, with expanded wings, forms a contrast to the thick fingers and heavy ploughman's wrist.

Westminster Review, n.s. 64 (July 1883), 287–91.

Specimen Days and Collect, by Walt Whitman, is in some sort the prose counterpart of his celebrated *Leaves of Grass*. The volume opens with an account of the parentage and ancestry of the author.

"The later years of the last century," he tells us, "found the Van Velsor family, my mother's side, living on their own farm at Cold Spring, Long Island, New York State, near the edge of Queen's County, about a mile from the harbour. My father's side—probably the fifth generation from the first English arrivals in New England—were at the same time farmers on their own land (and a fine domain it was, 500 acres, all good soil, gently sloping east and south, about one-tenth woods, plenty of grand old trees), two or three miles off, at West Hills, Suffolk County."

Next we have some reminiscences of Whitman's early life on Long Island, and afterwards at Brooklyn, where he attended the public schools, and began life in a lawyer's office. Two years later he went to work in a weekly newspaper and printing office to learn the trade. Of his amusements and tastes during this period we have many interesting details. His first subscription to a circulating library, when the "Arabian Nights," and Sir Walter Scott's novels, and after that his poems, laid the

foundation of a taste for the reading of romances and poetry which he retains to this day. The theatre, too, he delighted in, and saw all the great actors and singers, American or European, in their most celebrated rôles. We hear, too, of his passion for ferries. In his youthful years at New York and Brooklyn, his life was, he says,

curiously identified with Fulton ferry, already becoming the greatest of its sort in the world for general importance, volume, variety, rapidity, and picturesqueness. Almost daily, later ('50 to '60) I crossed on the boats, often up in the pilot houses, where I could get a full sweep, absorbing shows, accompaniments, surroundings. What oceanic currents, eddies, underneath the great tide of humanity also, with ever-shifting movements! Indeed, I have always had a passion for ferries; to me they afford inimitable, streaming, never-failing poems.

The Broadway sights, too, impressed him vividly. "Here I saw during these times Andrew Jackson, Webster, Clay, Seward, Martin Van Buren, fillibuster Walker, Kossuth, Fitz–Greene Halleck, Bryant, the Prince of Wales, Charles Dickens, the first Japanese ambassadors, and lots of other celebrities of the time." In 1848–9 he was editor of a Brooklyn newspaper, *The Daily Eagle*. In 1855 he sent to press *Leaves of Grass*, being then in his thirty-sixth year. In 1862 [*sic*] the Secession War broke out. Walt Whitman immediately abandoned his editorial and other avocations, and devoted himself during the whole continuance of the struggle to ministering to the sick and wounded in the military hospitals, living for the most part at Washington, and making occasional visits to the front. The scenes which came under his notice at this period are most vividly described in the present volume, and seem, as was but natural, to have left a profound and over-whelming impression on him, stirring his nature to the very depths, and exalting and intensifying his patriotic and demo-cratic sentiments. He even sees in the steadiness in action of American soldiers, and their heroic fortitude under wounds and sickness, a triumphant argument in favour of democracy; forgetting or ignor-ing that these same military virtues have been displayed by European troops in various ages, and under every form of government. Two facts concerning the Secession War deserve notice, as being in direct contradiction of the usually re-ceived opinion on the matter in England. First, we have it, on Mr. Whitman's testi-mony as an eye-witness, that an immense majority, quite nine out of ten, of the combatants on the side of the North were native Americans. Second, there were in the Northern army men from every State in the Union, without exception. Not one of the revolted States but had its contin-gent fighting under the Union flag. In a speech in the House of Representatives, April 15, 1879, Mr. Garfield said, "Do gentlemen know that (leaving out all the border States) there were fifty regiments and seven companies of white men in our army fighting for the Union, from the States that went into rebellion?" After the close of the war our author remained for some years in Washington, employed in the attorney-general's department.

"In February, 1873," he tells us, "I was stricken down by paralysis, gave up my desk, and emigrated to Cam-den, New Jersey, where I lived during 1874 and 1875, quite unwell, but af-ter that began to grow better; com-menced going for weeks at a time, even for months, down in the country, to a charmingly recluse and rural spot along Timber Creek, twelve or thir-teen miles from where it enters the Delaware river. Domiciled in the farm-house of my friends, the Staffords, near by, I lived half the time along the creek and its adjacent fields and lanes. And it is to my life here that I, per-haps, owe partial recovery (a sort of second wind, or semi-renewal of the lease of life) from the prostration of 1874 and 1875."

We may add, that it was not alone to the influences thus alluded to that this partial recovery was due, but in no small degree to the poet's own energy, good sense, and cheerful patience. Gallantly he has fought for his life, disputing the ground inch by inch, never yielding to impatience or discouragement, delighting in the joys still left him, and, as the homely proverb has it, "cutting his coat according to his cloth." Amid the notes on external Na-ture, on the songs and habits of birds, on the trees, the skies, the stars, of which a great part of the volume is composed, so rare and slight is the mention of his infir-mities that we might forget that the idyll was composed by a half-paralyzed man, were it not for such an entry as the fol-lowing:—

"September 5, 1877.—I write this, 11 A.M., sheltered under a dense oak by the bank, where I have taken refuge from a sudden rain. I came down here (we had sulky drizzles all the morning, but an hour ago a lull) for the before-mentioned daily and simple exercise I am fond of to pull on that young hickory sapling out there—to sway and yield to its tough-limber upright stem—haply to get into my old sinews some of its elastic fibre and clear sap. I stand on the turf and take these health-pulls moderately, and at inter-vals, for nearly an hour, inhaling great draughts of fresh air. Wandering by the creek, I have three or four naturally favourable spots where I rest besides a chair I lug with me and use for more deliberate occasions. At other spots I have selected, besides the hickory just named, long and limber boughs of beech or holly, in easy-reaching distance, for my natural gymnasia for arms, chest, trunk-muscles. I can feel the sap and sinew rising through me, like mercury to heat. I hold on boughs or slender trees caressingly there, in the sun and shade; wrestle with their innocent stalwartness, and *know* the virtue thereof passes from them into me—or maybe we interchange; maybe the trees are more aware of it all than I ever thought."

There is much in *Specimen Days* which we should like to quote, if our space permitted but little, comparatively, which calls for comment. The thought is often highly poetic, and always wholesome and unconventional. The form in which it is expressed is more open to criticism. At page 268 he says:—"Nothing is better than simplicity; nothing can make up for excess, or lack of definiteness." Now the want of definiteness is often painfully felt in his own style, while there is much of excess and redundancy. His sentences often read like lists of substantives; and both simplicity and definiteness are too often sacrificed to this heaping up of words, apparently with the view of more fully expressing something which after all remains obscure and intangible. Under the head of "Democratic Vistas" (p. 257), he gives us his idea of the literary style of the future:—

"Not merely the pedagogue forms—correct, regular, familiar with precedent, made for matters of outside propriety, fine words, thoughts definitely told out—but a language formed by the breath of Nature, which leaps overhead, cares mostly for impetus and effects, and for what it plants and invigorates to grow—tallies life and character, and seldomer tells a thing than suggests or necessitates it."

We conclude that *Specimen Days* are also a specimen of this new and especially democratic style. If so, we are not ripe for it, for it is, to us, the one great drawback to the book. Many of Whitman's criticisms on contemporary literature, society, and morals, in America, are very striking and original, showing great insight and considerable power of generalization; but their philosophical value is greatly lessened by his allowing his democratic enthusiasm to overspread the whole field of thought. For him it seems as though everything fell under one of two categories—democratic or feudal. Democracy, too, seems to him to exist nowhere but in America. Another very noticeable feature in his philosophizing is, that so much—nearly everything good or desirable—is in the future. He is perpetually violating the wise injunction of his countryman Artemus Ward: "Never prophesy, unless you know." Thus he paints the present state of American morality, political, commercial, and social, with quite as black a brush as did the author of "Democracy." "If I were asked," he says (p. 233), "to specify in what quarter lie the grounds of darkest dread, respecting the America of our hopes, I should point to this particular"—that is, the absence of "the primary moral element." But this is to be remedied in the future, *bien entendu*, by an "all-penetrating religiousness." But it is to be a democratic religion, apparently, without churches or religious machinery, for he elsewhere prophesies that before another century is past there will be no more priests. Will not the religious world be somewhat like an army without officers? In the future, too, and likely to be so for an indefinite period, is the American annexation of Canada, which the great prophet of democracy no less confidently predicts. But in a future more remote and dim than all the rest, is the "race of orbic bards, sweet democratic despots of the West," so eloquently apostrophized at page 241, and more fully described at page 253:—

"In the future of these States must arise Poets immenser far, and make great poems of death. The poems of life are great; but there must be the poems of the purpose of life, not only in itself, but beyond itself. I have eulogized Homer, the sacred bards of Jewry, Æschylus, Juvenal, Shakespeare, &c., and acknowledged their inestimable value. But (with perhaps the exception in some, not in all respects, of the second mentioned) I say there must, for future and democratic purposes, appear poets (dare I say so?) of higher class even than any of those— poets, not only possessed of the religious fire and *abandon* of Isaiah, luxuriant in the epic talent of Homer, or for proud characters as in Shakespeare, but consistent with the Hegelian formulas, and consistent with modern science."

The appearance of such poets as these, especially a class of such poets, can hardly be confidently expected; yet on this apparently remote contingency, the continued existence and greatness of the United States (we are elsewhere told) depends. Walt Whitman's critical remarks on the writings of Edgar Poe are well worth reading, as are also his criticisms on Carlyle and on Tennyson, but they are too long to quote. His remarks on British literature generally are not so happy; there is too much affectation of treating it as something foreign and alien. Here,

as elsewhere, his *idée fixe*, democracy, warps his judgment; his patriotism runs away with him. He claims for America as close kinship with the literatures of Italy, France, Spain, &c., as with that of England, yet naïvely avows their foreignness by wishing there existed better English translations of them. There is much truth in his strictures (page 231) on modern culture:—

"As now taught, accepted, and carried out, are not the processes of culture rapidly creating a class of supercilious infidels who believe in nothing? Shall a man lose himself in countless masses of adjustments; and be so shaped in reference to this, and that, and the other, that the simply good and healthy and brave parts of him are reduced and clipped away, like the bordering of box in a garden? You can cultivate corn and roses and orchards—but who shall cultivate the mountain peaks, the ocean, or the tumbling gorgeousness of the clouds?"

His judgment of Darwin's "Theory of Evolution" is insufficient and unsatisfactory. Probably the new idea reached him too late in life, when his mind had already taken too decided a bent to be fully penetrated and imbued by a new theory of the universe. He evidently regrets the old legends of man's descent from gods or demigods, and falls into the common error of supposing that Darwin makes man the descendant of apes and baboons. For his own part (p. 326), Whitman thinks—

"the problem of origins, human and other, is not the least whit nearer its solution. In due time the evolution theory will have to abate its vehemence, cannot be allowed to dominate everything else, and will have to take its place as a segment of the circle, the cluster—as but one of many theories, many thoughts, of profoundest value—and readjusting and differentiating much, yet leaving the divine secrets just as inexplicable and unreachable as before—maybe more so."

Evidently he has not taken in that the theory of evolution is not an ingenious word-system, like the metaphysical speculations of Kant or Hegel, but the discovery of a great natural law, like that of gravitation, dominating every form of life just as inevitably as gravitation reigns over matter. He does not see that man himself is but a small and fleeting phase of evolution, and his systems, religious and political, but the phases of a phase. One more quotation must close this notice, which our sense of the importance of the work under consideration has led us to extend to an undue length. In speaking of Protection (p. 332), Whitman asks the pertinent question: "Who gets the plunder?" "It would," he says, "be some excuse and satisfaction if even a fair proportion of it went to the masses of labouring men, resulting in homesteads to such men, women and children—myriads of actual homes in fee simple in every State. . . . . But the Act is nothing of the kind. The profits of 'protection' go altogether to a few score select persons, who, by favours of Congress, State legislatures, the banks, and other special advantages, are forming a vulgar aristocracy, full as bad as anything in the British or European castes of blood, or the dynasties of the past."

"Walt Whitman's Prose Works."
Spectator, 21 July 1883, pp. 933–5.

The admiration for the writings of Walt Whitman which has been expressed by several cultivated writers and critics of our time has been a matter of much surprise to us. That Mr. Swinburne should have been moved to eulogy of Whitman's "poems" is natural enough. There is an old proverb about the gregariousness of birds of similar plumage which goes far to explain it, and we can understand how it is that many of the less cultivated of Whitman's compatriots should be won over by his gorgeous anticipations of the "fruitage" of American democracy; but that Emerson and Mr. Ruskin, to mention no others, should be found quoted in the advertisement of his book has long puzzled us. Mr. Ruskin is reported to have said that "it carries straight and keen as rifle-balls against our deadliest social sins;" Emerson wrote that it is "the most extraordinary piece of wit and wisdom that America has yet contributed." And besides those and several other eminent authorities, there are not a few of our younger writers who regard Whitman as the great poet of democracy and the pioneer of a new literary era. According to the accepted canons of criticism and taste—canons to which the best minds of the best epochs of civilisation have successively added, or from which they have subtracted—we should have expected that the greater part of Whitman's "poems" would be set down as mere egotistical mouthing of sentiments either trite or untrue, sometimes deliberately nasty, and exhibiting very few traces of the inner qualities or external characteristics of true poetry. What, then, is the explanation of the admiration and eulogy which they have provoked? It seems to us to lie in the following considerations. In his essay *On Liberty*, Mill says that in an age of conformity "exceptional individuals, instead of being deterred, should be encouraged in acting differently from the mass. In other times, there was no advantage in their doing so, unless they acted not only differently, but better. In this age, the mere example of non-conformity, the mere refusal to bow the knee to custom, is itself a service." A half-unconscious conviction to this effect exists in most men; we often feel that we conform too much, although we see no point at which we had better cease to conform. There is a feeling of individualism, of self-assertion,—of manliness, if you like,—prompting a moment's sympathy with men or causes which reason immediately shows to be unworthy of it. It is hardly too much to say that for the first moment of thought upon a new subject—the Promethean moment—every man is a Radical. Defiance of established custom, though it may soon be seen to be mistaken and misleading, is, for the moment, a grateful testimony to the fundamental independence of our common nature. And the more closely any matter is confined within strict rules and customs, the more sure is any abrupt departure from these to secure a temporary approval and admiration. Now, in no field of modern thought is custom more imperious than in literature, and in no branch of modern literature is the tendency to lay down and follow strict rules so strong as in poetry. When, therefore, a writer appears, styling himself "poet," utterly defying and ridiculing all our rules and customs, he is almost certain to find a temporary circle of admirers who will exaggerate his merits and glorify his defects. This has been the case with Whitman. He comes with the latest version of the old heroic command, "Son of man, stand upon thy feet, and I will speak to thee;" and so at first men overlook all his defects and his emptiness,—they forget that they still find their daily spiritual and intellectual satisfaction in the long-accepted singers of mankind,—while the innate Radicalism of human nature is leading them to offer him a generous welcome.

The volume before us contains Whitman's complete prose works. The edition of Messrs. Wilson and McCormick is apparently printed from the same plates as the American edition, but upon better paper, with wider margins, and is therefore pleasanter to read. We may add, by the way, that the publication of Whitman's works by a Philadelphia house is doubtless accounted for by the fact that the Attorney-General of Massachusetts informed Messrs. Osgood and Co., Whitman's Boston publishers, that the issue of a second edition of *Leaves of Grass* would be followed by a prosecution for publishing obscene literature. Part of the present prose has appeared before in his books, part in the magazines, and part in the newspapers,—hence the title *Collect*—and the rest, consisting chiefly of items of autobiography, is now printed for the first time. *Specimen Days* occupy more than half the volume, and these are described as "a huddle of diary jottings, war-memoranda of 1862–65, Nature-notes of 1877–81, with Western and Canadian observations afterwards." They average about half a page each, and are impromptu, unrevised, bits of description or reflection "pencil'd" (or sometimes "pencill'd"), about any person, place, or thing to which the author "feels to devote a memorandum," falling for the most part under the three heads of himself, nature, and literature. The following "day" will give the reader an adequate idea of Whitman's descriptions of Nature; his days are joined each to each in natural common-place, and to have read half-a-dozen is to have read them all.

"A HINT OF WILD NATURE."

"As I was crossing the Delaware to-day, saw a large flock of wild geese, right overhead, not very high up, ranged in V-shape, in relief against the noon clouds of light smoke-color. Had a capital though momentary view of them, and then of their course on and on southeast, till gradually fading—(my eyesight yet first-rate for the open air and its distances, but I use glasses for reading.) Queer thoughts melted into me the two or three minutes or less, seeing these creatures cleaving the sky— the spacious, airy realm—even the prevailing smoke-gray color everywhere, (no sun shining)—the waters below— the rapid flight of the birds, appearing just for a minute—flashing to me such a hint of the whole spread of Nature, with her eternal unsophisticated freshness, her never-visited recesses of sea, sky, shore—and then disappearing in the distance."

One quality, however, saves this passage from being pure common-place, viz., its egotism, which makes it offensive. It is a fair specimen of the assurance with which the author sets forth trite reflections, dressed up in a sledge-hammer style, and constantly interrupted by trivial personal parentheses. Here is a typical example of Whitman's literary criticisms, exhibiting the same characteristics. It is typical, we should add, in every respect but one,—in this instance, the reader can discover a definite meaning on the part of the author:—

"There is, apart from mere intellect, in the make-up of every superior hu-man identity, (in its moral completeness, considered as *ensemble*, not for that moral alone, but for the whole being, including physique,) a wondrous something that realises without argument, frequently without what is called education, (though I think it the goal and apex of all education deserving the name)—an intuition of the absolute balance, in space and time, of the whole of this multifarious, mad chaos of fraud, frivolity, hoggishness,— this revel of fools, and incredible make-believe and general unsettledness we call *the world*; a soul-sight of that divine clue and unseen thread which holds the whole congeries of things, all history and time, and all events, however trivial, however momentous, like a leash'd dog in the hand of the hunter. Such soul-sight and root-centre for the mind—mere optimism explains only the surface or fringe of it—Carlyle was mostly, perhaps entirely without."

In this grandiloquent and verbose passage there is, at any rate, a very familiar idea to be found; but we have to confess that after careful reading we were unable to detect any definite meaning in the majority of Whitman's literary statements and prophecies, even in the cases where he puts a plain question, and professes to give a direct answer. As this may result from our inability to grasp the stupendous forecasts likely to be made by a man who calmly informs us that he found the Rocky Mountains to be the law of his own poems, we will leave our readers to judge between author and critic in a test case. Toward the end of "Democratic Vistas" (of which, by the way, we made a careful epitome, in a fruitless effort to follow the author's reasoning), Whitman says:—"Repeating our inquiry, what, then, do we mean by real literature? especially the democratic literature of the future?" This is admirably clear and to the point, but hardly has he asked the question before he begins to shuffle out of an answer to it. "Hard questions to meet," he goes on to say, and every succeeding clause takes us further from the point. "The clues are inferential, and turn us to the past. At best, we can only offer suggestions, comparisons, circuits." Then follows a page and a half of really eloquent tribute to the literature of the past, and an apostrophe to its great representatives:—

"Unknown Egyptians, graving hieroglyphs; Hindus, with hymn and apothegm and endless epic; Hebrew prophet, with spirituality, as in flashes of lightning; Christ, with bent head, brooding peace and love, like a dove; Greek, creating eternal shapes of physical and æsthetic proportion; Roman, lord of satire, the sword, and the codex."

This is good in itself, but the "circuit" is leading us further and further from the answer to the plain question with which the author started. When at length the answer does come, it is as follows (and who will interpret it for us?):—

"Ye powerful and resplendent ones! ye were, in your atmospheres, grown not for America, but rather for her foes, the feudal and the old—while our genius is democratic and modern. Yet could ye, indeed, but breathe your breath of life into our New World's nostrils—not to enslave us, as now, but, for our needs, to breed a spirit like your own—perhaps, (dare we to say it?) to dominate, even destroy, what you yourselves have left! On your plane, and no less, but even higher and wider, must we mete and measure for to-day and here. I demand races of

orbic bards, with unconditional uncompromising away. Come forth, sweet democratic despots of the west!

By points like these, we, in reflection, token what we mean by any land's or people's genuine literature."

In the regretted absence of the sweet democratic despots of the west, we should have been grateful if a little more simple meaning had come forth from the many pages of discourse like the above, which duty has compelled us to peruse. Mr. Stevenson, in his charming eulogistic essay, says, "Whitman is too clever to slip into a succinct formula;" we think it would be truer to say that he is far too unenlightened.

Taken as a whole, however, this volume shows its author in a pleasanter light than is shed upon him by his "poems." The personal element in it is more modest, less vulgar; there are passages of considerable power and original insight, although in most cases his descriptions still depend for their effect more upon a catalogue-like exhaustive enumeration, than upon selective acumen; and he is occasionally very happy in his epithets. But the most interesting parts of the book are those in which he really has something to tell; his reminiscences of the war and his description of the assassination of Lincoln are worth more than all his literary prophecies and political rhapsodies put together. These "war memoranda" suggest one rather unpleasant question; he seems to have done good service in visiting the hospitals and purveying small comforts to the wounded, but when we read his enthusiastic account of the young Union soldiers who faced death so simply and bravely, and bore their fearful sufferings and neglect without a word of complaint, it gives us rather a shock to find him saying immediately afterwards, "During the war I possessed the perfection of physical health," and, "There has lately been much suffering here from heat; I go around with an umbrella and a fan." We cannot help asking what would have become of the Union if many men in the perfection of physical health had contented themselves with an umbrella and a fan and "diary-jottings," instead of shouldering a musket and giving their lives in silence. And while we freely admit the merits we have mentioned, the examination of this volume has confirmed us in our conviction of the absence of any real and permanent significance in Whitman's writings. It is difficult to escape the belief that much of them has been produced with a view to effect. A man who was thoroughly actuated by the principles of democratic independence professed by Whitman would hardly have taken from a private letter of Emerson the over-generous words, "I greet you at the beginning of a great career," and have flaunted them upon the cover of his book. Occasionally he does give us what he terms "a radical utterance out of the emotions and the physique,"—a phrase intense in its expression, an idea startling in its originality and scope, an exhortation or an appeal powerful in its personal directness, but this is all.

But, in the first place, Whitman is ignorant: this book, with its scrawled title-page, furnishes abundant evidence that its author knows next to nothing of many things which he unhesitatingly exalts or denounces, and that he has no adequate conception of many of the problems he so confidently solves. He declares his determination to get "away from ligatures, tight boots, buttons, and the whole cast-iron civilized life;" he will have "no talk, no bonds, no dress, no books, *no manners*;" he tells us that Grant's life "transcends Plutarch," that "it was a happy thought to build the Hudson River railroad right along the shore," (what

deadly social sin will Mr. Ruskin think *that* statement carries against?) that "the time has arrived to essentially break down the barriers of form between prose and poetry," that "the Muse of the Prairies, of California, Canada, Texas, and of the peaks of Colorado. . . . . . soars to the freer, vaster diviner heaven of prose." What rubbish all this is! His grammar is constantly faulty, and much more so in his later works than in his earlier ones,— a suspicious inversion of the general rule. Why should any sane man prevent even his proof-reader from correcting blunders like "I do not know as," . . .? Unless, too, the reader possesses considerable familiarity with American slang, he will frequently be stopped by such expressions as "fetching up," "scooted," "derring-do," "out of kilter." But the English language, even when supplemented by the most forcible slang in the world, is still unequal to the expression of this man's thoughts, so that he is compelled to employ a large original vocabulary, *e.g.*, "jetted," "gaggery," "compaction," "out-croppage," "literatus," "ostent," "philosoph," "to promulge," and "memorandize." Even in his own name he perpetuates what was doubtless his familiar title among his fellow-compositors on the old *Long Island Patriot*. Moreover, just as his one successful lyrical poem, "My Captain," is enough to disprove all his theories of poetry, so we have noticed a curious slip, which, though small in itself, still tends to show that his outspokenness is an affectation rather than a genuine impulse. In describing the scene of wild excitement that followed the assassination of Lincoln, he says that the soldiers of the President's guard charged the audience in the theatre, shouting, "*Clear out! clear out! you sons of* ———. . . . . ." Think of this for a moment: "no bonds, no mannerisms, no fossil-etiquettes," and then,—"*you sons of* ———. . . . . ." Why, even Shakespeare, whom Whitman calls the "tally of feudalism," "offensive to democracy," or Tennyson, "lush-ripening," and "quite sophisticated," would have ventured to write "*Hell.*"

Whitman's second prominent characteristic is animalism, using the word in no specially bad sense. Not to renew an old and unpleasant controversy, we will let the statement pass that he has not written anything which is not pure in its intention although whatever the author's intention may have been, the intention of his American publisher is indicated by the announcement that the new edition of *Leaves of Grass* "contains every page, every line, every word attempted to be officially suppressed by the Massachusetts authorities." We will content ourselves with describing his characteristic as animalism—the emphatic expression of the simply animal side of human nature. His works simply raise again, with greater vehemence, perhaps, but with the same shallow views, the once famous cry, "Retourner à la nature!" If to sit naked on a gate in the sunshine, rubbing oneself scarlet with a flesh-brush—a process of which this volume contains a detailed account—were in any way symbolic of human life, then Whitman would be our proper teacher. But as far as this "*al fresco* physiology" is from being such a symbol, so far is Walt Whitman from holding such a position. And we have nothing to lose in discarding him; for all the radicalism, the love of truth, the independence, the faith in men, in democracy, and in America, which his admirers discover in him, is to be found in Emerson in purer, saner, higher form.

NOVEMBER BOUGHS (1888)

November Boughs

BY WALT WHITMAN

PHILADELPHIA
DAVID McKAY, 23 SOUTH NINTH STREET
1888

George Rogers.
"Walt Whitman Again: Another Volume by the Good Grey Poet, and Some Thoughts on His Writings Suggested by Its Appearance."
Philadelphia *North American*, 25 October 1888, p. 1.

Though it should do nothing else, the appearance of a new volume by Walt Whitman may be trusted to stir into renewed activity that interminable discussion as to the merit and meaning and value of his writings which is the most striking and trustworthy testimony to their originality and power. There must be something or even a great deal in an author who is able, if not to command the acceptance of his theories and ideas, at least to make them the subject of a controversy, which, after going on for more than thirty years, seems to be still as far as ever from reaching a settlement. *Leaves of Grass*, the book which first made Whitman a public character, was published in 1855, and after the thirty-three years which have elapsed since then its status as a literary production remains undetermined. There are those—and they include men of cultivated taste, enlightened judgment and unimpeachable integrity—who declare that, all things considered, Whitman is perhaps the greatest, the most original, the most characteristic poet that America has yet produced, and singularly enough the most eminent of the critics who hold to this opinion are Englishmen between whose high culture and the unpolished ruggedness of Whitman one would not expect to find any bond of sympathy. What, for example, within the compass of literary production could be further removed than the mellifluous strains of "The Princess" or *The Idylls of the King*, and the defiant rudeness of Whitman's writings, and yet it is said that Alfred Tennyson, influenced perhaps by a feeling akin to that which impels the curled darlings of civilization to seek in the primitive wilderness a respite from an excess of cultivation and refinement, is one of the "good grey poet's" most enthusiastic admirers.

On the other hand, there are those, and they also comprise men of honesty and discernment, to whom Whitman's so-called poetry is nothing but "a barbaric yawp," and the best of his lines little better than a senseless jargon. How can one account for opinions so widely dissimilar? Which of the two is right, and if neither, in what happy medium does the truth lie hid? Is Whitman a great poet, one of the inspired writers who once in a while appear among men to open up new hemispheres of thought, or is he a kind of monomaniac possessed and dominated by ideas which he is powerless to formulate, haunted by the vision of the great projects which he lacks the ability to execute; a man who, having just fallen short of being a genius, still has in his composition that strain of madness to which genius is said to be allied? Is he inspired or is he crazy, or what shall we say of him? It seems to me from what I have read of his writings, and of the commentaries and explanations by which he has, not unintelligently, thought well to supplement them, that Whitman is a man intoxicated with a single idea, that of the incomparable importance of the bare, the naked fact. He is essentially if not exclusively a realist, and by a realist as descriptive of Whitman I mean a man who is mistrustful of all things save those that can be seen and felt and handled; who is so enamored of the truth, the whole truth and nothing but the truth, that to him the graces of style are a snare and the adornments of fancy a delusion—a man whose impulse it is to get so close to nature that he is never satisfied to be any distance away from the great primary passions and the instincts of humanity.

Now this ardent devotion to the True, this noble abhorrence of anything that might savor of insincerity, is admirable and excellent, and so far as Whitman's poetry has made the impression it was intended to produce and has won the favor of readers it has done so by virtue of this very quality. There is so much insincerity in literature, and especially in the mass of what passes for a time as poetry; writers, and particularly second rate poets, are so prone to put forward as their own, thoughts and feelings and ideas that they have taken at second-hand from some one else; custom and convention play so large a part in the making of modern books that to turn to Whitman, whose work, whatever may be its faults and limitations, is wholly his own, and free from the smallest taint of imitation or conventionality, is like passing from a crowded and heated theatre into the open air. The bare fact unquestionably has an interest and power which are unsurpassed and unsurpassable, and no set of facts is more interesting to men and women than those facts which reveal the workings of the human mind and heart. The "study of mankind is man," and there is no study more fascinating—none that has to be carried on under greater difficulties. Men and women are so reluctant, or rather, perhaps, so unable to furnish one another with the necessary facilities for investigation. The great masters of the human heart must arrive at their conclusions and amass their knowledge by a

process of intuition, for it is the truth in another sense from that intended by the Apostle, that every man lives to himself and every man dies to himself. The spiritual isolation of each is ordinarily complete.

Such being the case a book which, like *Leaves of Grass*, is an unmistakably sincere expression of human feeling, a simple and unaffected revelation of the human soul, is sure to have a welcome and make some kind of mark. It is in this way, it seems to me, that such success as *Leaves of Grass* and the other of Mr. Whitman's books have had must be accounted for. They are made impressive by a devotion to fact so uncompromising that it rejects all the ornaments of rhetoric lest they obscure and distort or in the smallest degree modify the author's meaning. Whitman is mistrustful of rhyme and rhythm because he fears that if he uses them they will betray him into saying or suggesting something different from what he intended, a fear for which there is abundant reason. However gracefully the burden may be borne, however skilfully the chain may be concealed, the exigencies of verse, and especially of rhyme, are a burden and a chain none the less and it is their natural, their unavoidable tendency to restrict or hamper the free expression of a writer's ideas, and even to give a bias to his choice of language, which may sometimes lead him to present his thoughts with something less than perfect truthfulness and accuracy. I can understand, therefore, how a man like Walt Whitman, determined above all things to set forth his ideas with unswerving sincerity and absolute originality, should eschew the limitations of verse and prefer, even if he had to invent it, a literary vehicle which he could use with perfect freedom.

Yet assuming this to be the case, assuming that Whitman felt that he could not trust himself to write with force and faithfulness under the forms of verse, does it not follow that whatever other faculties he may possess, the true poetical inspiration has been denied him? He may be a great writer, a profound philosopher, a pregnant essayist, but surely if he does not employ a poetical method of expression he cannot be a poet, great or small. This, however, opens up a field of discussion upon which, however inviting the prospect, I do not at this time propose to enter. Let us assume for the present that Whitman is just as much of a poet as his most ardent admirers would have us believe, and having made that admission, pro forma, proceed to consider why his books have not attained—I will not say to a greater popularity, for popularity is far from being a criterion of merit—but to a more general and cordial acceptance at the hands of educated and intelligent people. I suspect that the most active reason is to be found in the circumstance that Whitman expects too much of his readers. He insists that they shall be partakers in his travail; that they shall both witness and have a share in the throes of his intellectual parturition. He uses language less to express than to suggest ideas, and to follow out the suggestions he makes involves a degree of mental toil to which few readers are willing to subject themselves. He does not arrange his words so that they shall the most clearly, the most happily, the most forcefully, convey his meaning, while at the same time drawing as little as possible upon the mental resources of the reader. Indeed he does not arrange his words at all. He piles them up: he throws them together; he scatters them broadcast. His poetry may not be void, but unquestionably it is without form. It is too often as though an artist should throw his paint brush at the canvas, and require the onlooker by the exercise of his imagination to evolve a picture out of the splash. So it is with these poems of Whitman. They contain the raw material out of which poems might be made; but the reader is obliged for the most part to do his own poetizing as best he can. Now the modern reader is accustomed to having things made easy for him. He will do no more private thinking of his own than is absolutely necessary, and when it comes to toiling in Walt Whitman's rough sketches of potential poems he respectfully declines the job.

As for Whitman's latest volume, while it contains nothing essentially new, it does contain a great deal that is interesting, notably the article "A Backward Glance O'er Travel'd Roads," in which the author expounds the methods and theories and purposes animating and underlying his literary work. Poetry, however, properly so-called, is not consciously written according to any method, or with any purpose, or upon any theory. It may be true, as Whitman insists, that this great Republic, in which men and women live out their lives under conditions different from and better than any heretofore existing since the world began, must produce such poetry as has never yet been known, although as poetry is the expression of human feeling, and human nature remains the same in a republic as in an empire, the point is at least debatable. But the great American poem when it comes will certainly not be written with deliberate intent. It will not be the work of anyone who shall say to himself: "Now upon this theory or that I will write an epic."

309

"The Latest Books . . . Walt Whitman on *Leaves of Grass*." Philadelphia *Times*, 27 October 1888, p. 4.

There is something pathetic—almost painfully pathetic—in "A Backward Glance O'er Traveled Roads," which serves as an introductory chapter to *November Boughs* (David McKay, publisher), a collection of Walt Whitman's later poems and other writings. This opening chapter can scarcely be called autobiographical. It is rather the poet's review in his old age of what he conceives were his intentions in his manhood's prime when he wrote *Leaves of Grass*. He confesses that as a poet he has not gained the acceptance of his own time—that from a worldly and business point of view *Leaves of Grass* has been worse than a failure. It is plain that even in his serene old age Mr. Whitman still feels the wounds made by the "marked anger and contempt" with which his book was received. What he considers that he has positively gained in the thirty years since *Leaves of Grass* was published is a hearing, and he is willing to leave the value of his work to be determined by time.

What Mr. Whitman claims as the motif of nearly all his verse is "the great pride of man in himself." The personality in his songs which such a motif implies the poet deliberately settled at the outset should be himself. *Leaves of Grass* he therefore claims as mainly the outcropping of his own emotional and other personal nature—as an attempt from first to last to put a person, a human being, himself, fully and truly upon record. Mr. Whitman does not deny but courageously

avows that *Leaves of Grass* is a song of sex and amativeness—even of animality. "Of this feature," he says, "intentionally palpable in a few lines, I shall only say the espousing principle of those lines so gives breath of life to my whole scheme that the bulk of the pieces might as well have been left unwritten were those lines omitted." And he stands by his guns to the last. "And in respect to editions of *Leaves of Grass* in time to come, if there should be such," he declares. "I take occasion now to confirm those lines with the settled convictions and deliberate renewals of thirty years, and to prohibit, so far as word of mine can do, any elision of them."

November Boughs is mostly made up of prose essays, the Bible as poetry, thoughts on Shakespeare, Burns and Tennyson, reminiscences of the Bowery Theatre, diary notes and war and Washington memoranda. The verse, "Sands at Seventy," occupies only a few pages of the book. But the volume is indispensible to every owner of *Leaves of Grass* and to every student of Mr. Whitman's claims as a poet.

"Walt Whitman's *November Boughs*." Philadelphia *Evening Bulletin*, 30 October 1888, p. 8.

No one can fail to be affected by the appearance of the latest writings of Walt Whitman, which are published by Mr. David McKay. Like all that he has written, they are not to be criticised, for the writer's literary creed denies and defies criticism. He is himself, and has the faith in his self-hood that every sturdy revolutionist or sincere reformer has. He may be right or he may be wrong, but his standard is his own, and he is brave enough to maintain it. This volume is a collection of bits that Whitman has published in magazines or newspapers. Many are in prose, in fact all may be so called, although some are poetical in their typographical arrangement. In the first twelve pages is an explanation or defence of his *Leaves of Grass*. This is in many respects a noble composition, in spite of its frequent disregard of literary and academic conventions. The collection of thoughts called "Sands at Seventy," cannot be called poetical, though the printed lines suggest it. Still there are occasional flashes of poetic light, which gleam through an excess of bigwordiness. But this remark borders on criticism, and that is forbidden when Whitman's contemporaries consider him. He has his own ideas of grammar, phraseology and the meaning of words, English and French, and he is not to be disturbed in his rights. What we especially admire in him is his stout, tough Americanism, his faith in his country, its government, and its people. His "War Memoranda," his reminiscences of his devoted labors in the army hospitals, and his noble tribute to Lincoln (not so tender as the really rhythmic verses "My Captain"), are things for young Americans to study. His literary essays on Burns, Tennyson and Shakespeare stir the sympathies of all lovers of the English language. More elaborate and long than all is the paper on Elias Hicks, which is a fervid tribute to one man, and a lesson to many. It is full of ideas and suggestions of ideas, which will work and bear fruit in the minds of the seriously thoughtful.

Hamlin Garland. "Whitman's *November Boughs*." Boston *Evening Transcript*, 15 November 1888, p. 6.

Walt Whitman has always been suggestive and usually felicitous in his titles, and there is something about *November Boughs* which arrests the attention of the reader.

"You lingering sparse leaves of me, on winter-rearing boughs" he writes in one place, and again in the "Carol at Sixty-nine" and other places, seems to hint that his work is nearly finished, yet the reader will find little sign of decay or weakness in this characteristic powerful volume of poems and essays. The design of the book is evidently to round out and comment upon his other works and to add a few more poems to the hitherto complete *Leaves of Grass*.

It is an admirable book for those to read who wish to know Whitman, to discover how calm, patient and philosophical he really is. It is no longer in order to assault him, even if we do not agree with him, and the number of people who begin to understand and admire this great personality is increasing. As Stedman has said, "Whitman cannot be skipped," he must be studied by whomever would lay claim to the name of critic or student of American thought, and such person cannot do better than begin study by reading *November Boughs*, and especially the calm estimate which the author himself puts upon his work, in the initial essay, "O'er Travelled Roads."

"So here I sit gossiping in the early

candle-light of old age—I and my book—casting backward glances over our travelled road. . . . That I have not gained the acceptance of my own time but have fallen back on fond dreams of the future; that from a worldly and business point of view, *Leaves of Grass* has been worse than a failure; that public criticism on the book, and myself, as author of it, yet shows marked anger and contempt more than anything else; and that solely for publishing it I have been the object of two or three pretty serious official buffetings—is all probably no more than I ought to have expected. I had my choice when I commenced. I bid neither for soft eulogies, big money returns, nor the approbation of existing schools and conventions."

In calculating the decision of the world upon his book, he says William O'Connor and Dr. Bucke are far more peremptory than he, and regards the fact that he has obtained a hearing as of prime importance:

"Essentially that from the first, and has remained throughout the main object. Now it seems to be achieved, I am certainly contented to waive any otherwise momentous drawbacks as of little account. Candidly and dispassionately reviewing all my intentions, I feel that they were creditable, and I accept the result, whatever it may be."

Surely these are dignified and reasonable words, with which no one can quarrel. People in general are coming to think that his intentions were creditable, and no one who has really known him or brought himself to the poet's point of view has ever thought otherwise. The supreme barrier has been ignorance of the poet's real life (his service to his fellows, the ready self-sacrifice and the boundless love for all conditions of life), which has always barred the way to knowing his works. In the bitterness of the controversy the critics befogged the public mind, at times wilfully misrepresenting him, leaving out of their columns all reference to his sublime service to men during the civil war and his never-failing sympathy towards the poor and ignorant, as well as his tolerance of beliefs opposed to his.

The admirers of Whitman (if I may be allowed to represent them) do not complain at the non-acceptance of his work as poetry, but they do complain, and have reason to complain, of the distortion of the poet's intention and the misrepresentation of his private life. I for one have no quarrel with any one who honestly objects to Whitman's being called a poet, but with those who raise the point (happily they are few now) that his intentions were not creditable, I certainly do take decided issue.

After all, the controversy about poetry is mostly a contention about a word. I read a passage from Whitman like this:

"I stand as on some mighty eagle's
  beak,
Eastward the sea absorbing, viewing
  (nothing but sea and sky)
The tossing waves, the foam, the
  ships in distance,
The wild unrest, the snowy curling
  caps—that inbound verge of
  waves,
Seeking the shore forever."

I say this is poetry, you say "it is passionate descriptive speech." Very well. It doesn't matter what you call it. A great picture is there. Emotion is there, and a certain resonant, free song is there. The name does not matter. This example will do as well as hundreds to illustrate the present attitude of those who call Whitman a poet and those who do not. Opponents no longer find it necessary to assault the poet's character in order to justify their dislike of his writings, and on the other hand the "Whitmanites" are ready to make certain concessions, and altogether an understanding is being reached. I think no one can read *Specimen Days*, and especially the war memoranda, without coming to venerate the man who spent years in the hospitals (visiting the bedsides of over one hundred thousand soldiers), laying the foundations for the sickness which chained him to his chair before he was sixty years of age, despite a magnificent physique.

There is a very significant memorandum in this last volume touching the physical effect of his experience in the hospital:

"WASHINGTON, May 26, '63. It is curious: when I am present at the most appalling scenes, deaths, operations, sickening wounds (perhaps full of maggots), I keep cool and do not give out or budge, although my sympathies are very much excited; but often, hours afterward, perhaps, when I am at home or out walking alone, I feel sick and actually tremble when I recall the case before me." This gives us a glimpse of the horrors of the labor which undermined one of the superbest physical organizations.

Coming at Whitman from this side (through his prose) the student will get close to the author of *Leaves of Grass* and be prepared to look from the same height upon the "objectionable" passages. Appreciating his motive and catching somewhat of the same breadth of view, the reader will find no line with a downward tendency.

Here, again, the time has come for the correction of an error. *Leaves of Grass* is now a volume of over four hundred pages, and yet in the midst of this unparalleled grouping of great thoughts and superb images, there are not ten lines to which the ordinary reader of Shakespeare could consistently point as objectionable. This must not be forgotten. Waiving the claim that it is not "poetry," as com-

monly understood, and agreeing that to many people there are objectionable passages, it still appears to me unreasonable to hold a prejudice against a most remarkable outpouring of exalted passion, prophecy, landscape painting, songs of the sea and, above all, calls for deeper love for Nature and for men. I have faith to believe that the circle of readers who feel this toward Whitman is constantly growing and must continue to grow as men grow to know him.

The advocates of Whitman's case have demanded too much of the public; they have not taken into account as well as he has the inertia of the average mind, whose thinking is necessarily along well-worn grooves, and can be but slowly and unwillingly turned aside. We insist now on the critics taking a new stand on the matter. Whitman is no longer a mystery; he is a serene, gentle, grand old man, living in Camden, who sends us what he thinks in his final volume, desiring readers and friends amidst the democracy, which he loves so well, his faith not shaken by all the buffetings, unkindnesses and neglect which he has received. We should hasten to do him honor while he is with us. Praise too often builds monuments when it should buy bread; furnishes tombstones where it should warm houses. Royal praise for the hearing ear, I say, flowers of love for the throbbing sense of the living poet. I present my tribute, drop my bit of laurel into the still warm, firm hand of the victorious singer.

I copy one of the poems of the present volume, which contains nearly a score of essays:

OF THAT BLITHE THROAT OF THINE.

[More than eighty degrees north, Greely, the explorer, heard the sound of a single snowbird, merrily sounding over the desolation.]

Of that blithe throat of thine from
    Arctic bleak and blank,
I'll mind the lesson, solitary bird—let
    me, too, welcome chilling drifts,
E'en the profoundest chill as now—a
    torpid pulse, a brain unnerved,
Old age land-locked within its winter
    bay. (Cold, cold, oh cold!)
These snowy hairs, my feeble arm,
    my frozen feet,
For them thy faith, thy rule, I take
    and grave it to the last;—
Not summer zones alone, not chants
    of youth, or south's warm tides
    alone,
But held by sluggish throes, packed in
    the northern ice the cumulus of
    years,
These with gay heart I also sing.

The poet's optimism can rise and does
rise above pain and weakness and all be-
setting ills with a positive sublimity of mien.
May he live to enjoy the ever-growing respect of the thinking men of his day.

"Whitman's *November Boughs*."
Literary World 19 (8 December 1888), 446–7.

After all, what one finds most worthy of
study in the works of Walt Whitman is
Walt Whitman himself. The aggressive,
virile personality of one who brooks no
conventional limitations has here free
and ample expression; and while we may
question the literary value of much or of
all that he has written, we cannot, if we
are impartial in judgment, fail to recognize and in some sort to admire the native goodness of heart and the lofty ideals
of the man. Through his printed words,
from the introduction to *Leaves of Grass*
to his latest messages inscribed in the volume now before us, there runs the self-
same vigorous reiterated note—the note
of comradeship, the yearning after that
ideal democracy where fraternity shall be
something more than a name and where
each shall give of his best for the good
of others. In this sense, as a prophet of
the new era for which so many now long
and wait, Walt Whitman stands on the
whole preëminent among moderns. He
has failed and failed lamentably in his attempt to construct a new technique in
verse, but at least he has shattered the old
bonds, he has broken the outworn mold,
he has cast his ideas into natural forms,
and in this he has conferred a benefit
upon the world of writers which will
in time be recognized. At a period filled
to overflowing with the pettiest manifestations of art that ever stifled the intellect of humanity, he alone has dared to
be wholly and entirely himself. He has
taught, as far as his voice has reached,
that literature is something more than a
playing with words, that it is a vital thing,
the expression of a nation's thought, and
that before we can have a national literature we must think great thoughts and do
great deeds. Success in barter does not
make a nation and the heaping up of material luxury cannot make a national literature. The form of expression is something, but the idea back of the form is the
main thing, and that is what the world,
or at least the western part of it, has been
prone to forget. "I say the profoundest
service that poems or any other writings
can do for their reader," Whitman remarks, "is not merely to satisfy the intellect, or supply something polish'd and
interesting, nor even to depict great passions, or persons, or events, but to fill
him with vigorous and clean manliness,

religiousness, and give him *good heart* as a radical possession and habit." To give good heart as a radical possession and habit—that is not an ignoble standard in literature certainly, and yet how few there are in these days who even keep it in view. To satisfy the superficial appetite for sensation, to please, to cajole, to flatter, to titillate—to this end is the generality of literature in this country now produced. Whitman sounds the note of revolt against universal self-indulgence and boredom. To read him, even when he is at his worst, is for a healthy mind to get a bracing tonic. His poems (for we must call them so) are as suggestive in their way as the cartoons of the old masters. They foreshadow possibilities, they appeal in some inscrutable way to the imagination, they stimulate, for they are inspired by the optimism which sees in man something more than the grovelling component of a selfish herd, and which, looking to wider horizons and heights yet unattained, urges him onward in the struggle toward liberty. For these reasons we can welcome in behalf of reason and sanity whatever Walt Whitman chooses to give us, even these fruits of later years from *November Boughs*. Whether he is taking "A Backward Glance" over the road he has traveled; or poetizing in the old, familiar vein; or discoursing of the Bible, and Shakespeare, and Burns, and Tennyson; or giving reminiscences of Father Taylor, and Lincoln, and Elias Hicks; or detailing his memoranda of the war, he is in every instance supplying some hint or record which we should be sorry to lose. If we can thank the author for nothing else we can at least thank him for the candid revelation of his inmost thought, for the attempt, however ineffective, faithfully to portray the aspect of the universe as reflected from the mirror of his own soul.

New York *Tribune*, 9 December 1888, p. 14.

It seems probable that this volume will be the last published by Walt Whitman, and it is a gathering together of many fragments, mostly in prose. The verse consists of the short pieces under the head "Sands at Seventy," a little collection which fairly exhibits the poet's strength and weakness, and in proportions indicating the maintenance by him of a curious stability of quality. In the prose part of *November Boughs*, the opening paper entitled "A Backward Glance O'er Travel'd Roads" will be to many readers the most interesting, for the reason that it is a restatement of the considerations which, in his eyes, justify the peculiarities of this form and method. Here, too, is to be noted evidence of an unchanging point of view which in Whitman's case is more than the effect of advancing age—though that, too, is partly accountable for it. The poet himself ingenuously supposes that his departure from accepted methods and his effort to resurrect our archaic form of expression, together with his insistence upon a realism which is so exaggerated as to be unnatural, arise wholly from a radical spirit of reform. In this he has always been to a great extent mistaken, for his peculiarities are at bottom much more the results of a certain narrowness and want of both sympathy and elasticity than of originality and the zeitgeist.

The very fact that his strongest poems are those in which he displays his eccentric method least should have bred mistrust in him of the soundness of his theories. The fact that, while believing himself the poet of the people, he has never been accepted by the people as their poet, should have led him to question the infallibility of his inspiration, and above all have forced him to ask himself whether, after all, he saw the democratic movement of his time as it really was. But it is clearly enough shown in this, his last volume, that Walt Whitman's fundamental misapprehensions are ineradicable, and no stronger proof of this could be adduced than his declaration of belief that the future progress of the United States is to be largely spiritual, and the parallel implication that his poetry represents a step in this direction. Age, indeed, has sobered him considerably, and in his last poems we miss the defiant tone with which he was wont to reinforce his assaults upon all the conventionalities. There is, too, less crudeness and more melody in his verse, and less, be it said also, of that impetuous panoramic tendency which formerly converted some of his most ambitious pieces into the semblance of fantastic catalogues. His prose style is marked by some, but not all, of the defects which mar his poems, but it is generally clear enough in meaning, and at times vigorous, if never graceful.

"The Newest Books."
Book Buyer 5
(January 1889), 584–5.

Time only can determine the exact place which Walt Whitman is to occupy among the world's thinkers; and meanwhile it is instructive and interesting to learn from this volume something of the origin, growth, and purpose of his *Leaves of Grass*, the volume of verse around which so much controversy has raged. In the opening essay, entitled "A Backward Glance o'er Travel'd Roads," the author discusses this work with candor and

at length, explaining the motives that prompted it and the philosophy of life that it attempts to expound. The essay is certainly interesting and throws a great deal of valuable light upon the spirit that pervades the *Leaves of Grass*, as well as upon its peculiar form. The first quality which the author claims for this body of verse is its suggestiveness, and as regards the lines that have called forth the most criticism, he says "the work must stand or fall with them, as the human body and soul must remain as an entirety." The author's later verse makes the second division of the book, and is gathered under the title, "Sands at Seventy." The latter half of the book consists of papers of varying length on literary, personal, and other themes, much of it vigorous in expression and full of suggestiveness. A portrait of the author taken from life in his seventieth year is the frontispiece of the book, and is reproduced on the opposite page.

San Francisco *Chronicle*, 13 January 1889, p. 7.

The best things in *November Boughs*, by Walt Whitman, are a few sonnets and prose articles. The bulk of the book will prove tedious to all except his admirers, and nothing that he might write will daunt this loyal band. Those who have established the cult of any author always go to the extreme of hero-worship. This is seen in the Browning societies of England and this country, and it finds equal expression in the Whitman coterie. The very uncouthness of Whitman appears to give pleasure to these people, and they are never tired of praising what has been called his "heroic nudity." In the first article in this volume, written at 70, Whitman attempts again to justify *Leaves of Grass*. To use a phrase of Henry James, "he regards himself too seriously," and it makes one smile to read the frequent references to Goethe, Milton and other bards with whom Walt compares himself. What he says about his motive in writing this work which has called down on him so much orthodox condemnation is honestly and plainly stated, but we think he values the poem too highly and that it cannot in any sense be taken as the voice of a representative American of the latter half of this century. Whitman has always seemed very un-American in many of his traits, notably in his acceptance of gifts from friends and in his lack of ambition. That he has many genuine poetic ideas, even in his old age, is evident to any one who reads this collection of his later writings, but these ideas seldom find adequate expression. The mannerisms, both of his prose and his verse, check all perfect development, and one can only fancy what they might have been put in rhythmical verse or prose. The book has a good portrait of Whitman taken in his seventieth year.

[W. Harrison]. "Walt Whitman's *November Boughs*." *Critic* [New York] n.s. 11 (19 January 1889), 25.

Ordinarily, one associates 'November boughs' with flown birds, vanished scents, tattered foliage, skies of steel. Nature like a Greek athlete is stripped for the winter wrestle. Already there is a shimmer of frozen rivers in the distance, a ripple of soft reverberations from vanished summer echoing in memory only—even a prophecy of the boreal flare in the northern sky. The sap is down: the skeleton arms are up: all the infinite articulations of tree and leaf, the lovely geometries of interlacing branches, bare to the quick: everything is ready for the long, long sleep.

Is this true of Walt Whitman's book? In a sense; it is a preparation for the long sleep—a touching, *ave et vale*; apparently the author's greeting and salutation and—good bye. But in another sense it might just as well have been christened 'May-blossoms' or 'Leafy June,' or anything else suggestive of richness, luxuriance, juice and bloom, for all are there in springtime abundance, even a group of new poems—'Sands at Seventy,'—delectably sandwiched between the Introduction and 'Our Eminent Visitors' (republished from *The Critic*). Sap at seventy is seldom so affluent as it is in this striking volume, binding up the life-long thoughts of a revolutionist in verse, an evolutionist in belief; and it runs up and along these 'November boughs' with a great urge and palpitation that expands and freights them to bursting. One can fancy them all over tingling with red blood to their pith. Themistocles drank bull's blood and then died of it as a poison. Here there is no thought of poison or death except as the horizon of all things, the *garde-fou* that like a banister keeps men from tumbling over into annihilation. Succulence, marrow, poetic feeling course through the book exultantly.

All the author's essential things are here: beliefs, faiths, theories, practices; monologuing, apologuing; strong-hearted democracy; camaraderie and bonhomie; interspersed with wonderfully graphic tableaux of memoranda (if one may so speak) gathered and grouped from his hospital and Indian Bureau memories. So the prophets spake: in brief puffs and pulsations like these: Orphic utterances that expire in a sigh or a hexameter: moods of norn and sibyl run into speech as molten glass is run into forms; short, quick, pregnant flashes of reminiscence that expand into a picture or a pictured paragraph without a moment's hesitation. The most remarkable part of the book is its first heart-beat: 'A Backward Glance o'er Travel'd Roads,' which one might number as strophe α in a Greek ode, all the other essays and fragments being epodes, after-songs, echoes of the initial trumpet-blast. In this preface the author reaffirms himself, his poetic position, his heresies, his art theory, his democratic dreams: he stands or falls by *Leaves of Grass*, and he denounces with a Shakspeare-like malediction all who would disturb the 'bones' of his work or who would fig-leaf or expurgate it. Whether his theory of verse-form be true or false, it finds its justification in the times, which demand something new, and has at least a foundation in the noble unmetered verse of the Bible.

Along with this 'Everlasting Yea' or chapter of re-affirmation go little singing essays and excerpts in marvellously nervous prose labelled with this or that title: 'The Bible as Poetry'; 'Father Taylor and Oratory'; 'A Word about Tennyson' (originally published in this journal, together with 'What Lurks behind Shakspeare's Historical Plays,' 'Five Thousand Poems', and 'Yonnondio'). The soul looks out through these jewelled eyes: they are windows of the poet's soul looking toward Jerusalem. Father Taylor moved the 'good gray poet' as no orator had ever done before. In the essay on 'Slang in America,' there is food for the philologist. The War memoranda and glimpses of hospital life contained in them are Tacitean in brevity and picturesqueness, everywhere quick and alive with pathos and pity.

The woes of Andromache quail before these. It is this great fiery chasm of woe into which the artist looked for an instant, with all its Dantesque horror, and then, brooding over brotherhood, union, democracy, sang *Leaves of Grass*, 'My Captain,' 'Calamus,' and all that *me quoque* which forms the essential germ of the Whitman gospel: egotism not as an abstraction but as an intensely concrete, kindled, personal necessity of modern democratic verse asserting itself triumphantly. Other blossoms of these *November Boughs* are 'Abraham Lincoln,' which is as beautiful as an epigram of Simonides; 'New Orleans in 1848'; 'Last of the War Cases'; 'Elias Hicks'; and 'The Old Bowery.' The latter is a theatrical efflorescence: full of notes and historiettes of the magical times of the elder Booth, Charles Kean, Mario, Alboni, and the old Park Theatre: a 'bough' hung thick with leaf and fruit and clustering recollection.

On the whole, all these 'boughs' together make a very rich bouquet, tied at every twig with a love-knot for the reader, and full of the unction and eloquence of a most sweet personality.

[Oscar Wilde]. "The Gospel According to Walt Whitman." *Pall Mall Gazette*, 25 January 1889, p. 3.

"No one will get at my verses who insists upon viewing them as a literary performance, or as aiming mainly towards art and æstheticism. *Leaves of Grass* has been chiefly the outcropping of my own emotional and other personal nature—an attempt from first to last to put a *Person*, a human being (myself, in the latter half of the nineteenth century, in America) freely, fully and truly on record. I could not find any similar personal record in current literature that satisfied me." In these words Walt Whitman gives us the true attitude we should adopt towards his work, having indeed a much saner view of the value and meaning of that work than either his eloquent admirers or noisy detractors can boast of possessing. His last book, *November Boughs* as he calls it, published in the winter of the old man's life, reveals to us, not indeed a soul's tragedy, for its last note is one of joy and hope and noble and unshaken faith in all that is fine and worthy of such faith, but certainly the drama of a human soul, and puts on record with a simplicity that has in it both sweetness and strength the record of his spiritual development and of the aim and motive both of the manner and the matter of his work. His strange mode of expression is shown in these pages to have been the result of deliberate and self-conscious choice. The "barbaric yawp," which he sent over "the roofs of the world" so many years ago, and which wrung from Mr. Swinburne's lips such lofty panegyric in song and such loud clamorous censure in prose, appears here in what will be to many an entirely new light. For in his very rejection of art Walt Whitman is an artist. He tried to produce a certain effect by certain means and he succeeded. There is much method in what many have termed his madness, too much method indeed some may be tempted to fancy.

In the story of his life, as he tells it to us, we find him at the age of sixteen beginning a definite and philosophical study of literature:—

Summers and falls, I used to go off, sometimes for a week at a stretch, down in the country, or to Long Island's sea-shores—there in the presence of outdoor influences, I went over thoroughly the Old and New Testaments, and absorb'd (probably to better advantage for me than in any library or indoor room—it makes such difference *where* you read) Shakspere, Ossian, the best translated versions I could get of Homer, Æschylus, Sophokles, the old German Nibelungen, the ancient Hindoo poems, and one or two other masterpieces, Dante's among them. As it happen'd I read the latter mostly in an old wood. The Iliad I read first thoroughly on the peninsula of Orient, north-east end of Long Island, in a sheltered hollow of rocks and sand, with the sea on each side. (I have wondered since why I was not overwhelmed by those mighty masters. Likely because I read them, as described, in the full presence of Nature, under the sun, with the far-spreading landscapes and vistas, or the sea rolling in.)

Edgar Allan Poe's amusing bit of dogmatism that, for our occasions and for our day, there can be no such thing as a long poem, fascinated him: "The same thought had been haunting my mind before," he says, "but Poe's argument, though short, work'd the sum out and proved it to me:" and the English translation of the Bible seems to have suggested to him the possibility of a poetic form which while retaining the spirit of poetry would still be free from the trammels of rhyme and of a definite metrical system. Having thus to a certain degree settled upon what one might call the *technique* of Whitmanism, he began to brood upon the nature of that spirit that was to give life to the strange form. The central point of the poetry of the future seemed to him to be necessarily "an identical body and soul," a personality in fact, which personality

319

he tells us frankly, "after many considerations and ponderings I deliberately settled should be myself." However for the true creation and revealing of this personality, at first only dimly felt, a new stimulus was needed. This came from the Civil War. After describing the many dreams and passions of his boyhood and early manhood he goes on to say:—

These, however, and much more might have gone on and come to naught (almost positively would have come to naught) if a sudden, vast, terrible, direct and indirect stimulus for new and national declamatory expression had not been given to me. It is certain, I say, that, although I had made a start before, only from the occurrence of the Secession War, and what it showed me as by flashes of lightning, with the emotional depths it sounded and arous'd (of course, I don't mean in my own heart only, I saw it just as plainly in others, in millions) that only from the strong flare and provocation of that war's sights and scenes the final reasons-for-being of an autochthonic and passionate song definitely came forth. I went down to the war-fields of Virginia, lived thenceforward in camp, saw great battles and the days and nights afterwards—partook of all the fluctuations, gloom, despair, hopes again aroused, courage evoked—death readily risked—the *cause* too—along and filling those agonistic and lurid following years, the real parturition years of the henceforth homogeneous Union. Without those three or four years and the experiences they gave, "Leaves of Grass" would not now be existing.

Having thus obtained the necessary stimulus for the quickening and awakening of the personal self, some day to be endowed with universality, he sought to find new notes of song, and passing beyond the mere passion for expression— he aimed at "Suggestiveness" first. "I round and finish little, if anything; and could not, consistently with my scheme. The reader will have his or her part to do, just as much as I have had mine. I seek less to state or display any theme of thought, and more to bring you, reader, into the atmosphere of the theme or thought—there to pursue your own flight." Another "impetus word" is Comradeship, and other "word-signs" are Good Cheer, Content, and Hope. Individuality, especially, he sought for:—

I have allowed the stress of my poems from beginning to end to bear upon American individuality and assist it— not only because that is a great lesson in Nature, amid all her generalizing laws, but as a counterpoise to the levelling tendencies of Democracy—and for other reasons. Defiant of ostensible literary and other conventions, I avowedly chant "the great pride of a man in himself," and permit it to be more or less a *motif* of nearly all my verse. I think this pride indispensable to an American. I think it not inconsistent with obedience, humility, deference, and self-questioning.

A new theme also was to be found in the relation of the sexes, conceived in a natural, simple, and healthy form, and he protests against poor Mr. William Rossetti's attempt to Bowdlerize and expurgate his song.

From another point of view "Leaves of Grass" is avowedly the song of Sex, and Amativeness, and even Animality— though meanings that do not usually go with these words are behind all, and will duly emerge; and all are sought

320

to be lifted into a different light and atmosphere. Of this feature intentionally palpable in a few lines, I shall only say the espousing principle of those lines so gives breath to my whole scheme that the bulk of the pieces might as well have been left unwritten were those lines omitted. . . . Universal as are certain facts and symptoms of communities there is nothing so rare in modern conventions and poetry as their normal recognizance. Literature is always calling in the doctor for consultation and confession, and always giving evasions and swathing suppressions in place of that "heroic nudity" on which only a genuine diagnosis can be built. And in respect to editions of "Leaves of Grass" in time to come (if there should be such) I take occasion now to confirm those lines with the settled convictions and deliberate renewals of thirty years, and to hereby prohibit, as far as mine can do so, any elision of them.

But beyond all these notes and moods and motives is the lofty spirit of a grand and free acceptance of all things that are worthy of existence. "I desired," he says, "to formulate a poem whose every thought or fact should indirectly or directly be or connive at an implicit belief in the wisdom, health, mystery, or beauty of every process, every concrete object, every human or other existence, not only consider'd from the point of view of all, but of each." His two final utterances are that really great poetry is always the result of a national spirit, and not the privilege of a polished and select few; and that the sweetest and strongest songs yet remain to be sung.

Such are the views contained in the opening essay, "A Backward Glance o'er Travel'd Roads," as he calls it: but there are many other essays in this fascinating

volume, some on poets such as Burns and Lord Tennyson, for whom Walt Whitman has a profound admiration: some on old actors and singers, the elder Booth, Forrest, Alboni, and Mario being his special favourites: others on the native Indians, on the Spanish element in American nationality, on Western slang, on the poetry of the Bible, and on Abraham Lincoln. But Walt Whitman is at his best when he is analyzing his own work, and making schemes for the poetry of the future. Literature to him has a distinctly social aim. He seeks to build up the masses by "building up grand individuals." And yet literature itself must be preceded by noble forms of life. "The best literature is always the result of something far greater than itself—not the hero but the portrait of the hero. Before there can be recorded history or poem there must be the transaction." Certainly in Walt Whitman's views there is a largeness of vision, a healthy sanity, and a fine ethical purpose. He is not to be placed with the professional *littérateurs* of his country, Boston novelists, New York poets, and the like. He stands apart, and the chief value of his work is in its prophecy not in its performance. He has begun a prelude to larger themes. He is the herald to a new era. As a man he is the precursor of a fresh type. He is a factor in the heroic and spiritual evolution of the human being. If Poetry has passed him by, Philosophy will take note of him.

"Books and Authors." London *Echo*, 26 January 1889, p. 1.

One other book from America. Walt Whitman's *November Boughs*, a story of the poet's life, has been published by Mr. Gardner, of Paternoster-row. Written in the poet's declining years, it is imbued with the sanguine, generous faith in man which characterised his youth. In which respect he differs considerably from his English brother poet—who should have been done with Amy's cousin where he left him nearly half a century before. These *November Boughs* are a fascinating and most suggestive record of the history of a mind—for of external effect and event there is but little, save the poet's experiences in the great Civil War, the drama of which it was that first made Whitman poetically vocal. In his talk about his reading habits when a boy—reading his Shakespeare, Homer, Dante, Bible—in scenes appropriate to them, there are some delightful passages and expressions that haunt the memory—as when he tells us how he studied Dante in "an old wood." The subject is by far too complex for treatment in a paragraph; and we can only say that orthodox critics may, quite possibly, reconsider their judgment of him after they have read the poet's own explanation of how his choice of theme determined the form of expression—justified his rejection of the old-world restraints of rhyme and metre. You may or may not call Whitman a poet—the poet of Democracy—but, if not a poet, he is a prophet of the new time.

[William Dean Howells]. "Editor's Study." *Harper's New Monthly Magazine* 78 (February 1889), 488.

Mr. Walt Whitman calls his latest book *November Boughs*, and in more ways than one it testifies and it appeals beyond the letter to the reader's interest. For the poet the long fight is over; he rests his cause with what he has done; and we think no one now would like to consider the result without respect, without deference, even if one cannot approach it with entire submission. It is time, certainly, while such a poet is still with us, to own that his literary intention was as generous as his spirit was bold, and that if he has not accomplished all he intended, he has been a force that is by no means spent. Apart from the social import of his first book ("without yielding an inch, the working-man and working-woman were to be in my pages from first to last"), he aimed in it at the emancipation of poetry from what he felt to be the trammels of rhyme and metre. He did not achieve this; but he produced a new kind in literature, which we may or may not allow to be poetry, but which we cannot deny is something eloquent, suggestive, moving, with a lawless, formless beauty of its own. He dealt literary conventionality one of those blows which eventually show as internal injuries, whatever the immediate effect seems to be. He made it possible for poetry hereafter to be more direct and natural than hitherto; the hearing which he has braved nearly half a century of contumely and mockery to win would now be granted on very different terms to a man of his greatness. This is always the way; and it is always the way that the reformer (perhaps in helpless confession of the weakness he shares with all humankind) champions some error which seems as dear to him as the truth he was born to proclaim. Walt Whitman was not the first to observe that we are all naked under our clothes, but he was one of the greatest, if not the first, to preach a gospel of nudity; not as one of his Quaker ancestry might have done for a witness against the spiritual nakedness of his hearers, but in celebration of the five senses and their equal origin with the three virtues of which the greatest is charity. His offence, if rank, is quantitatively small, a few lines at most; and it is one which the judicious pencil of the editor will some day remove for him, though for the present he "takes occasion to confirm those lines with the settled convictions and deliberate renewals of thirty years." We hope for that day, not only because it will give to all a kind in poetry which none can afford to ignore, and which his cherished lines bar to most of those who read most in our time and country, but because we think the five senses do not need any celebration. In that duality which every thoughtful person must have noticed composes him, we believe the universal experience is that the beast half from first to last is fully able to take care of itself. But it is a vast subject, and, as the poet says, "it does not stand by itself; the vitality of it is altogether in its relations, bearings, significance." In the mean while we can assure the reader that these *November Boughs* are as innocent as so many sprays of apple blossom, and that he may take the book home without misgiving.

We think he will find in reading it that the prose passages are, some of them, more poetic than the most poetic of the rhythmical passages. "Some War Memoranda," and "The Last of the War Cases"—notes made twenty-five years ago—are alive with a simple pathos and instinct with a love of truth which recall the best new Russian work, and which make the poet's psalms seem vague and thin as wandering smoke in comparison. Yet these have the beauty of undulant, sinuous, desultory smoke forms, and they sometimes take the light with a response of such color as dwells in autumn sunsets. The book is well named *November Boughs*: it is meditative and reminiscent,

with a sober fragrance in it like the scent of fallen leaves in woods where the leaves that still linger overhead,

"Or few, or none, do shake against the cold— Bare ruined choirs where late the sweet birds sang."

It is the hymn of the runner resting after the race, and much the same as he chants always, whether the race has been lost or won.

[William S. Walsh]. "Book Talk." *Lippincott's Monthly Magazine* 43 (March 1889), 445.

Here is Walt Whitman's *November Boughs*, a collection of pieces in prose and verse. To the people who live in the appearances of things, to the people who love shams and conventions, to the people who worship the isms which the past has bequeathed, Whitman has no message to convey. He does not live in the trim little parterre which human genius has reduced to order, he is a portion of the great unconquered chaos that surrounds us here, there, and everywhere. His voice comes far away from the distance. You have to pause to listen, and are not always sure you have heard aright, but somehow you feel that the very Distance is the truest part of yourself, and that the far-off voice reveals to you the deeps of your own soul. The things you have vaguely felt are here uttered, and then for the first time perhaps you recognize that you have felt them. Whitman himself tells us in his excellent preliminary essay "A Backward Glance o'er Travelled Roads" that the word he would put primarily for the description of his *Leaves of Grass* is the word Suggestiveness. "I round and finish little, if anything; and could not, consistently with my scheme. The reader will always have his or her part to do, just as much as I have had mine. I seek less to state or display any theme or thought, and more to bring you, reader, into the atmosphere of the theme or thought,—there to pursue your own flight." But the most characteristic and illuminating passage in this essay is where Whitman tells us, "Ever since what might be call'd thought, or the budding of thought, fairly began in my youthful mind, I had had a desire to attempt some worthy record of that entire faith and acceptance ('to justify the ways of God to man' is Milton's well-known and ambitious phrase) which is the foundation of moral America. I felt it all as positively then in my young days as I do now in my old ones; to formulate a poem whose every thought or fact should directly or indirectly be or connive at an implicit belief in the wisdom, health, mystery, beauty of every process, every concrete object, every human or other existence, not only consider'd from the point of view of all, but of each. While I can not understand it or argue it out, I fully believe in a clue and purpose in Nature, entire and several; and that invisible spiritual results, just as real and definite as the visible, eventuate all concrete life and all materialism, through Time. My book ought to emanate buoyancy and gladness legitimately enough, for it was grown out of those elements, and has been the comfort of my life since it was originally commenced."

"*November Boughs.*" *Saturday Review* 67 (2 March 1889), 260–1.

In this small volume, by a man whose name has been the occasion of as much pen-and-ink fighting as most names in the last half of the nineteenth century, there is extremely little contentious matter. Most of it is prose—to anticipate the rather superfluous and stale jibes on the subject, let us say intentional prose—and the small section which is not contains nothing aggressive. Most of it is, again, a mere collection of the casual articles for newspapers and magazines by which the author is known to eke out his means of subsistence. Only in the first article, perhaps, which is a kind of review or reflection upon his own literary history, does Walt Whitman make much addition to his characteristic work; and this is not in the least combative. On the contrary, it seems to us to be singularly modest—not at all with the sham modesty which a vain old man who is proud of what he has done sometimes affects. Mr. Whitman says, in a manner which, if irony were not a mode rather foreign to him, we should consider ironical, that "William O'Connor and Dr. Bucke are much more peremptory" in estimating his value than he is. We should be very much surprised if they were not. William O'Connor and Dr. Bucke (we use these names with all apologies to the eminent possessors, of whom we know very little, as types) usually *are* "more peremptory," and may usually be neglected. We have no concern with William O'Connor and Dr. Bucke. If we have concern with Mr. Whitman (he would not like to be called Mr., but he has done what he likes himself for the most part, and we shall imitate him), it is less with this particular little volume than with his whole work. That work, or rather the important part of it—for little that has appeared since makes much difference—was reviewed in the earliest days of the *Saturday Review* by a very eminent hand. We shall not say that it was unjustly reviewed, nor do we think so. From certain points of view Walt Whitman deliberately laid himself open to what he has abundantly received—the process technically known as "slating." If a man will, by no means without truth, announce his completed intention of emitting a "barbaric yawp," he must reckon with the expression of the sentiments of persons who do not like barbaric yawps. If he will, in season and out of season, praise an irrational variety of polity, which has never yet been tried with real success in any age of the world's history, he must lay his account with harsh answers from people who utterly decline to sacrifice the freedom of forty-nine wise men to the tyranny of fifty-one fools. If he chooses to dilate on subjects which the world usually keeps *sub rosa*, for many wise reasons—not the least wise being that they lose half their charm and interest if the Rose presides not at the discussion of them—here, too, he must take the consequences. If, desiring to be new, he rushes to cheap and obvious ways of being, not new, but merely novel, employs a grotesque vocabulary, and discards the ornaments of rhyme and of recognized verse, he cannot eat the cake of eccentricity and yet have that of classic recognition. And we conceive that a critic has a right, if he likes, to visit all these provoked consequences on the provoker's head, whatever William O'Connor and Dr. Bucke may say. We must repeat that it does not in the least matter what they do say. The whole tale of this new "Backward Glance o'er

Travel'd Roads" amounts to an acknowledgment by Walt Whitman himself, not that his critics were right—very far from that—but that he had nothing else to expect. Of course he reiterates—not vehemently, as of old, but vigorously enough—his standard doctrines that democratic America wants something newer and better than the old poetry, and that his poetry is not an achievement (William O'Connor and Dr. Bucke say that), but an experiment in the way of giving a new form to democratic America. There are even faint glimpses (though he seems to recoil from them with horror, and says "Great is democratic America!" as his new Om-mani-padmi-hom, many times to wash himself clean of the fact of sin) that "modern science and democracy appear to be eliminating something that gives the last majesty to man."

Now it seems to us that Walt Whitman's unfavourable critics hitherto have rather failed to distinguish between the faults which false premises to start from and a misconceived aim to tend to have produced in him on the one side, and the faculties, and even to a certain extent the accomplishments as a poet, which in spite of all these evil influences he has displayed on the other. It is very rare, indeed, to find an admirer of his who does not sympathize with some, at least, of his principles; it is almost an unknown thing to find a critic who dislikes him, and whose dislike is not based either on dislike of his political, religious, and moral standpoints, or else on an unwillingness to admit the "barbaric yawp" because there is so much yawp in it, and it is so barbaric. Yet this is certainly wrong, nor is it quite universal. We, for instance, who write here to-day willingly make a present of almost every general principle of his to the enemy to be given up to chaos and old night. So far is it from being the case that the United States of America present a higher type of civilization and of humanity, that we should count the grey New Yorker rather lower than the European child. Democracy, instead of being a great and beautiful goddess, is a dirty, half-witted trull. Instead of its being a good thing to do as Whitman has tried to do, to put a person fully, freely, and truly on record, the first and the last rule of the poet should be, not indeed to work impersonally, but to pass every personal emotion through the sieve of the universal, to "disrealize" everything, to bring it into union with the whole. We hold that, whether it is desirable or not to say to "the perfect girl who understands you" the things that Whitman says, it is infinitely better not to shout such conversation on the housetops; that to talk about "me imperturbe" is silly, not impressive; that rhythmical staves of prose are infinitely more difficult, as well as much more rarely effective, than the common rhyme-assisted measures, and so forth. All this is granted by us, or rather spontaneously asserted, and if William O'Connor and Dr. Bucke do not like it, we cannot help that. And then we face round, and ask simply whether this is not poetry?—

> Come, lovely and soothing Death,
> Undulate round the world, serenely
>   arriving, arriving,
> In the day, in the night, to all, to
>   each,
> Sooner or later, delicate Death.
>
> Praised be the fathomless universe,
> For life and joy, and for objects and
>   knowledge curious;
> And for love, sweet love—but praise!
>   praise! praise!
> For the sure-enwinding arms of cool-
>   enfolding Death.
>
> Dark Mother! always gliding near,
>   with soft feet,
> Have none chanted for thee a chant

> of fullest welcome?
> Then I chant it for thee—I glorify
>   thee above all;
> I bring thee a song that when thou
>   must indeed come, come
>   unfalteringly.
>
> Approach, strong Deliveress!
> When it is so—when thou hast taken
>   them, I joyously sing the dead,
> Lost in the loving floating ocean of
>   thee,
> Laved in the flood of thy bliss, O
>   Death!
>
> From me to thee glad serenades,
> Dances for thee I propose, saluting
>   thee—adornments and feastings for
>   thee;
> And the sights of the open landscape,
>   and the high-spread sky, are fitting,
> And life, and the fields, and the huge
>   and thoughtful night.
>
> The night, in silence, under many a
>   star;
> The ocean shore, and the husky
>   whispering wave whose voice I
>   know;
> And the soul turning to thee, O vast
>   and well-veiled Death!
> And the body gratefully nestling close
>   to thee.
>
> Over the tree-tops I float thee a song!
> Over the rising and sinking waves—
>   over the myriad fields and the
>   prairies wide:
> Over the dense-packed cities all, and
>   the teeming wharves and ways,
> I float this carol with joy, with joy to
>   thee, O Death!

This exquisite poem—for we do not hesitate to call it so—was indeed not in the original *Leaves of Grass*, as it appeared more than thirty years ago, nor were the "Sea-shore Memories," the next best thing that Whitman has done. But the quality, less conspicuously present and alloyed with much more base matter, is almost everywhere. That the alloy is almost everywhere, also, is perfectly true. But, when we are asked whether soil is auriferous or not, we do not pause to inquire whether it is nothing but auriferous. It may be annoying enough to come, after such a passage, upon such another as this:—"Thumb extended, finger uplifted, apron, cape, gloves, strap, wet-weather clothes, whip carefully chosen, boss, spotter, starter, hostler, somebody loafing on you, you loafing on somebody, headway, man before and man behind, good day's work, bad day's work, pet stock, mean stock, first out, last out, turning in at night." But for what was the divine art of skipping created, if a reader is not able to dodge things like this, and to go straight to others which the theory of poetry (and of common sense) will allow?

We cannot, for our part, conceive any theory of poetry which shall shut out stuff such as the Death Carol, because it is not in any of "the four-and-twenty measures," as Welsh critics say, or because it finds itself in the company of unwise laudations of a (to speak mildly) imperfect state of politics and manners, unwise excursions into *tacenda*, unwise catalogues of names and trades, and other unwisdoms not a few.

No; let us, if it be ours to lecture on poetry, hold up Walt Whitman as much as any one pleases for an awful example of the fate that waits, and justly waits, on those who think (idle souls!) that there is such a thing as progress in poetry, and that because you have steam-engines and other things which Solomon and Sappho had not, you may, nay must, neglect the lessons of Sappho and Solomon. But let us none the less confess that this strayed reveller, this dubiously well-bred truant in poetry, is a poet still, and one of the remarkably few poets that his own country has produced.

William Morton Payne. "Recent Books of Poetry." *Dial* [Chicago] 9 (April 1889), 323–4.

November Boughs is a title due to the same sense of literary fitness as that which inspired the naming of Landor's "Dry Sticks" and "The Last Fruit off an Old Tree." Indeed, paradoxical as the statement may seem, a sense of fitness is the predominant impression remaining from the study of Whitman's work, and this in spite of its indefensible rhythmic and verbal vagaries. It is the fitness, in the large sense, of thought and language to the character and mood of the writer. "Unstopp'd and unwarp'd by any influence outside the soul within me, I have had my say entirely my own way, and put it unerringly on record"—this is what Whitman tells us in the "Backward Glance o'er Travel'd Roads" which prefaces the new volume. The absolute honesty of his work, coupled with the genius for style which it displays, ensure for it both permanence of influence and the respectful consideration of future years. Enlarge upon its faults as we may, the work still has rare qualities of power and beauty which it takes no extended search to discover. Let us quote the two poems entitled "Halcyon Days" and "Queries to my Seventieth Year." He must be dull of soul who has no sense of the beauty of the one or the power of the other.

"Not from successful love alone,
　　Nor wealth, nor honor'd middle
　　　age, nor victories of politics or
　　　war;
　　But as life wanes, and all the

turbulent passions calm,
As gorgeous, vapory, silent hues
  cover the evening sky,
As softness, fulness, rest, suffuse the
  frame, like fresher, balmier air,
As the days take on a mellower
  light, and the apple at last hangs
  really finish'd and indolent-ripe
  on the tree,
Then for the teeming quietest,
  happiest days of all!
The brooding and blissful halcyon
  days."

It is the reverse of the shield that comes
to view in the other poem:

"Approaching, nearing, curious,
Thou dim, uncertain spectre—
  bringest thou life or death?
Strength, weakness, blindness, more
  paralysis and heavier?
Or placid skies and sun? Wilt stir
  the waters yet?
Or haply cut me short for good? Or
  leave me here as now,
Dull, parrot-like and old, with
  crack'd voice harping,
  screeching?"

The poems in this volume fill but a score
of pages, but every page has its charm.
Upon one we find this faultless epigram
on "The Bravest Soldiers":

"Brave, brave were the soldiers (high
  named to-day) who lived through
  the fight;
But the bravest press'd to the front
  and fell, unnamed, unknown."

Upon another we are greeted with this
word for Lincoln's birthday:

"To-day, from each and all, a breath
  of prayer—a pulse of thought,
To memory of Him—to birth of
  Him."

Still another gives us this picture of the
resurrection that comes with the spring-
tide:

"Then shalt perceive the simple
  shows, the delicate miracles of
  earth,
Dandelion, clover, the emerald grass,
  the early scents and flowers,
The arbutus under foot, the willow's
  yellow-green, the blossoming
  plum and cherry;
With these the robin, lark, and
  thrush, singing their songs—the
  flitting bluebird;
For such the scenes the annual play
  brings on."

We find verses like these, scattered in rich
profusion through the songs:

"Possess'd by some strange spirit of
  fire."
"With husky-haughty lips, O sea!
  Where day and night I wend thy
  surf-beat shore."
"Old age land-lock'd within its
  winter bay."
"Isle of the salty shore, and breeze,
  and brine."

It is the very magic of style that informs these lines. For the rest, these
"Sands at Seventy" contain no word that
is objectionable as certain passages of the
Leaves of Grass were objectionable. Nor
do we find in them the violent distortion of speech—the "barbaric yawp,"—
or the endless catalogues of attributes
and things which made the poet's earlier
work æsthetically offensive. Of the prose
work which makes up the greater part of
the volume, this is not the place to speak
at length, and we will only remark that
much of it seems to us as suggestive and
beautiful as the poetry. The writer takes
occasion, in his preface, to justify the

328

passages in the *Leaves of Grass* which have been the subject of so much discussion, and "to confirm these lines with the settled convictions and deliberate renewals of thirty years."

Scottish Review 14 (July 1889), 212–13.

In this volume the author has gathered together a number of pieces both in prose and verse, written at different periods extending over a considerable number of years. The topics are varied, but chiefly of a literary, or biographical kind. There are poems entitled 'Sands at Seventy,' and others with the leading 'Fancies at Navesink.' Then there are prose essays, some of them covering little more than a page, and others extending to several pages on such topics Our Eminent Visitors, The Bible as Poetry, Burns as Poet and Person, Tennyson, Shakespeare, English Books, Slang in America, Abraham Lincoln, and a number of War Memoranda. But the most interesting as well as the most important of the Essays is the one with which the volume opens, 'A Backward Glance o'er Travell'd Roads.' In this the author reviews himself and his work, and notwithstanding all that has been said against his poetical beliefs and methods, reiterates his persuasion of their truth and appeals from the present to the future. Here also he repeats his demand that America should possess a literature peculiarly and exclusively its own, saying, 'No law or people or circumstances ever existed so needing a race of singers and poems differing from all others, and rigidly their own as the land and people and circumstances of our United States.' At the same time he restates his belief that science instead of superseding poetry will only open out fresh and more extensive fields to which the poetic imagination must emigrate. 'Whatever,' he remarks, 'may have been the case in years gone by, the true use for the imaginative faculty of modern times is to give ultimate vivification to facts, to science, and to common lives, endowing them with the glows and glories and final illustriousness which belong to every real thing, and to real things only.' The papers on Shakespeare and Burns are suggestive, but there is little new in them. On such subjects much that is new can scarcely be expected from anyone.

Checklist of Additional Reviews

"Books and Authors," New York *Home Journal*, 24 October 1888, p. 2.
American 17 (24 November 1888), 91.

COMPLETE POEMS & PROSE OF WALT WHITMAN (1888)

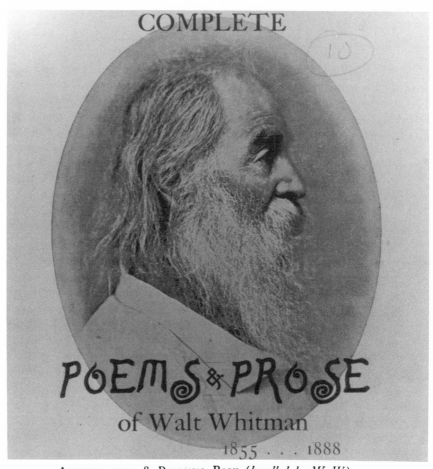

COMPLETE

POEMS & PROSE
of Walt Whitman
1855 . . . 1888

AUTHENTICATED & PERSONAL BOOK (*handled by W. W.*) . . .
Portraits from Life . . . Autograph.

The complete edition of Walt Whitman's
works, just issued by the poet himself in
one volume, is a book to be prized by the
bibliophile as well as treasured by Whitman's friends. The plates of the three uniform volumes comprising Whitman's writings are used, but with the broad margins
and finer paper of the uncut sheets, the
guise seems an entirely new one. The text
has received a final revision, there is the
charm of certain additions, there are several portraits of Whitman ranging from
his early prime to one taken in his 70th
year, and there is the great value of the
direct association of the poet's personality, as guaranteed in the words of the
handsome title page, with its fine profile
reproduced from a photograph: *Complete Poems and Prose of Walt Whitman.
1855–1888. Authenticated and Personal
Book (Handled by W. W.) Portraits from
Life. Autograph.* On the first fly leaf
of the copy before the writer are the
words, written in the poet's familiar hand:
"S—— B——, from his friend, the author, Walt Whitman, with affection and
memories.—Dec. 21, 1888." The hand-
writing is strikingly firm and bold, showing that the paralysis that afflicts the author has not affected his firm hand.

The cover is a plain one, with marbled
sides and back of dark olive, with the
title pasted on in plain white paper: *Walt
Whitman, Complete Poems and Prose—
Leaves of Grass, Specimen Days and
Collect, November Boughs with Sands at
Seventy, Annex to L. of G.—Portraits*

from Life, and Autograph Ed'n 1888–9.
Altogether, the volume combines the
homely democratic simplicity associated
with Whitman's name with the essential
features of a handsome book—a worthy
garment for the great thoughts presented.
The note at the end, written for this edition on Nov. 13, 1888, states the author's
motives for publishing it, and may be
called

HIS LITERARY VALEDICTORY

As I conclude—and (to get typographical correctness,) after running
my eyes diligently through the three
big divisions of the preceding volume—the interrogative wonder-fancy
rises in me whether (if it be not too
arrogant to even state it), the 33 years
of my current time, 1855–1888, with
their aggregate of our new world doings and people, have not, indeed, created and formulated the foregoing
leaves—forcing their utterance as the
pages stand—coming actually from
the direct urge and developments of
those years, and not from any individual epic or lyrical attempts whatever, or from my pen or voice, or any
body's special voice. Out of that sup-
position the book might be considered
an autochthonic record, and expression, fully rendered, of and out of
these 30 to 35 years—of the soul and
evolution of America—and, of course,
by reflection, not ours only, but more
or less of the common people of the
world. Seems to me I may dare to
claim a deep native tap root for the
book, too, in some sort. I came on the
stage too late for personally knowing
much of even the lingering revolutionary worthies—the men of '76. Yet, as
a little boy, I have been pressed tightly
and lovingly to the breast of Lafayette
(Brooklyn, 1825), and have talked
with old Aaron Burr, and also with

those who knew Washington and his surroundings, and with original Jeffersonians, and more than one very old soldier and sailor. And in my own day and maturity, my eyes have seen and ears heard, Lincoln, Grant and Emerson, and my hands have been grasped by their hands. Though in a different field and range from most of theirs, I give the foregoing pages as perfectly legitimate, resultant, evolutionary and consistent with them. If these lines should ever reach some reader of a far-off future age, let him take them as a missive sent from Abraham Lincoln's fateful age. Repeating, parrot-like, what in the preceding divisions has been already said, and must serve as a great reason why of this whole book—first, that the main part about pronounced events and shows (poems and persons, also) is the point of view from which they are viewed and estimated: and second, that I cannot let my momentous, stormy, peculiar era of peace and war, these states, these years, slip away without arresting some of its specimen events—even its vital breaths—to be portrayed and inscribed from out of the midst of it, from its own days and nights—not so much in themselves (statistically and descriptively our times are copiously noted and memorandized with an industrial zeal), but to give from them here their flame-like results in imaginative and spiritual suggestiveness, as they present themselves to me, at any rate, from the point of view alluded to.

Then a few additional words yet to this hurried farewell note. In another sense (the warp crossing the woof and knitted in) the book is probably a sort of autobiography, an element I have not attempted especially to restrain or erase. As alluded to at the beginning, I had about got the volume well started by the printers, when a sixth recurrent attack of my war paralysis fell upon me. It has proved the most serious and continued of the whole. I am now uttering

"NOVEMBER BOUGHS"

and printing this book in my 70th year. To get out the collection—mainly the born results of health, flush life, buoyancy and happy outdoor volition—and to prepare the *Boughs* have beguiled my invalid months the past summer and fall. ('Are we to be beaten down in our old age?' says one white-haired old fellow remonstratingly to another in a budget of letters I read last night.) Then I wanted to leave something markedly personal. I have put my name with pen and ink with my own hand in the present volume. And from engraved or photographed portraits, taken from life, I have selected some, of different stages, which please me best, (or at any rate displease me least), and bequeath them at a venture to you, reader, with my love. W. W., Nov. 13, 1888.

Leaves of Grass has the following prefatory verses in this volume:

Come, said my soul,
Such verses for my body let us write
    (for we are one),
That should I after death invisibly
    return,
Or, long, long hence, in other
    spheres,
There to some group of mates the
    chants resuming,
(Tallying earth's soil, trees, winds,
    tumultuous waves.)
Ever with pleased smile I may keep
    on.
Ever and ever yet the verses

owning—as, first, I here and now,
Singing for soul and body, set to
   them my name,
                          Walt Whitman.

The second book, *Specimen Days and
Collect*, contains two things which alone
would make it invaluable, the preface to
the first issue of *Leaves of Grass*, that of
1855, and the great essay, "Democratic
Vistas." Since Whitman included verse only
in the final form of *Leaves of Grass* the
original preface is given in the prose
book. It is known as a masterpiece of composition in the grand style. Its thoughts
borne free on the wings of a spontaneous
rhythm. Many of its passages will be recognized as having been worked over into
later poems. "Democratic Vistas" is one
of the greatest essays ever written concerning America. Whitman speaks here as
a seer. Probably no one has ever taken a
more comprehensive, far-seeing national
view. It is a paper for statesmen in the
highest sense. With his healthy, strong,
optimistic mind, he looks far ahead through
the centuries and perceives the grand destiny of our country, but this does not
make him ignore the shadows of the picture, and the very clearness of his prophetic vision shows to him, also, the
plainer the perils that beset the road to
the goal, as in these words of warning:
"Shift and turn the combinations of the
statement as we may, the problem of the
future of America is, in certain respects,
as dark as it is vast. Pride, competition,
segregation, vicious willfulness, and license beyond example, brood already
upon us. Unwieldy and immense, who
shall hold in behemoth, who bridle levia-
than? Flaunt it as we choose, athwart
and over the roads of our progress loom
huge uncertainty, and dreadful, threaten-
ing gloom. It is useless to deny it: Democracy grows rankly up the thickest, noxious,
deadliest plants and fruits of all—brings

worse and worse invaders—needs newer,
larger, stronger, keener compensations and
compellers."

November Boughs begins with a review
of the poet's career, and works from
the standpoint of the journey's close: "A
Backward Glance O'er Travel'd Roads."
There is humility and modesty in its tone,
as well as hopefulness, assertion and a
brave, serene confidence. Characterizing
his poems, he thus prescribes his purpose
and his method: "The word I myself put
primarily for the description of them
as they stand at last is the word suggestiveness. I round and finish little, if anything, and could not consistently with
my scheme. The reader will always have
his or her part to do, just as much as I
have had mine. I seek less to state or display any theme or thought, and more to
bring you, reader, into the atmosphere
of the theme or thought, there to pursue your own flight. Another impetus
word is comradeship as for all lands, and
in a more commanding and acknowledged sense than hitherto. Other word
signs would be good cheer, content and
hope. The chief trait of any given poet is
always the spirit he brings to the observation of humanity and nature, the mood
out of which he contemplates his subjects. [. . .] Universal as are certain facts
and symptoms of communities or individuals at all times, there is nothing so
rare in modern conventions and poetry
as their normal recognizance. Literature
is always calling in the doctor for consultation and confession, and always giving evasions and swathing suppressions
in place of that 'heroic nudity' on which
only a genuine diagnosis of serious cases
can be built. And in respect to editors of
Leaves of Grass in time to come (if there
should be such) I take occasion now to
confirm these lines with the settled convictions and deliberate renewals of 30

years, and to hereby prohibit, as far as word of mine can do so, any elision of them."

He continued with the following reverent words: "Then still a purpose inclosing all, and over and beneath all. Ever since what might be called thought, or the budding of thought, fairly began in my youthful mind, I had had a desire to attempt some worthy record of that entire faith and acceptance ('to justify the ways of God to man' is Milton's well known and ambitious phrase) which is the foundation of moral America. I felt it all as positively then in my young days as I do now in my old ones: to formulate a poem whose every thought or fact should directly or indirectly be or connive at an implicit belief in the wisdom, health, mystery, beauty of every process, every concrete object, every human or other existence, not only considered from the point of view of all, but of each. While I cannot understand it or argue it out, I fully believe in a clew and purpose in nature, entire and several; and that invisible spiritual results, just as real and definite as the visible, eventuate all concrete life and all materialism, through time. My book ought to emanate buoyance and gladness legitimately enough, for it was grown out of those elements, and has been the comfort of my life since it was originally commenced." He ends with the words: "In the free evening of my day, I give to you, reader, the foregoing garrulous talk, thoughts, reminiscences,

As idly drifting down the ebb,
Such ripples, half-caught voices echo
    from the shore.

"Concluding with two items for the imaginative genius of the West when it worthily rises—First, what Herder taught to the young Goethe, that really great poetry is always (like the Homeric or Biblical canticles) the result of a national spirit, and not the privilege of a polished and select few. Second, that the strongest and sweetest songs yet remain to be sung."

The latest poems, given under the title of "Sands at Seventy" are like the voice of an old friend whose tones we have learned to love for the sake of the words they have conveyed, the thoughts they have clothed. So ever after, whatever the words be, the tones have a welcome sound. It is so with all old poets; their message has been spoken, their great harvest has been gathered, but the aftermath is to be valued, and scant though it may be, it still contains the quality, the savor of the rich soil that has rejoiced us with its abundant yield. These latest poems of Whitman's are fragmentary utterances; they have the old character of form and expression, but are intermittent flashes; detached images, brief glimpses. As with Dr. Holmes, these songs are pervaded by the reminiscent atmosphere of sunset hours. In one of the traits that have strongly characterized Whitman there is no perceptible decline—that of graphic, terse and vivid delineation with a word or phrase that both depicts and suggests, like the sure brush stroke of a master painter. An example of this is to be found in the stately beginning on the poem of the death of Gen. Grant: "As one by one withdraw the mighty actors," striking at once the keynote of a majestic theme that is sustained with the same power to the close:

Thou from the prairies!—tangled and
    many-veined and hard has been
    thy part,
To admiration has it been enacted?

It is a glorious calm that pervades these four lines:

After the dazzle of day is gone,
Only the dark, dark night shows to
    my eyes the stars;

336

After the clangor of organ majestic,
    or chorus, of perfect band,
Silent, athwart my soul, moves the
    symphony true.

And, in these lines called "Halcyon Days" the re [sic] is manifest what was once said of Appollonius of Tyana, that old age, as well as youth, has its bloom:

Not from successful love alone,
Nor wealth, nor honored middle age,
    nor victories of politics or war,
But as life wanes and all the
    turbulent passions calm,
As gorgeous, vapory, silent hues
    cover the evening sky,
As softness, fullness, rest, suffuse the
    frame, like fresher, balmier air,
As the days take on a mellower light,
    and the apple at last hangs really
    finish'd and indolent ripe on the
    tree,
Then for the teeming quietest,
    happiest days of all!
The brooding and blissful halcyon
    days!

A strong group of poems are the "Fancies at Navesink;" reflections on the meanings of the ocean rides as the pulse of the power that vivifies all—the "fluid, vast identity, holding the universe with all its parts as one." Then the ebb, with its images of death, failure and despair swept on to oblivion—but that not the end, for

Duly by you, from you, the tide and
    the light again—duly the hinges
    turning.
Duly the needed discord parts
    offsetting, blending,
Weaving from you, from Sleep,
    Night, Death itself.
The rhythms of birth eternal.

The six-line poem on Whittier's 80th birthday is a beautiful tribute. Those fond of drawing analogies might find much satisfaction in the resemblance in the names of the two poets, one a Hicksite Quaker, the other the son of Hicksite Quakers. Whitman passing his last years across the river from the great Quaker City, always using the quaint Quaker terminology of "Fifth Month," etc., and devoting the last pages of his "November Boughs" to a collection of notes on Elias Hicks, of whom he says in his prefatory note: "As myself a little boy hearing so much of E. H., at that time long ago in Suffolk and Queens and Kings counties— and more than once personally seeing the old man—and my dear, dear father and mother faithful listeners to him at the meetings—I remember how I dreamed to write, perhaps, a piece about E. H. and his look and discourses however long afterward—for my parents' sake—and the dear Friends, too! And the following is what has at last but all come out of it—the feeling and intention never forgotten yet!"

Whitman's opinion of Tennyson is of particular interest, since the British laureate is one of our great American's most intimate, though never beheld, friends across the Atlantic. In the brief paper, "A Word About Tennyson," Whitman says:

Let me assume to pass verdict, or, perhaps, momentary judgment, for the United States on this poet—a removed and distant position giving some advantages over a nigh one. What is Tennyson's service to his race, times, and especially to America? First, I should say—or, at least, not forget— his personal character. He is not to be mentioned as a rugged, evolutionary, aboriginal force—but (and a great lesson is in it) he has been consistent throughout with the native, healthy patriotic spinal element and promptings of himself. His moral line is local and conventional, but it is vital and genuine. He reflects the upper crust of his time, its pale cast of thought—even its ennui. Then the simile of my friend, John Burroughs, is entirely true. 'His glove is a glove of silk, but the hand is a hand of iron.' He shows how one can be a royal laureate, quite eloquent and 'aristocratic,' and a little queer and affected, and at the same time perfectly manly and natural. As to his non-democracy, it fits him well, and I like him the better for it. I guess we all like to have (I am sure I do) some one who presents those sides of a thought or a possibility, different from our own—different, and yet with a sort of home-likeness—a tartness and contradiction offsetting the theory as we view it, and construed from taste and proclivities not at all his own. [. . .] Yes, Alfred Tennyson is a superb character, and will help give illustriousness, through the long roll of time, to our 19th century. In its bunch of orbic names, shining like a constellation of stars, his will be one of the brightest. His very faults, doubts, swervings, doublings upon himself, have been typical of our age. We are like the voyagers of a ship casting off for new seas, distant shores. We would still dwell in the old suffocating and dead haunts, remembering and magnifying their pleasant experiences only, and more than once impelled to jump ashore before it is too late, and stay where our fathers stayed and live as they lived. May-be I am non-literary and non-decorous (let me at least be human and pay part of my debt) in this word about Tennyson. I want him to realize that here is a great and ardent nation that absorbs his songs, and has a respect and affection for him personally as almost for no other foreigner. I want this word to go to the old man at Farringford as conveying no more than the simple truth: and that truth (a little Christmas gift) no slight one, either.

There are many other words worth reading in this new section of the volume; papers on Shakespeare, Robert Burns, Fr. Taylor, remarks on "The Spanish Element in Our Nationality," and various random notes and reminiscences, including some additional ones about the war. It is all pervaded by the healthy personal feeling, lofty patriotism and deep spirituality inherent in Whitman. Altogether, this complete edition may be called monumental in our literature.

DEMOCRATIC VISTAS, AND OTHER PAPERS (1888)

Democratic Vistas, and Other Papers. By Walt Whitman.

[*Published by arrangement with the Author.*]

LONDON
WALTER SCOTT, 24 WARWICK LANE
TORONTO: W. J. GAGE & CO.
1888

Walter Lewin.
Academy 33
(30 June 1888), 441–2.

A complete edition of Whitman's prose writings in the useful and convenient "Camelot" series would be very acceptable; and, as one more volume would secure this, I hope the publisher will see his way to it. There is a suggestion of incompleteness about this otherwise excellent series. The number of volumes of selections included in it seems rather excessive. It provides the British public with admirable samples of many authors, but even the British public cannot live well on samples alone. Complete sets of Landor, Swift, Leigh Hunt, and the rest, would, of course, be out of the question in such a series; but it might sometimes be better to give one complete work of an author than cuttings from half a dozen. At any rate, in the case of Whitman, the whole of his prose works are within reach; and, as the two volumes already issued omit several important pieces, there is a special reason why a third and concluding volume should follow. Perhaps the very best piece of prose from Whitman's pen is the preface to the first edition (1855) of *Leaves of Grass*. Much of the substance of it appeared in another form in the second and subsequent editions, chiefly in the pieces which now bear the titles "Song of the Answerer" and "By Blue Ontario's Shore." It was, however, never reproduced in its original shape until 1868, when Mr. W. M. Rossetti gave an incomplete version of it in his English volume of *Selections*. In 1881, at the suggestion of the late Thomas Dixon, of Sunderland (to whom Ruskin's letters—entitled *Time and Tide*—"to a working man of Sun-

derland" were addressed), and, by permission of the author, I myself reprinted this preface unmutilated; and Whitman includes it in his *Specimen Days and Collect*. But, for some reason or another, it does not appear in either of the "Camelot" volumes. Other valuable prefaces and essays are also missing, quite enough in quantity, and quite good enough, to make a volume. Perhaps author, editor, and publisher, will consider the suggestion.

Leaving now the omissions, we find there is plenty of excellent matter in the present volume. Next to the "Preface" above named, "Democratic Vistas" is quite the best thing Whitman has produced in prose. Whatever may be said for the genius that created the peculiar style of *Leaves of Grass* (and, for my part, I think a great deal may be said on this point) Whitman's essays do not mark him out as a master of style in prose. They are fittingly described by a favourite word of his own—jottings. But what they may lack in style is more than compensated by the abundance of thought they contain. Jottings so valuable will easily pass muster, even though they be not arranged in accordance with high literary art. "Democratic Vistas" consists of jottings on the future of democracy and, incidentally, on many topics not suggested in the title. The "other papers" in the volume consist of jottings, variously named, on Shakspere, on Tennyson, on Burns, and on other subjects, including the author himself and his writings. Yet it would be wrong not to correct my criticism about Whitman's style by pointing out that there are numerous passages scattered through all these essays which are remarkable not only for the ideas they express, but for the finished beauty of their form as well.

The poet of the modern has some interesting things to say about those poets of other days whose reign is now drawing to a close; the singers of "those beautiful, matchless songs adjusted to other lands than these—other days, another spirit and stage of evolution." "What," he asks, and proceeds to answer,

"is Tennyson's service to his race, times, and especially to America? First, I should say, his personal character. He is not to be mentioned as a rugged, evolutionary, aboriginal force—but (and a great lesson is in it) he has been consistent throughout with the native, personal, healthy, patriotic, spinal element and promptings of himself. His moral line is local and conventional, but it is vital and genuine. He reflects the upper crust of his time, its pale cast of thought—even its *ennui*. . . . He shows how one can be a royal laureate, quite elegant and 'aristocratic,' and a little queer and affected, and at the same time perfectly manly and natural" (p. 127).

Admitting that he may be himself "non-literary and non-decorous," Whitman is able and willing to appreciate in Tennyson that "latent charm in mere words, cunning collocutions and in the voice ringing them, which he has caught and brought out beyond all others." Burns, in some respects, comes closer to Whitman's heart. "There are many things in Burns's poems and character that specially endear him to America," he says. For one thing, he was "essentially a republican"; for another, he was "an average sample of the good-natured, warm-blooded, proud-spirited, amative, alimentive, convivial, young and early middle-aged man of the decent-born middle classes everywhere and anyhow" whatever all this may mean. In better style Whitman remarks, later on:

"There is something about Burns peculiarly acceptable to the concrete human point of view. He poetises work-

a-day agricultural labour and life (whose spirit and sympathies, as well as practicalities, are much the same everywhere), and treats fresh, often coarse, natural occurrences, loves, persons, not like many new and some old poets, in a genteel style of gilt and china, or at second or third removes, but in their own born atmosphere—laughter, sweat, unction" (p. 118).

Yet, while anxious to give full honour to all poets of the past, Whitman does not forget for a moment that poetry of the future whose pioneer it is his mission to be. "Even Shakspere," he says, "belongs essentially to the buried past."

As to this mission of his, and the way in which he has fulfilled it, Whitman has several things to say—more, perhaps, than was necessary. For in these latter days, without explanation—which he never condescended to give while he was abused—he and his work have come to be pretty well understood. One of the best possible evidences of the inherent strength of *Leaves of Grass* and its author is that, under circumstances the most unfavourable, and against all kinds of impediments, they have held their own, and come to be esteemed. But Whitman, who would explain nothing in answer to abuse, is prepared to explain much in answer to sympathy; and, accordingly, in three separate articles in this volume, he discourses of himself and his book. *Leaves of Grass*, he says,

"is, or seeks to be, simply a faithful and doubtless self-willed record. In the midst of all it gives one man's—the author's—identity, ardours, observations, faiths, and thoughts, coloured hardly at all with any colouring from other faiths, other authors, other identities or times. Plenty of songs had been sung—beautiful, matchless songs—

adjusted to other lands than these, other days, another spirit and stage of evolution; but I would sing, and leave out or put in, solely with reference to America and myself and to-day. Modern science and democracy seemed to be throwing out their challenge to poetry to put them in its statements in contradistinction to the songs and myths of the past. As I see it now (perhaps too late), I have unwittingly taken up that challenge, and made an attempt at such statements, which I certainly would not assume to do now, knowing more clearly what it means" (p. 87).

The book is valuable precisely because it is a faithful and self-willed record. It is, as I have said elsewhere, a biography, in poetry, of the human soul—of Whitman's own soul, ostensibly; really of all souls, for the experience of the individual is simply the experience of the race in miniature. That the record is "self-willed" is undeniable; and, in these days, when few persons dare to utter their own thought, while most are mere echoes or, at best, speak only when they are quite sure that their opinions are supported by precedent, surely the faithful, honest, uncompromising Whitman is a much-needed teacher.

GOOD-BYE MY FANCY (1891)

Good-Bye

My Fancy

2D ANNEX TO LEAVES OF GRASS

PHILADELPHIA
DAVID McKAY, PUBLISHER
23 SOUTH NINTH STREET
1891

"Whitman's Farewell:
A Melancholy Book."
New York *Tribune*,
16 August 1891, p. 14.

A dreadful photograph resembling nothing so much as a death-mask serves as grim frontispiece to this ultimate publication by Walt Whitman. According to the practice of his later years the volume is written partly in prose and partly in Walt Whitman's peculiar idea of poetry. There is a melancholy flavor about the whole of it, though the old man tries very hard to be cheerful. More than once, however, he refers to the world's refusal to recognize him as a poet. All the great magazines, he declares, have declined to print his lucubrations, and apparently the general public have not fatigued his publisher with orders for his books. The so-called poetry in this volume is naturally of a valedictory character to a considerable extent, and though it is not less prosaic and unmelodious than the writer's earlier productions, the circumstances under which it was written impart a certain suggestion of pathos to it. Walt Whitman does not indeed face the Unknown with apprehensions and misgivings. If he does not appear to cherish Christian hopes and expectations, his Pantheism has not prevented him from maintaining a belief in another existence, and an existence not less adapted to and filled with activity and energy than the present one. Yet he does not speculate much upon the future. Rather does he seem to be chiefly interested in forecasting the ultimate destiny of *Leaves of Grass*, which he does not like to think will be relegated to the limbo of unused or unreadable books.

This question is of course not one upon which those who like or who dislike Walt Whitman's writings can pass final judgment. Posterity often does surprising things and adopts queer views. Among its peculiarities is a tendency "parcere subjectis et debellare superbos" [to spare the conquered and vanquish the proud]; and for all any one living knows this proclivity may be exercised on behalf of Walt Whitman. As regards his contemporaries, they certainly have not discovered in him the music of the future, and the reasons which have determined the prevailing judgment upon him do not appear weak or capricious. Walt Whitman himself retains a consolatory assurance of his own position, and it is not worth while to attempt to disturb his faith. In the concluding pages of the present volume he gives some autobiographic memoranda which will be found interesting and quaintly illustrative of character. As for the more pretentious papers—attempts at essay-writing and the like—perhaps the less said about them the better. For it is unfortunately the fact that when Walt Whitman tries to be profound he commonly becomes unintelligible, seeming to lose his footing in a bag of verbiage. His passion for stringing words together in catalogue-form recalls old Burton at times, though of course Whitman has nothing of Burton's erudition. Let us hope, however, that his last booklet may contribute somewhat to the comfort of his age and the assuagement of his infirmities.

Sidney Morse. "The Second Annex to *Leaves of Grass*." *Conservator* 2 (September 1891), 51–2.

In one way Walt Whitman may be said to be very unlike his poet-compeers, ancient or modern—in his inability in any sort to efface, in prose or poem, his own personality. It is all a part of him. His life is in it all: 'tis what he is, thinking, seeing, hearing, feeling—more outwardly than inwardly, perhaps. He has no characters; is never dramatic. He is always on the march—

"I tramp a perpetual journey;"—

going somewhere—seeing somewhat, hailing, greeting, saluting—reverencing, too, in the good sense of the term. One may not care for this or that so-called poem—think it no poem, for that matter; but take his book, with its accumulating "annexes," for all in all, and you cannot well get away from it, are glad to have it around, lying near handy; and are more apt than otherwise to light on a line, or many lines, that go to the spot, as he himself might say, and yield full satisfaction. In reading Emerson's verse to others, I have at times found a disturbance from the thought and beauty of it all (with a secret wish that I had not begun to read and a vow that I would never do the like again), by my auditor's smile or half sneer at the author's sometimes forced rhymes or prosy lines; as though that were the point, and mattered at all. To hear a poem only with the outer ear is not to hear it at all—nine times in ten. And the tenth time, more than likely, there is no poem to hear. Reading Whitman aloud is even more difficult. Not for the faulty rhyme—for the absence of any intention of that sort eliminates that difficulty—but for the same inability of average mortals to detect beneath the strange in form, or the supposed want of proper poetic form, the breathing of a poet-spirit. Lowell voices in the best way it can be voiced this limitation, or to my mind wrong poetic notion, in his "Fable for Critics:"

"Then comes Emerson first, whose
    rich words, every one,
Are like gold nails in temples to
    hang trophies on;
Whose prose is grand verse, while
    his verse, the Lord knows,
Is some of it pr—— No, 'tis not
    even prose."

The critic could hear the poem underneath Emerson's prose, because

"Aye climb for his rhyme,"

closes the finer ear to the revelation.

"In the worst of his poems are mines
    of rich matter.
But thrown in a heap with a crash
    and a clatter."

And beyond, amid, or underneath the "crash" and the "clatter" there is no vibratory soul-music. And yet—

"Now, it is not one thing nor another
    alone
Makes a poem, but rather the
    general tone,
The something pervading, uniting
    the whole,
The before unconceived,
    unconceivable soul."

When the critic in the next line intimates that this "something pervading, uniting the whole" may be lost "just in moving this trifle or that," and so you

> "Take away, as it were, a chief limb of the statue."

he is intent on the perfection of the artificer or builder, so seeking the poem's life, loses it. Lost to him because of faulty form; but for another, willing the "unconceivable soul" should build its own form, not dictatory, not outwardly measuring, there may abide all the force and beauty of a spiritual or poetical vision; the glimpsing of that which, after all, for the most part, lies beyond the ken of sight, or power of words or painter's brush to report,—"the unconceived, unconceivable soul." Poetry is ever suggestion; never "a twice-told tale of God." There is Lowell's "Foot-Path."

> "It mounts athwart the windy hill
>   Through shallow slopes of upland
>   bare,
> And fancy climbs with footfall still
>   Its narrowing curves that end in
>   air."

What lies beyond?

> "What Nature for her poets hides,
> 'Tis wiser to divine than clutch."

The "prying, peeping critic" here takes to his heels; the poet comes joyously forward, and modestly:

> "The bird I list hath never come
>   Within the scope of mortal ear;
> My prying step would make him
>   dumb,
> And the fair tree, his shelter, sear
> "Behind the hill, behind the sky,
>   Behind my inmost thought, he
>   sings;
> No feet avail; to hear it nigh,

> The song itself must lend the
>   wings."

*   *   *   *   *

> "I know not, and will never pry,
>   But trust our human heart for all;
> Wonders that from the seeker fly
>   Into an open sense may fall."

The culture, the skill, the art, that close this "open sense," turns the poet blind from his vision.

Art lies in knowing how little is needed. A new vista, and the work is done. This is the "open secret" in all true civilizing—to get rid of the superfluous and be not only content but well supplied with little. Neither too much, nor too much finish. Whitman speaks of "the last polish and intellectual 'cuteness of Emerson," but just whether to like it or not, I don't make out. To my reading the "polish" and the "'cuteness" both go to rendering best things in smallest compass. In this respect Whitman does not himself, certainly, err. He owns up for himself: "I have probably not been enough afraid of careless touches from the first—and am not now—nor of parrot-like repetitions, nor platitudes and commonplace." And yet, perhaps again, he would have spent it all or very much of it had he faltered for such "intellectual 'cuteness" or to give a "last polish." One may with profit to himself do considerable editing, abbreviating or omitting altogether phrases and lines. But solely, as I think, it is their redundancy that is disturbing—this however, in his longer poems, wherein one at times loses himself in nothing special or tires of too much "cataloguing." Whitman says, "Perhaps I am too democratic for such avoidances." (Of this much talk of the "democratic" there may be something to say another time. Just now to say that it sometimes reminds me of my Sunday-school teacher's encomium of the universal, democratic, paternal idea of "the good God, who knows and has numbered every hair on your head, even the hairs of your eyebrows, and each drop of blood in your entire system." But it always seemed to me there was no small "waste of powder" in such exactitude: as though a few hairs more or less, or drops of blood, much mattered—to the soul of me!)

To leave preface just at the end and come to the book—most welcome is this 'Second Annex.' No, you had "not better withhold." There is no "old age" nor "paralysis" here that tires, or makes me sorrow that you have kept and given forth these

"Last droplets of and after
    spontaneous rain."

"This little cluster" brings fragrant memories and old-age excellencies— "from sane, completed, vital, capable old age." Well, I agree (and it please me)— "The final proof of song or personality [and I have but stumbled on this now after penning the above] is a sort of matured, accreted, superb, evoluted, almost divine, impalpable diffuseness and atmosphere or invisible magnetism, dissolving and embracing all—and not any special achievement of passion, pride, metrical form, epigram, plot, thought, or what is called beauty." You have done well to "improve to-day's opportunity;" but do not "wind up"—till you do wind up. All these last little chants, songs, greetings, come with especial flavor of friendliness, as do all the bits of reminiscence. Especially have I enjoyed "Old Actors, Singers, Shows, etc."—you say in "New York;" but I had my hearing of most of those you mention elsewhere. The sad thing of it all is the "sooner or later inevitably wending to the flies or exit-door— vanishing to sight and ear—and never materializing on this earth's stage again!"

Why things cannot stay and be and remain on and on, when once they come— that is the question. And the answer is, "Perhaps, most likely, they do—and will, forever!"

The two poems that always appear to my mental view when I think of or turn *Leaves of Grass* are: "The Song of the Open Road" and "The Mystic Trumpeter." That they are so much different from or superior to others in the same volume, I do not presume to say; but they for some reason have fixed themselves in among my likings, and I turn the leaves sometimes with a sort of half fearing they may have some way escaped their rootings, and are no longer there. I am sorry the book is not now before me, that I may refresh myself with lines that it would also be here a pleasure to quote. But here at hand is "When the Full-Grown Poet Came"—a short poem, but one that holds philosophy for all—poet or non-poet—if such there be—equally concerned with the same reconciliation and harmony. I will read it again for myself and write it out as I read:

"When the full-grown poet came,
    Out spake pleased Nature (the
        round, impassive globe, with all
        its shows of day and night),
            Saying, *He is mine*;
    But out spake, too, the Soul of man,
        proud, jealous and unreconciled,
        Nay, he is mine alone;
    —Then the full-grown poet stood
        between the two, and took each
        by the hand;
    And to-day and ever so stands, as
        blender, uniter, tightly holding
        hands,
    Which he shall never release until he
        reconciles the two,
    And wholly and joyously blends
        them."

350

Literary News n.s. 12 (September 1891), 282 [reprinted from *Commercial Advertiser* (unlocated)].

Walt Whitman still lives. One more utterance from our old original individualistic American poet, now, as he tells us, in his seventy-second year, and not expecting to write any more; this, indeed, written as it were in defiance of augury. The grand old fellow in that little of new he gives us is in good fettle and equal to himself. Most of the volume is made up of recollections, memories not only of facts, but of thoughts, and they are not the least interesting, especially his recollections of persons once famous, but long since gathered in by the reaper. The following is mystical, indeed everything that Whitman has written is mystical, a shadowing forth of a half comprehended entity in thought:

LONG, LONG HENCE.

"After a long, long course, hundreds
    of years, denials,
Accumulations, rous'd love and joy
    and thought,
Hopes, wishes, aspirations,
    ponderings, victories, myriads of
    readers
Coating, compassing, covering—
    after ages' and ages'
    encrustations,
Then only may these songs reach
    fruition."

Critic [New York] n.s. 16 (5 September 1891), 114.

The Greeks put in their graves an image of Hermes the *psychopompos* to convey the spirit over into the land of shades. '*Good-bye, my Fancy!*' is Walt Whitman's Hermes-image to convey his parting salutations to the afterworld. In its sixty-six pages we have a medley and motley of prose and verse like what the countryman calls the rich 'strippings' of the cow's milk, the last and oiliest, the most nutritious and creamiest of the lacteal fountain. A few things here have been published before. *The Critic*'s readers have tasted and enjoyed the uncloying 'Old Man's Rejoinder,' 'For Queen Victoria's Birthday,' 'The Pallid Wreath' and 'Unassail'd Renown'; but the bulk of the book—its stem, stalk and flower—is new to the public and has not before tempted the intellectual palate.

I sing of life, yet mind me still of
    Death,

is the keynote of the volume, in which the author humorously calls himself a sea-shell cast up by the sea. Yet does he not remember the wonderful *susurrus* of that Wordsworthian shell which, though far inland, whispered of its native place even as that *susurrus* in the soul whispered of immortality? The almost dead shell of the 'greybeard sufi' has a live soul in it capable still of radiant abalone-like iridescences. The chemist's tincture brings out these wondrous tints even as opportunity will elicit them from the 'conch' of Camden.

In fact, here I am these current years 1890 and '91 (each successive fortnight getting stiffer and stuck deeper), much like some hard-cased dilapidated grim ancient shell-fish or time-bang'd conch (no legs, utterly non-locomotive) cast up high and dry on the shore-sands, helpless to move anywhere—nothing left but to behave myself quiet, and while away the days yet assign'd, and discover if there is anything for the said grim and time-bang'd conch to be got at last out of inherited good spirits and primal buoyant centre-pulses down there deep somewhere within his gray-blurr'd old shell. . . . And old as I am I feel to-day almost a part of some frolicsome wave.

The 'shell' is indeed a part of the 'frolicsome wave' which laves it into exquisite curves and colors. This is Whitman's universal quality, his sympathy, his worldwide hand-clasp, his general salutation to the universe. The shell and the sea are comrades, and so is every creeping and smiling or sailing and winged creature—comrades all in that catholic-apostolic *camaraderie* which includes every sprout and germ of the divine energy—a *camaraderie* as close and as kind as that which clasped hamadryad and enclosing oak together. Death, which inspires so many of these beautiful irregular lines, looms up magical and benign before a mind simply wondering, not abashed—the 'eidólon-yacht' of his soul ready to put forth on its mirage-haunted seas with utmost trustfulness. Whitman's beliefs come out singularly strong and triumphant here and there among the creed-leaves of the book: beliefs in future personality, identity, immortality, a merciful and loving God, progress, consciousness: he peoples that dim world with these, and it becomes immediately lustrous. These brave beliefs ring almost gayly through 'An Ended Day,' 'The Pallid Wreath,' 'My 71st Year,' 'Shakespeare-Bacon's Cipher,' and other

protests against materialism, often as beautifully expressed as Tennyson's or Whittier's vital faith. Indeed, the whole book is a book of 'last words' from dying lips sealing a life that has been blameless.

There is no sound of lamentation or Job-cry in it, pervaded as it is with bright, broad optimism, the grace of benignant utterance, the egoism of a healthy and gracious child. Almost the only querulous note is the plaintive reference to rejected MSS. sent in to the 'great magazines.' The generous recognition of Tennyson and Ruskin and the other English and American admirers has offset this, and kept the paralyzed author from real want. The last twenty pages or so are full of Pascal-like *pensées* grouped in paragraphs, vividly poetic, many of them, with Whitman-esque threads and colorations running all through. Such are 'A Death-Banquet,' 'Some Laggards Yet,' 'Splinters,' 'Health,' 'Crossing from Jersey City,' 'An Engineer's Obituary' (his brother), and the 'Old-Age Jottings.' Histrionic New York of thirty or forty years ago reappears delightfully in 'Old Actors, Singers, Shows, etc.'—a tell-tale bead of personal recollections in which the author suspends a votive offering before each vanished image and lingering voice, all quaintly carved in his own rich involved English. Much ruddy philosophy courses through these recollections—healthy love of the drama, love of a beautiful voice, love of Shakespeare and the great artists—of Alboni and Jenny Lind and Fanny Kemble and fine reading.

The author turns the kodak on himself and reveals each inner sanctuary of his moral and physical nature. Now in his seventy-third year, he is as fresh and piquant as ever, as devoted to his great 'America,' his ideal Democracy, his poetic theories as he was in 1855, when he began jotting down his revolutionary memoranda. And at the forefront of it all looks out a portrait—profile rounded like the arch of the full moon, nebulous, Ossianlike, but striking in its filmy vagueness.

Independent 43 (10 September 1891), 1355.

Of Walt Whitman we could say nothing unkind—we could speak with sincere and sympathetic respect. His latest book does not challenge criticism; it is evidently the work of a mind sorely diseased, worn out indeed. The fragmentary, disjointed essay entitled "An Old Man's Rejoinder," is suggestive of unmitigated pathos. There is just enough in it to show how deeply Walt Whitman has suffered because he has not been able to convince competent critics of his ability as a poet, and there is enough there as well to make one sympathize with the old poet, no matter how much one may feel the justice of what the critics have done. There is nothing of any value whatever in this book. One reads parts of it with a twinge of curiosity tempered with sadness. So far as what purports to be literature is concerned here is the end of a wasted life. "I have been and am rejected by all the great magazines," he says, and the saying suggests untold pangs of defeat. That the great magazines were right and Walt Whitmon [*sic*] wrong the contents of this thin, crazy-quilt volume amply prove without the trouble of calling upon *Leaves of Grass* for more convincing testimony. We wish Walt Whitman every good that life can bring; but it will be well for the world when his writings disappear and are as little talked of as they always have been little read.

"Good-Bye My Fancy." Literary World 22 (12 September 1891), 305.

There is something at once very pathetic and courageous in this definitive leave-taking by the poet Walt Whitman. His traits and his place in literature need no farther discussion at present; neither does his absorbent personality that has desired to assimilate the world, or the singular contests of praise and blame which have been waged about him. Such as he is—and surely he is unique—he now bids farewell, and yet not farewell, to his gift of utterance:

On, on the same, ye jocund twain!
My life and recitative . . .
. . . I and my recitatives, with faith
and love
Waiting to other work, to unknown
songs, conditions,
On, on, ye jocund twain! continue on
the same!

And again:

Good-bye my Fancy,
Farewell dear mate, dear love!
I'm going away, I know not where
Or to what fortune, or whether I may
ever see you again,
So Good-bye my Fancy. . . .

If we go anywhere we'll go together
to meet what happens,
Maybe we'll be better off and blither,
and learn something,
May-be it is yourself now really
ushering me to the true songs (who
knows?)
May-be it is you the mortal knot
really undoing, turning—so now
finally
Good-bye—and hail, my Fancy.

353

Other poems in this small but characteristic collection continue the design of the author's previous work, completing the message "today at twilight . . . with vital voice, reporting yet"—the brave veteran! More than half the volume is made up of prose articles and fragments. In these Mr. Whitman's manner remains much the same as in his chants, while the reader is at least spared the continual negation of the laws of the technical art of poetry. In an essay on "National Literature" he finds the essential traits of the American people to be good-nature, decorum, and intelligence, and bases his hopes upon these qualities. In music, despite the critics who assure him he belongs to the worship of Wagner, he dwelt under "the old Italian dispensation," as he calls it, and wishes that he might thank the composer Verdi for "much noble pleasure and happiness." The somber velvet of the voice of Signora Alboni also charmed him; and the brave songs of the Hutchinsons, with their sister, "the red-cheeked New England carnation, sweet Abby." Kean in King John, and Fanny Kemble in Fazio, "a rapid-running, yet heavy-timber'd, tremendous, wrenching, passionate play," and the comedy of Hackett, appealed, in their

day, to Mr. Whitman; and were followed in his theatrical enjoyments by a long list of other artists. He describes his habitation, "a rather large 20 by 20 low-ceiling'd room something like a big old ship's cabin," in literary disorder of papers and books, with its three windows, the stove and oak-wood fuel, and the great arm-chair spread with a "wide wolf-skin of hairy black and silver."

If this volume shall be, as the author appears to intend, his last literary effort, it closes firmly and fitly the literary career of a poet who has with pride and fidelity obeyed his own genius, and who has sought to collect within himself, and to understand and speak—in his oracular, strange voice—the experiences of common humanity.

Checklist of Additional Reviews

"The New Books . . . Walt Whitman," *Review of Reviews* 4 (September 1891), 227.

Index

Academy, xix, 211–13, 281–5, 341–3
American, xviii, 252–5, 329
American Phrenological Journal, 23–6
Athenæum, 159–63

B., 121–2
[Baxter, Sylvester], xix, 333–8
Book Buyer, 316
Boston *Banner of Light*, xiv, 85–6
Boston *Commonwealth*, xvi, xviii, 120–1, 135–7, 255
Boston *Cosmopolite*, 108
Boston *Evening Transcript*, xix, 311–14
Boston *Herald*, 333–8
Boston *Intelligencer*, 55
Boston *Sunday Herald*, xviii, 273–9
Boston *Wide World*, 108
Broadway Magazine, 137–43
Brooklyn *Daily Eagle*, 18–21
Brooklyn *Daily Times*, xiii, 21–2, 66–7
[Browne, Francis F.], 240–3
Buchanan, Robert, xv, 137–43
Burroughs, John, xv–xvi, 123–30, 135–7

Canadian Journal, 50–55
Catholic World, xviii, 249–50
Chambers's Journal of Popular Literature, Science, and Art, xvi, 168–77
Chicago *Tribune*, xviii, 233–7
Christian Examiner, xiii, 59–60
Christian Spiritualist, 55
Cincinnati *Daily Commercial*, xiv, 71–3
Clapp, Henry, 79–81
Conservator, xx, 348–50
[Conway, Moncure D.], xv, 105–6
Crayon, 27–34, 91
Criterion, 26–7
Critic (London), xii, 43–6, 96–100
Critic (New York), xvii, xix–xx, 223–5, 293–5, 317–18, 351–3

Dana, Charles A., xi, 3–8
Detroit *Free Press*, xviii, 243–4
Dial (Chicago), xvii, 240–3, 327–9
Dial (Cincinnati), 105–6
Dowden, Edward, xix, 181–208, 281–5

Examiner, xii, xvii, 41, 177, 213–16

F., 118–20
Fern, Fanny, xii, 46–8
Fox, William J., 41

Galaxy, 123–30
Garland, Hamlin, xix, 311–14
Gordon, T. Francis, xviii, 252–5
Gosse, Edmund W., xvii, 211–13
Griswold, Rufus W., xii, 26–7

Hale, Edward Everett, xi, 34–6
Harper's New Monthly Magazine, 322–3
Harrison, W., 317–18
[Hearn, Lafcadio], xviii, 250–2
Higginson, T. W., 239–40
Hill, A. S., 131–2
H[owells], W. D., xv, 112–14, 322–3
Howitt, William, 41

Independent, xx, 353

[James, Henry], xv, 115–18

Leader, xii, 48–50
Leader and Saturday Analyst, 89–91
Lewin, Walter, 341–3
Liberty, xvii, 237–8
Life Illustrated, xi, 8
Lippincott's Monthly Magazine, 323–4
Literary Gazette, 91–2
Literary News, xx, 351
Literary World, xviii–xx, 225–7, 279–81, 314–15, 353–4
Lloyd's Weekly London Newspaper, xvi, 157–9
London *Echo*, 321–2
London *Morning Star*, 177
London *Review*, 177
London *Sun*, xvi, 149–57
London *Sunday Times*, 147–9
London *Weekly Dispatch*, xii, 41

Macaulay, G. C., 256–69
McCarthy, J. H., xvii, 213–16

Mace: A Weekly Record of the Glasgow Parliamentary Debating Association, 285–9
M[itchell], E[dward] P., xxi, 227–33
Monthly Trade Gazette, 55
Morse, Sidney, xx, 348–50

Nation, 115–18, 239–40
New Orleans Times-Democrat, xviii, 250–2
New Orleans Weekly Mirror, 108
New York Daily Times, xiii–xiv, 60–6
New York Daily Tribune, xi, 3–8
New York Examiner, xviii, 244–9
New York Home Journal, 329
New York Illustrated News, 86–7
New York Ledger, 46–8
New York Saturday Press, xiv–xv, 74–6, 79–81, 87–9, 118–20
New York Sun, xvii, 227–33
New York Times, xiv–xv, xviii, 82–5, 118, 289–92
New York Tribune, xviii, 273, 315–16, 347
Nineteenth Century, 256–69
North American Review, xi, 34–6, 131–2
Norton, Charles Eliot, xi, 14–18

P., C. C., 87–9
Pall Mall Gazette, xix, 318–21
Payne, William Morton, 327–9
Philadelphia Evening Bulletin, 310–11

Philadelphia North American, 307–9
Philadelphia Press, 255–6
Philadelphia Times, 238–9, 310
Putnam's Monthly, 14–18

Radical, xv, 121–2
Review of Reviews, 354
Rogers, George, 307–9
Round Table, 112–14

San Francisco Chronicle, xx, 316–17
Saturday Review, xii, xiv, xvi, xx, 55, 92–6, 163–8, 324–7
Scottish Review, xx, 329
Secular Review, xvii, 216–20
Spectator, xiv, xix, 100–5, 299–304

United States Review, 8–14

W., D., 50–5
[Walsh, William S.], 323–4
Washington Daily National Intelligencer, xii, 37–40
Watson's Weekly Art Journal, xv, 111–12
Westminster Review, xiv, xix, 107, 181–208, 295–9
White, W. Hale, xvii, 216–20
Whitman, Walt [as reviewer], xi–xiii, xx, 8–14, 21–6, 74–6, 79–81
Wilde, Oscar, xix, 318–21